DAK
92
YOUN

Collin, Andrea Winkjer

Mr. Wheat.

(YOUNG)

(+ 1 DVD)

Mr. Wheat

A Biography of
U.S. Senator Milton R. Young
By Andrea Winkjer Collin
with Richard E. Collin

also

Race of the Century: *Guy vs. Young* *1974 North Dakota* *U.S. Senate Election*

By Allan C. Young

Bismarck, North Dakota

Mr. Wheat
A Biography of
U.S. Senator Milton R. Young
By Andrea Winkjer Collin with Richard E. Collin
Book and DVD
Copyright © 2010
Smoky Water Press

Race of the Century:
Guy vs. Young
1974 North Dakota U.S. Senate Election
By Allan C. Young
A thesis submitted to the graduate faculty of the University of North Dakota in partial fulfillment
of the requirements for the degree of master of arts, Grand Forks, North Dakota, May 1989.

Published by Smoky Water Press
Post Office Box 2322
Bismarck, ND 58502-2322
info@dakotabooknet.com
www.dakotabooknet.com
701-222-0947

Smoky Water Press is a division of Capital Communications, Inc.
Bismarck, North Dakota

Printed in the United States of America
Printed and perfect bound at Niess Impressions
Minot, North Dakota 58701
www.niessimpressions.com

Cover design by Sydney (Bren) Winkler. Front cover farm photograph by Andrew Young, Napoleon,
North Dakota. Front and back cover photographs of Senator Young from the Milton R. Young Photograph
Collection, North Dakota State University Libraries, Institute for Regional Studies.

ISBN: 978-0-9820752-2-7

Dedication

To John (Scoop) and Marcia Young

Contents

Mr. Wheat:
A Biography of U.S. Senator Milton R. Young

Race of the Century:
Guy vs. Young 1974 North Dakota U.S. Senate Election

About the Authors

Andrea Winkjer Collin was born and raised in Williston, North Dakota. She earned a journalism degree from the University of North Dakota in 1976, and has worked the years since as a newspaper reporter, magazine editor, business communications specialist, legislative assistant, development consultant, teacher, freelance writer and publisher. She is presently editor of *North Dakota Horizons*, the state magazine of North Dakota, and senior editor for the *North Dakota Blue Book*, published by the North Dakota Secretary of State's office.

Richard E. Collin was born in Minneapolis, Minnesota, and raised in suburban Washington, D.C. He earned a bachelor of arts degree in American history from the University of Maryland in 1977, and a master of science degree in Space Studies from the University of North Dakota in 1991. A U.S. Army veteran, Collin was stationed in Erlangen, West Germany, from 1979-81. He then attended Brown Institute of Broadcasting in Minneapolis and worked as a radio news reporter, media relations coordinator, and NASA video conference coordinator for 10 years in North Dakota and Oklahoma. From 1993-95, he served as communications director for Governor Edward T. Schafer of North Dakota. Since 1995, he has worked at the State Historical Society of North Dakota, where he is communications and education director. He is also on the adjunct faculty at the University of Mary in Bismarck, where he teaches history and political science.

The Collins live in Bismarck with their three daughters.

Introduction

A vivid memory of my college years is attending the 1974 Republican State Convention in Minot when U.S. Senator Milton Young accepted the nomination to run for his sixth and final term in the U.S. Senate.

He was 76 years old, and he knew it would be a tough fight against our popular former Governor William Guy. But Senator Young didn't back away from this challenge. With his powerful seniority, he knew that another term in the Senate was in the best interests of North Dakota. Today, it remains one of the most memorable political races in North Dakota's history.

A few years later, when I was a law student at the University of North Dakota, Senator Young helped me secure an internship in Washington, D.C. That summer, I saw firsthand how effective a Senator he was. With his friendly nature and unassuming personality, Senator Young commanded the respect of his colleagues in Congress, of every President in the White House during his 36 years in office, and others throughout the nation's capitol.

Unassuming and a bit shy at home, powerful and highly effective in Washington, Senator Young set the standard for constituent service, never forgetting the people of his home state who sent him to the nation's capitol year after year.

He influenced me and countless other young North Dakotans who aspired to a life of public service. He showed us that a plain-spoken farmer from a state like North Dakota–who always had a warm handshake and kind word for his constituents – could become one of the most powerful lawmakers in the nation.

My longtime friend, Andrea Winkjer Collin – with the able assistance of her husband, Rick Collin – has dedicated several years to writing this book about one of North Dakota's most distinguished public figures. This book will remind all of us how fortunate we are to claim as our very special legacy the 56 years of elected public service of this outstanding North Dakotan – "Mr. Wheat" – United States Senator Milton R. Young.

Wayne Stenehjem
North Dakota Attorney General

Foreword

As the story of North Dakota in the 20th Century continues to be written and interpreted, a number of political figures will be remembered for their contributions to the state and the nation beyond our state's borders.

These people will be noted for a number of reasons. Most listings are likely to include the distinguished public career of John Burke, the charisma and controversy of William L. Langer, the national political platforms of William F. Lemke and Gerald P. Nye, and the dozen years as governor of William L. Guy.

Near the top of this list the name of Milton R. Young must be placed. Born in 1897, as the 19th Century was waning, Young held an elected office for more than half of the 20th Century. He was the last person born in the 19th Century to serve in the United States Congress.

The stature to which he rose in the United States Senate may have surprised no one more than Young himself. As a young man, he recalled never thinking of being anything more than a LaMoure County farmer. The speech impediment he had since childhood kept him from seeking the limelight and speaking in front of crowds, and could have possibly discouraged others so afflicted from pursuing a lifetime of public service. Yet, his first elective office to his farm township board in 1924 sparked a desire for public service that moved him from township, to county, to state, and then to national elected positions.

In the United States Senate, Young forged a coalition early on with colleagues from other farm states, and developed some rather unorthodox personal and professional friendships that may not have been expected from a Senator from North Dakota. Except for the 80th Congress of 1947-49 and the 83rd Congress of 1953-55, Young's Republican Party remained in the minority during his years in the Senate. Yet, he became a recognized authority on both sides of the aisle in agriculture and agriculture policy. The affectionate nickname of "Mr. Wheat" given him in his early years in Washington is an indication of the high regard to which he was held for his knowledge of farm issues.

In addition to agriculture, Young's influence in the Senate reached into other state and national issues. His admiration for President Abraham Lincoln sparked a dogged determination to restore Ford's Theatre in Washington, D.C. He was an early promoter of the U.S. space program. His interest in military, defense and foreign policy issues took him around the world. And, his interest in karate captured the bemused attention of those who knew him.

If each state in America could custom design a United States Senator based on its own characteristics, attributes, and its image across the country, Milton Young may have been that perfect match for North Dakota. He was a hard-working, unassuming farmer who had a commitment to public service and who gained the respect and admiration of colleagues throughout the United States Congress. Often he was called one of the Senate's "work horses," deferring the spotlight to the "show horses."

Milt Young's 36 years in the U.S. Senate ranks him as North Dakota's longest-serving Senator, and when he retired, the 14th longest-serving Senator in U.S. history. But his heart was never far from his Berlin, North Dakota, farm. He relocated some of his Washington staff to LaMoure in the summers, and despite a daily schedule that included world and national political leaders, the first question he asked in weekly telephone calls to his family back home was "How are the crops?"

It has been 65 years since Milt Young was appointed to the United States Senate on March 12, 1945, and nearly 30 years since he ended his extraordinary 56-year career as an elected official in January 1981. This time span has been difficult for me to grasp, considering that my age is equal to his years of public service.

A biography of Senator Young has been long overdue, and by all rights should have been published decades earlier. The span of time between the end of his public service and the completion of this book has brought both disadvantages and advantages. The main disadvantage has been the natural fading of public awareness that comes during these years. Also, many good primary sources, such as family, friends, staff members and political colleagues, are no longer living. Senator Young's widow, Pat, who has long been supportive of seeing a biography on him published, has faced deteriorating health issues and was unable to actively participate as a primary source for this book. His son and daughter-in-law, John (Scoop) and Marcia Young, and other family and friends who did step forward with information and personal anecdotes have greatly enhanced this book.

The advantage to writing this biography after such a span of time is the perspective that these passing years have brought to Senator Young's years of public service. It allowed me to consider such questions as: What did he contribute to our state and nation? How did his years of service affect state and national politics and policy? How would North Dakota be different today without the military bases and other installations, or without the water projects and research laboratories he helped bring to the state? How would agriculture be different today without the target price support concept he championed that has been part of agriculture policy for the past three decades?

This book falls short of definitively answering these questions and giving Senator Young's life and accomplishments the thorough illumination and interpretation he so rightly deserves. It is, however, my hope that this book will impress upon its readers the extraordinary times in state, national and world history in which he had a front-row seat during his years of public service. There is much more about the life of Senator Young that deserves to be explored by future biographers.

In the early stage of this project, I grappled with how to effectively tell Senator Young's story with the available sources and material. I decided to not actively seek to interview an extensive number of former colleagues and acquaintances. Instead, due to the vast amount of primary source information that was collected in the oral interviews that then-University of North Dakota history professor Dr. D. Jerome Tweton conducted with Senator Young in 1979 and 1980, I made the decision to use these interviews as the corpus of this book. I laboriously typed into my computer most of the contents of these extensive interviews, grouped them by topic and from there developed the chapters. I supplemented this with the personal interviews my husband, Rick, and I conducted, with selected material from the 800 boxes comprising the Milton R. Young Papers in the Orin G. Libby Manuscript Collection at the University of North Dakota, and with accounts from state newspapers dating back to the early 1900s.

I also decided to include in every chapter direct quotations from Senator Young taken from the oral interviews with Dr. Tweton. They are shown throughout the text in italics and have been edited for syntax and sentence form.

Because my professional training and experience have been in the field of journalism, I have written this book in a journalistic style, citing sources in the body of the text, with supplemental citations in the chapter notes at the end of the book. This does not pretend to be a scholarly work. I leave that to others.

The story of any individual, whether it is a public or private life, is always told through the lens of the times during which it is written. As a North Dakota native who met Senator Young several times at political events in high school and college, and while working for Senator Mark Andrews on Capitol Hill in Washington, D.C., my hope is that for those who did not know him, this book will help define his personality, his character and his accomplishments during a lifetime dedicated to public service.

Andrea Winkjer Collin
March 12, 2010

Acknowledgments

When I began this book project, my twin daughters, Sonja and Elizabeth, had just turned 12, and daughter Karen was nearly seven. As we complete it, the older girls are freshmen in college and Karen is well-entrenched in middle school. This project has been part of their lives for more than seven years, and by now they likely have absorbed more about the life of Senator Young than most people three times their age. No writer could ask for a better partner than my husband, Rick Collin, who from start to finish has been a steady sounding board, advisor, fact checker, proofreader and rich source of historical perspective. My two sisters, one brother and their spouses, especially brother-in-law Steven Allen, have given ongoing support, as has my mother, Betty Winkjer.

I am certain I would not have been interested in writing this book without the respect for both public service and the political process that was instilled in me by my father, Dean Winkjer of Williston, North Dakota. In addition to his 52-year professional career as an attorney, he taught college level political science classes for more than a dozen years, served in the North Dakota House of Representatives for eight years, and was active in civic and political causes throughout his life. He took his children to political functions as soon as we could walk, and relished political conversations with anyone who would engage him, whether or not their views matched his. He died on April 25, 2009, and it is one of my greatest regrets that I cannot place in his hands a copy of this book.

Thank you as well, to:

The Young family, especially Marcia and John (Scoop) Young, their son Than, grandson Andrew, and niece Susie Meier, who supported this project by providing family information, materials and photographs.

Dr. D. Jerome Tweton, Professor Emeritus of History, University of North Dakota, for his extensive interviews of Senator Young in 1979 and 1980, and support throughout this project. His meticulous research prior to conducting these oral interviews provided a factual structure and invaluable primary source material detailing the Senator's life and years of public service. The value of these oral interviews will continue to increase for generations to come. What Dr. Tweton did should be an inspiration and impetus for others to follow in collecting the stories of public figures while they are still with us.

Senate Historian Donald Ritchie, from the Office of the Historian of the U.S. Senate; former Senate Librarian Greg Harness, a Fargo native who had worked in the Senate Library since 1975 and served as the Senate's 17th Librarian from 1997 until his retirement in January 2008; and Jamestown native Jim Ramstad, who served in the U.S. House of Representatives from Minnesota's Third District from 1991 to 2009, for their early encouragement and support.

Allan C. Young, of Grand Forks, whose 1989 University of North Dakota master's thesis on the "Race of the Century," provides a comprehensive recount of the 1974 Young-Guy race, for his permission to reprint it as part of this book.

Louise Aandahl Stockman of Fargo, daughter of Governor Fred Aandahl and longtime family friend, who provided valuable perspective on her father's years as a political colleague of Senator Young.

The always helpful staff at the Orin G. Libby Manuscript Collection, Elwyn B. Robinson Department of Special Collections at the University of North Dakota Chester Fritz Library; John Bye, archivist and director of the North Dakota State University Institute for Regional Studies; present and former state archives staff at the State Historical Society of North Dakota, including Gerald Newborg, Ann Jenks, Jim Davis, Sharon Silengo, Shane Molander, Greg Wysk, Sarah Walker, Lottie Bailey, and Reference Librarian Marilyn Johnson from the North Dakota Legislative Council.

The ever-dependable source of North Dakota information not easily found elsewhere that is contained in the *North Dakota Blue Books*, published by the North Dakota Secretary of State.

Sydney (Bren) Winkler, a talented young graphic designer with a bright future ahead of her, for her patience and professionalism through this long production process.

And, from the beginning to end of this project, Attorney General Wayne Stenehjem and Bob Christman, former agricultural aide to Senator Young, now Deputy North Dakota Agriculture Commissioner, for their wise counsel and steady encouragement.

A Dakota Pioneer Family Since 1880

The story of the Young family and the journey that brought it to what is now North Dakota is not unlike many pioneer families in the 1800s. North Dakota was one of the last states to be populated, with the late 1800s just beginning to see settlers move into the state, first in the east and then onward west for the next 50 years. Figures from the U.S. Census Bureau showed the population of the portion of Dakota Territory that is now North Dakota dramatically increased from 36,909 in 1880 to 646,872 in 1920.

An 18-year-old John Young came to Dakota Territory in 1881 and began farming in LaMoure County near the town of Grand Rapids. John's spirit of adventure was evident early in his life. He was born January 23, 1863 in Read's Landing, Minnesota, which is located along the Mississippi River near Lake City, about 30 miles south of St. Paul. His father, Frederick, was born in Gailsbach, Wurtenberg, Germany, and immigrated to the United States on a sailing ship as a boy. The family settled in Buffalo, New York, where Frederick grew up and worked in a saw mill as a young man.

In Buffalo, Frederick met and married Barbara Schlaider, also a native of Germany, and the couple moved west to Minnesota, settling in Read's Landing in the mid-1850s. They purchased a farm that was mostly timberland, some of which Frederick cleared and farmed. Frederick and Barbara had five children, Catherine, who died in infancy; Charles F., George, John and Henry. Barbara died at a young age in the mid-1860s, and is buried in Read's Landing.

Frederick married a second time to Eliza Flemming. She helped raise his children, and they had 10 children of their own, three who lived to adulthood. Frederick and Eliza moved directly across the Mississippi River, to Pepin, Wisconsin, where he operated a keelboat and wood yard along the Chippewa River north of Pepin. When steamboats replaced the keelboats on the river, he discontinued his keelboat operation and sold wood to fuel them. When the railroad came through and took the steamboats off the rivers, Frederick continued farming his land, raising grain, hogs and cattle. Frederick died in 1880 at the age of 47, and is buried in Pepin.

As they were nearing their teenage years, John Young and his brother, George, who was 15 months older, were having their own adventures. They worked with their father floating logs down the Mississippi River. In 1880, John moved to Dakota Territory to work on another river, the Red, in Grand Forks. After his father died later that year, he returned to Minnesota for a short time. That following spring, John, age 18, and George, age 19, decided to leave their home and go to LaMoure County, Dakota Territory. Fredrick's brother and their uncle, Charles F. Young, had already settled there and had begun acquiring many sections of prairie land. The young men boarded an emigrant train car with some of their horses, farm machinery and a wagon, stopping in Jamestown, Dakota Territory. From there they drove overland the 45 miles to their Uncle Charles's farm in Grand Rapids, arriving on June 1, 1881. The legal description of Charles's farm was Sec. 1, Twp 134, R. 62. Not wasting any time, John and George broke 170 acres of prairie by that fall.

Before the arrival of the railroad to LaMoure County, John hauled groceries the 35 miles between Jamestown to Grand Rapids by oxen. Among the stories passed down through the family about John's early years in Dakota Territory includes one that occurred a cold, winter night while hauling groceries. While he was sleeping under the wagon, a snowstorm came up and the oxen got loose, forcing John to spend most the next day locating them across the frozen prairie.

The Northern Pacific Railroad had arrived in Dakota Territory in 1872, but its southwestern branch didn't come through LaMoure County until the summer of 1887, when it ran through both the towns of LaMoure and the future town site of Berlin. In 1882 George "squatted" on a pre-emption claim, buying two yoke of oxen and beginning his own farming operation.

Throughout the 1880s, brother Charles purchased a significant amount of land in LaMoure County. He purchased several parcels from the Northern Pacific Railroad at a price ranging from 60 cents to a dollar per acre, and he worked with land agents and the Northern Pacific to lure prospective settlers to the area, taking them around and earning a small commission on the land he sold for the railroad.

In Henrietta Township, Charles owned every odd-numbered section, and several sections in some of the other townships in the county. He later was to acquire property in several other states and spent his time managing his property holdings. Charles died in 1889 at the age of 49 at a sister's home in St. Paul.

John did not take out his own homestead, but instead worked on Charles's farm for three years, breaking, cultivating and farming three quarter sections. In the spring of 1885, John purchased from Charles the south half of Section 33 in Henrietta Township. He built a 24-by-60-foot barn on the southwest quarter of his new land, and with his horses and farm machinery, John broke the prairie sod and began farming his own land.

He was elected to the Henrietta Township School Board in 1890 and was re-elected to a three-year term in 1891. At that time the population of LaMoure County was 3,061.

In the spring of 1891, John seeded 425 acres of farmland. When that was done, he traveled to Minnesota to get married. On May 14, 1891, John married Rachel Zimmerman at her home in Elizabeth, Minnesota. During his trips back home, they had met in St. Paul, where she had lived for four years as a dressmaker and seamstress. Rachel Zimmerman was born in Osseo, Minnesota in Hennepin County, February 9, 1867, the daughter of Elsbeth and Casper Zimmerman, who both were

3

from County Glorious in Switzerland, known as the German part of Switzerland. In 1870, her family, which was to grow to eight children, moved to Elizabeth, near Fergus Falls and her brother, Casper, was considered to be the first white child born in Otter Tail County. When she was 20, Rachel moved to St. Paul to become a dressmaker.

The newlyweds moved into the front part of John's barn, in separate quarters, which he had built to separate them from his horses and oxen. Rachel's memories of those early days were of the oxen rubbing their horns on the wall during the night, once even knocking down the alarm clock. Not unlike the brides of other early settlers, Rachel was discouraged and yearned to move back to St. Paul. But like most of the other homesick women, she stayed, and in her case shared her sewing skills with others, making everything from wedding dresses to funeral shrouds in the 59 years she lived in LaMoure County.

The *LaMoure County Chronicle's* "Personals" column of May 29, 1891, announced the arrival of the newlyweds back to the county: "John Young and his bride have come to their Berlin home, and John has been 'setting up' the cigars for a week."

Known as prudent and hard-working people, John and Rachel were good neighbors, helping others as they were able. Neither was educated past the third grade, but even as a young man, John was considered a good businessman and entrepreneur who had an interest in books and reading.

Soon after their wedding, John built the first brick farm house in LaMoure County, a large, square structure on the edge of what was to be the townsite of Berlin. This has since been the home to several generations of the family. The May 22, 1891, *LaMoure County Chronicle* carried the following item in its "Personals" column: "John Young expects to build a fine, two-story brick veneered dwelling, to contain eight rooms, on his Berlin farm and contractors are now figuring on the job."

In 1892, John became his area's postmaster, and the mail was brought to his farm, which he then distributed to the neighbors.

On May 28, 1894, John and Rachel's first son, George H., was born, and Charles F. arrived two years later on May 14, 1896. On December 6, 1897, Milton Ruben Young made his entrance into the world in the midst of a snowstorm. At the time, John was ill and in the hospital in Edgeley, some 11 miles west of the farm. Mrs. Ole Horsager, the neighborhood midwife and mother of three who lived three miles away, was on call to deliver the newest Young child.

A favorite family story is told about Rachel asking the farmhand, an older German bachelor uncle, to hitch up a team of horses and get Mrs. Horsager. "It's storming outside," he told Rachel. "You might as well wait until morning." He was apparently not aware that babies come when they are ready and don't wait for storms to subside. Rachel's powers of persuasion prevailed, Mrs. Horsager was retrieved and, with the snow flying outside, the third of John and Rachel's four sons came into the world.

On January 18, 1900, their fourth son, Raymond, was born on the farm in Berlin, where for the next 16 years, John and Rachel raised their family. A daughter, Irene, was born in 1902 and died in infancy.

Before the turn of the century, John had already expanded his interests beyond his farm. He had begun selling real estate, town lots and farmland, and was responsible for many new families settling in Berlin and its area.

A two-column ad that ran nearly halfway down the front page of the *LaMoure County Chronicle* on December 31, 1897, proclaimed John's real estate ventures. It read:

Westward the Star of Empire
Takes its Way!
Forty Thousand Acres!!
Choice James River Valley Land
in
LaMoure County, North Dak.

THE YOUNG ESTATE
This land is situated in the southern part of LaMoure County, and is mostly tributary to the town of Berlin. The Fargo & Southwestern Railway traverses the land east and west, and every acre of it is convenient to market.

5

The soil is of the far famed fertility of North Dakota land, and is adapted both to grain and stock raising.

NORTHERN PACIFIC LANDS

I have the agency for about 25,000 acres of Northern Pacific lands in this vicinity --- most of it south of Berlin --- whose soil is of the quality of that described above.

Also several small tracts of land contiguous to Berlin and very desirable for farm and stock purposes.

TERMS:

These lands will be sold on very liberal terms.
Correspondence regarding prices, etc., solicited.

Address,
JOHN YOUNG,
LAMOURE, NORTH DAKOTA

In the same issue of the newspaper, the editor wrote:

"As before stated, the Chronicle has been retained for a nice consideration to assist in the prosecution of John Young's immigration work. Read that double half column ad on the first page of the paper this week.

"LaMoure and LaMoure county will be strictly in the push next year. Prosperity has already come rolling in, and right at its heels is a big tidal wave of immigration that will break and dissipate itself all of LaMoure county. Happy New Year!"

In 1897, John bought for $1,200 the north half of the same section he bought in 1885 from the Minnesota Loan and Trust Company. The Northern Pacific Railroad ran through the center of this section between LaMoure and Edgeley.

In the spring of 1903, John had this section of land surveyed and plotted, founding the town of Berlin. Originally it was to be called Youngstown, but he decided to call it Berlin, most likely because the birthplace of his father, Wurtenburg, Germany, was 30 miles north of Berlin.

In 1905, John built a two-story brick building in Berlin, and he and Herman Goehl helped organize the State Bank of Berlin. He and his brother-in-law, Henry Zimmerman, founded an implement business in 1906, when he moved his family to Berlin, along with his and Rachel's mother. He also went into the machinery business with Zimmerman.

They sold Har-Par tractors, which Milt called the noisiest tractor ever made. *"An early memory of mine was hearing my father and uncle discussing tractors. This turned into an argument, with my father saying they would never be any good. Uncle Henry argued, 'They are here to stay.' It was a prophetic statement."*

True to his beliefs, during his years of farming John never owned a tractor, using instead his 30 horses. Along with his farming operation, also John custom threshed for some neighbors. *"Threshing with heavy steam-powered machinery was difficult, requiring good management and good mechanical skills. Many of the people who did custom threshing at that time lost money, especially if there was too much rain and there was a whole crew to feed through a long, rainy spell."*

John helped build the Methodist church in Berlin, where Rachel regularly brought her sons for Sunday School and worship services. Rachel was very religious and had been raised a Lutheran. John, however, was known to like to play cards, and to gamble a little. Although personally opposed to smoking, drinking and playing cards, Rachel was tolerant of those who did, especially her husband.

At that time, Methodist preachers were strongly opposed to working on Sunday. *"I remember as a young boy attending church with mother one Sunday during harvest. My father was threshing about a half mile away with his steam rig. When the engine needed water or he needed a grain hauler or something else, he would send a signal by the way he blew the steamer's whistle. The preacher was annoyed with this whistle blowing that was disturbing the church service and devoted his sermon to how bad John Young was to be threshing on Sunday. I never thought much of that preacher after that!"*

While Milt was still a child, a Latter Day Saints missionary came through the area and converted Rachel, with John to follow. The Reorganized Church of the Latter Day Saints (LDS), headquartered at Independence, Missouri, became the family's religious denomination. This branch of the Latter Day Saints did not follow the teachings of Brigham Young and broke away when he and others who believed in polygamy moved to Salt Lake City. Unlike its better known counterpart, the Church of Jesus Christ of Latter Day Saints, the Reorganized branch of the church eschewed polygamy.

The Youngs and other families in the area established a church in Berlin in a building that was vacated by the Lutherans when they built a larger church. The Youngs often hosted the Latter Day Saints Sabbath School at their home on Sunday mornings, and elders were their house guests for as long as two weeks. Milt continued his LDS affiliation throughout his life, donating to the church and attending services about once a month as an adult.

In 1909, John quit active farming and rented out his land so he could devote more time to his business interests, which by now included selling automobiles. He carried many different models of cars, the Whippet, the EMP, the Flanders, the Velie, the Little and the Rambler, but he sold Studebakers for the longest period of time. At one time John had an agency for the county and he had sub-agents selling cars for him. Most of the roads in the area were full of wagon-ruts and very poor. *"Our family also had a motorcycle for a while, and whoever was driving that would take many tumbles trying to follow the ruts."*

In 1910, the town of Berlin had a population of 137. It also had a weekly newspaper, *The Berlin Record*, which was published from June 1910 to April 1912. On the pages of this newspaper unfolded the life of this town, and the Young family was one of the families mentioned in nearly every issue.

The July 1, 1910, issue reported, "John Young is having his house remodeled throughout – a new kitchen and bathroom being added. A heating plant is to be put in, also a laundry in the basement, making a very comfortable and commodious dwelling, when completed."

Beginning with the newspaper's first issue, John ran an advertisement for his automobile business.

> **AUTOMOBILES**. A Car Load of Velies has just been received. Absolutely the greatest value for the money ever seen in any automobile manufacturer. Look them over and see them run. Their best selling argument

is the way they work. JOHN YOUNG, Berlin.

Other frequent early advertisements were from the Northern Pacific Railroad, for its passenger service; Lovett Brothers General Store, for its straw hats and work gloves; the Hamilton Drug Store and G.D. Enyart Auctioneer, both of Edgeley; R.G. Dripps Blacksmith Shop, for its specialty of horse shoes; the Murfin and Doane Attorneys at Law of Edgeley and Berlin; the State Bank of Berlin; C.W. Klenk and Company, for its gasoline stoves; the Bereman and Johnson short order restaurant, which had just opened below the State Bank of Berlin; Willis Chamberlin's Dray Line; Dr. Cresten Olson, a physician and surgeon who treated eyes and fitted glasses, and dispensed his own drugs; the City Meat Market; and the Hotel Berlin.

The newspaper's "Local Doings" column tracked the life of the community, and it frequently mentioned that John Young had traveled out of town that week to tend to business affairs. Sometimes he drove and other times he took the train, either freight or passenger, taking one one-way and the other on the return trip. Many of the trips were to area towns such as Edgeley, LaMoure, Forman, Monango and Rutland, with the purpose of travel sometimes stating that he was contracting workers for his farmland, or checking on the threshing of area farms. One weeklong trip was to Minneapolis. Another was to Detroit, Michigan, in the fall of 1911.

The "Local Doings" column of October 27, 1911, reported:
> John Young boarded the train last Friday for Detroit, Mich., where he will attend a meeting of the various agents of the E.M.F. and Flanders automobiles, both which are manufactured in that city.

Two weeks later came the report:
> John Young returned Saturday from his trip to Detroit, Mich., and other points. The Studebaker Co. surely knows how to show their agents around and give them all a good time when they see them.

Rachel traveled, as well. When her husband was in Detroit, *The Berlin Record* reported:
> Mrs. John Young, accompanied by her sons and the Berlin teachers, autoed to LaMoure Saturday to witness

the football game between LaMoure and Jamestown which resulted in the victory for LaMoure.

Milt was 13 years old, and his older brothers were attending high school in LaMoure, most certainly the reason for the trip.

The previous year, Rachel and her mother, Elsbeth Zimmerman, took a trip of their own. She had moved to Berlin in 1906 with her son, Henry and his family, after living with them in Spokane, Washington, for four years. Rachel's father had died in 1888 and Elsbeth had continued to live in Ottertail County until 1902. In 1910, Henry and his family moved to Bismarck and Elsbeth moved in with Rachel and John and their sons.

That fall of 1910, Rachel and her 70-year-old mother made a trip to northwestern North Dakota, where three of Rachel's brothers lived in Minot and Flaxton, in Ward and Burke counties. How they traveled is unclear. The "School Notes" column in the October 28, 1910, *Berlin Record* made mention of Milt, likely referencing the fact that his mother and grandmother were out of town. "Milton Young looks cheery, in spite of the fact that he is still batching."

The November 11, 1910, *Berlin Record* reported on their return:
> Last Wednesday Mrs. John Young and mother returned from their trip northwest. They found their friends and relatives well and prosperous. Grandma Zimmerman stood the trip fine for one so feeble.

Two months later, on January 24, 1911, Elsbeth Zimmerman died at John and Rachel's home. The funeral service was conducted by Reverend Wildermuth of Fargo, from the Church of the Latter Day Saints, and she was buried in the Berlin cemetery. Her five sons and Rachel attended the funeral, although her two other daughters were unable to attend.

While growing up on the farm, the Young boys got along well with each other, and although they didn't do much fieldwork, they helped with some dragging or haying. Mostly, they had quite a few cows to milk. *"Milking time was the our chance to fool around, postponing this chore for as long as possible. We would chin ourselves on the hook hanging from a post in the barn and try all kinds of gymnastics. The milking always got done, but it sometimes was late when it was completed."*

As long as they lived there, the Berlin farm home did not have toilet facilities or a bathtub. *"We would bath in a washtub, and on cold evenings we would lay around the hard coal burning stove before eventually going to bed, sometimes with a heated brick from the stove to warm our beds."*

While John was more business-minded, Rachel devoted her life to raising her four sons. Considered kind, compassionate and understanding, she was also frugal, and did not buy Milt a shirt from a store until he was 15 years old. Prior to that, she made clothes for her sons from the old clothes of the hired men during the many years she washed for them. Rachel was a large and tall woman, whom Milt resembled, and he was always close to her throughout his life. She wanted her sons to have good educations, and whenever they were away, she would write them many letters, encouraging them through the rough times in their lives. When they were away at college, she'd write them to "study hard" and "keep your clothes washed."

Rachel took butter or eggs to the local merchant trading them for groceries. The area residents were dependent on trains because they were the only means of getting groceries or any freight. *"During one particularly bad storm the town didn't have a train for five weeks. Then it came for a couple of days before another storm closed the tracks again for two more weeks."*

Milt first attended Plum Grove School, which began as a one-room country school in Henrietta Township in 1884, and later relocated to Berlin in 1904. One teacher taught all of the grades until a newer, larger school was built in 1908. The original school building was sold to the Equity Elevator and Trading Company of Berlin, remodeled and used for a house.

When he was 11 years old, Milt's class most likely participated in a statewide observance of the February 12, 1909, centennial of the birth of President Abraham Lincoln. North Dakota's Superintendent of Public Instruction Walter L. Stockwell directed that all schools throughout the state read the Gettysburg Address on that day. This may have been the beginning of Young's interest in the sixteenth President, which would play a prominent part during his public service later in his life.

Before he started school, he had begun stuttering, which he struggled with throughout the rest of his life. *"I remember being asked to make a recitation in a fourth grade school program. I tried to get started, but I just couldn't get a word out. I went back and sat down beside our hired man and he talked me into trying it again. I did, and when I got started I went very fast – and that is one of the reasons why I have talked fast ever since."*

The social life in Berlin involved whist playing and frequent get-togethers with neighbors. Picnics and baseball were very popular, with the big event of every Sunday in the summer being a baseball game between the area teams. The Young boys often walked to these events because their father wanted his horses that worked so hard all week to rest on Sundays.

After completing eighth grade in Berlin, Milt and his brothers went on to high school in LaMoure. The family moved to LaMoure in 1913, while continuing to farm the land in Berlin. *"On many Friday nights, my brothers and I would strike out from LaMoure and walk – or partly run – the 10 miles home to the farm."*

In 1912, at the age of 15, Milt landed a job as a section hand putting down ties for the Northern Pacific Railroad. *"I was the youngest one on my crew, and the section boss wanted to help me learn how to drive the railroad spike. On my first attempt, I missed the spike, hit the rail and broke the handle on the spike hammer. That was the end of my career as a spike driver."*

Milt characterized himself as a high school student who didn't get the best grades, but could always pass the examinations. Miss Kaiser, his English teacher, kept him after school many afternoons to help him with English, which was difficult for him. They were to meet again in Washington, D.C., when he was in the Senate and she, now known as Mrs. Mountain, was living only a block from him in the city.

LaMoure High School offered an agriculture course that required only three years of English and one year of mathematics, allowing Milt to graduate in three years in 1915. Perhaps the only student in LaMoure up to that time to graduate in three years, Milt had to carry a greater course load than the average student.

"More than once, Mr. McMillan, the school superintendent, called me into his office and told me to drop a course because I was taking too many. I ignored him and kept taking the classes. I saw myself as a farmer and wanted to finish high school as soon as I could."

It was a decision he would regret throughout the rest of his life.

The first office to which Milt was elected was president of the LaMoure High School Athletic Association, aided by classmate Louise Bennett, who was his campaign manager.

The Young brothers were involved in school sports. In Milt's senior year, the LaMoure High School football team was unbeaten – until it traveled to Ellendale in the fall of 1914 to play the team at the Normal School. The LaMoure team was soundly defeated, but while there for the football game, Milt met his future wife, Malinda Benson, whose parents farmed seven miles northeast of LaMoure. Of Norwegian descent, Malinda's parents had immigrated to Spring Grove, Minnesota, where she was born on October 16, 1895. They then moved to the Davenport, North Dakota, area before buying the farmland near LaMoure in the Verona-Benson Corners area. After high school, she attended Ellendale Normal School.

In 1915, during his last year in high school, Milt took about three weeks off school in the spring to put in the crops. He farmed it from then on, renting it from his father for some 20 years before eventually owning it in the early 1940s.

Milt and Malinda began dating about six months after they first met, but only sporadically for quite awhile. A quiet person who loved to dance, she and Milt, who was only good at the waltz, spent time together at area dances. *"Fortunately for me, the bands would play a waltz every third number, and that's when I would look for dance partners. I didn't*

13

practice the other dances enough to become good at them, including the polka. Sometimes older women would pull me into the square dances, but I was shoved around more than I knew what I was doing. The summer barn dances around the area were well attended, and some dances even continued throughout the winter."

In 1916, at the age of 18, Milt got his first car, which began a tradition of his father giving him a new car every summer, taking it back in the fall and getting him another one the next summer. After high school, Milt enrolled at the North Dakota Agricultural College (NDAC) in Fargo, now North Dakota State University, and joined the football team. It was then that he realized he did not have the English and geometry credits he should have had to be prepared for college and that he would need to take additional classes to get caught up with the other freshmen. As he considered what he would have to do have a successful college experience, his regret about his decision to finish high school in three years had already begun.

Soon after the NDAC football season ended, on Halloween night, Milt left college in Fargo. He drove out of town in his Studebaker with wire wheels, which he considered to be one of the fanciest cars he would have for many years. He drove to Iowa to join his brothers at Graceland College in Lamoni, which was affiliated with the Reorganized Church of the Latter Day Saints. His sole purpose for going there was to play football longer into the season. Once that football season ended, Milt joined the wrestling team. During a wrestling match he acquired a scar on his lip that he covered up for many years with a moustache.

At Graceland the three Young brothers, who resembled each other and often wore each other's clothes, made an impression with the faculty and students at the school. When oldest brother George first arrived, he acquired the nickname, "Skinny." So when Charles joined him he became, "Skinny the Second," and predictably, Milt became "Skinny the Third." *"Once when walking down the street near the campus, someone hollered to me from the window, and said, 'Wait a minute, Skinny.' I waited and the fellow said to me, 'Oh, I thought you were Skinny Young,'*

'I am,' I replied. I just wasn't the right 'Skinny Young.'"

Brother Charles had moved on to the University of Iowa to study dentistry, and while there he competed on the university's swimming, wrestling and gym teams at the same time.

At Graceland, Milt took one business course, but didn't continue college beyond that. Discouraged that at Graceland, also, he would have had to make up the high school courses that he needed to continue with a higher education, Milt abandoned the idea of going to college. Throughout his life, he regretted not pursuing a higher education, considering it a handicap that his formal education was virtually no more than three years of high school.

Milt returned home to farm. Always interested in mechanics, he believed there would be a future in learning more about it, especially for farming. That led him to Kansas City for a few months during the winters of 1916 and 1917 to attend the Sweeney Auto School in Kansas City. *"I wasn't overly impressed with the school and what I learned there, and during my second year of school after completing the classes, I worked at the Montgomery Ward store for about a month before going home to put in the crop."*

While in Kansas City, Milt had his first drink of alcohol. *"An older roommate from Alabama did a bit of drinking and we went out one night and both imbibed too much. I had a hangover the next day, and said to him, 'I will never take another drink as long as I live.' The friend replied, 'Oh, you will be a soak the rest of your life." That prediction didn't hold true, although I continued to drink as an adult."*

He smoked his first cigarette when he was 21. *"I began smoking like a trooper and chewed snuff for seven years. I tried to quit smoking in the 1930s and 1940s but it didn't work. I wasn't successful until the late 1950s."*

When he was 21 and she was 23, Milt married Malinda Benson on July 9, 1919. They eloped, driving Young's Whippet to Moorhead, Minnesota. This wedding made the front page of the *LaMoure County Chronicle* later that week in a story headlined "Dan Cupid Makes More

Conquests." The other weddings reported were of Bertha Simonsen and Clarence L. Finch at the bride's home in LaMoure, and of Gustaf Sand of Black Loam and Marie Paulson of Litchville before Judge Murfin.

This is the report on the Benson-Young wedding:

> There was a pleasant stir of interest in local circles when it learned of yet another conquest of the busy and untiring archer (Dan Cupid).
>
> On Monday forenoon, very quietly, at Moorhead, Minn., Miss Malinda Violet Benson, daughter of Mr. and Mrs. Peter E. Benson of LaMoure and Milton Young, son of Mr. and Mrs. John Young of this city, were united in the holy bonds of wedlock. The ceremony was performed at the pastorate by Rev. Martin Anderson, Norwegian Lutheran pastor of Moorhead. Charles Young, brother of the groom, appeared as witness.
>
> The young couple returned to LaMoure the same day by auto.
>
> The bride is a native of LaMoure county having spent her girlhood at the parental home near Verona. She graduated from the commercial course at the N.I.S. [Normal and Industrial School] of Ellendale. For the past five years she has been a resident of LaMoure, making her home with her parents. Possessing striking personal charms and the infectious and always engaging spirit of youth, she was warmly welcomed into the society of LaMoure's younger set. With her to her new environment go the cordial good wishes of the many friends acquired during her residence in the city and indeed wherever she has resided in the past.
>
> The groom is a young man upon whom good fortune has bestowed much honesty. Good looking, exhaling good humor, boyish sincerity and an engaging manliness withal, having won the heart of a charming life consort, Mr. Young has indeed made an auspicious start in life. He is also a native of LaMoure county, having been born upon the farm at Berlin. Having spent most of his life upon the farm he may well be termed a son of the soil. For the past eight years he has been a resident of LaMoure and the greater part of the time. He is a graduate of the LaMoure High School, was a student at the N.D.A.C. and took a commercial course at Graceland College of Lamoni, Ia. The past year Milton has assumed no small

responsibility for a young man, having rented his father's extensive farming estate of about nine hundred acres near Berlin, the cropping of which he has superintended. He will continue farming operations in this capacity.

Tuesday evening the young couple autoed to the farm near Berlin where they will set up housekeeping immediately. The Chronicle is pleased indeed to join in the hearty congratulations and good wishes extended to the young couple by their many friends throughout the county.

A Dirt Farmer During the Depression

In 1916, North Dakota political legend William Langer is said to have sat back and charted every step of his political career that would eventually lead him to the United States Senate, including a stop in the governor's office. As audacious as this may have seemed, this map of his future took him down the road he aspired, notwithstanding a few bumps along the way.

This could not be more different than the dreams of Milton Young. As a young man he considered no other profession than being a LaMoure County farmer, even rushing through high school to begin this vocation. That Langer and Young, who had such different early aspirations and personal styles, would become two of the most dominant figures on North Dakota's political landscape in the 20th Century and eventually become colleagues in the U. S. Senate is one of the ironies in the state's political history.

The newly married Milton and Malinda Young began the decade of the 1920s in the brick farm home his father had built at the edge of Berlin in Henrietta Township nearly 30 years before. John Young had been renting that land to his son for the past decade, and he offered the newlyweds the farmhouse as their home. It would be another 20 years before John Young would officially deed the land to them.

John and Rachel Young had built a modern frame house in LaMoure in 1916, which was their home for the rest of their lives. From 1922 to 1935, the elder Youngs spent most of the winter months in Miami,

Florida, and the rest of the year in LaMoure.

In 1922, Young followed in his father's footsteps and began a 25-year stint as a custom thresher. With his newly purchased threshing machine, called a separator, Young had an ambitious year. He shipped his threshing rig up to Noonan, in the very northwest corner of the state near the Canadian border, to work on some fields owned by Malinda's family and their neighbors. He unloaded the equipment in the nearby town of Kermit, threshing in that area for about four or five weeks. He finished in mid-November, quitting only because of the cold weather. Harvest at that time was a much slower process, without the benefit of today's fertilizers and varieties of grain that mature earlier.

Back home, while taking care of several neighbors' crops, he also traveled 60 miles south and east to farms near the Sargent County communities of Forman and Rutland, especially in 1939 and 1940, when he didn't have much of a crop to harvest. In 1943 he did custom work for 18 neighbors, in 1944, for 12 and in 1945 he threshed for nine neighbors.

Although he never invested in the stock market, Young dabbled in the grain markets – once. *"I bought 10,000 bushels of oats on the futures market in 1923, when I was shredding corn for neighbors and making about $20 a day. At that same time, I was losing nearly that much every day on the oats market. On the day before Christmas, the money I put up for margins ran out and I received a telegram that day telling me I was closed out. I learned a hard lesson and never put money in the grain futures market again."*

In 1927, Young purchased a 20-35 Allis Chalmers tractor which, like his threshing separator, was to last him well beyond two decades. Known for the meticulous care he gave his machinery, he and Malinda also worked hard to keep their farmyard clean and neat.

Young's love of baseball carried into his early farming years. Although an early ambition in life to become a baseball pitcher never happened, that didn't stop him from enjoying the sport. He became manager of the Berlin baseball team, partly to give him a better chance to play. Many area teams, Berlin included, hired some players, and Young gave special consideration to those who played baseball when he hired men for farm work.

"LaMoure was always the town for Berlin to beat, but other area teams that were also good included Rutland, which had a battery of black players, and the town of Medberry, located between Berlin and Edgeley. Although there was a regular schedule of summer baseball games, these towns were too small to be part of a league, and most of the time we would play each other on an informal schedule."

Young played his last game when he was 29. *"I was playing left field, although I ordinarily played right field. A high fly ball was completely lost in the sun as I tried to catch it. It hit my glove, but could just as well have hit my head because I didn't see it. The ball was dropped and the game was lost. I was not too good at hitting. I always wanted to be a pitcher because I was all arm and no body. I often thought that if I had coaches like they have now where every pitcher learns to get his whole body into the throw, I might have been able to pitch much better."*

Attending that last game was a new LaMoure resident who was to be a political contemporary of Young's decades later. He was the Reverend Leslie R. Burgum who served the LaMoure Methodist Church from 1927 until 1930. Burgum had also trained in the field of law, and in 1930 was appointed to a parish in Larimore, where he was able to complete studies at the nearby University of North Dakota Law School in Grand Forks. Burgum passed the bar exam in 1933, although he continued in the full time ministry for some time after that. In 1940 he was the unsuccessful Democratic candidate for lieutenant governor and in 1954 he was elected attorney general, serving in that position until 1962.

The stock market crash of October 1929 ushered in the Great Depression, and the severe drought that followed throughout the next decade was to affect LaMoure County deeply. It influenced Young and his political philosophy the rest of his life.

Although he didn't have much money in banks, he watched how the economic crisis of the Depression affected his father and other family members. Because John Young suspected there might be a Depression, he scattered what little money he had in seven different area banks. All but two went broke. When his banker, David Lloyd of LaMoure, left to go get that money, he dressed like a poor person on the train, hiding the money in his pockets so he wouldn't get robbed.

The Depression had a profound impact on the population of North Dakota. LaMoure County lost about a third of its farmers, and between the years of 1930 and 1944, North Dakota's overall population decreased from 682,000 to 534,000.

As many as half of the population in North Dakota during the Depression received some kind of relief through a New Deal program. They had their critics, but Young recognized that without these programs many more people would have left the state.

"Some of my neighbors hunted jackrabbits and dug wells to make money. One program paid farmers to kill their cattle and pigs, which bothered many, including our Congressman William Lemke, because of the paltry $20 that was offered as the top price."

Young remembered how discouraged his neighbors were after every harvest during those years. *"They would vow not to put in another crop. But by the time spring came, they would be in their fields again. Because everyone was so broke, men would stop by the farms and beg to stay over the winter and work for as low as $12 a month and even furnish their own clothes."*

In the 1930s Young raised mostly grain, but had a few dozen dairy cows for several years, about the most one person could milk by hand. *"I had a milking machine, but during the worst times the electricity bill was so high that it forced me back to hand-milking. Dairying was a losing business for the first 10 years I had dairy cows."*

Young also raised a few sheep, but too many were being killed by dogs, and there wasn't enough feed during the drought years. *"I got rid of them, figuring it would be easier to get back into the sheep business when the drought ended than to build up a new dairy herd.*

"There were two years when I had no crop at all, except for a little

'header,' which grew in the sloughs and would produce enough for about half of my seed for the next year."

As difficult as life was during the Depression, some of Young's neighbors kept their sense of humor. *"One planted cactus he was going to use to winter his cattle. I watched it turn brown and I told him the cows would never eat that brown cactus. The neighbor replied, 'Then, I will put green glasses on them!'"*

While growing up, the subject of partisan politics was not discussed in his home. Although his father served on the township school board, Young never knew the politics of either his father or mother. He assumed his father was quite independent, but becoming involved in politics was not something they had encouraged him to do, or that he did to please them.

"When I first voted in 1920 at the age of 22 I had decided I was a Republican. But I was too proud to carry a voter's guide into the voter's booth with me the first time I voted, and later I realized I voted for some of the wrong candidates."

The Nonpartisan League (NPL) was organized by A.C. Townley in 1915 and 1916. LaMoure County, especially Berlin, was considered one of the hotbeds of the NPL in its early days, with many area farmers joining its ranks. By the 1920s it had become the dominant political force in the state and was aligned with the Republican Party. *"I was uncomfortable with many of the liberal platforms of the NPL, so I supported the non-NPL Republican candidates"*

It was the poor wheat prices in the 1920s, a result of the post-World War I domestic economy, that drew Young into politics, and his political views throughout his life were to be shaped by his early years of farming in the 1920s and 1930s.

In 1924, Young followed the McNary-Haugen farm bill in Congress closely. Senator Charles McNary from Oregon was chairman of the Senate Agriculture Committee and Representative Gilbert Haugen from Iowa was chairman of the House Appropriations Committee. Both Republicans, they proposed creating a federal farm board with a revolving fund that would dispose of surplus farm commodities to markets overseas.

In presenting the legislation to the House, Representative Haugen outlined some of the issues in agriculture he hoped his bill would address. These issues included there being half as many bank failures between 1920 and 1923 as in the whole period from 1902 to 1923; that four-sevenths of the total farm income was being used to pay taxes and interest on mortgages and debt; that farm labor had become so costly the average farmer could not afford to hire; that more than 1.1 million farmers and hired men had deserted the farm in 1922 to seek industrial employment; that one-quarter of the farm owners in the corn and wheat states were bankrupt; and, that the purchasing value of farm products was less than half what it was before World War I.

This legislation was made to address these issues by declaring that a general emergency existed in agriculture; creating a $2 million corporation funded by the federal government with a board of directors consisting of the Secretary of Agriculture and four members appointed by the President; empowering the corporation to buy and sell wheat, flour, rice, corn, wool, cattle, sheep, swine and food products of cattle and swine whenever a special emergency was declared in one or more. When the market price fell below the ratio price, the corporation would buy enough of the commodity for export to restore the domestic price. The ratio price would bear the same relation to the pre-war price as the current-average price of all commodities bears to the average prewar prices of commodities. And, to protect the ratio price from foreign competition, the Secretary of Agriculture could declare prohibitive or embargo tariff rates.

The legislation was supported by a group of Republicans in May 1924 who had gathered in Jamestown to organize efforts to promote a slate of "independent" or "real" Republicans in the June primary election. The group sent a telegram to North Dakota Congressman Olger B. Burtness and encouraged other commercial clubs and civic organizations in the state to also show their support.

The bill passed Congress twice, in 1927 and 1928, but Republican President Calvin Coolidge vetoed it both times.

It was two decades later that Young was to realize the significant role Burtness played in drafting this legislation. In a December 2, 1946, letter to Young during his second year in the Senate regarding an agricultural price support bill, Burtness wrote:

> . . . [this bill] has the underlying principles of the old McNary-Haugen Bill, in which I was tremendously interested. In fact, I might tell you that I was the one who got then-Secretary (Agriculture Secretary Henry C.) Wallace to put his economists to work to draft the bill, and the one with whom the department cooperated until the bill was in shape, and Secretary Wallace and myself then agreed that the way in which to give it the greatest possible prestige was to have it introduced by the chairman of the agricultural committees of both houses. The fact is that McNary and Haugen knew nothing about it until the secretary mailed them proposed copies. This situation came about not because of any particular modesty on my part, but because I had the firm belief that such procedure would serve our ultimate purpose the best.

In his reply to him on December 7, 1946, Young wrote:

> . . . I hadn't realized, Olger, that you were this much interested in agricultural problems, particularly, dating way back to the days of the McNary-Haugen bill. In all probability, Olger, if you hadn't been quite so modest in subordinating your work on this bill by giving authorship to McNary and Haugen, it might had made a great difference in your political future. This bill was popular in North Dakota for a good many years.

Burtness served in Congress from 1921 until defeated for re-election in 1932, swept aside in the national landslide that elected Democrat Franklin D. Roosevelt to the White House that year.

In 1924 at the age of 27, Young decided to seek public office. Although his stuttering bothered him, he had come to terms with it and determined it would not keep him from aspiring to a life of public service. Throughout his life, he took his stuttering in stride, observing several times that it kept him humble and kept his speeches shorter.

Longtime LaMoure friend Claire Sandness remembered hearing Young speak at a LaMoure County Fair in the 1930s when he was a candidate for office. Standing on a grain truck, Young made his speech. When he was finished, he stopped to visit with Sandness, and said, "Claire, it would have been a lot easier to shovel grain off this truck than it was to speak off it."

He began his political career at the grassroots level, becoming a successful candidate for both the Henrietta Township board and its school board. Young and the other members of the school board faced a tough challenge to manage the school district during the Depression. By watching the spending very closely, this was one of the few solvent districts in the state. It even paid teachers $10 more a month than the required minimum wage of $45 a month.

A policy of the board was that township residents who needed relief could not go directly to a welfare agency. It was the responsibility of Young and the other township board members to first try to locate any relatives who could help them before they could approve assistance.

In 1933, he was elected to the Corn and Hog Board, and for a time served as president of the LaMoure County group. *"This was a new federal program that created much interest among farmers because they received small payments based on the number of hogs they had or acres of corn they had planted."*

A similar federal wheat program was also implemented at about the same time. In 1934, LaMoure County producers were paid more than $200,000 for these programs, with the entire state receiving payments of $3.95 million.

Joining Young on the county board were A.J. Sandness, from Litchville; A.A. Brunsman, from LaMoure; E.G. Nicolai, from Deisem; J.J. Wells, from Edgeley; H.B. Struble, from Marion; and Victor Kelder, from Verona. Each board member was responsible for getting information to a designated part of the county. Young's district covered the townships of Henrietta, Willow Bank, Wano and Badger. *"Board members spent a lot of time arguing with the federal statistician and the state agency that oversaw the program. The biggest problem in running the board was farmers claiming to have more hogs than they actually had in order to receive higher payments."*

While serving on this board he first met Fred Aandahl, who would later play an important role in Young's political career. Aandahl was president of the Corn and Hog Board in Barnes County, which bordered LaMoure County to the north. Young and Aandahl formed an immediate bond. *"We shared the same views about the benefit federal money could have on struggling farmers."*

During the Presidency of Franklin Roosevelt, the Corn and Hog Board became part of one of his New Deal programs, the Agricultural Adjustment Agency, or AAA. It included all grain crops.

He remained on it until he was elected to the state legislature and a state ruling made elected legislators ineligible to serve on that board. He also helped organize the Farmers Union in Berlin, including its grain elevator, and was the group's secretary for awhile. He called a meeting to help organize the Farmers Union Insurance Company and took out a $1,000 policy, which he carried throughout his life. Young remained a member of this Farmers Union chapter until about 1940, even though he had long since realized that the organization's politics had become too liberal for him, and the organization opposed him in some of his campaigns.

The petite Malinda, who barely reached to her husband's shoulders, was quiet and a hard worker, although she did not take to farm life as well as had Young's mother. She was known for the hearty meals she cooked for the farm workers and the threshing crews, and she was active in the Berlin Homemakers Club and the Berlin Legion Auxiliary. Later in life she was involved with the Zoar Church of LaMoure, LaMoure Fortnightly Club, and the Organization of Eastern Star.

Although he was known as an amiable neighbor and good citizen, Young had his share of human frailties. *"Once I got into trouble gambling in a tavern in Berlin, running up a fairly sizeable debt. My gambling habit was cured after a collector came to the farm and took a few pigs to pay the debt."*

Another time he had to pay a $75 fine for getting into a scuffle with the grain elevator operator over a payment dispute. As he was paying his fine, Young told the clerk of court, "You might as well double that because I'm going to go hit him again!"

Along with their crops and livestock, Young and Malinda raised three sons on the family farm. The oldest, Wendell "Mix," was born December 18, 1919. Duane Charles "Toad," was born November 28, 1921, and John Milton "Scoop" was born on November 26, 1923.

Their unusual nicknames had interesting origins. "Toad" came from the way Duane walked as a toddler as a result of the bowlegs he developed from the braces he wore to help him walk. "Scoop" was the name of a popular comic strip character. And "Mix" was the name of a friend of Young's at Graceland College.

The Young boys attended school in Berlin, and one vivid memory Scoop has from his childhood was when he nearly died of pneumonia when he was 12. His father stayed with him day and night in the hospital until he recovered, bringing the two closer than ever.

Young's first two decades as a full-time farmer taught him many lessons he would carry with him the rest of his life. They included how to persevere through a crippling Depression, the value of neighbors and family during rough times, and the role government should play in agriculture policy.

An Emerging Political Figure

As the 1930s emerged, William Langer had established himself as a dominant force who was to ride the highs and lows of a colorful North Dakota political career. It began with his first statewide election as Attorney General in 1916 and lasted until his death in 1959. As Langer's power and influence increased throughout the 1920s and into the 1930s, the political philosophies and allegiances of most other politicians in the state were defined by whether they were pro-Langer or anti-Langer. By the mid-1930s, Young had decided he was anti-Langer.

The Nonpartisan League's (NPL) record of supporting what were considered radical social programs is well documented — founding the Bank of North Dakota, the State Hail Insurance Department, and the State Mill and Elevator, among other projects. This philosophy of state ownership turned many against the NPL, including Young. *"I was no tough conservative. I was broke. I probably should have been as liberal as the rest of them, and I was in some respects. But the thinking of many I knew in the NPL, and I had many good friends among them, was pretty much Socialist and it turned me against them."*

One of Young's first political influences was an older neighbor, August Schockman, who lived three miles north of Berlin. A successful farmer who bought cattle and was president of the bank in Berlin, Schockman was active in the anti-NPL movement, and he insisted on taking Young with him to county political meetings. Young became involved on the precinct level before elections, attending meetings with Schockman, and it wasn't long before he was being eyed by party leaders as a potential candidate.

He attended his first state Republican convention in Valley City in 1932, when President Herbert Hoover was endorsed for re-election. *"I was broke at the time, and I was bothered by a resolution that was passed at that Convention saying how wonderful everything was in the country. Everyone I knew was broke, and I decided that I could not vote for Hoover."*

This was an early indication of his political personality, which was marked by an independent streak that decade after decade was tempered with his desire to keep the Republican Party from being too conservative.

In the spring of 1932, Young and two other friends from Berlin went to visit Edgeley physician, Dr. Lee Greene, at his office. Greene was from a politically active family. His father, James, had been a member of the first North Dakota legislature after statehood in 1889, and Dr. Greene was the county leader of the Independent Voters Association (IVA), which since 1918 had been an anti-Nonpartisan League force in the Republican Party. Young and Greene also shared a mutual love of baseball. *"During that visit, Dr. Greene said to me, 'You are going to run for the House of Representatives.' I answered, 'The hell I am!' About a month later I learned that Dr. Greene had already circulated petitions for me to be a candidate. I went along with it, however, and officially announced my candidacy for the North Dakota House on March 31, 1932."*

In the early days of his first campaign, Candidate Young stopped to see Al May, a conservative Dickey banker. From him he received one of his first stern lectures in the realities of politics. *"He asked me if I was supporting Hoover. I replied, 'Mr. May, I'm afraid not. I probably should not say this but I am not voting for him.' He then forcefully let me know how important it was to be loyal to the party ticket, and it taught me a lesson. I was very careful about ever talking about not voting for another Republican again."*

Also on the campaign trail Young met Charlie Nelson, a man who told him that he sold Flanders automobiles as one of the agents for John Young's automobile business. Nelson joked to Young, "If the Lord ever forgives me for selling those automobiles, I will never do anything wrong again!"

Young announced his candidacy in some advertisements in the *LaMoure Chronicle*. One advertisement that ran on May 26, 1932, was joined by similar ones from other candidates, including T.S. Hunt for County Auditor; De Forest French for County Treasurer; B.W. Boyd for Clerk of Court; N.J. Crudden for Sheriff; M.C. Aahl for County Superintendent; M.A. Buechler for County Judge, and Charles E. Crist for Register of Deeds.

Young's announcement read:

> To the Voters of LaMoure County: I am a candidate for Representative on the Republican ballot to be voted on at the Primary Election on June 29, 1932. I am an active farmer and was born in LaMoure County. Have served on the township and school boards of Henrietta Township for the past 8 years.
>
> It is my sincere belief that I can and will serve the best interest of this community, if elected.
>
> Your cooperation and vote toward my election will be appreciated.
>
> Respectfully,
> MILTON R. YOUNG

A week before the election, Young wrote the following letter he mailed to voters.

> MILTON R. YOUNG
> (Farmer)
> Berlin, N. Dak. June 23, 1932

Dear Voter:

> I am a candidate for the office of State Representative for this district and my name will be on the Republican Ballot. My occupation has always been a farmer and I have no other interests. I have lived continuously on the farm, where I now live, except for a few years away at school.
>
> I have served on the township and school boards for the past eight years and have been chairman of the township board for the past seven years consecutively.

We have good reserves in both township and school treasuries. The average tax per quarter section of land in the township where I reside, and for, at least, the past three years is the lowest of any consolidated school district in the county.

I am for good, sane government and am against wild plunges in any direction. It is time we get down to common sense. If there is a man in your party or mine that doesn't deserve to be there, it is time to vote him out. He is a detriment to both you and your party.

You may rightfully say: "well, if he wants the office he should come and see me." It is almost impossible to cover the entire county in these kind of times for an office, to which, I am elected, pays only expenses and would take me away from my farm work for a period of 60 days.

I don't know why I would be interested in any legislation that wouldn't be good for all the farmers of North Dakota. I am having just as much trouble trying to make ends meet, in raising 30 cent wheat and $2.00 hogs, as any of the rest of the farmers.

Your vote and support will be sincerely appreciated and if elected, I promise you a square deal.

Respectfully submitted,
Milton R. Young,
Republican Candidate for
Representative this district

Young's mention of the incumbent who was a "detriment to both you and the party" referred to William H. KaDell, who was a farmer north of Edgeley. Before the election, Young asked his friend Ed Reed from nearby Grand Rapids about how many votes he would get in his township. Reed replied, "You would get all but two, and Christ himself wouldn't get them if he ran." Young got all but one.

In that summer's primary election, Young's 1,667 votes made him the second highest vote getter, behind incumbent Carl Opdahl's 1,856 votes. Young edged out the other incumbent, W.H. KaDell, who received 1,511 votes. This guaranteed him a place on the general election ballot. Because of the strength of the Republican Party and its Nonpartisan League faction, contests among Republicans to win the Party's primary election constituted almost a more hard-fought battle than the general election contest between the Republican and the Democrat.

That election resulted in a sweep of NPL candidates to top state offices, including Langer as governor. An original member of the NPL, Langer left it in 1919 to unsuccessfully run for governor as an IVA candidate in 1920, only to return to the NPL in the late 1920s. The 1932 NPL sweep was a setback for the IVA Republican candidates, who in the 1920s had dominated the state legislature.

The *LaMoure Chronicle's* June 30 recap of the primary election noted Young's victory. "Milton Young of Berlin, making his debut in political circles, showed up brilliantly in the Republican race for the legislature, running close behind the popular veteran Carl Opdahl. W.H. KaDell, incumbent, was eliminated."

The *Chronicle* that day also noted, "Milton Young crashed into politics, successfully defeating the incumbent, W.H. KaDell, and will run with C.H. Opdahl against the unopposed Democrats."

A week later on July 7, another *LaMoure Chronicle* article recapping the election wrote said, "The League swing takes with it a comfortable working majority in the Legislature, as well, with 21 of 28 senatorial candidates elected and 80 for the House. Milton Young of LaMoure county was one of the very few Independent endorsed candidates for representative who came out successful."

In that same issue, Assistant Editor W.S. Hancock wrote in his "Bill Sez" column, "For a novice in the political game, Milt Young struck a gait that makes even the old timers sit up and take notice."

The LaMoure County Auditor tabulated the money spent by the 34 candidates during the primary campaign. It was $930.49. Young was the top spender with a total of $79.50. He and only three others spent more than $70.

During the fall campaign, Young tried to visit every farmhouse in the county. He also ran a large, two-column by seven-inch display advertisement in the newspaper on October 27. It read:

MILTON R. YOUNG
Republican Candidate
FOR REPRESENTATIVE

I am a native of LaMoure County; have lived my entire life on the farm where I now reside, with the exception of a few years at school. I have farmed seven to nine quarters of land myself for the past 14 years.

I have been Chairman of Henrietta Township Board for the last seven years; am a member of the School Board of Henrietta Township; serving in that capacity for the last three years.

Following this service to the people of the Township, they were kind enough to give me 118 votes in the June Primary, out of a total of 158. The taxes of Henrietta Township have been the lowest of any Consolidated School District of the County for the past three years.

If elected, I will sincerely work for the interests of the LaMoure County Farmers. I sell my products on the same market as the rest of the farmers in LaMoure County, and have as much trouble making "ends meet."

Why can't we forget politics for the time being, and work for our common interest – agriculture.

Being short of both time and money, it will only be possible for me to see a small percentage of the voters of the county. I hope you will over look this, and give me the same consideration as if I had the privilege of seeing you personally.

I respectfully solicit your vote and support at the General Election, November 8, 1932.

Respectfully Yours,
MILTON R. YOUNG

P.S. My name will appear on the Republican column on the Ballot.

Running as an Independent, Young was considered an unsponsored candidate, the only one in the county to have no political organization backing him on the ticket. His name, however, was on the Republican ballot because state law allowed Independent candidates to designate what type of party affiliation they wanted on the ballot.

That didn't seem to matter to the LaMoure County voters comprising Legislative District 24. Opdahl was the top vote getter with 2,177 votes, and Young took the second most votes, 1,963. He defeated William

Boardman, the Democratic candidate, by 42 votes to win a seat in the House. W.H. KaDell, who was defeated for re-election in June, ran again as a write-in candidate but came up short again, polling 1,164 votes. The fifth candidate, J.W. Kniefel, took 739 votes.

In addition to Langer's win in the race for governor, voters returned Senator Gerald P. Nye to the Senate with 100,000 more votes than his Democratic opponent, P.W. Lanier of Jamestown. Young's victory notwithstanding, the 1932 election swept NPL candidates into control of the entire state administration, winning majorities in both houses of the North Dakota Legislature and every state office. At the national level, Democratic Presidential nominee Franklin D. Roosevelt easily defeated President Hoover, carrying North Dakota as well.

Young was the only IVA candidate to win in the state, and the results of this election signaled the virtual demise of the IVA.

The front pages of the January 5, 1933, *LaMoure Chronicle* carried articles on the plenary sessions of the Legislature with Young and Opdahl as the county's representatives. In a fitting contrast to the news of Young's political success was another front-page article in the same newspaper on the success of Young, the farmer:

Rep. M. Young
Breaks Record
Berlin Man's Fed Lambs
Lead Receipts in St. Paul Market

Rep. Milton Young of Berlin may be a legislator these days, but he is first and foremost one of the most progressive and successful farmers in LaMoure county. Just now he is congratulating himself on his lamb feeding undertaking this fall, not to mention receiving the congratulations of his admiring friends.

Cause for the celebration is the carload of feeder lambs which Legislator Young last week sent to the St. Paul market. Of the 270 lambs sent down, every single one of them topped the market except one animal which was a cripple!

Records show that the lambs, which averaged an average of 20 pounds apiece in the 75 days that Young has been feeding them – considered a remarkably fine record by sheepmen.

In spite of the fact the Mr. Young had a run of bad luck when he first received the shipment of lambs to feed, he found the experiment successful. After all shipping costs had been paid and allowance made for his original losses, Mr. Young netted $244 – more than enough to cover the feeding charges and still leave a nice profit to pay himself for his labor.

Milton Young is one of the most enthusiastic proponents of the contract lamb feeding system which County Agent Wayne Weiser has been promoting in LaMoure county for the last several years.

In January, Young and Opdahl drove to Bismarck for the opening of the North Dakota Legislative Session on January 3. An influenza epidemic in the state had stricken the newly elected Governor Langer, who was too ill to attend any inaugural festivities and didn't appear at his office until the second week of January. The Legislature was still meeting at the World War Memorial building in downtown Bismarck. The spectacular fire that destroyed the Capitol Building on December 28, 1930, had displaced the Legislature, along with other state offices, until the new 19-story building was occupied in late 1934.

One of the first votes by the 1933 House of Representatives elected NPL Republican Representative Minnie D. Craig of Esmond Speaker of the House. Craig, a former Republican National Committeewoman, became the first woman legislator to hold this position of leadership in North Dakota. Ironically, the same NPL caucus that nominated Craig for Speaker also adopted a motion to prohibit the employment of married women in the Legislature "except where they are shown to be in need of work."

In his freshman year, Young was assigned to the Judiciary, Revision and Corrections of the Journal, Temperance, and Ways and Means committees. Because North Dakota voters had just repealed Prohibition in the general election, the Temperance Committee's work no longer had much relevance.

Serving in the Legislature throughout the 1930s was difficult. *"North Dakota had $40 million in state debt in 1933, and Golden Valley County was the only county in the entire state without a deficit because* *of the efficient strip crop farming practices the Swedish immigrants to that area used long before they were implemented anywhere else. Sioux County was at the other extreme – for awhile it didn't have enough money to buy postage stamps."*

Legislators from the eastern part of the state were more conservative, while those from the west tended to have more liberal views. Williams County Representative Ben Fedje served in the House three terms between 1923 and 1936. *"Fedje liked to lecture the members, especially those from the Red River Valley and other eastern parts of the state, who were faring better through the Depression years than their western neighbors. He said, 'If you had no crop and all the cactus we have, you would be just as radical as we are!'"*

It was another example of the political attitude Young had observed in his home area during the years of the greatest struggles on the farm – *"when people go broke, they tend to get more liberal."*

During his first term as a state legislator, Young was able to observe Governor Langer closely. *"In his speeches during the Legislative Session, the Governor would advocate a lot of liberal ideas. But, he would expect the legislators to be more conservative and kill many of these proposals. Once in awhile, when they didn't, Governor Langer would send a top lieutenant over to the legislative chambers to see that those bills were killed. It was an example of Langer's keen political instincts – advocating legislation that was popular with many voters, while also working behind the scenes to ensure that it not be passed."*

By 1934, Young had decided he was going to speak out as an anti-Langer candidate. *"He had gotten into all kinds of trouble and advocated some things I couldn't stand for. I first publicly attacked Langer in the LaMoure area, and he in turn called me a 'trickster and a liar.'"*

After two years in the House of Representatives, Young decided to run for the State Senate in 1934. His *LaMoure Chronicle* advertisement in the June 21, 1934, issue that ran prior to the June 27 primary election stated:

Milton R. Young
CANDIDATE FOR
STATE SENATOR

As a Farmer I'm naturally most interested in Legislation affecting Farm interests.

I challenge any one to show where I voted wrong on Farm Bills in the last session. As a Farmer I have no objection to legislation Towns and Cities need to carry on their governments.

We have a common interest and there should be no hard feelings or conflicting ideas.

For years I have been a member of both school and township boards.

Your confidence and support is always appreciated.

37 Years on the same LaMoure County farm.

The primary election results put Young ahead of the Democratic incumbent, Nick W. Schommer, with 1,978 and 1,487 votes respectively. For this election, Young spent $29.50 to Schommer's total of $8.

North Dakota has had many significant political years since becoming a state in 1889. The political chaos that ensued in 1934 must qualify as near the top of that list. That was the year North Dakota had four governors in seven months. Even as a freshman legislator, Young was drawn into the fray.

In April 1934, Governor Langer and eight others from his administration were indicted by a grand jury for misuse of federal funds. They were charged with soliciting funds from federal employees for political purposes and conspiring to corruptly administer federal funds. This legal action was supported by two diverse groups, the state's conservatives and the Roosevelt Administration.

Statewide newspaper accounts of these days presented daily updates on this political chaos. A trial began on May 22, and the jury found Langer guilty. He was sentenced on June 29 to 18 months in a federal prison and fined $10,000. Langer immediately appealed.

Lieutenant Governor Ole Olson arrived in Bismarck to take the office of governor, but was told by Langer's people that because the sentence was being appealed, Langer did not need to leave office.

Olson appealed to the state Supreme Court, which ruled on Tuesday, July 10, that Langer was disqualified to continue to hold the office of governor. Following this decision, Langer, who said he feared the danger of rioting and bloodshed, proclaimed martial law, which brought 20 National Guardsmen to the capitol.

Langer also called a special session of the Legislature to convene at noon on July 19, saying that it was needed to deal with specific tax and other state issues, but the general belief was that Langer hoped that League-dominated legislators would somehow find a way to keep him in office.

Believing that he was the legitimate acting governor, Olson contacted state legislators himself, revoking Langer's call for a special session. Langer countered with personal letters and telegrams telling them to "pay no attention to any message that the session will not convene."

"I was still a state representative when I received the messages, and decided to go to Bismarck, even though I was broke at the time, and had to borrow $60 to make the trip."

The heat wave that gripped the Great Plains that week matched the political heat in Bismarck. The *Bismarck Tribune* reported that on July 18 Napoleon's high was 108 degrees, and Bismarck, Wishek and Jamestown recorded temperatures of 106 degrees. All other points in the state reporting temperatures were also above 100 degrees, except for Crosby's 95 degrees, Williston's 96 and Max's 99.

The national press was following the hunt for Public Enemy Number One, John Dillinger, which ended in the shooting death of the notorious Depression-era gangster in Chicago on July 22. At the same time, several national newspapers and magazines dispatched reporters to Bismarck to cover the chaos at the state capitol.

The lawmakers who traveled to Bismarck gathered for the first time in the legislative chambers of the new North Dakota Capitol. The furnishings in the chambers were described by the *Bismarck Tribune* on July 19:

> Desks for the solons in both chambers are of pine
> – small rather insecure affairs, stained to hide their

newness. Set before the majestically rising columns behind the platform of the Senate is a simple kitchen table of wood – the dollar ninety-eight kind to serve as the president's desk.

A miscellaneous collection of folding chairs, camp chairs, kitchen chairs and just plain chairs has been provided, completing the setting for a session, the first to be held in the state's new $2,000,000 capitol.

Notices on the capitol pillars posted by Acting Governor Olson suspending the session were ignored as people entered the new building on July 19. Joining the assembled legislators when the session convened at noon were interested onlookers who crowded each chamber's galleries. With 59 House members answering roll call in the House a quorum was reached, enabling the session to convene. The 17 senators who assembled fell short of a quorum. The session was quickly recessed with plans to reconvene the next day. This dashed the hopes for a legislative remedy to his situation for Langer, who had barricaded himself inside his office behind heavy bronze doors, with guards posted in his office and at all entrances to the Capitol.

In addition to the legislators, 700 Langer supporters had gathered at the Capitol that day. Usher L. Burdick, the president of the Farm Holiday Association and the Langer-endorsed Republican candidate for Congress, had called the Farm Holiday members to Bismarck. They were demanding that Acting Governor Olson support farm legislation that would establish a five-year farm foreclosure ban during the special session of the Legislature that was scheduled to reconvene the next day.

Young remembered years later the tense and angry feeling among those supporters that day, who were shouting, "We want Langer." He was among those who worried that the crowd could have erupted into a serious and dangerous situation. Olson, who a few days earlier had feared that federal troops would need to be called to remove Langer from his office, faced the angry horde in front of the Capitol. Olson, an anti-Langer Republican, was a longtime dirt farmer near New Rockford, and also a member of the Farm Holiday Association.

An account of Olson's July 20 confrontation with the Farm Holiday

Association members appeared in the July 21 *Bismarck Tribune*:

HOLIDAYITES TOLD EXTRA SESSION
OF SOLONS NOT NEEDED
Acting Governor Olson Pledges All Possible Aid to Farm Cause

Efforts of members of the Farm Holiday Association to induce Acting Governor O.H. Olson to call a special session of the state legislature failed Friday.

In unmistakable terms Olson told them in a speech delivered at the capitol, that he would not do it. And they cheered him when he finished.

As a result the "demonstration" counted on by Langer partisans to create an atmosphere favorable to him, fizzled dismally. Many of the holiday members were on their way home Saturday.

When the demonstrators, shepherded by J.H. Miller, Bismarck, arrived at the capitol building, Olson told their leaders that it was the people's capitol, paid for it with their taxes, and invited them in. The crowd came in a milled around but maintained perfect order. National guardsmen who were on duty paid no attention to them.

In the governor's office Olson talked with the committee appointed to see him, explained why he could not call a special session. The argument waxed warm but the farmer governor was unmovable.

Later Olson went out and addressed the group. In a voice wracked by emotion he asked for peace and a calm appraisal of the situation in which North Dakota finds itself.

"I will do all I can to help anyone who needs help," he said. "As long as I am acting as governor the full power of the state will be behind the effort. I do not tell you I will not sign bonds. If the people of this state need help I will sign bonds or do anything else that may be necessary."

Asserting that he intends to cooperate with the national government in its effort to help the people of the state, particularly those in need, Olson pointed out that the government is and has been financing relief work in this state and said such cooperation seemed not only advisable but his duty.

Describing his own difficulties in meeting taxes and paying expenses, Olson assured them that he understood their plight and sympathized with it fully, since he suffered from the same set of circumstances.

As a member of the Holiday Association, he said, he had participated in five different movements to prevent foreclosures ad the eviction of farmers.

The cheers at the finish seemed to surprise the acting governor. He was greatly pleased.

Having heard Olson speak, the crowd left in an orderly manner, returning to downtown Bismarck.

A touch of drama marked Olson's conference with the committee, composed of Mat Mulholland, Wells county; H.J. Fisher, Bowman county; John Hagan, McHenry county; D.D. Barkman, Burleigh county; F.J. Graham, Ellendale and J.H. Miller, Bismarck.

Mulholland said the farmers believed that certain interests are "crucifying Langer," that Olson "is being hoodwinked by the other crowd," but if he calls a special session, the people will back him.

"There is no thought to do anything disgraceful to the state," Mulholland said. "I told our people we are here to ask for certain things, but we are here, too, to protect the American flag. The Holiday Association respects you and we know you respect us."

"If you don't call a special session," said Dr. Miller, "sentiment against you will go down; if you call it, sentiment for you will go up."

Rising at the end of the conference table, his face showing the strain he had been going through for several days, Olson said with quiet emphasis:

"We must recognize constitutional government. When I took the oath of office," – and his right hand unconsciously was raised –"I swore to uphold the constitution of the United States."

In a May 30, 1981, letter to Olson's daughter, Martha Olson Nelson of Towner, North Dakota, Young wrote about Governor Olson on that day in 1934: "In his down-to-earth, common and effective way which was so typical of him, he talked to them in a way that created a completely different atmosphere. His speech left a great impression with these people and soon most of them returned home peacefully."

The turmoil of the events in July had no sooner begun to subside than Young found himself answering to what he viewed as an insult to the state in general and agriculture in particular by some eastern journalists who had come to the state to cover the removal of Governor Langer from office. He responded to this with a letter to the *LaMoure Chronicle* on August 16 that demonstrated Young's astute grasp of agricultural issues in the 1930s:

Dear Editor:

Enclosed you will find a newspaper clipping an old schoolmate sent me from Oklahoma City, Oklahoma, written by Gerald W. Johnson in the Baltimore Evening Sun. This and many other articles appearing recently in eastern papers and magazines can't help but make us wonder if they are really so grossly misinformed as to the true conditions or is it another vicious program to keep the government from aiding agriculture. The one appearing recently in the Saturday Evening Post was probably the most damaging of all.

To the greater portion of North Dakota this drought is only of two years duration and not four as claimed. To a part of it there has been no drought at all. Why just look at the last two years? Why not look back 50 or 60 years to judge the future of North Dakota. On the one hand we have the eastern Brain Trusters telling us the reason we are broke is because we have over-produced. We have their program of crop reduction on our hands now. About the time we begin to believe them along comes this propaganda by a different group of doctors and writers. They believe it is all a mistake this country was ever put under cultivation. Dr. [Elwood] Meade [federal reclamation commissioner] on a recent trip to the state recommended a rehabilitation program because we could not produce enough.

Contrary to the article, our soil is not light, it has not blown away as he claims. Few if any states can boast of a heavier soil as an average of the whole state. The Red River Valley for its size has the richest soil in the world. The subsoil in the balance of the state, even if the top soil had blown away, compares favorably with its ability to produce with most other states' top soil.

Many times in the past 53 years our family has farmed in this county, we have had acres of the top soil blown away as deep as it was plowed. We plowed up the sub soil and there was little if any difference in the crop on that land compared to other land that had not blown.

Undoubtedly the Red River Valley with its real heavy soil blew as had any farm land in the state. This is because it was highly cultivated. The same year the valley had one of the biggest crops it ever produced.

The real trouble with North Dakota today is not the drought. We would not have been in this deplorable condition had it not been for the years of bankrupt prices that preceded it. Years during which the government stood idly by and watched its greatest industry go to complete poverty. Poverty so complete that farmers could not keep on their farms the good barley and oats crops of 1932. It had to be sold to pay the thresh bills at prices of from 4 to 12 cents a bushel in the local elevator. During the winter of 1933-34 southeastern North Dakota shipped hundreds of thousands of tons of hay to South Dakota. This would be on our farms today had we not been so desperately in need of cash. Cash to pay more interest on bills contracted during years of starvation prices. All because they said we produced too much.

Commencing about 1929 and 1930 the farmers filled their granaries machine sheds and even bought more steel bins to store their grain. Two or three years of this was all the best of them could stand. They unloaded. The Farm Board unloaded, sold part of its wheat to China on long time credit. If we were only Chinese now we could get that long time credit for some seed wheat!

All we ask in North Dakota is a price for our grain when we do raise it. We then would be in a position to be more provident and provide for the lean years.

If it were possible to have a law in this state barring the use of combines and the burning of straw stacks then there would always be enough rough feed on hand to winter the live stock.

We would not be so overstocked on cattle at the present time had it not been for prices that at times would not pay the freight to So. St. Paul. The farmer just kept the old cow year after year thinking that some time the price would be better. She kept on raising more calves. In the meantime South America was supplying our canned beef.

We are still accepting rye from Poland, a country which pays its farmers a bounty on export grain and flax into Minneapolis from India while Secretary Wallace claims flax cannot be profitably grown in the United States.

Two years ago and less barley in this state ranged in price from 2 to 12 cents a bushel. Now it is about 60 cents. Is there any sense to that? Must it all be supply and demand on a world market or is it a government problem at times? Most other nations have a high import duty and others have a bounty on exports paid to the farmer.

We have the greatest system of all. A large majority of our people are wanting for more food and clothing in a land of plenty, another big class of people – the farmers trying to reduce because they produced so much it broke them. All this in a nation which is spending more than a billion dollars a year getting ready for a future war.

The big newspapers and magazines say it's all a mistake we farmers are out here in North Dakota. They are afraid now that we might not produce enough in the future.

Personally I would like the present allotment program if it had cost of production added to it and have the program handled by farmers themselves and not by statisticians and others who know nothing about farming and care less. Our president as least is trying to do something for agriculture.

We may have to change our system of farming to be more along the lines of dry farming as carried on in parts of Montana. We may have to keep trench silos filled to meet emergencies. We can carry over more feed from year to year if necessary. Certainly the last thing we can think of is to move to other states where generally they are worse off financially than we are.

All we ask of the industrial east is to tell the true facts about us and give to us that same measure of government protection and aid they have so richly enjoyed the past 15 years.

Although bewildered as to which line of thought to believe – if either the group of doctors who believe our troubles is in over production or the more recent group who are afraid we won't produce enough – we are still going to farm in North Dakota.

M.R. YOUNG

LaMoure Chronicle editor H.R.S. Diesem commented on Young's letter in the same issue of his newspaper that it appeared. He wrote:

A "Dirt Farmer" Answers

The William Langer rumpus, which entailed the proclamation of martial law and presence of a handful of troopers for only a few feverish days, had an unfortunate secondary effect none could foresee.

Some of the big eastern papers sent staff correspondents, the boys who get "By Lines" on their special stuff wired east, to cover the Langer "tempest in a teapot." Soon running out of verbal thunder, the correspondents began telling about North Dakota dust storms and dismally announcing that the state is nearly done for – agriculturally. They have cast North Dakota in a future role of cattle grazing – a synthetic cow country.

Journalistic guns fired by eastern staff correspondents have a fashion of going off "half-cocked" like the wordy blasts of the fellow who wrote the Hired Man – his work – in North Dakota, and again the not too accurate Morris Markey who can count banks in North Dakota where even a Burroughs adding machine differs widely.

After all this stuff, the statements of a "dirt farmer" of LaMoure County – namely Milt Young, representative in the legislature and now G.O.P. nominee for state senator, are both refreshing and illuminating. If you want the low down on dust storms, on soil blowing, drought effect and the future of agriculture in the County of LaMoure and other counties of North Dakota, what more could one offer than the conclusions of an honest-to-goodness farmer himself, who in plowing one windy day has probably has gained more knowledge of soil shifting than eastern journalists in a lifetime!

Mr. Young in the front page article in this issue makes several points, namely:

The so-called drought period is two years, not four.

Even in drifted spots the remaining subsoil is better than many eastern soils.

The soil of North Dakota is not light – as an eastern writer so boldly states – but is heavier than in most other states.

The worst thing from which North Dakota is now suffering is the long spell of producing farm commodities at reduced prices, says Mr. Young.

This farmer-legislator thinks we may have to resort to dry farming methods, and certainly be more provident in the future.

He makes a timely plea that easterners tell the real facts – and that means that eastern reporters will have to put in more than a few days to check up facts – and seek them not in hotel lobbies but among farmers themselves.

But read Milt Young's article for yourself.

H.R.S DIESEM, editor

The *Bismarck Capital*, one of the capital city's daily newspapers, commented on Young's letter in its August 30, 1934, edition. It wrote:

Milton R. Young, state representative, in an article printed in the LaMoure County Chronicle, says the eastern writers have overemphasized the drouth in dwelling on the plight of the farmer.

Mr. Young is a farmer. He would know what he is talking about. He claims that low prices of farm products have been more harmful than the drouth itself.

The writer explains the East was aroused by the dust storms and promptly concluded that all of the western soil had been blown away. This is not true, because, as Mr. Young says, "many times in the past 53 years our family has farmed in this country, we have had acres of top soil blown away as deep as it was plowed. We plowed up the subsoil and there was little, if any difference in the crop on that land compared to other land that had not blown."

The farmer has complained for years of the prices. He has gone unheard. Now that the East is doing our complaining for us about the drouth, maybe we will get some reaction. Perhaps we could bargain that if the East fixed up the prices we would be glad to take care of the drouth. Impossible? Well, it's a good thought anyway.

Young was not the only person objecting to unfair press the state was receiving by journalists who had come to the state to cover the William Langer story. The *Saturday Evening Post* writer Morris Markey, who Young referenced in his letter, was roundly criticized by others in the state for the article he wrote in the July 21, 1934, issue. An article published in the August 23, 1934, issue of the *Bismarck Capital* reported that North Dakota Bank Examiner Adam A. Lefor and St. Paul Association Vice President A.B. Lathrop complained to the magazine's editor. In response, *Saturday Evening Post* editor George Horace

Lorimer apologized for the errors, acknowledging that drouth had not made a desert of Minnesota and the Dakotas; ninety-nine percent of North Dakota's banks were not closed, and farmers in the northwest were not completely insolvent. He also said the magazine would send another writer who was "western-born and reared" to the area "to retrace Mr. Markey's steps and correct any false impressions his articles may have left."

The fall months of 1934 found Young campaigning for his district's Senate seat. He again used newspapers ads, which were identical to those used in the primary campaign. He also, for the last time, mounted a vigorous house-to-house campaign. Future campaigns were to use more letters to constituents, and beginning in the 1940s, the radio emerged as an important campaign tool.

In the November election Young defeated Lee R. Herring, a Langer Leaguer, with 2,836 and 1,266 votes, respectively. The *LaMoure Chronicle* called it "one of the greatest victories for anti-Langerism that ever happened." Young's campaign expenses totaled $40.88 to Herring's $32.60.

Acting Governor Olson, who was not on the general election ballot, was replaced as governor by Williston newspaper editor Thomas Moodie, a Democrat. He defeated NPL candidate Lydia Langer, the wife of the deposed former governor, who ran in his place.

But William Langer scored another political coup in early 1935, discovering that Moodie had voted in Minneapolis three years earlier while working for a newspaper there. This disqualified Moodie from being governor because of a state law that required a candidate for governor to be a resident of the state for five years prior to his election. As a result, Moodie was forced to resign, after serving in office for less than two months.

On February 16, 1935, Republican NPL Lieutenant Governor Walter Welford, a Neche cattle and grain farmer, became North Dakota's fourth governor in seven months.

In 1933, Governor Langer had issued an executive order, which called for a moratorium on farm foreclosures. During the 1935 Legislative Assembly, Senator James Cain from Dickinson asked Young to co-sponsor legislation that addressed how to handle court-ordered farm sales. *"Sponsoring this Young-Cain Moratorium Bill was good for me politically, but I believed it was necessary, because I could personally relate to farmers who were broke."*

Langer's moratorium required individuals to submit their case directly to the Governor to be considered for protection, essentially allowing the executive branch to act for the judicial.

This legislation called for a "legal moratorium," and was similar to legislation that had been advocated by Governors Moodie and Olson. It applied not only to mortgage foreclosures, but to tenants in possession of land and vendees in contracts for the purchase of land. Similar moratorium bills were passed in legislative sessions until 1943.

Later in the session, Young sponsored and worked for the passage of legislation that gave those who had lost their farms because they couldn't pay their taxes the first right to purchase back this land from the county.

Also in 1935, Young was one of only a few legislators to vote against the Hopton Hail Risk Bill, legislation named for the state's Insurance Commissioner Harold Hopton that forced all farmers to take out hail risk insurance. *"It required that all farmers pay $4 an acre, and when the year was over the state had taken in 10 times more than it had paid out. This went against my political philosophy of not mandating programs for farmers."* In comments he shared with his constituents through the *LaMoure Chronicle* on February 21, 1935, Young said he didn't believe state farmers were able to stand the extra load it would impose on them. He also feared the possibility that the fund created by the law would present possibilities for political machine building.

In the same newspaper article, Young also commented on other legislation during the session. As a member of the Game and Fish Committee, Young and the majority of the committee supported a dog tax bill. "It seems to me we have come to the point where we have to decide which is the most important in the state – the sheep industry or dog industry," he wrote. As a sheep farmer, Young had lost sheep to dogs. He believed taxing them would limit their numbers and keep them better controlled. The bill, S.B. 290, had Young as the primary sponsor and Senators Oswald Braaten from Thompson and Otto Topp from Grace City as the other sponsors. It passed the Senate but was indefinitely postponed in the House.

This bill created an opportunity for his colleagues to tease Young. *"One morning when I came into the chambers, I found a half dozen dogs tied to my desk."*

As legislators grappled with the appropriations bill and language that would provide funds to cover the costs of the special session held the previous July, Young announced that he would ask to be excused from voting on it as it would mean an additional $40 to him if it passed.

In a March 14 article in the *LaMoure Chronicle*, Young defended the legislature's appropriation bill that was $2 million higher than the previous biennium:

> Our appropriations committee was composed of old, experienced legislators. Let me say that they were as hard boiled as any could be. It was a case of appropriate this much or close up the institutions entirely. For instance, the Old Soldiers Home at Lisbon ran far short this last year and was borrowing from the Bank of North Dakota, as were most of the other state departments. Shingles were off the roof at the Soldiers Home, plaster was spoiled and other buildings going to ruin for lack for money to repair them.

He also offered words of support for Governor Welford:

> I have every reason to believe we have a very good Governor. He is in a hard place and should be given every consideration by all good citizens. If he is unable to bring peace and harmony in state government, then there is small chance of some one else being able to do it. Anyone could feel proud to possess a record such as his has been in this state for more than half a century. In my judgment, the job hunters will cause him more trouble than all the rest of us put together.

The 1935 Legislature passed a two percent sales tax to support the financing of school and welfare programs. In May, citizens began circulating petitions to refer the sales tax, as it had successfully done in 1933 when the Legislature approved a similar tax. Young opposed the referendum and shared his reasons in a May 15, 1935, article in the *LaMoure Chronicle*. He wrote:

> It is hard to keep still at this time when the Sales Tax bill is about to be referred.
>
> The people who are sponsoring the referendum are using misleading and incorrect statements.
>
> The Sales Tax bill was passed by this legislature only after a careful study of the state's needs and the sources to derive the money from were carefully studied. It was passed by a non-partisan controlled legislature. From this county, Clark's a Democrat, Shockman a Non-Partisan, and myself elected as an Independent, voted for the measure.
>
> Practically all the Farmers Union members, although bitterly opposed to it in principle, voted for it as they could see no other way to raise money to run the state — the schools in particular.
>
> I have not seen one of the circular letters being sent out over the state but if it is as incorrect and misleading as their article in The Fargo Forum, it is not worthy of consideration.
>
> Federal aid by which most of the schools in the western part of the state have operated in the last year, was cut off. The legislature had notice of this about a month before the money was stopped. Most counties in western North Dakota have long since exhausted every available way of raising money. Sioux county, for instance, borrowed more than $2,000 from the Bank of North Dakota to pay compensation insurance on work relief projects. They could borrow no more and had to quit all their projects. The chairman of the Sioux county commissioners told me they hadn't money to buy postage stamps to answer the letters from the different parties they owed money to. He said they hadn't money enough to hold a term of court for three years and consequently the law breakers were never given a trial. They had no money to keep them in jail.
>
> Yet, this group sponsoring the referendum would have you believe that the state's finances are the best in years.

The population of Sioux county is half white and half Indian. The Indians in the past paid practically no taxes. The delegation from Sioux county figured it might be possible for them to operate with a sales tax, as the Indians would then help pay.

Practically every school district in LaMoure county will receive more than $1,000 a year. They can at least levy this much less this year. The high school tuition for every rural student is paid out of this fund.

The sales tax could be entirely a replacement tax if it were not for the terrible financial condition of the state. Most all political sub-divisions levy the limit under the initiated law.

It is easy to say to tax the property more – raise the levy. That doesn't always raise the money. Too much property already has been lost for taxes.

Minnesota can hardly be compared to North Dakota even if [Minnesota] Governor [Floyd] Olson acted wisely. They do have a few millionaires there. They could raise more money on taxes from their iron mines alone than we could in the entire state. Their state has not experienced the drouth we have and their type of farming has fared better than ours.

South Dakota has had a gross earnings tax and now has switched to a sales tax. Ask the people who live in South Dakota what they think of their sales tax and invariably the answer will be O.K. Ask the people of Iowa and you will have a like answer.

If the sales tax is referred it will mean a special election and a special session of the legislature, both with a tremendous cost. Why not try it out for a year at which time we will have another election and it could be voted on without much added cost.

I would like to ask the people of LaMoure county to study the school situation in the state and then if in their judgment they want the sales tax referred it still can be done and I will say – no more.

The group sponsoring the referendum says that the legislature appropriated $600,000 for this fund to have the state relief setup called SERA instead of FERA. This is dirty propaganda if you ask me.

This was a definite demand from the Federal Government if the relief money was to continue coming into North Dakota. For the amount of money this state appropriated to meet federal money we now receive more in return than any other state in the union.

The members of the legislature from LaMoure county voted for this measure only after a careful study of the facts. It was our best judgment.

If we did wrong we can only say we did the best we knew how to leave the state in a position to operate for the next two years and honorably pay the bills for schools and relief of the poor.

Sincerely yours,
Milton R. Young

Unlike the referendum that defeated the state sales tax measure in 1933, the 1935 vote on July 15 did not pass, so the sales tax was adopted.

In 1935, Young introduced a bill that would tax chain stores, and he appeared before the House committee chaired by Representative L.L. Twichell of Fargo. *"After my testimony, Twichell said to me, 'Milt, you are a good legislator, but you sure are cracked on this subject.' I remembered that remark later in my career, when I saw that even the best legislators can be 'cracked' on some issues, even myself, when I was considered a fanatic on farm issues."*

With his move to the North Dakota Senate, Young was emerging as a public servant who had an ability to deal with the issues of the day in a public forum, but also – perhaps surprisingly to some considering his speech handicap – an emerging political figure in state issues who would be rubbing shoulders with the other prominent political figures of his day for the next five decades.

Through all of this, Malinda remained home on the farm, steadfast in her lack of interest in politics, and rarely attending political gatherings with him. She had married a farmer, not a politician, and she had preferred that Young not get into politics at all. During his years in the Legislature, her lack of interest in politics, along with the responsibilities of raising their sons and her work on the farm resulted in only a few trips to Bismarck with her husband.

When not in Bismarck and out in the fields, Young kept his name before the public through more letters to the editor and staying active in activities in Berlin. He chaired the charity drive for infantile paralysis in honor of the birthday of President Roosevelt in 1935, and pinch hit for Governor Welford before the Berlin Community Club. Young had invited the Governor as a favor to his brother, Charles, now dentist Dr. C.F. Young, who was president of the club. When Welford couldn't make it, State Senator Young filled in and, according to a March 18, 1935, report in the *LaMoure Chronicle*, he surprised the crowd with "unsuspected oratorical powers." Young explained these powers as being developed through "arguing with traveling men and other visitors with whom I came in contact on the streets of Berlin during the Depression."

His legislative colleagues were not always as kind. Several years later in 1941, when Young, as floor leader, was presenting a gift at the end of the session to Minority Leader Senator Edmund Stucke of Garrison, Young's two seatmates, Senator Jonathan "Mike" Flatt of Sheldon and Senator William "Billy" Braun of Wahpeton, each pulled on his coattail and teased him. *"They said to me, 'Sit down you S.O.B! You sound like hell.'"*

Later in 1935, Young made a trip to Bismarck with the Berlin Superintendent of Schools and some students. There he ran into William Langer in the pool room of the Grand Pacific Hotel. *"We leaned on the edge of the pool table and discussed politics, and Langer asked me, 'Milt, do you think I have any chance of coming back?' I replied, 'I think you have, but you will have to get around the state.' I never forgot that conversation. Here was William Langer, when he was at his all-time political low – asking me, of all people, if I thought he had any chance of coming back!"*

By the end of 1935, Langer had been cleared of all his legal problems through the courts. By 1936 he was back in the political fray, receiving yet again the NPL endorsement for governor. With Langer back on the ballot, that meant Young and other who were anti-Langer were again campaigning against him. *"Once during the campaign, I brought some anti-Langer speakers to town. The next day the NPL had a meeting in town. It was a cold and windy day, and I was looking after the community hall my father owned, so I invited them to use the hall. Sitting in the back row, I was surprised to hear Langer spend about half his speech taking after me, vowing to leave no stone unturned to defeat me.*

"After the rally, the group met for lunch at the basement of the Oasis Restaurant. Langer was sitting at the end of one room and called me over. He put his arms around me like an old friend. I said to him, 'Bill, why do you have to give me hell every time you come to LaMoure County?' Langer looked at me and replied, 'Milt, did I give you any hell?'"

Langer lost to Governor Welford in the primary, seemingly ensuring Welford's success at being elected to a full second term. However, Langer ran as an Independent in the general election and won, becoming the first Independent in the history of North Dakota to be elected governor.

In 1936, Democrat Franklin D. Roosevelt won re-election and again carried North Dakota, winning a second term by prevailing over the Republican candidate Alfred M. Landon. In North Dakota, he drew 163,000 to Landon's 73,000 votes. This is the only election to date in the state's history that a North Dakotan has been on the ballot for President. Congressman William Lemke ran as the candidate for the Union Party, a third party that supported farm aid; the Frazier-Lemke refinance bill that stopped foreclosures on farmers who could not make their mortgage payments; the Townsend Plan old-age pension proposal that was to influence the shaping of the Social Security system in the Roosevelt Administration; and a demand that the government stop issuing interest-bearing bonds. Lemke polled more than 900,000 votes in his campaign for the Presidency, and even though he was not elected, North Dakota voters re-elected him to another term in the U.S. House.

The 1937 session that convened on January 5 presented several difficult issues to the 113 representatives and 49 senators in the Legislature. As reported in the December 31, 1936, *LaMoure Chronicle*, the issues included how to provide funds for nearly half the counties to buy livestock, feed and provisions for needy persons; pressure by sheriffs and peace officers to seek "radical changes" in law enforcement; and how to provide state compliance with federal unemployment insurance legislation regulations. The positions Governor-elect Langer would take on these issues was unknown, because the article reported he had been away from Bismarck much of the time since his election on November 3. "Political 'grapevines' indicate Governor-elect William Langer will control the House, while his control of Senate strength is uncertain," said the report.

During the 1937 session, Young continued to advocate chain store tax legislation, and he re-introduced with Senator Cain from Dickinson a bill that would re-enact the state's legal moratorium law giving courts the right to sit as courts of equity in mortgage foreclosure cases. The first law was passed in 1935 but was limited to a two-year period.

In the summer of 1937, his hometown of Berlin celebrated its 50th anniversary, and Young emceed the celebration.

The 1938 election put Young in a tight race for a third term in the Senate. He ran against Joe Johnson, the county chairman of the NPL and county president of the Farmers Union. Except for his first legislative election in 1932, it was one of his closer races of the 1930s, with Young winning by 154 votes.

Langer did not seek re-election as governor that year. Instead, he was the NPL-endorsed candidate to run against Senator Gerald P. Nye for the U.S. Senate seat. Nye had held the seat since November 1925 when he filled the vacancy caused by Senator Edwin Ladd's death in June of that year. Nye had been elected in 1926 and again in 1932. He defeated Langer in the primary, but Langer ran as an Independent in the 1938 general election. A coalition of anti-Langer forces, described by Elwyn B. Robinson in his 1966 book, *History of North Dakota* as "conservative Republicans, Democrats, and Lemke-Frazier-Nye Leaguers," successfully returned Nye to a third term. That same coalition elected Democrat John Moses governor, defeating the NPL candidate, the Republican Agriculture and Labor Secretary John Hagen of Deering. Young's own campaign was affected by political machinations of trying to keep Langer out of the Senate.

"When I was asked which candidate I was supporting, I didn't want to take sides. I was in a tough battle myself, and although I was always a Nye supporter, I decided to concentrate on my own fight and not get involved in others. This also caused a little trouble for me while campaigning in LaMoure. When I was asked how I was going to vote for governor at a public meeting, I gave a very short answer, 'Moses is a hell of a lot better than his opponent.'"

At the time, Young had no idea the role Moses would play in his own political future seven years later. *"I liked Moses. He was a fine governor. A very honest, decent fellow, and after all the turmoil of the Langer years, people were pleased with the quiet type of government Moses gave us. He was very popular and could have been elected for years and years."*

Young's committee appointments in the 1939 Legislative Session were Appropriations, Game and Fish and State Affairs. On these committees were some of his closest colleagues, Fred Aandahl from Litchville; Joe B. Bridston, a Grand Forks insurance agent; and Rilie Morgan, a Grafton newspaper editor.

During the session, Young supported establishing voter registration, an idea he championed throughout his political career. *"At that time, it was considered an anti-Langer reform, because of the frequent claims of misuse and fraudulent votes being cast in state elections. It didn't pass."*

Young also introduced a bill to give 18-year-olds voting rights. *"I believed that if 18-year-olds were old enough to be drafted and fight and defend their country they were old enough to vote."* The bill did not pass either, but it showed how Young was ahead of his time on this issue. Eventually, giving 18-year-olds the right to vote was championed by President Richard Nixon, becoming the 26th Amendment to the U.S. Constitution in 1971.

In the late 1930s, Young was active in trying to bring tax reform to the state. He was especially unhappy with the fact that foreign corporations received tax relief while North Dakota farmers didn't receive any.

This was one example of his independent thinking and perhaps radical thoughts as it related to agriculture, which weren't always shared by his Republican colleagues. This issue did not get the support or attention he wanted. "If this is a progressive state, I am a shave-tailed Chinaman!" he said in frustration to those who wouldn't give it the attention he thought it deserved.

Back before the LaMoure Community Club in March 1939, Young spoke about the current legislative session. The *LaMoure Chronicle* report on his remarks in its March 16 edition:

> Senator Young spoke with spirit, deploring delays, log rolling, lobbying and trading tactics, and the League caucuses with their nearly autocratic predetermination of voting in the House.
>
> He admitted it was a hard session on solons, necessitating frequent and long conferences and brain-fag. He praised Gov. John Moses for his efforts to compose differences. The tired legislators got within about $3,000,000 of figuring things out.
>
> Sen. Young deplored the loss of civil service, upheld his chain store tax bill, explained tax case laws, decried high government costs and mounting bond interest burden, mill losses, significantly heavy in election years, and the state hospital mess. He declared the relief burden is staggering and mounting, with administration cost too high. He thought the gross income tax unwieldy with grievous "pyramid effect."

The decade of the 1930s was coming to a close. It was a tumultuous one for the state, politically and economically. Newspaper articles the end of December 1939 covered the annual economic review of the state that had been compiled by the Greater North Dakota Association, the state's chamber of commerce.

"This past year has brought very substantial increases in farm income, the greatest since 1929, increased livestock on farms, reductions in debts and taxes, increased private building, boosted retail sales, greater freight car loadings, lower relief requirements, larger tourist travel and resulting receipts, and a generally heightened morale to the state as a whole," said the report. It gave the 1939 gross farm production total as $218.3 million. Not since 1929 had the state production total even equaled $200 million, the report stated.

With the early 1940s came rain that ended the drought and brought a stronger national and state economy.

Milt Young's first eight years as an elected member of the North Dakota Legislature had prepared him well for the challenges and opportunities he would face in the 1940s.

From One Senate to Another

The campaign of 1940 found William Langer back in politics, this time running for the United States Senate seat held by Lynn Frazier, one of the founders of the early Nonpartisan League movement. Frazier was seeking his third term in the Senate after first being elected in 1922. The year before, he had been recalled by the voters and removed as governor. He is the first of only two governors recalled in American history. The second would not be until California's Governor Gray Davis 82 years later, in 2003.

In another attempt to form an anti-Langer faction of the North Dakota Republican Party, Young managed the primary election's "Whelan-Orlady" campaign. Thomas Whelan was an active Republican and successful potato farmer from St. Thomas who would later make a name for himself for the "To Hell With Hitler" slogan he printed on his potato sacks during World War II. His running mate, Benjamin Orlady, was a Jamestown merchant.

Whelan was running as a Progressive Republican for Frazier's Senate seat, and being his campaign manager gave Young one of his first statewide tastes of politics. *"The headquarters was at Jamestown where Orlady was a merchant. This was not a well organized campaign from the start. I, of course, took over the job of managing it when the campaign was well under way. During about the last three weeks of that campaign, Tom Whelan set up another headquarters in Fargo and did most of his campaigning from there. This was the primary election and, of course, Langer defeated both Whelan and Frazier. Senator Frazier did not have the endorsement of either organization and was running as an Independent and lost."*

Speculation was that Whelan was Langer's candidate to help siphon votes from Frazier in the 1940 general election. *"Tom Whelan was a strong Republican. I think, of the two, he probably did favor Langer over Frazier. Frazier was real liberal and, I think, honest, but he wasn't a party man either."* Whelan remained active in state politics and was the first North Dakotan to be appointed a U.S. ambassador, serving in Nicaragua from 1951 to 1961.

Langer defeated Frazier in the fall election. A 1936 law enacted by Independent Voters Association (IVA) supporters prevented a candidate defeated in the primary election to run for the same office in the general election, which would have disqualified Frazier. This is one of the reasons North Dakota Republicans threw their support for Langer. They also wanted a unified ticket to ensure the victory of Wendell Willkie and Charles McNary on the Republican Presidential ticket against Franklin Roosevelt and Henry Wallace in Roosevelt's bid for a third term. Despite an independent challenge by William Lemke that was supported by Langer's opponents, Langer at last reached his long-held goal to be elected to the United States Senate.

In 1941, Young was president pro tempore of the North Dakota Senate, and in 1942, he was instrumental in the organization of a new faction of the party, which a year later was to take on the name of the Republican Organizing Committee – the ROC. It was another anti-NPL/ anti-Langer organization, which replaced the IVA, and declared as its purpose to "unify all Republicans under the banner of Republicanism."

Agnes Geelan, in her 1975 Langer biography, *The Dakota Maverick*, identified the six individuals who were to dominate the Republican Party and North Dakota politics for the next 20 years. Along with Young, Geelan named:

- Joseph Bridston, a Grand Forks businessman, who served in the State Senate from 1939 to 1956, was interim president pro tempore from 1947 to 1948, and president pro tempore in 1949;

• Rilie Morgan, Grafton newspaper publisher, who served in the State Senate from 1939 to 1954 and was its majority leader in 1951;

• Norman Brunsdale, from Mayville, who served in the State Senate from 1927 to 1934, and 1941 to 1950, was president pro tempore in 1943, majority leader from 1945 to 1949, Governor from 1951 to 1957, and a U.S. Senator from 1959 to 1960;

• Fred Aandahl, Litchville, who served in the State Senate from 1931 to 1932 and 1939 to 1942, Governor from 1945 to 1951, and U.S. Congressman from 1951 to 1953; and

• Clyde Duffy, from Devils Lake, who joined the group when he was later elected to the State Senate, where he served from 1949 to 1956, as minority leader in 1953 and 1955, and as Lieutenant Governor from 1957 to 1959.

In the 1940s, the ROC was using radio regularly for campaigning. Young became involved in an anti-chain store campaign led by Senator Bill Braun of Wahpeton. He and Senator Joe Bridston of Grand Forks used the radio for this campaign. *"I don't know why a farmer like me was so concerned about these small town merchants. We thought the chain stores were going to wipe out all the smaller businessmen. We didn't have any money, but we did collect a little money to tell our story. The newspapers weren't much interested in carrying what we had to say because the chain stores were good advertisers."*

In 1943, Young was elected the majority floor leader in the Senate. Joe Bridston wrote in a letter in 1943 to a woman who thought Young should be the candidate for governor in 1944. *"He wrote, 'Milt is fine and would help on the ticket but I can't see him for governor. His handicap without gossip would be bad enough but both are impossible.' "*

Young believed Bridston was right in that assessment. *"My speech defect was a problem. The other thing he probably had in mind was that he probably thought I was not sedate enough. My speech handicap was worse then and I never had any ambitions to become governor. I don't think I ever could have been elected because I think that people look for a different type person for governor than they do as a legislator. I remember a dry lobbyist who was a good supporter of mine. He knew I drank some but he supported me as a legislator. I don't think he would have ever supported me for governor and I think that is true of many people."*

There was some concern within the ROC that Young would be upset and leave the ROC if he were not endorsed as the candidate. Bridston wrote in 1944 that "the ROC can't afford to lose him and he is too valuable to the party to lose." Young believed Bridston was right on that, too – to an extent. *"There were some with the ROC who had become too conservative and I had some arguments with them. There was a period then when I thought that I had about enough of politics and I was thinking of quitting – not necessarily leaving the ROC – but not running for the State Senate again and getting out of politics."*

During the 1944 campaign Young was campaign manager for the ROC and reluctantly filled out the ticket for the United States House seat. *"I didn't seek the endorsement but was practically forced into it by the leadership at the ROC convention. As a candidate I had to step aside as campaign manager."*

Bismarck businessman Milt Rue took over managing the primary campaign until the fall. Young lost in a close primary vote against Charles R. Robertson by some 2,200 votes, less than half-a-vote a precinct. Following his first defeat in an election, Young considered getting out of politics. *"But that changed when Fred Aandahl asked me to meet at the Gardner Hotel in Fargo and convinced me to manage the fall's ROC campaign. As we talked, Aandahl asked if there was anything he could do for me. I replied, 'Well, if there is a vacancy in Congress sometime you might consider me.' I didn't realize until later that a vacancy in the House was not filled by appointment. Nothing more was said about that conversation."*

Young was vocal about his concern that the ROC not become a businessman's party, which he believed was the downfall of the now defunct IVA. *"I was a farmer and farmers were a much bigger percentage of our state population than they are now. I always thought the Republicans made a mistake in having mostly businessmen and few farmers as delegates to their conventions. As campaign manager, I strongly urged that each county have as many farmers in their delegation as they represented in the total population of the county. This new procedure, I believe, more than anything else, accounted for the ROC winning and becoming a power in North Dakota politics for 20 years or more."*

In the 1944 election, Aandahl became the ROC candidate for governor, hoping to win the seat that John Moses vacated to run for United States Senate. The ROC also endorsed Nye for the Senate and Lemke for re-election to the United States House. Young knew Lemke was known as a radical but believed he had become more conservative by 1944. However, not all the ROC Republicans agreed, quietly supporting Moses over Nye. *"A lot of ROCers voted for Moses, which helped him since Moses usually never carried his own Mercer County because it was very strong Republican."*

Young was campaign chairman for Nye's 1944 campaign for a fourth Senate term against the Democrat Moses. Nye was a Cooperstown native who served in the United States Senate from 1925 to 1945. He was a "Rumper Leaguer," a term for anti-Langer Nonpartisan League members, and the ROC needed their votes. *"That was during World War II and a lot of people were bitter toward Nye because of the position he took after the declaration of war. He didn't go all out like he might have. Congressman Lemke was an isolationist, too, but his attitude was different and he was endorsed by the ROC and elected. Aandahl usually listened to me on strategy and we agreed that he and Nye should travel together all the time. They did and they got good crowds."*

The Senate race was between Nye, Moses and Lynn Stambaugh, who entered as an Independent. *"There was some suspicion that Stambaugh entered with Langer's financial backing and the promise of a job if he lost in order to beat Nye. I believe Langer would have gone to that extreme to beat Nye. When Stambaugh later got a good job with the Import-Export Bank, it almost looked as if there was something to that story. Stambaugh was never a strong Republican and not active in the Republican Party. He probably thought he had some chance of being elected but Nye won the nomination. Langer always liked a three-way race. The more candidates he could get in there, the better. He had a lot of people who despised him bitterly, but then he had the most loyal following of anyone in politics."*

Stambaugh's vote total in the general election was considerably less than the votes cast for the winner, John Moses. However, the vote total for Stambaugh and Nye was larger than Moses. *"But, I always thought that even if Stambaugh hadn't run, Moses would have won."*

The 1944 election was a big victory for the ROC, with Aandahl being elected governor and many more ROC candidates to state offices and the Legislature. While some people in the state, including some newspaper editors, credited the success of the ROC to him, Young believed Bridston probably had more to do with starting of the ROC. *"He despised Langer more than anyone else and he was close to Harold Stassen in Minnesota, who reorganized their Republican Party. I suppose the fact that I managed the campaign and developed most of the strategy was probably the reason for the editorials. I could be a good fundraiser. But I had some help. Milt Rue and I could sit at the telephone and call people all over the state. Milt was a demanding type person and he would tell them to send so much money and most of them would do it. Our campaign, when I managed it, was the first one that wound up in the black. All of the elections before that I had anything to do with wound up with sizeable debts."*

With the new session of the Legislature, Young as Senate Majority Leader was dealing with re-enacting the state two percent sales tax and increasing the tax base on real and personal property from 50 per cent to 75 percent of the assessed valuation. A February 28, 1945, article in the *Bismarck Tribune* reported that both measures had previously been killed passing in reconsideration. In the article, Young was quoted as saying he voted for the bill "because it is the only remaining piece of legislation left for action which will provide sufficient revenue to meet the cost of state and local government."

During the campaign in September 1944, Moses had surgery in Rochester, Minnesota, for a stomach condition. On January 18, just 15 days after taking his Senate seat, Moses returned to Rochester for a series of x-ray treatments. His condition was made worse by an attack of pleurisy. He died March 3, 1945, at the age of 60.

"When it was apparent that Senator Moses would only live a short time longer, out of the blue sky Aandahl called me into his office and said, 'If the state constitution does not prohibit me, I am going to appoint you to the Senate.' The state constitution did prohibit the appointment of a legislator but the Senate is the sole judge of the qualifications of its members. This nullified the state constitution."

The conversation Young had with Aandahl took place about a month before Moses died. Since the Legislature was in session, Young often socialized with other legislators at their hotels in the evenings. *"Everyone was speculating about who would get the appointment if Moses died. There were many who thought that there were others more qualified than I was and they were probably right. I was always quite a ways down on their lists. There were quite a few strong Nye supporters as well as supporters for Brunsdale and Bridston. Brunsdale supported me."*

Young thought at the time that Joe Bridston, probably more than anyone else, wanted to see Young appointed to the Senate, especially since Young had been the first ROC campaign manager, and the ROC was responsible for Aandahl being elected governor.

"Somehow or other Bridston seemed to like my judgment on some things. Quite often when we were both in the State Senate, he would come ask me how I was going to vote and what I thought. He wouldn't always vote the way I did but he asked me. He was interested in my judgment."

In a March 3, 1945, article about the death of Senator Moses, the *Bismarck Tribune* reported that Aandahl had told Nye a few days earlier that he would not appoint him to the seat. "The Governor feels that the people decided Nye's immediate political future at the election last November and that to appoint a man who has been rejected by the voters would be unwise," the article said. "He also made clear at the same time that he had no intention of resigning as Governor to accept appointment to the Senate from his successor in office. This he has indicated is not in accord with his ideas of clean politics."

Nonetheless, Nye campaigned very vigorously for the appointment to the Senate. A group led by Ashley Republican Max Wishek wanted Nye appointed, and Aandahl held up announcing the appointment to give them the opportunity to meet with him. *"But once Aandahl had made up his mind, he wouldn't budge at all. Fred Aandahl was a real good friend of mine, strictly honest, and with a lot of courage. I used to play quite a lot of poker and things like that which was quite a lot different from Aandahl. He was more religious but still we were very similar in our political thinking. He was a little more conservative than I."*

On March 12, 1945, Young's political leadership in the Republican Party for the past dozen years elevated him from the North Dakota Senate to the United States Senate. That was the day when Governor Fred Aandahl, his Barnes County neighbor who had farmed 960 acres near Litchville, and who he first met when they served on their respective county Corn and Hog Boards, and later in the North Dakota Senate, appointed Young, age 47, to the U.S. Senate.

Young had enjoyed his service in the State Legislature. *"They were a hard working group of people. No matter what party they belonged to there was usually a good friendship between all of us. Most of them had a good sense of humor and some were pretty smart."*

When he was appointed in 1945, Young remembered that there was some animosity among the party devotees, but generally good support. *"There were many who wanted the Senate appointment and some of them never quite forgave me for it."*

Nye was very upset. His comment upon hearing of Young's appointment to the Senate was, "This is a hell of a way to run an election campaign for the United States Senate. The candidate is licked and his campaign manager gets the job."

The appointment guaranteed Young his Senate seat until the next general election, which was in June 1946, and he would have to run again for the full term in 1950.

"If a humble spirit and an open mind are assets, I feel that I have some qualifications justifying acceptance of the appointment," Young was quoted as saying in state newspapers as he accepted the appointment.

He resigned from the State Senate two days later on March 14. On that day the editorial in the *Bismarck Tribune* wrote about Aandahl's appointment of Young:

> This is proof that Aandahl is completely orthodox in his political thinking. He evidently felt that the post should go to one of the group which had supported him in the campaign . . . It is significant that no one in the group most closely associated with Gov. Aandahl has raised his voice in protest. Others doubtless would have liked the appointment, but their comment about Mr. Young has been distinctly favorable . . . The acclaim which has come to Mr. Young is of the hopeful variety. He has served well as a state senator, but his record in the United States Senate has yet to be made. Upon it, doubtless, will depend his chance of election when his name comes before the voters in June of 1946, which is the present prospect.

On February 1, 1945, a news article published in *The Bismarck Tribune* reported on the annual economic review compiled by the Greater North Dakota Association, the state chamber of commerce. The headline read, "1944 Was a Year of Big Prosperity."

The following highlights from the economic review as reported in the news article give a snapshot of the condition of the state as the new U.S. Senator took office.

Agriculture: North Dakota had $515 million in agricultural income in 1944. Income had steadily risen between 1936 and 1943, from $127 million to $549 million. The 1944 income showed a drop of $34 million. 1944 was the fifth consecutive year in which precipitation was above normal, averaging 21.6 inches in the state. It was distributed throughout the year and small grain crops and corn were good. Excessive rain in the eastern part of the state damaged some harvested grain and some crops in the eastern part of the state were under water and not worth harvesting. The average temperature for the year was 41.1 degrees Fahrenheit, and pastures were good throughout the summer and fall.

Financial: One measure of the North Dakota's prosperity was shown in its purchase of war bonds, which since 1941 had totaled $280 million. Of the six war bond drives to date, North Dakota topped the nation in percentage of E bond quotas met in the first four drives. The state's 151 state and national banks and the Bank of North Dakota had deposits, as of December 1, 1944, totaling $377 million which, when added to the savings in building and loan associations of $17 million, brought a grand total of bank deposits of $394 million. On December 12, 1944, the balance in all state funds was $33 million, an increase of $9 million from the beginning of the year.

Transportation: Railroads were commended for handling the near record grain crop with less confusion than in prior years. Northwest Airlines increased service to North Dakota, providing two additional daily flights, one east and one west, giving the state five flights daily each way. The airline reported a 25 percent increase of passengers carried over the previous year. Truck and bus lines operating in North Dakota reported a volume increase of 10 to 15 percent over 1943 and a 20 percent increase over 1941.

Recreation: Hunting, fishing and trapping was a $10 million industry, with more than 1,600 non-resident hunting licenses totaling $40,000 sold in 1944. This was despite gas rationing and a shortage of shells. The average amount of money each non-resident hunter spent in a day during hunting season was $100.

Natural resources: Approximately 2.5 million tons of lignite coal was produced in the state in 1944, and natural gas was sold from a dozen heavy-producing wells.

Water development: New flood control legislation passed by Congress funded the construction of four dams in the Red River Valley, and Missouri River development was expected to make North Dakota the mecca for labor nationally when dams were built in the state.

Milton R. Young was entering the United States Senate at a very compelling time in the history of both his state and nation.

A Washington Newcomer

The new Senator from North Dakota took the train to Washington and moved into a suite at the Shoreham Hotel, located on Calvert Street Northwest and overlooking Rock Creek Parkway. He was sworn in by Vice President Harry Truman on March 19, 1945, as the 40th Republican Senator in the 79th Congress. Following the ceremony, Senator Langer hosted a luncheon in Young's honor for all Republican Senators. Langer invited Truman to a dinner he held in Young's honor later that day, although Truman did not attend.

Langer was criticized in the Nonpartisan League newspaper, *The Leader,* because of the luncheon and dinner. *"Langer responded to this criticism by saying 'North Dakota is too small a state not to get good appointments to the Senate, even though you didn't always agree on everything.'"*

In a strange twist of fate, two long-time political nemeses, Milton Young and William Langer, found themselves as colleagues in the United States Senate, representing the same party from the same state – a relationship they would share for the next 14 years. Young believed Langer was sincerely pleased with his appointment to the Senate. *"I was the ROCer and Langer was the NPLer, and neither of us had an interest in affiliating with the other faction of the Republican Party. I believe Langer was more comfortable serving with me rather than another Leaguer or a Democrat."*

At the time, it was customary for a Senator to be assigned to three major and two minor committees. Young's first assignments on April 5, 1945, were to the Agriculture, District of Columbia, Immigration, and Manufactures committees (in 1946 this last committee became part of the Commerce Committee). Other early committee appointments were Appropriations, Education and Labor, and Banking and Currency. *"I hadn't been in the Senate for two or three days when Senator Edwin Johnson from Colorado, who was presiding over the Senate, called me up and said, 'Take over for me, I have to leave.' I replied, 'I don't know a damn thing about the Senate rules.' He said, 'You'll do all right,' and left me to preside over the Senate."*

The first correspondence Young received as a Senator included hundreds of letters of congratulations on his appointment to the Senate.

Harry Tenborg, an insurance salesman from Carrington and longtime Young supporter, wrote on March 10, 1945:

> Dear Milt: Or possibly I should say "Sir" to a United States Senator. But the Hell with that noise, as you are still Milt to me. At any rate, old man, my strongest congratulations. Now go to it, and so mold your career, that the people will want Senator Young, rather than the Senator wanting the people and especially just and only around election time.
>
> I was talking to Schaeffer and Nels Kunkel this morning, and we were feeling happy that our choice had proven to be the Governor's choice. I really think that such was the case from the outset.
>
> Then one of the boys spoke up and said, well, he is a farmer and he might have some manure on his shoes, and we all laughed and I said that is just another one of those attributes that Milt Young has to his credit, which will more than ever help him to keep his feet on the ground.
>
> So, Skipper, with kindest regards and very best wishes,
> As ever, Harry.

A letter dated March 13, 1945, came from Ferd A. Pansandak of Fullerton. "Was very glad to hear of your appointment, congratulations," he wrote. He continued to urge Young to give immediate action to some subsidy or acreage payment to North Dakota farmers who were interested in beginning to grow a new state crop – sunflowers.

Chester W. Hamblin, of Salem, Oregon, the pastor of the First Presbyterian Church, knew Young from when he had lived in North Dakota. He sent a letter dated March 14, 1945:

Last Saturday evening Mr. George Aiken, who is the State Budget Director and the Governor's Executive Secretary, and a former newspaperman, spent part of the evening at our home along with his wife. I mentioned the fact that I would like to be in Bismarck for a time to give Gov. Aandahl an idea or two about the senatorship. He said, 'The appointment was announced today.' I said, 'Who is it?" He replied, 'He was a man by the name of Young.' I said, 'That is one of the very men I was thinking about.'

All of which leads to his next remark, which I am going to send you with the hope and fervent prayer that you may always remember it. Mr. Aiken looked at me and said in his direct and frank way, 'Chet, I do not care about other things. I want to know – IS HE HONEST! They have strange ways of influencing one at Washington. Can he be influenced, or is he sound?'

You know of course what I think of you, and for that very reason I thought you would be interested in this question . . .

The new Senator replied to him on March 24, 1945:

The last paragraph in your letter in which this friend of yours asks whether or not I am honest I believe is very significant of your views about public officials. This I, too, believe is the most important qualification for any public official. I hope above everything else that I will remain honest, as I think I am now. Other mistakes can be forgotten, I believe, if a public official is honest and in the long run the best interest of the nation will be served.

J.A. Gilje, the editor of the *Foster County Independent* in Carrington, more than once called Young "fiercely independent" in his editorials. In keeping with his independent nature, one of the first votes that Young cast in the Senate, on March 23, 1945, was to support the confirmation of Aubrey Williams as head of the Rural Electrification Administration. Senator Moses had supported him in committee before his death, and Young felt an obligation to vote for him also, even though he was rejected by the Senate by a 52-36 vote. Williams had been a Farmers Union organizer, was deputy administrator of the Works Progress Administration and executive director of the National Youth Administration in the FDR Administration.

"This was viewed as a liberal vote. I didn't know at the time that Aubrey Williams had gotten Langer into trouble on relief programs during the Thirties, because he was one of the people who investigated the use of relief money. Langer, however, also supported the Williams confirmation, and his defeat came from southern Democrats and other Republicans."

Because of the Williams vote, Young was to find out that many people in Washington thought he was going to be a liberal. Prominent national newspaper columnist Drew Pearson, who wrote the well-known political column, *Washington Merry Go Round,* invited him over to his Georgetown home along with a group of liberals. *"I suppose they thought I was going to be quite a liberal Senator. Actually, from that time on I voted pretty much middle-of-the road – far more on the conservative side."*

His early vote for Williams might have pleased more liberal-leaning Farmers Union members in his state, which might have been helpful in the election that was to occur shortly, although Young doubted that. *"Glenn Talbot was President of the Farmers Union and there was no way that he would ever support me. In fact, my vote on farm matters was quite liberal and I was often in trouble with some of the more conservative Republicans."*

Back home to harvest

During the summer of 1945, Young decided to return home to again help his son, Scoop, and his 18 neighbors with threshing. Throughout the 1940s, the Senate was in session only three to four months at a time, taking long breaks. And, as a new member of Congress, Young had few important assignments right away. The most pressing issue was shortages of many commodities and goods because of the war.

"My neighbors couldn't buy machinery and would have had to wait

a long while to get their crops in if I hadn't come home and done it for them."

This was the first year the newest of modern farm machines, the combine, was used on the Young farm. As its name implies, this machine "combined" the work of two vital farm machines, the thresher and the swather. During that 1945 harvest, three-fourths of the Young family's crop was taken with the new machine. The combine was purchased over the objections of his 83-year-old father. *"He thought I had gone to the dogs by getting that combine. He couldn't see its value. I said I needed it because of my greater absences from the farm now that I was in Washington."*

The 1945 crop was a surprising success. *"It hadn't looked very good in July when I was visiting. It was starting to head and it needed rain, badly. I thought the crop was done. My crop that year yielded more than 60 bushels to the acre of oats. Wheat averaged 20 bushels per acre, and with more than 1,000 acres, the farm brought more income to our family than did my salary from the Senate."* In the 79th Congress that salary was $10,000 a year.

While working in one of his neighbor's fields on August 14, 1945, Young heard the news about Japan's surrender to the Allies, which marked the end of World War II.

By the time World War II had ended, all three of Young's sons had returned home from military service to the family grain farm, where they also fed cattle for many years, raising as many as 2,000 head a year. Each son farmed about 500 acres around Berlin. In those early years, Scoop did a lot of driving back and forth from Washington with his father. The sessions began January 2, and they would drive back to Washington, even during the winters. Scoop would fly out and the two would drive back, or vice versa.

Establishing an office

Young was inspired by the way Senator Langer ran his Senate office, which included an emphasis on constituent services that at the time was much more aggressive than what many other Senators provided.

For Young to emphasize good constituent services matched his personality well. He possessed the Young family trait that whatever task was taken on was done meticulously and to perfection. His ability to read people well – to see through their motives – had helped bring him to this office in Washington. And his ability to analyze personalities and detect disingenuous people or social climbers was being put to the test in a much larger arena. He also was a good listener, which family members believed was partly because of his speech impediment, making him more comfortable listening to others than talking himself.

Young's attention to detail is apparent through the emphasis he put on answering the correspondence to his office. He was involved in answering the letters promptly, and often apologized when there was not a quick turnaround on a reply.

As was the case with her support of her husband's political career up to this point, Malinda didn't enjoy Washington when she visited. *"One time Mrs. Langer arranged for her to go to several parties and meetings to get acquainted. This may have been one of the reasons she didn't visit very often. She didn't like the Washington social life. Mrs. Langer had her busy from morning until night."*

His initial Senate staff had mostly been hired by Senator Moses and had Democrat ties. After a few months, Young began to look for staff with Republican connections. He called some Republican county chairmen and asked them if they knew of any good secretaries. Mark Amundson, Bowman County chairman, recommended Pat Byrne, daughter of M.S. Byrne, a Bowman lawyer of Irish background. Many of her family members had served in the Navy, and Amundson told Young, "If you can get her, she would be real good."

"It was nine o'clock in Washington the morning I called Pat, but the time was two hours earlier at her home in Bowman. She had been to a barn dance the night before and had gotten a little head cold, but her dad liked to get her up early after she had come home late from dances. Her dad was coaching her while we were on the phone. He told her to

ask me how much the job paid. I said $3,600 a year, which was pretty good wages then. Her dad then told her to ask if it was permanent. I was up for election the next June, but I assured her it was."

Pat was 22 years old when Young called her. She had gone to Dakota Business College in Fargo and had been a court reporter for Cass County Judge P.M. Paulsen in Fargo for three years. She knew shorthand, an office skill that was valued on Capitol Hill. Although hesitant at first about moving to Washington, her father "insisted I try it for six months," Pat recalled in a *Fargo Forum* news story in December 23, 1969. She accepted the job, and she and a friend moved out to Washington together. She served in his office the remainder of his Senate career, and married the Senator on December 27, 1969, six months after the death of Malinda Young on June 3, 1969.

Pat is credited with encouraging Young to take up golf. The new Senator worked hard at his job and didn't delegate as much to his staff as did other members of Congress. There was nothing too trivial for him to handle. His reasoning was that there were many farmers in the state and if he took care of their concerns they would be loyal to him.

However, this affected his staff, because he worked many Saturdays and Sundays and expected some of the staff to work, too. Pat and other staff members thought if he had golfing to look forward to he wouldn't work so much on weekends. Their reasoning was sound, and Young golfed the rest of his life. Two courses in Washington where he often golfed were the Congressional Club and the Old Soldiers Golf Course.

One of the practices Young began early was to bring editors from North Dakota to work on his staff for two-week periods of time. *"It was a way to develop a good relationship with the press, and they usually did some writing for me."* One who came and stayed for a while was *Bismarck Tribune* Assistant Editor John Hjelle, who became Young's first administrative assistant. Hjelle had been active in ROC circles, and he stayed in Washington until the death of *Bismarck Tribune* Editor Ken Simons in 1948, when he became editor.

Early Senate influences

Politically, Young leaned toward isolationism. But he distanced himself from the extreme isolationism of former Senator Nye, who represented North Dakota in the 20 years prior to Young. Republican Senators Arthur Vandenberg of Michigan and Everett Dirksen of Illinois were among those who were also at one time strong isolationists like Nye. *"But they came to realize that we had to live in a changed world and we couldn't go back to being isolationists. This was strong in the Upper Midwest states, and at least in North Dakota because of its population of Germans and Germans from Russia. Many of them migrated to the Ukraine to get away from being drafted into the Army there and other military. Isolationists considered themselves Progressives – they were people who wanted more domestic kinds of programs than involvement in foreign wars."*

The influence of Vandenberg was significant, especially in foreign policy. Young credits him as the Senator who converted him from being an isolationist to more of an internationalist, even though he would retain some of his isolationist views later during the Korean and Vietnam Wars.

"I pretty much agreed with him on foreign policy when I first got to Washington. We were involved in this war and paid a hell of a price and we had better salvage something out of it. We both were living at the Wardman Park Hotel [on Woodley Road Northwest] and would often ride to and from work or have dinner together. The hotel string orchestra often played his favorite song for him, 'The Whippenpoof Song'"

He also admired Vandenberg's speaking ability. *"He was a great speaker. His speeches were only 15 minutes long, 20 minutes at the most. But for each speech, almost every Senator would be on the Senate floor to hear him. I remember hearing him give his speech in 1948 in favor of The Marshall Plan, where he said, 'politics stops at the water's edge.' Senator Russell, probably the greatest historian in the Senate, said to me when it was over, 'that will go down in history as one of the greatest speeches ever made in the Senate.'"*

Young was impressed with the new phrases Vandenberg, who was a former newspaper editor, was always coining. *"One time I said to him,*

'Art, coining new phrases must come easy for you as well as making speeches.'" "No," he said, "I sometimes sit up until 2 or 3 o'clock in the morning preparing a three or four-minute speech."

He was also a great admirer of Senator Robert Taft of Ohio, who was his seatmate on the Senate floor during much of the time they served together. Taft was the one who made Young Secretary of the Republican Senate Conference Committee – a position he kept for 24 years, longer than any other Senator.

Just three months into his fourth term, on April 12, 1945, President Franklin D. Roosevelt died, and Vice President Harry Truman became President. Roosevelt's Agriculture Secretary had been Claude Wickard, and Truman's appointment of South Dakota native Clinton P. Anderson to be the new Secretary of Agriculture drew Young's praise. He wrote to Anderson in a May 29, 1945, letter:

> Allow me to express my most sincere congratulations upon your appointment by President Truman to the post of Secretary of Agriculture.
>
> I was born and raised on a farm in North Dakota and have been engaged in farming all of my life. I have gained a firsthand knowledge of the many problems which face the farmers of the northwest states and of the many factors which are involved in a practical and successful farm program. For these reasons I think that I am in a position to speak for the greatest majority of North Dakota farmers.
>
> I am confident that because of your experience and your interest in our sister state of South Dakota, and because of your own firsthand knowledge of farming problems, your appointment will be as gratifying and encouraging to other North Dakota farmers as it has been to me.
>
> May I assure you of my desire to cooperate with you to the fullest possible extent in the exercise of your duties as Secretary of Agriculture.

In September 1945, Young was asked by members of the Minot American Legion Post to invite General Omar N. Bradley, the Administrator for Veterans Affairs, to be their guest for several days of upland game hunting sometime that fall. In his September 15, 1945, letter inviting General Bradley, Young wrote:

> Perhaps you already are acquainted with the opportunity afforded hunters by North Dakota's unique upland game possibilities. I do not believe that it is possible to find the variety of hunting anywhere else in the nation that you can find in North Dakota. In one afternoon you may be able to shoot pheasants, grouse and partridge, as well as geese and ducks. However, each and every one of these species of game is more than plentiful and only in rare instances need the sportsman return home without his bag limit.
>
> Minot is situated in the heart of this great game country. Hunters headquartering there find both marvelous opportunities to enjoy the sport and unusual cordial hospitality ... Minot's particular brand of western hospitality would be turned loose for you, of course.

He added that on this trip to North Dakota, Bradley could also view the sites chosen by the Veterans Administration for new veterans' hospitals at Minot and Valley City.

In General Bradley's September 22, 1945, reply he wrote:

> ... You have inerringly discovered my Achillean heel. There is nothing I enjoy more than hunting, especially in such a paradise as the country around and about Minot. You know with the stepped up rate of demobilization, our work for veterans has been greatly increased. Accordingly, I shall find it necessary to restrict my travel and activities essentially to our immediate operations during the next few months.

A crucial early decision

Although General Bradley did not accept Young's invitation, three Senators agreed to join him hunting in the sand hills of LaMoure County that fall – Homer Capehart, a Republican from Indiana; Guy Cordon, a Republican from Oregon, and Allen Ellender, a Democrat from Louisiana. Joining them were Young's old North Dakota Senate seatmates Mike Flatt of Sheldon and Billy Braun of Wahpeton.

Flatt and Braun had heard that Dick Barry, a businessman and campaign and finance chair for Cass County Republicans, had recently been in Montana and got into a discussion about the Missouri Valley Authority (MVA) with Lief Erickson, who had just lost a bid for the U.S. Senate in Montana's primary election. The MVA was a proposal championed by Montana's Democrat Senator James E. Murray that would coordinate dams, irrigation and flood control projects throughout the Missouri River Basin.

"Barry told Erickson that when the chips were down, Milt Young would have to be against the MVA. This was reported in a news story carried by the Associated Press. Later, the AP called me and said, 'Is that true?' Well, I hadn't made any decision at that time. Really I leaned the other way a little bit but when it was put the way Barry did, I said, 'I am for MVA.' This created a lot of enemies among the more conservative people, but that was far preferable to being some kind of a stooge."

Young was concerned that the ROC might not support him because of his support for the MVA. *"There were many important influential people in the ROC who were strongly opposed to MVA but Fred Aandahl did an unusual thing then. We didn't have television at that time but he went on a statewide radio hookup on his own and in his speech said he totally disagreed with the position I took but defended my right to make whatever decision I deemed was right. That was an unusual speech and one which Aandahl had not even discussed with me. This was typical of Fred Aandahl and it had considerable influence with some disappointed ROCers."*

In mid-January 1946, Young hosted a luncheon at the Capitol in honor of Governor Aandahl, which was attended by several Senators.

Young himself received many invitations to speak at national and state events, especially those related to agriculture, such as 4-H camps and annual meetings of elevators and veteran's groups, cattlemen's associations, state automobile leaders, letter carriers and college homecomings.

In his early months in Washington Young tried to avoid these parties. One was from Senator Robert Taft of Ohio at his home. *"I knew it was a white tie affair and I didn't even have a tuxedo. When he asked if I was coming, I told him why and he said, 'Don't pay any attention to that. I will just be wearing business clothes.' So I went to the party and there*

were Supreme Court justices, members of Congress and many other
prominent people – most of them in white tie and tails. But Bob Taft, just
to make me comfortable, wore a business suit."

One invitation in early 1946 was from the National Press Club for
him to attend its "Baby Senators Night," which would bring to the Press
Club some of the newest members of Congress. Young declined.

Early correspondence with William Guy

During his first year in Washington, Young and a 26-year-old North
Dakota farmer named William L. Guy, Jr., exchanged a series of letters
covering a number of issues.

The first letter was dated December 19, 1945:
Dear Senator Young:

> I am a recently discharged Lieutenant in the U.S.
> Navy. I've spent a little over three years in the service
> of which two of the years have been at sea on a destroyer.
> At present I am taking life easy while I wait for the winter
> quarter of Graduate School at the University of Minnesota
> to open. Because of this leisure time I am writing you a
> few opinions which I hope help you to gauge what the
> public and servicemen think about a few of the problems
> which confront legislation in Washington. I stopped
> in your office this fall with my wife but your morning
> schedule seemed too full to bother you. Our visit to your
> office was fruitful, however, as we were able to meet
> again friends John and Alice Hjelle.
>
> 1. Army Navy merger: I am most disgusted with
> the Navy point of view on this matter. I think all of
> the servicemen of this war have seen the tremendous
> overlapping and consequent inefficiency of the two
> services. The success of the operation of the Marine
> Corps is enough to demonstrate how easily land, air and
> sea forces can manage under one management. This is
> one point on which nearly all servicemen I have talked
> to are firmly agreed upon. We want the Air, Sea and Land
> forces merged under one department – Navy tradition
> and trade school inertia be damned.
>
> 2. I hope that Congress will see fit to maintain the
> large Navy we have. Of course drastic reductions in
> personnel are in order but the ships and equipment

should be put in a reserve which our present means of preservation would allow us to do.

3. We have developed many bases in the Pacific and Atlantic. Those bases should be kept as most of them represent a blood and cash outlay by this country. If the rest of the world is depending on the United States to disentangle their problems every time their inadequately protected investments are endangered, then we should not have to fight for a place to stand in order to deliver our blows.

4. We need universal military training in this country. Every fit boy out of high school or 18 years of age should have to spend a year in the armed services. At least one half of this training time should be spent out of the United States in training at some outlying base. The experience and new grasp on the scope of this country's foreign situation would be invaluable to him and the United States.

5. We have a group of professional soldiers and sailors in this country who have been trained for years in the art of defending the United States. Please don't let the Pearl Harbor investigation wind up on the key that the people of the United States were to blame for the loss directly of several thousands of lives at Pearl Harbor on December 7, 1941, and the consequent lengthening of the war. It is apparent to most of who have served under the systems of the Army and Navy that the top brass can do a good job, the kind that the taxpayers have been hiring them to do through their lifetime, or they can be holding down their top jobs as the result of the common interdepartmental politics and Officer's Club stool-perching ability. Just as I believe many of our commanders richly deserve credit for their efforts in this war, so do I believe that the top Commanders at Pearl Harbor at the time of the attack deserve the most severe censure for allowing their stupid inability to spell the difference between life and death to soldiers and sailors under their commands.

I guess by now you must believe this the letter of a chronic griper. But I imagine that most of your letters are from those who want something if only to complain. Up until the last few months it was considered poor form to write a congressman without an endorsement by a superior officer. Now that I am free, I feel that it would be worthwhile to express the above sincere thought to you.

I hope you have a relaxing Holiday Season and the New Year full of success.

> Respectfully
> William L. Guy, Jr.
> Formerly of Amenia, N.D.

Young's reply on January 24, 1946:

... Today has been the first time I found an opportunity to take care of my correspondence. I would like to answer your good letter in considerable detail, but this will be impossible and I am sure you would agree with me if you had an opportunity to look at the stack of letters before me to say nothing of all the important legislation including appropriations for the Garrison Dam. Also the truck strike, the potato car situation and so forth call for much time and energy.

I fully agree with you that we must maintain a strong military force so that our leadership in the world will not suffer. However, I believe this can be accomplished by making voluntary enlistments far more attractive, which enlistments reached some over 200,000 during December. Along with this, the National Guard should be greatly enlarged and certainly in this respect an increase in pay should be made immediately, since as I understand it, there has been no raise since 1916. We can have military training compulsory in all colleges and even in high schools for that matter if necessary. Subjects such as radar, photography and many other sciences should be made compulsory in both colleges and high schools or subsidized by the government so that there will be a far greater number with training necessary for war duty if necessary.

I do not think, however, that a one-year program of military training could pass Congress at the present time. Most members, including myself, would much rather see a program whereby college students could take their military training during the summer vacation months and farm boys during winter slack periods. I do think, though, that the majority of Congress, including myself, would go for the one-year plan if the same results could not be accomplished otherwise.

Thank you for writing me in detail concerning your ideas, Mr. Guy, as I am most anxious to know what you servicemen are thinking. I knew your father very well a few years back when we came in contact quite often over farm problems."

In a June 3, 1946, letter from Guy he told Young that he was days away from receiving a master's degree in agricultural economics at the University of Minnesota, and again talked about the armed forces merger, military training, price controls, and labor problems in the country. He ended the letter, "I expect to be back in North Dakota in a few days. It will feel good to get back home and worry about rust, hail and drought again after the past few months of worrying over school work. I imagine you would welcome the opportunity to worry only about rust, hail and drought."

Young's June 8, 1946, reply: "Yes, as you say, I would welcome the opportunity to worry 'only about rust, hail and drought.' There have been so many issues of transcendent importance before the Senate in recent weeks that it has been most wearing. Other Senators who have been here for years and years tell me that never have they seen conditions such as exist today – speaking of the number of controversial bills which have been up for consideration and the amount of mail they have received. It has been a terrific job, I can assure you. I expect that the Senate will adjourn some time in July and I hope to spent the rest of the year, until the next session convenes, at my farm at Berlin."

1946 Senate campaign

Outside of the day-to-day issues in the Senate, Young's attention was focused on the June 25, 1946, primary election. This was the first of what was to be six re-election campaigns in his Senate career. It was critical that he win. He knew losing could mean the end of his political career.

Also up for re-election was Langer, and as had been the case for many years, the most heated contests were in the primary campaigns, where the factions of the Republican Party battled over whose candidate would be on the November general election ballot.

Young had begun making radio broadcasts from Washington that ran on state radio stations. They covered a variety of issues in Congress that he thought were of interest to his North Dakota constituents. The topics ranged from the black market of beef to recognizing the Senate pages who were from North Dakota. In March 1946, he suspended these radio broadcasts until the end of the primary election.

Young wrote about this decision in a March 1946 letter to John Alm of Page, ". . . Inasmuch as we are now about to embark upon another political campaign in North Dakota, I think these Washington Reports will be discontinued, at least until the campaign is over. It seems to me that this is no less than proper since, certainly, people would not appreciate being exposed to these reports simply for political reasons. It is for this reason that I have attempted to make my own reports strictly non-political and interesting, as well as informative."

The March 11, 1946, issue of *Life* Magazine profiled the 35 Senators who were up for re-election that year. One of Young's closest colleagues, Senator Arthur Vandenberg of Michigan, was featured on the cover. His profile talked about his success as a newspaper publisher, being an expert on finance and international law and being known as "one of the crack speakers in the Senate."

Seven of the Senators, Young included, were featured in photographs from their home states. Portraits of the others, including Langer, who was also up for re-election that year, were featured with shorter profiles.

Young was pictured at a table playing cards with some neighbors from home. The text read, "Young of North Dakota, Republican, is a vigorous, raw-boned farmer considerably more at home with his friends than in Washington drawing rooms. He was appointed last year by North Dakota's able Governor Aandahl to take the seat of Senator Moses until a special election this June. He owns a 1,300-acre farm, works it himself, has retired its indebtedness. As a Senator he has supported MVA, gone along with internationalism, proved himself sincere, a hard worker, congenial, well-liked. Last summer he left the Senate for a few months to get the harvest in on his farm. Opinion: Still unknown. He is feeling his way. Against Langer and Nye, he stands out like a beacon."

Langer's profile read: "Langer of North Dakota, Republican, is a shrewd, sharp lawyer with chameleonesque variability and a left-wing, isolationist background. In 1934, while governor of North Dakota, he was convicted of levying a 5% 'political contribution' against salaries of relief workers. He defied the court, declared martial law. Later his conviction was reversed. After election to the Senate, his right to a seat was unsuccessfully challenged, the Elections Committee charging him with "continuous, contemptuous and shameful disregard of high concepts of public duty.' He introduces more trivial bills than any other senator. Opinion: Take him out."

The process for nominating a candidate for the Senate seat was to be made by the precinct committeemen of each political party prior to the next statewide election. This nomination was made at the state conventions of each political party. The Republican convention was March 11 to 16 in Bismarck. If Young had lost at that convention, where the Nonpartisan League had a two-thirds majority, he would have lost the nomination. Had he run without the party endorsement, it would have had to be as an Independent, and he doubted he could have won.

Young was the ROC-endorsed candidate. Challenging him for the seat was Dr. George Schatz of Fargo, the NPL-endorsed candidate. And Nye was making another attempt to return to the Senate. *"A few months before the convention Nye came to me and said, 'Wouldn't you run against Langer and let me run for my old spot? You could win easily.' I was no pro in politics at that time by any means but I mentioned it to Langer one day and, typical of him, in the hard-boiled way he had, he said, 'Do whatever you think best.' I decided against it."*

In mid-February, Nye announced he would be a candidate for either Young's or Langer's seat. Days before the Republican convention, however, Nye announced he would run for Young's "short-term" Senate seat, instead of Langer's.

"I expected Nye to get a fair amount of support at this NPL-dominated convention and was concerned about getting a majority of votes. I worked hard to establish a record in little over a year's time in the Senate, and needed the support of both the League-controlled Republican Party and the ROC." He figured he had 172 votes, but

needed 191 for the endorsement.

For the two or three weeks prior to the Republican convention, a heavy winter snowfall had blocked Highway Two entirely across the state. To meet delegates across the northern tier, Young secured a plane equipped with skis. He began his meetings in Williston and moved on to Stanley, Minot, Rugby and Devils Lake, trying at each one to placate Republicans to vote for him, especially in light of his support of the Missouri Valley Authority, which most Republicans strongly opposed.

The North Dakota Farmers Union was a strong supporter of the MVA, and in an interesting political twist, because of Young's support for the MVA, some of the Leaguers who belonged to the Farmers Union supported him at the convention. *"Something significant happened the evening before the convention that may have decided the party vote. The delegates from Grant County – all who were Leaguers and many who were Farmers Union members – asked to come up to my room to visit. They asked questions for nearly an hour, and said they might vote for me the next day. Their support went back to my stand on MVA, which they strongly favored. When I voted for MVA I wasn't thinking about Farmers Union votes. The only thing that caused me to come out for MVA was that I couldn't be in a position as had been claimed – that 'when the chips are down, Milt Young would have to be against MVA.'"*

Young wanted an open ballot at the convention but by tradition it was usually a secret ballot. *"I fought for an open ballot because I thought I would get the 172 votes and scratch for the rest of them and I wanted to know where they were. I believed an open ballot would give me more information as to where to get the additional votes. The convention voted to have a secret ballot, which proved lucky for me. I had more luck than sense because I got votes from many of the Farmer Union delegates who supported MVA, and some Leaguers who wouldn't dare vote for me in an open ballot, but on a secret ballot they did."*

Erich Zieman of LaMoure County, who called him "a real farmer who can serve North Dakota farmers best," placed Young's name in nomination. The second ballot of the convention elected the candidate.

Young received 195 votes, four more than were required to win, and 24 more than the first ballot total. Schatz had 151 votes on the second ballot, up from 139 on the first ballot, And, Nye's vote total was 34, down from 66 in the first round of balloting.

In a recap of the week's political events, the "North Dakota Whirligig" column in the March 17, 1946, issue of the *Fargo Forum*, wrote about Young's strong showing:

> ... Surprises of the week were confined largely to the official Republican convention. The strength mustered by Milton Young to win the nomination, and the weakness of the Nye group, were tops as Nye slid from 66 to 34 in one ballot.

The following weekend the state Democrats gathered in Fargo for their convention. In the keynote address, the delegates heard Minneapolis Mayor Hubert H. Humphrey tell them that their party in North Dakota "faces the greatest opportunity in its history and the eyes of the nation are upon it to return the state to sound progressive hands." He said the fact that both Senators are on the ballot, "makes your state doubly crucial in this all important year."

David Kelly of Grand Forks, the state's Democratic National Committeeman, was the early favorite to be endorsed to run against Young. But he removed himself from consideration and political newcomer Bill Lanier, Jr., of Fargo received the endorsement. A 33-year-old World War II veteran, the former Marine earned a Purple Heart for his combat duty as a first lieutenant. Born in 1913 in Memphis, Tennessee, Lanier's grandfather was a corn and cotton grower. A move to North Dakota was precipitated by the need for his mother to move to a drier climate for her health. He moved to Carrington in 1923 with his father, Powless William Lanier, Sr., who set up a law practice. His mother and sister soon joined them and they lived there for three years before moving to Jamestown. As a teenager, he campaigned for his father, who was the unsuccessful candidate for the U.S. House in 1930, and who two years later moved his family to Fargo to became the U.S. Attorney in for North Dakota. In 1932, the senior Lanier seconded the nomination of Franklin D. Roosevelt for President at the National Democratic Convention in Chicago.

Young Bill Lanier graduated from Jamestown High School, and he worked part-time as a semi-pro baseball player and opera singer, putting himself through the University of North Dakota and George Washington University School of Law in Washington, D.C. Lanier was offered a professional contract by the Metropolitan Opera Company, but chose law as a career. He was practicing law with his father, who remained active in Democrat Party politics throughout his life, at the time of his nomination. This was the first of three of Young's re-election campaigns in which Bill Lanier, Jr., would play a prominent role.

Also on the ballot would be Nye, who had unsuccessfully sought the endorsement of the NPL, but who instead began circulating petitions immediately following the convention to place his name on the ballot as an Independent. Nye claimed there had been a misunderstanding at the Republican convention, when the state's National Republican Committeeman Fred Graham told convention delegates that he had assurances from Nye and Dr. Schatz that they would "abide by the wishes of the convention."

Some of Young's observations about the campaign were apparent in his correspondence with constituents. Lewis Baertsch of Jamestown, a frequent letter writer and Young supporter, had the following observations about Lanier and the upcoming election in a March 28, 1946, letter:

> A democrat I talked to said even though he can't stomach his father, the son is a fine young man and will make it and said you can be assured that he will be elected if it's a three-cornered race. It is probable that should Senator Nye be a candidate you would have to plan your campaign to miss no opportunity to cover every angle to the last ditch.
>
> There is no question whatsoever but what you can be the winner on June 25 if you will carry on a strenuous dignified clean campaign. People like dignified clean campaigns. I recall so well some years ago when Senator Nye made a speech in Jamestown in the NPR park, a beautiful day, that lost him votes, a remark that he made

that Langer has "ants in his pants" didn't set with the crowd even though they may have been on the fence, perhaps a few dozen laughed and most of them were disgusted. Many made remarks that I heard as follows, 'it's getting pretty rotten when a candidate for the U.S. Senate has to make such remarks.' Others said 'here is one vote he won't get.' Others said, 'what has that to do with the issues?' I merely mention this to show that most people even though they are common everyday working people like a dignified campaign.

In an April 8, 1946, reply to Baertsch, Young wrote:

I noted with considerable interest your statements about what Nye had to say in one of his campaigns about Langer "having ants in his pants." I, too, had heard many times about this statement and that it did Nye a lot of harm.

The clean manner in which Aandahl carried out his campaign of two years ago, in my opinion, had much to do with his successful election. I am going to carry mine on in exactly the same way and ignore entirely some critical remarks, which Nye, I am sure, is bound to make about me. Of course, if it gets too tough, I may have to answer occasionally.

I am in full agreement with you, Lewis, that even though the prospects look good, it will be necessary to put on the best possible campaign. I understand that Nye will announce his candidacy over the radio tonight and, also that he plans to campaign continuously from now until election. He does have a great ability and that together with his desperation should make him a dangerous candidate.

Going into the election campaign, Young knew it would be a tough race. Again he had to appear fairly independent, running against both the attractive newcomer Lanier, and Nye. "I was not in a position to antagonize any one of the major factions of the party supporting me."

It disturbed Young to have Nye as his opponent. *"It was disheartening in a way because I was a strong supporter of his for many years. I managed his 1944 campaign against Moses, which he lost, and he wanted to blame someone. He, himself, caused his defeat but it was a little difficult for him to take. He was pretty vicious in his attack against me. I think that the way he went about it he helped me more than he hurt me. He pictured me as a pretty bad character, a great liberal, and he quoted various liberal columnists – one being Walter Winchell. Nye received considerable national attention because he was perhaps one of the most quoted men in America in his last term in the Senate."*

ROC activist Clyde Duffy called this contest between Young and Nye "the most bitter battle in North Dakota history."

In a May 3, 1946, letter to Baertsch, Young wrote:

> . . . I certainly am most happy to have the good will and support of you and people like Reverend Bergum [with whom Young had played baseball during his early years of farming] . . . I am inclined to believe that the good vote I received for Congress two years ago was largely due to the fact that I was a farmer. In fact, I received more farm votes than did Robertson even though he was quite well known and endorsed by the League, which has most of its strength in the rural areas. I believe it would be wise on my part to stress this farm angle more than anything else.
>
> For the most part, all the news I have received has been most encouraging except yesterday, when I received a report that many Leaguers in the Minot and Grand Forks area were going for Nye. He is fairly strong in the Minot area; in fact, I believe that this is his best part of the State. Even if he should receive 50 percent of the League vote, it still wouldn't be enough to elect him.

More of Young's concerns about Nye's campaigning were expressed in a May 11, 1946, letter he wrote to Donald Wanner, who worked for the Farm Security Administration in the state. This was in reply to a letter he had received from him.

> I am happy to know that you find such favorable sentiment for me in your travels around the state . . . Nye is causing me considerable trouble, particularly among businessmen who seem to think that I am far too radical. Of course, I am somewhat on the liberal side and Nye is making the most of it among the conservatives.

As his party's endorsed candidate for the Senate, Young had many Republican factions to please during the campaign. This resulted in him working out of three campaign headquarters. Langer and the NPL insisted there be a Republican campaign manager, and they, not Young, selected Roy Frazier, an active League member, and secretary-treasurer of the state party, as manager for that headquarters. Other campaign work was done out of a separate ROC headquarters at the GP Hotel in Bismarck, and he also had a smaller personal campaign office.

Because of Frazier's ties to the NPL, Young was not initially sure whether to consider him a friend or foe. *"I was in Washington and he called me up quite often. He swore at me and called me names over the phone and you would think judging from the telephone conversation that he was against me. I checked on him and found out that right after leaving the telephone where he called me everything under the sun, he would go out in the street and be plugging for me."* Young later came to regard him as a loyal supporter.

On the campaign trail, Young ran into opposition to him and support for Nye. Among the Nye supporters were the *Minot Daily News* and some prominent state businessmen. One day he was campaigning in Watford City, an area he was to decisively carry in the election. He was with Speed (Rollis) Nelson, a recently discharged sailor, who had been editor of the *Non Partisan Leader* before going into the service, and his friend, Freddie Compton. *"I went up and down the streets visiting with businessmen and they went into the beer parlor. We met later and were driving out of town when I said, 'I'll get the hell beat out of me here. Everywhere I went they were all Nye.' But Speed and Freddie said where they were they were all for me. We were two or three miles out of town and turned around and went back to the beer parlor. I bought a round of drinks."*

On May 9, 1946, Young contacted *Look* Magazine in New York and sent a check for $400 for 10,000 reprints of an article called "Your Last Chance," about atomic energy. He said it was urgent he had them by June 5, and asked that they be shipped to the ROC headquarters in Bismarck. The article talked about the threat of atomic war in the future. It said, "Now victory has brought a breathing spell. You have a last chance to save your civilization . . . And you have the choice of three ways to use that last chance. Few things in your life are more important than which choice you make."

The choices were to try to conquer the world, try to defend yourself, and put an end to war. In promoting the third choice, it gave suggestions about what different types of Americans –"the insurance man, teacher, mechanic, salesman, utility worker, scientist, merchant, newspaperman and clergyman" – can do to bring it about.

"A few weeks before the election, the Fargo Forum *ran an editorial that said I would probably lose, unless I got out and got to work – then I might win. That kept me campaigning."*

Young tried to keep the campaign issues centered on agriculture as a way to counter accusations that he was too liberal. He talked about his record and what he expected to do for North Dakota.

Langer, who was being challenged by the ROC candidate Joe Bridston of Grand Forks in the primary campaign, seemed to be supportive of Young in his speeches. *"I think after I got the nomination he wanted me elected. He certainly didn't want Nye. I don't think he wanted Bill Lanier, a Democrat, and one he didn't know very well."*

In early June, Young sent the following statewide campaign letter on his United States Senate letterhead:

> Dear Friend:
>
> Two years ago, I wrote you in behalf of my candidacy for Congress. Although I was little known over the State then, and was able to put on only a meager campaign, I lost by about only one vote per precinct. I attribute much of this fine vote to the good work people like you saw fit to do for me.
>
> Since that time, a vacancy occurred in the United States Senate because of the death of the late Senator John Moses. Our Good Governor Fred Aandahl appointed me to fill that position, and I have devoted every energy to merit his confidence and faith in me.
>
> This past year in the United States Senate has been a most difficult one because of the tense international situation and the many complex national issues. But I have tried hard to do a good job for you and to represent you in a way as to bring credit to 650,000 people of our State. True, being a farmer, I naturally directed much of my attention to farm problems, which are so vital to the

prosperity of everyone in North Dakota. At the same time, I have worked hard on the problems of businessmen and veterans, education and other state interests, including $500,000,000 in authorized water projects in North Dakota. I would like to go into more detail regarding my work in Washington, but limited space in this letter will not permit.

I am enclosing a pamphlet prepared by my good neighbors in LaMoure County regarding my activities and objectives in the United States Senate. I hope you may find time to read it. Should you feel inclined, I would appreciate it so much if you would pass it on to your friends.

I sincerely hope my record as your United States Senator has been such to merit your support in this coming election. Surely you know that anything you may find possible to do for me will be greatly appreciated."

A few days before the election Young was at the Elks Club in Fargo with Ken Fitch, a Fargo insurance executive and longtime Republican member of the North Dakota House, and Ben Stern, Dakota National Bank president and Republican National Committeeman. *"Some out-of-state newspapermen – one from New York, one from Pittsburgh – and two other big newspapers were there, as was Bill Lanier. We sat down with them. Lanier told these newspaper people that he would probably carry every county in the state. Well, I said, 'Won't I carry my own county?' 'Well, you might,' he said. That was an example of how cocky he was. I think he went a little too far that way."*

Years later, Pat Young recalled during that campaign when Lanier stopped by Young's Senate office in Washington to look it over. He told them he wanted to see what his new office would look like.

The election turned out to be a landslide for Young, who scored an easier victory than anyone had anticipated, with more votes than the total of both his opponents. The final vote total was 75,998 for Young, 37,507 for Lanier, and 20,848 for Nye. Young received 67 percent of the vote.

Young expected to win but was surprised that the election wasn't closer. *"I thought Bill Lanier would be stronger than he was. He was talented, good looking, a good singer – he had everything – and was just out of the Marines. But somehow or other he didn't conduct his campaign as well as he might have . . . he was a very able person, but he never caught hold. Most of his campaign was one of attacking my voting record and me personally and I think he went too far with it. Vicious attacks and inaccurate statements on my voting record hurt him more than it helped him."* This was not the only time Young and Lanier would oppose each other on a statewide ballot.

Young believed he won because of the positions he took on issues and the good friends he had made. *"The press, with the exception of* The Minot Daily News, *which supported Nye, was pretty much all on my side. Being a farmer and being a more 'middle-of-the-roader' and independent also helped me win. I don't know of any other candidate for major office in North Dakota who faced as complicated and difficult a situation as I did in this campaign – or one who had to be somewhat independent and even antagonize some friends."*

The support Lanier received from the national political action committee of the Congress of Industrial Organizations – the CIO – which was one of the nation's largest labor unions, was also an issue in the campaign. The Republican Party took out statewide newspaper ads to counter the support former U.S. Secretary of Agriculture Henry Wallace gave for Lanier in radio ads.

Also on the ballot were three measures, including a constitutional amendment making a county manager form of government mandatory without an election when the assessed valuation of the county dropped below $2.5 million; and another one to authorize a two-mill property tax levy for a veterans' rehabilitation fund up to $8 million or 10 years, whichever came first. The third, a referendum measure, called for an increase in taxable assessed valuation on all property from 50 percent to 75 percent of true value. All three were soundly rejected.

Because North Dakota's Republican primary was traditionally the election that would guarantee a general election victory, Young focused almost exclusively on his own campaign. Bridston came closer to defeating Langer than most challengers, losing to him by only 5,000 votes. However, Bridston criticized Young for not campaigning hard enough for him and other ROC candidates, and Young believed that some of this criticism was justified. But he bristled at Bridston's charge that he had made a deal with Langer to not campaign against him.

"I had no idea I would win as big as I did. If I thought that I could have won and get almost as many votes as Nye and Langer put together, I probably would have tried to help Joe Bridston more. But there was no deal between me and Langer. None whatsoever."

Perhaps to soften this criticism, on July 5, 1946, Young wrote letters to State Treasurer H.W. Swenson, Secretary of State Thomas Hall, Attorney General Nels Johnson and Insurance Commissioner Otto Krueger who, along with Governor Aandahl, ran on the ROC ballot with Young:

Congratulations on your splendid victory in this campaign. I am not unmindful of the prestige it gave me to be on the ticket with winners such as you. My only regret is that I wasn't able to help all the ticket a little more. In this election with a CIO candidate running against me who had all kinds of money to spend - a Democratic slate with no contest, and Nye firing on the other side - I had about all I could do to take care of my own campaign. Surely no one could have predicted two weeks before the election that I had an easy race.

A press release of July 25, 1946, announced that Young was establishing a state office at LaMoure for the balance of the summer, upon the adjournment of Congress:

Senator Young said he would spend most of his time on his farm in Berlin, where he will put on his overalls and work in the harvest fields for the balance of the season.

"I will maintain an office in LaMoure, however, and will try to spend some time there each week taking care of such business and may come up," Senator Young said. "My Washington office will remain open, and operating, of course."

The Senator said he hoped to "make a couple of swings around the state," as soon as he has finished harvesting his crop. "The session of Congress just concluded has been one of the most important and consequently grueling ever held," Senator Young said. "Senators who have been in Washington for several sessions confirm that.

Congress has had to pass upon such pressing questions as international cooperation, peacetime conscription, retention of price and other wartime controls, the control of atomic energy, new social, economic and scientific legislation, and scores of other important matters. More than 10,000 bills were introduced. Tons of mail poured in on the members.

Withal it has been a most interesting and educational experience for all members. I have learned much during my first session here but now look forward to returning home. I think it will be a healthy thing for the country to have their representatives in Washington spend some time among the people. They will return to Washington when the next Congress convenes having a better knowledge of the needs and thinking of the people."

Here is a summary of some other early issues Young faced in his first years as a new Senator from North Dakota, and his views on them:

Equal Rights Amendment

In May 1945, Young joined about a dozen Senators who sponsored a Resolution proposing a Constitutional amendment providing Equal Rights for Women. *"Among the Senators signing it were Bill Langer, Jim Fulbright, Millard Tydings, Claude Pepper, Art Capper, John McClellan, Warren Magnuson and Homer Capehart – a mix of Republicans and Democrats. Of these supporters, two of them, Capehart and McClellan, I considered to be very conservative Senators. I continued to support it through my years in the Senate, although I believe that it was perhaps needed more in the mid-1940s than it was a few decades later."*

UN Charter in 1945

The United Nations was an issue that came up just after the 1946 election. *"Langer voted against it, but I voted for it. I was a strong isolationist, but after all the blood and money we spent, I thought we should try to do something to prevent another war. Langer called it a 'square peg in a round hole.' But I supported it because we had gotten into this bitter war – the Second World War – and I was sympathetic in trying to do something on a worldwide basis that might prevent future wars. I made a short speech on the charter – my first in the U.S. Senate."*

Dropping the Bomb on Japan

"My first reaction in early August 1945 when I heard that Truman ordered the dropping of the atomic bombs on Japan was that it was a dreadful thing. Many thought we shouldn't have done it, we were sure of winning the war anyway, but in retrospect, it was the right thing to do. There were no more American lives lost. There were at least 90,000 Japanese killed, but it did end the war. If we had not dropped the bomb and ended the war quickly, Japan would have fought on for some time and the destruction and loss of life would have been much heavier. Germany fought until about everything was destroyed. Without dropping the bomb, people would never have realized the tremendous damage it could do, and those were very small bombs compared to what Russia and the United States have now."

Yalta Agreement

Shortly before the end of World War II, President Roosevelt reached agreements at Yalta with Soviet Premier Joseph Stalin and British Prime Minister Winston Churchill that ceded control of Eastern Europe to the Soviet Union. The United States began the policy of containment of Communism. In 1947 the Truman Doctrine, with aid to Greece and Turkey, formalized this containment policy.

"The Yalta agreement gave Russia such tremendous power and complete domination of Eastern Europe and the Yalta agreement pretty well determined which countries would have influence and control. In this case, Roosevelt voted with Stalin, and Churchill voted the other way. If Churchill had had his way, Russia wouldn't have had nearly the power and influence that it wound up with in Europe. I believe the aid to Greece and Turkey was necessary. We saved Greece from becoming a Communist nation and we helped some others, and I think a certain amount of that was necessary. I think the policy of John Foster Dulles,

who became Secretary of State after Dean Acheson, went too far. He had
a policy of containment of Communism all over the world. I remember
his argument yet that with the British pulling out of countries all over
the world this did create a power vacuum. He believed if we didn't move
in, the Russians would and that was probably true to some extent. But
we never were powerful enough and never had the resources to try to
contain Russia all around the world alone."

End of War Price Controls

"World War II had just ended when I first came to the Senate. It was
probably one of the easiest times of all to serve in the Senate. Congress
had just appropriated all the money that the military wanted. There were
not many other problems. The big issue at the end of the war was price
controls. The Office of Price Administration (OPA) became a big issue
in the election of 1946. Republicans generally were opposed to OPA and
they proved to be right because that was the year the Republicans gained
control of both Houses of Congress. I was opposed to continuing OPA
after the war was over because it slowed down production and much of
what the people needed had to be bought on the Black Market. I became
involved in some of those investigations. Some of my best friends told
me I was wrong on OPA. But it proved that the overwhelming majority of
people had enough of OPA. It ended shortly after the election when the
80th Congress met. That's the Congress Truman called the 'Do Nothing
Congress.' He was smart in coining that phrase, but that was one of the
best Congresses I ever served in."

Anti-Monopoly Program

In 1946, Young co-sponsored legislation which did not pass that
would have established a consistent and coordinated anti-monopoly
program to protect against monopolistic practices, and protect the public
interest whenever necessary through methods of public control over
monopoly. Young joined with many liberal Senators like Republicans
Langer, George Aiken from Vermont and Dean Taylor from New York,

along with Democrats James Murray from Montana, Hugh Mitchell from Washington, and Harley Kilgore from West Virginia.

"I was always quite an independent but I probably was somewhat influenced on that particular subject by Teddy Roosevelt, whom I admired and who was a trustbuster. I viewed North Dakota as being an anti-monopoly state. That is one of the reasons for the origin and the strength of the Nonpartisan League. It was sort of anti-Twin Cities with the banking interests and the grain trade against the railroads. All had great influence on North Dakota politics and our economy."

The Taft-Hartley Bill

In 1947, when Congress passed the labor legislation called the Taft-Hartley Bill, Young was a seatmate of one of its co-sponsors, Senator Robert Taft. *"Several amendments were made to the bill that placed more restrictions on labor and I voted for maybe four or five of them. The next day when more amendments were introduced, I took the floor and said, 'One of the most vicious of commentators is Mr. George Taylor. I listened to his remarks last night. First he attacked labor and then he attacked farmers. I shall now make a statement about labor I had not intended to make.' I continued that I was not an expert on labor and had tried to study the proposed labor legislation and to be fair with labor, but when men like Taylor representing industry are as unfair to labor as they are to farmers then these labor bill amendments have gone far enough. My position from now on will be to oppose all amendments. If the bill is presented without any further amendments I shall vote for it even over a Presidential veto, but if it is made one bit tougher my position will be against it all the way through."*

Young believed it was one of his better early speeches. He supported two additional amendments, and in the end voted for the entire bill. *"This probably had quite an effect on the bill, too, because it only passed over the President's veto, as I recall, by one vote. I was a key vote at that time. At that time there were more Senators closer to farmers than there are now, and this Taylor was viciously against farm programs. So the fact that*

I was a farmer myself made me more adamant in my opposition to Taylor and could well have affected a few other Senators. I just felt strongly about this issue. I never felt in my life that I was anti-labor even though most of them opposed me. I never had that kind of feeling toward labor."

George W. Taylor was an industrial relations expert who had arbitrated many labor disputes. In addition to being a fierce opponent of the Taft-Hartley Act, Taylor was the official arbitrator of internal Congress of Industrial Organizations (CIO) jurisdictional disputes. He also was a strong advocate of private sector collective bargaining and held labor-related positions in the Roosevelt, Truman, Eisenhower and Kennedy administrations.

One of the amendments Young voted against lost by one vote and his was the swing vote again on an amendment that would have damaged the union movement. It was vesting bargaining rights in the local union, making it an unfair labor practice for the parent union to prevent the local union from making agreements. *"I wasn't that anti-union. I didn't think that Taft-Hartley really hurt the unions. Of course, they put on a strong campaign in succeeding years in opposition to Taft-Hartley but it really has never hurt the unions. It helped industry sometimes, I think. And it gave employees some long-needed help."*

'First A Farmer'

The first item on Milt Young's agenda when he returned home was to drive around his farm and look at the crops. When he was in Washington, the first question he would ask his son, Scoop, and his wife, Marcia, in his weekly phone call to them on Sunday nights was, "How are the crops?" The second question was, "What's the price of wheat?"

Once, when Marcia complained about how rainy it had been, he scolded her and said, "Don't ever say that. You can never have too much rain. Anyone who has lived through the Depression would tell you that." One year when the barley was shredded from hail on three quarters of their farmland, he advised, "Don't do anything. Keep it and it will come back." He was right.

He discontinued his membership with the local Farmers Union organization in the early 1940s because he believed it was more interested in social programs on the national level than it was in farm matters. Later in the 1970s, Young was dismayed when his liberal Democrat colleague, Abraham Ribicoff of Connecticut, who had been a vocal opponent of farm programs in the Senate, received a higher ranking for his voting record from the Farmers Union than he did. This happened because the ranking also factored in a Senator's support for social, welfare and government programs.

Despite his differences with the Farmers Union, Young defended the organization in September 1945 when Senator Henry Bridges, a Republican from New Hampshire, said on the Senate floor that the

Farmers Union membership included many Communists. *"I stood up and said, 'according to FBI records there were only 70 known Communists in the whole State of North Dakota and the Farmers Union wasn't any more Communist than any other organization in the whole country.'"*

Young admired Senator Bridges. *"He was a great Senator and a good friend of mine, but he was quite conservative and very strong anti-Communist. But I thought Senator Bridges was going too far in accusing the Farmers Union of being Communist. They were some very liberal thinkers – probably even Socialist – but I didn't think that the Communist charge was justified. Many people from that part of the country looked at our area as very liberal. In fact, Senator George Moses from New Hampshire once labeled North Dakota's Senators as 'sons of the wild jackasses.'"*

Young had philosophical struggles with the role the federal government should have with farm programs. *"Lincoln said something to the effect that the federal government should do only those things the states themselves could not do alone. That is a good philosophy. I still believe more in state's rights and the fewer federal programs the better. But there are many things that the federal government must do – such as interstate highways and various water projects – which affect all states. If each state had its own way, you would never have a good highway system. You could hardly go from one state to the other on a direct route.*

I believe that farm programs had their place in the federal government. I would have been much more popular in the Senate if I could have gone along with no farm programs at all. Having lived through the Thirties, I knew the necessity of the government doing something. Senator Dick Russell and I both said so often that farmers would be willing to go it alone if the rest of the country would do the same. I think that is true yet. With its tremendous power, labor can to a large extent set their members' wages and hours . . . So when almost everyone else can set their prices and the farmers can't, you have to have legislation. This can only be done through a government program.

You cannot get several million farmers to organize and agree on what they want or need. I came to the Senate with this philosophy."

The McNary-Haugen Bill of the late 1920s, which first generated Young's interest in national politics, was sponsored and bore the names of two Republican Senators. President Coolidge, also a Republican, vetoed the bill twice, believing that it would result in government management of markets and showed favoritism for farmers that was not in the best interests of the rest of the population. Young disagreed, believing that had it become law, it would have helped fight off the ensuing years of drought and depression. And, he believed Republicans would not have suffered the disastrous defeats they did in succeeding years.

Throughout his entire Senate career, Young was a member of the Senate Agriculture and Forestry Committee, with his first appointment effective April 5, 1945, taking the seat held briefly by Senator Moses before his death. At his retirement in 1981, Young had earned the distinction of having been the committee's longest-serving member at 35 years and nine months.

For many years he was the committee's ranking minority member. Besides the short tenure of Moses, since statehood, only seven other North Dakotans had served on the committee, and two had chaired it, by the time he joined the committee. These Senators and their years on the committee were Republican Lyman R. Casey, 1891 to 1893; Democrat William Roach, 1983 to 1899; Republican Henry C. Hansbrough, 1893 to 1909, and chair from 1908 to 1909; Republican Asle J. Gronna, 1911 to 1921 and chair from 1919 to 1921; Republican Edwin Ladd, 1921 to 1925; Republican Lynn J. Frazier, 1927 to 1941, and Republican Gerald P. Nye, 1943 to 1944.

When he came to Congress, Young was surprised that Senator Langer and Congressmen Usher Burdick and William Lemke, the other members of North Dakota's Congressional delegation, were not members of Congressional Agriculture committees. *"Langer, Burdick and Lemke all came up through the League. You would think that they would know farm programs and specialize in them, but not one of the three did or ever served on the Agriculture Committee. They represented a farm state, and the strength of the League was farmers. The strangest thing was that none of them knew much about farm programs or paid much attention to them."*

Young also served on the Senate Appropriations Committee from 1947 through retirement, and became the committee's ranking minority member in 1973. He was the third North Dakotan to be on the committee, following Asle Gronna, who served from 1919 to 1921, and Gerald Nye, who served from 1927 to 1945. Over the years, Young was on several appropriations subcommittees, including agriculture during his entire Senate tenure, as well as defense, interior, and army and military construction.

Some Senators were familiar with North Dakota and its agriculture issues because they had worked harvests in it or neighboring states. They were Senator Joseph McCarthy, who worked in North Dakota the summer of 1950, and Senator Wayne Morse of Oregon and Senator Fred Harris of Oklahoma, who hauled bundles in North Dakota while working their way through college. Harris began in Oklahoma and combined all the way north to Scranton in southwestern North Dakota. Senator Allen Ellender of Louisiana also worked his way through college hauling bundles, beginning in Kansas and traveling as far north as South Dakota.

Since his first days in the Senate, Young showed an interest in food, farming and agriculture issues. Among the early legislation that Young successfully sponsored was the renewal of the federal food stamp program. Senator George Aiken approached Young soon after his arrival in the Senate in 1945 about co-sponsoring legislation to reestablish this program that had existed in the 1930s and early 1940s. Although funded through the federal government, it was administered through the states, and Aiken, who administered it while Governor of Vermont, thought highly enough of the program to reestablish it. Young and Aiken even went to the White House one day to try to convince President Truman that he should get behind this legislation. According to Young's aide, Neil

Bjornson, Truman told them, "Get out of here with that damn Socialist idea!" But they persevered and gathered enough support to pass a pilot program, which later was established as a permanent program.

"I sponsored it then partly because of surplus food issues, but also because I thought it would be a better way of distributing food to needy people than just handing out commodities, but over the years I believed it got out of hand and I became less supportive of it."

The old farm block that had shepherded farm policy through the first half of the 20th Century had, for the most part, left the Senate by the time Young joined its ranks. The few remaining were Burton Wheeler, a Democrat from Montana; Hiram Johnson, a Republican from California; Robert La Follette, a Republican from Wisconsin; and Arthur Capper, a Republican from Kansas.

"I followed them closely and was quite sympathetic with them. Most of them were isolationists and I was always some kind of isolationist. But there were some able men among them. The older La Follette was one of the all-time great leaders of the Senate. Senator Capper was getting pretty old and a little senile. Hiram Johnson from California was a brilliant man but had a stroke and could hardly talk. Wheeler was still very strong then with quite a little influence and was highly respected. He was one who had the courage to go against President Roosevelt in the so-called packing of the Court." This happened in 1937 when Roosevelt unsuccessfully proposed, in the wake of several Supreme Court rulings against his New Deal programs, that as many as six justices be added to the Supreme Court if any justice over the age of 70 refused to retire.

These Farm Block Senators had been involved in setting the farm policies and farm commodity programs that had been established following the Depression. The first mandatory price support legislation was established in the Agricultural Adjustment Act of 1933, part of President Franklin Roosevelt's New Deal legislation. Young's arrival in the Senate just as World War II was ending came at a time of concern that greater crop surpluses would bring the return of depressed prices.

This Steagall Amendment, named after longtime Alabama Democrat Representative Henry Steagall, was part of the Agricultural Adjustment Act of 1938 that continued the wartime price support levels of 90 percent for basic commodities for two years after the official end of the war, December 31, 1946.

Post-World War II Agricultural Challenges

On February 21, 1947, Young spoke on the floor of the Senate about proposed cuts in the federal budget.

> Mr. President, Congress has pledged itself to a program of extreme economy. I am thoroughly in accord with that objective. It is time that we cut down from wartime levels of expenditures. It is time that steps be taken to eliminate unnecessary government controls, services, and outlays necessary to maintain its services. We should demand efficient and economical administration from every governmental department and agency. All requests should be subjected to an intelligent and exhaustive study, but it is with great concern that I view the steps that have been taken to arbitrarily slash the budget without that intelligent study necessary to determine where the cuts can be made and how much those cuts should be.
>
> . . . As a farmer, coming from an agricultural state, I am naturally concerned about the welfare of agriculture. This should also be of great concern to every Member of Congress, since there never has been any long-sustained period of prosperity in this nation when farm income was low. Farmers everywhere – and particularly in the Midwest and West – are naturally concerned about reclamation, flood control, and irrigation. These worthy projects are not merely an expenditure, but rather an investment in the economic security of all who live within deficient rainfall areas.
>
> These programs must not be abandoned. We cannot expose our resources and our farmers to the drought, dust storms, erosions, and floods which have devastated our economy in the thirties. I cannot forget those years, but apparently others have.

Young made another speech on the floor of the Senate on May 6,

1947, this time decrying what he believed was "... the adverse publicity agriculture has been receiving in the past months":

Nearly every magazine, and many columnists and radio commentators, are constantly making public statements which, for the most part, I know to be most unfair and not based on facts.

Through this publicity, the consumer is led to believe that our government is using the United States Treasury, in a big way, to raise farm prices, at a time when a drive is being made to reduce industrial prices. I regret that almost everyone making public statements on the farm price situation does not take the time to make a fair and unbiased study of the actual circumstances.

... In 1946, this nation produced its greatest wheat and corn crop, along with record-breaking quantities of other food crops. Through this great production, it has been possible for the United States to export more foodstuffs in a single year than all other nations of the world combined have exported throughout all history. We have exported tremendous amounts of meats, farm products, and grains of all kinds.

... There are some extremists who, in their ardent support of the free enterprise system, would at this time eliminate all export controls. If that were done at this time, our exports would increase and food prices would rise sharply, since it is estimated that the world food demand exceeds by three trillion tons the world food supply. Naturally, without export controls the drain on our production would increase, resulting in far greater food cost in the United States. The plain, unadulterated fact regarding the rise in the cost of foods in this nation is that it is almost entirely due to our tremendous shipments abroad. While I believe that helping feed the rest of the world is important, particularly if we are to stave off Communism, I think it should be understood, here in the United States, what effect great exports have in America, where all foodstuffs are sold on the open market, and where the farmer has nothing to say about the price he receives. So long as we export down to a level where a home scarcity is created, we can expect nothing but the resulting high prices.

... Mr. President, there are many columnists and radio commentators who suggest that we should adopt the corporation method of farming at this time. Perhaps in some phases of agriculture cheaper prices might result; but if that were the case great numbers of our farmers would have to leave their farms, which would result in making this nation possibly an entirely industrial nation; something which, in time of war, would, I think, make the United States very insecure.

In December 1947, Young was successful in reducing the carryover provision for wheat from 150 million bushels to 125 million bushels in the Appropriations Committee. In a speech on the Senate floor on December 19, Young explained his actions.

I think it is entirely unreasonable that we should carry over 150 million bushels of wheat when Europe is starving. I likewise think it is unreasonable to carry over that great amount of wheat, since that is contrary to any previous regulation. In fact, I know of no time in the history of the United States when there was legislation to control any carryover as is provided in this bill.

. . . Not in 30 years has there been a year in which we did not export wheat. Also, I believe it is unreasonable to impose a provision of this kind upon the wheat farmers of the United States at a time when they have produced approximately 500 million more bushels of wheat than can possibly be consumed within the United States. This is a time when there are more controls now over the price of wheat than there are with respect to any other commodity produced in the United States. It would be impossible for me to believe that Congress would impose upon, say, the automobile industry, when they had a surplus, a provision that would require them to carry over $450 million worth of automobiles they could not possibly use with the express purpose of depressing prices.

. . . For the last six years the price of wheat has been controlled, by one means or another, and has been held down to a level far lower than it would have reached had it been allowed to seek its level in a world market. I have no serious objection to that if the Congress, in the future, will consider support prices. I wish to add also that, in the last year, the prices of merchandise the farmer has to purchase have increased 13 percent more than the prices of the products he has to sell.

The Brannan Plan

President Truman proposed a number of initiatives he called the Fair Deal. One championed by his Secretary of Agriculture Charles Brannan was proposed in April 1949, and was called the "Brannan Plan." It replaced price supports with a direct payment to farmers to make up the loss when prices dropped. Brannan argued it would cost less than price supports and still subsidize farmers when they needed assistance. Young was among the plan's vocal opponents. *"I believed the current price support plan was better and once said the Brannan Plan reminded me of 'police-state' regulations. Once on the Senate floor I said about Brannan, 'Only a pure demagogue could be in possession of the facts and not use them properly.'"*

Young personally liked Brannan, who belonged to the same Reorganized Church of the Latter Day Saints as Young did, although they only spoke about this shared religious affiliation once. *"Brannan was a very decent fellow, but I wasn't for the Brannan Plan. I believed the existing 90 percent price supports worked so well because they held the price up. We didn't have the problem that would come later of needing to meet export prices of other countries, and there was no surplus problem then and no world prices to compete with."*

Despite several attempts, the Brannan Plan never passed Congress. In the 1970s, Young came to appreciate it when he championed what became known as the target price concept, recognizing then that the plan was ahead of its time in the 1950s. Brannan remained active in influencing agriculture legislation for several years following his time as Secretary of Agriculture. In the 1970s, Brannan lobbied for the sugar beet industry and Young credited him with helping get the sugar beet refinery established in Drayton, North Dakota.

The Hope-Aiken Bill

The Agricultural Act of 1948 was called the Hope-Aiken Bill, named after Representative Clifford Hope, a Republican from Kansas and Senator George Aiken, a Republican from Vermont. Signed into law on

July 3, 1948, it included the first extension of the Steagall Amendment. It also provided that, beginning in 1950, average prices of the previous 10 years be taken into consideration, as well as the 1910 to 1914 base period. Young supported the Hope-Aiken Bill because it provided close to $2 for wheat, which he believed was a good price. *"At that time, $1.75 or $2 was a good price. You could make money at it."*

Young sent a Western Union telegram to the North Dakota news media on June 21, 1948, following the bill's passage by Congress. It read:

> In closing hour of forty-four hour continuous Senate session, five Senate conferees on continuation of price support legislation, of which I was a member, were able to prevail upon House after three previous conference broke up in bitter arguments, to accept continuation of price supports at 90 percent of parity until January 1, 1950, and permanent support program thereafter. This is the first time in history of the United States that the farmer will have a guarantee of at least a fair price for the things he has to sell. It is the greatest victory farmers have ever attained. This will, for example, guarantee price support levels for wheat in 1949 at least $2.00 or better a bushel and 1950 and later years supports cannot drop more than 5 percent each year and could be raised over present supports.
>
> All other grains will be supported at levels comparable with wheat. Flax, which is supported at 154 percent of parity at present time, can be supported at discretion of Secretary of Agriculture at these same levels in the future. Wool, which never has had a permanent status, now is assured of continued price supports in years to come unless some future Congress unwisely repeals this legislation.
>
> Milton R. Young
> United States Senator

Young also supported the reestablishment of the Commodity Credit Corporation, which was first created in 1933, and whose charter act was signed into law on June 29, 1948. It specified that the corporation should carry out price and income support activities.

Foot and Mouth Disease

At the end of 1948, Young released information from his office on a probe he conducted on foot and mouth disease, "following hearings I held in three states after traveling more than 12,000 miles and conferring with Mexican officials and field forces of the U.S. Bureau of Animal Industry to chart a future coarse on eradicating the most dread disease known to the livestock industry now knocking at our door along the Rio Grande."

He said the Senate Appropriations Subcommittee, of which he was a member, had the unanimous opinion that the program should continue, "as long as there is hope of success and the amount of expenditures are not prohibitive." Young described the fight against the disease being in two phases: "control and eradication of the current outbreak in Mexico to prevent it entering the U.S., and a long-range program aimed at developing a vaccine that will offer permanent immunity."

Fighting 'Butterlegging'

Another issue of concern in the late 1940s affected the dairy industry. It involved repealing a tax on oleomargarine. Young supported the dairy industry in its opposition to the tax repeals. However, a total of 15 separate bills providing for its repeal had been introduced in Congress the first 10 days of the 81st Session of Congress that began in January 1949. President Truman even expressed support for the tax repeal in his economic report to Congress at the beginning of the new session.

On May 19, 1948, John Burnham, executive secretary of the North Dakota Dairy Industries Association, presented a statement to the Senate Finance Committee at a hearing to weigh the merits of the proposed repeal of certain taxes levied on vegetable oil substitutes for butter.

Burnham said in his statement:

> We, as champions of the butter industry, are not hostile to any food product, nor do we uphold punitive taxes and fees levied against any food product. However, we do believe that every food product offered the American people be sold on its on merits, without discrimination

but also without access to facilities for substitution or imitation of other food products. We favor only such taxes as shall protect the consumer from such substitutions and imitations. Butter made from cream is produced on five million American farms in every state of the union.

Butter is needed in the milk production cycle because without a copious market for butter all milk production would be cut to the average needed for other uses. This would result in severe fluid milk shortages in our urban centers at season of slack production. Oleo has found its friends among northern senators from our large cities. May I point out to them – and to their constituents – in a friendly way that a blow at butter today may take away the baby's milk bottle next winter. This is not emotion – that is a prediction based on an appraisal of statistically correct factors of production and marketing.

. . . The desire of those who produce cream and make butter is that no substitute for butter be permitted to imitate butter in a manner designed to fool the housewife. Certainly, then the housewife should agree with our premise: Allow all wholesome substitutes, but insist that they sail under their own colors, that they not be permitted to falsify their true content by imitating a product of entirely different content.

Butter through Mother Nature has been given the color yellow. Yellow is our trademark. It has been the color of butter for four thousand years. For comparison, consider a taxicab company, which for scarcely forty years has used yellow as its color and its name. If some of you gentlemen, Senators though you be, were to go into Chicago today and start a cab company, painting your cars yellow, you well know there would be a court injunction issued against you before your cars had been on the streets an hour. That is because of a record of forty years. Ours is four thousand.

Allow us to keep our trademark, and to insist that no substitute be given carte blanche right to take our markets and fool the housewife. The makers of oleomargarine say it is a good, nutritious food. If so, it should have not hesitancy in selling for what it is, adopting its own color trademark, its own individualized package and container.

The butter industry seeks nothing, save a chance to live and to be a friend of its associates, including its competitors. It would bar no competitor from the market. But it must insist that each food be identified in the marketplace, in fairness to such food, but especially in fairness to the consumer.

In a news release on June 10, 1948, Young weighed in on the oleo issue:

The oleo industry should abandon its defensive tactics and seek by self-regulation to identify its product for what it is, preferably by a distinctive color all its own. The consumer has a right to know what she is buying, and to be protected against the palming off of yellow oleo as butter – at butter prices. The 10-cent tax on colored oleo is not a tax on food, it is a tax on fraud. Remove or lower the tax and you will provide a positive incentive to fraud and deception. Butterlegging will thrive and grow by leaps and bounds.

The tax was repealed in 1950.

Marshall Plan Concerns

In February 1949, Young called for an investigation of financial support the United States was providing to European nations under the Marshall Plan, which was established in April 1948 to help Europe recover from World War II. When it concluded in 1952, the United States had provided European countries $13.3 billion in support.

A news article that appeared in the February 18, 1949, *Jamestown Sun* reported on the investigation: "Senator Young, always on the lookout for slip-ups in farm matters by the government, discovered that American dollars were being used in foreign countries to purchase crops of which the United States already has a surplus."

Young discovered that the Economic Cooperation Agency (ECA), the temporary U.S. agency created to implement the Marshall Plan, had approved a $55 million loan to the United Kingdom for the purchase of wheat in Canada. When he questioned ECA Administrator Paul Hoffman about this, Hoffman acknowledged making the loan, in addition to similar ones that totaled $618 million for the purchase of foreign food supplies under the Marshall Plan.

A hearing was ordered by Senator Elmer Thomas, a Democrat from Oklahoma who chaired the Senate Agriculture Committee, with the main goal to determine the effect this ECA policy was having on depressed farm commodity prices and the farm price support program. At the hearing, Secretary of Agriculture Brannan acknowledged that his department had not objected to the purchase of $354 million worth of Canadian wheat. According to the *Jamestown Sun* report:

> Young asked Brannan how this deal could be engineered when farmers had been asked to reduce their wheat acreage last fall. Brannan's answer was that there is presently a carryover of around 300 million bushels of grain in the U.S., which he terms "not a surplus," and opined that a shortage of shipping facilities prompted the Canadian wheat purchase. This is an idea strongly protested by Senator Young, who declared, "We have been able to handle large crops with a greater shortage of boxcars than we have now. It seems to me that foreign purchases are largely responsible for our drop in prices now and that they may eventually wreck our agricultural economy.

Young addressed this in a statement he had placed in the *Congressional Record* for February 21, 1949:

> While farm prices have declined from 20 percent to as high as 60 percent in the past year, the things that the farmer has to purchase in the everyday operation of his farm have increased tremendously in the past six years. Even worse, during this past year when farm commodity prices were dropping, the prices of the industrial goods the farmer has to purchase have increased at an accelerated rate. Even at this time farmers are producing practically at cost and there is no indication that the things he must buy will drop in price. Indeed, there is every indication that they will continue to increase.
>
> As a result of accumulating surpluses in almost every farm commodity, there is little likelihood that the price of farm commodities will increase in the near future or, perhaps, for years except for occasional rises in the price of certain commodities for which there may at times be a temporary increased demand.
>
> Since last April there was made available to European nations $1.18 billion in Marshall Plan funds

for the purchase of United States farm commodities. Had it not been for these purchases, agriculture today would be in even worse condition than it is. At the same time, however, that ECA made this $1.18 billion available for the purchase of United States food supplies, they also and, in my opinion, unwisely and directly contrary to the ECA authorization, bought $617 million worth of food supplies in other countries. During approximately this same period, the Army Quartermaster Corps made food purchases in foreign countries in excess of $50 million for use of the armed forces in the occupied areas.

If this total of approximately $667 million had been made available for the purchase of additional farm commodities within the United States, there would not have been this drastic decline in farm commodity prices, especially in wheat and all other grains.

ECA and the United States Department of Agriculture officials used an escape clause in the ECA authorization which permitted them to buy in off-shore countries if supplies were not available in the United States. Both contended that there was a shortage of shipping facilities which made wheat, for example, not available in the United States beyond the amount which they purchased.

Secretary of Agriculture Charles Brannan even went so far as to say that he expected 300 million bushel carry-over as of July 1 next would not be a surplus. Yet, at the same time that these heavy purchases were being made in off-shore countries, he asked the American wheat farmer to reduce his acreage.

In the last four or five years, February and March have been the months when Europe was in greatest need of food and during these years the United States Government made its greatest effort in this period to export the greatest amount possible of wheat and other foods. It should be noted that in April of 1946 the United States Government even offered a bonus of 30 cents a bushel to secure additional supplies of wheat for European aid. And the Office of Defense Transportation, at President Truman's request, issued an emergency order to make available more cars to get wheat to the seaboard.

It is rather strange indeed that during this period of greatest need, and when both ECA and the United States

Department of Agriculture claim that shipping facilities are not available, that I should receive a letter this week from John Haw, a high official of the Northern Pacific Railway Co., which entirely refutes this claim of a shortage of shipping facilities.

. . . It is difficult for me to understand why on the one hand this Government is attempting to support farm prices and on the other hand it is doing everything it can to hold farm prices down.

With this type of administration of our Federal Government, the outlook for the future prosperity of farmers does not look too bright. The situation could become even worse in future years when foreign countries with their low standard of living and thus cheaper production costs again have surpluses which they undoubtedly will dump in the United States at prices far more favorable than their own. Frankly, I cannot see how any high level price support program can be maintained in this country under that type of policy. Farmers have not forgotten that period from 1932 to 1940 when prices were low for agriculture commodities and commodities were stored in every city and hamlet in the United States in large quantities. And at the same time, this, the greatest agricultural Nation in the world, actually imported more farm commodities than it exported.

It is abundantly clear that without an adequate price support program in the future and favorable action by every department of our Government, this Nation will face an even worse depression than the last.

Expanding price support programs

Richard Russell, the Georgia Democrat who was Young's closest Senate friend, served on the Appropriations Committee during his entire 38-year Senate career, and chaired it from 1969 to 1971. A longtime member of the Agriculture Appropriations subcommittee, Russell was known as a strong advocate of farm programs, especially those affecting agriculture in the South. Largely through Russell's influence, Young often aligned himself with Southern Senators on many agricultural issues.

Through the end of the 1940s, Young worked hard to win support for a long-range farm program that would run for three to five years instead of the traditional one-year programs. He believed that farmers needed a longer period of farm programs to plan for their own security, and opposed special legislation for just one commodity, instead supporting a program to cover all agricultural products. This brought disagreements with Senator Russell, who supported legislation for crops grown only in the South, such as cotton, tobacco and peanuts. *"The Southerners were close to agriculture and were very able and very active on agricultural legislation. They were able to get things for the South that we could not get in the rest of the United States."*

Twice Young and Senator Russell were able to get one-year extensions to the 90 percent support level in the Steagall Amendment. The second extension was in the Agricultural Act of 1949, which was signed into law on October 21, 1949, and was the second major farm legislation Congress considered since Young came to the Senate. The bill also designated mandatory support for some non-basic commodities such as wool and mohair, tung nuts, honey, Irish potatoes, and milk, butterfat, and their products.

In the late 1940s, Young began writing columns entitled, *On Capitol Hill with Senator Young,* which he sent to North Dakota media outlets on a regular basis for the next 30 years. These columns covered many topics, but predictably, he wrote extensively on the agricultural issues that occupied so much of his time and energy, and he gave his opinion about what they meant to North Dakota farmers.

In a column sent out on October 26, 1949, Young shared his views on the Agricultural Act of 1949:

> My undying gratitude goes to the House Conferees on the long-range farm price support legislation, and particularly to the four Southern Democrats who at no time would yield to the Senate's position of lower flexible supports. The seven Senate conferees, who must vote as a unit, stood 4-3 for lower supports until the very end of these long and bitter hours of conferences. After four days of almost continuous and bitter conferences our Senate minority, of which I was a member, was

able to gain the additional vote to give us a majority. On basic farm commodities, which include wheat, the final compromise provides a level of supports averaging as much as would the Russell-Young amendment. The greatest accomplishment in the case of wheat was allowing the Secretary of Agriculture to use either the present parity formula or the Anderson modernized parity formula, whichever is the higher. The present parity formula for full or 100% parity is $2.15 a bushel. The Anderson modernized full 100% is $1.90 a bushel.

Young and Russell sponsored an amendment to that bill that would have set a level of support at 90 percent of parity per crops of any basic agricultural commodity for which marketing quotas are set. However, despite their best efforts of speaking out in support of it, the amendment did not pass. Most of the opposition came from their own colleagues in the Great Plains and the South.

As agricultural legislation evolved into multi-year farm bills, six main commodities were mainstays of the farm program. Much of the work Congress did before the Watergate scandal of the 1970s was handled behind closed doors, and each Senator on the Agriculture Committee was given the responsibility for crafting the legislation for that year's farm bill for a specific crop. Because of Young's expertise on wheat, that crop became his responsibility for each farm bill, and his nickname of "Mr. Wheat" stuck with him during the rest of his Senate career.

Grasshopper Threat

The decade of the 1950s began with a grasshopper threat. Young wrote about it in his March 1950, *On Capitol Hill* column:

Recent surveys indicate there is a threat of another devastating grasshopper infestation this year if we have a favorable hatching season. In several areas of North Dakota, and particularly in states to the west and southwest of us, egg deposits are as heavy or heavier than in past years when the Great Plains areas suffered most severe damage. Securing a federal appropriation to carry out an adequate grasshopper control program is becoming increasingly difficult . . . If the grasshopper menace becomes more real, there is a possibility of securing

119

greater federal appropriations and more assistance to individual farmers. It will require an all-out effort, however, on the part of state and local officials from the many states affected to secure this necessary, and increased federal assistance.

Rural Electric and Telephone Cooperatives

In June 1950, Young announced that the first loan under the Rural Telephone Act to be made in North Dakota would be to the Abercrombie Telephone Company in Abercrombie. Young had been a co-sponsor of the Rural Telephone Act, and a strong supporter of rural electric legislation, which by the mid-1950s had brought an $11 million transmission loop into the state, as well as many other transmission lines.

His support of rural electric and telephone cooperatives continued throughout his Senate career. During those years seven lignite-based power plants were built, and one was named the Milton R. Young Station, near Center. Owned by the Minnkota Power Cooperative, it began operating in 1970.

During Young's tenure in the Senate, from 1945 to 1981, North Dakota rural electric cooperatives received more than $3 billion in loans. Rural telephone cooperatives in the state received loans of $150 million during those same years.

Battles with Benson

Dwight Eisenhower became President in January 1953, and despite Young's great admiration for him, he had frequent clashes with Eisenhower's Secretary of Agriculture, Ezra Taft Benson. *"He was a very opinionated person. He was very stubborn. He didn't believe in any farm programs at all. He wanted a free market for everything and I made many speeches saying I would be willing to have the farmers go it alone if the rest of the country would. But Benson was an unusual person in a way. He made many speeches and got good coverage on them, always saying exactly the same thing in a little different way."*

In 1954, Young said in a television interview about the Benson price support proposals: "In effect, Ag Secretary Benson is asking for lower price supports and in the economic situation in which we are in now, when there is no other way for farmers to receive a fair price through farm price supports. Any lowering of price supports now would be lowering of farm income. It would be disastrous for farmers and it would be disastrous for our entire economy, and certainly for everyone living in a state like North Dakota, Minnesota or the Middle West."

Many of their arguments were over the level of price supports. *"Benson didn't believe in any farm program at all, and the need for good farm programs was the major reason for me getting into politics. Most members of Congress from farming areas, especially the Plains states and the Upper Midwest, were anti-Benson."*

This put Republicans who supported farm programs, like Young, in a difficult position. They did not want to criticize their political party's President, but they disagreed with Benson. Some very conservative Republicans who didn't believe in federal support for agriculture were strong Benson supporters. *"Eisenhower got a lot of pressure to remove Benson, but he stayed with him, although he intervened a couple of times. One time we were arguing about the level of price supports. I wanted something quite a little over $2 and Benson wanted it about $1.75 and Eisenhower made the decision to compromise it at $2 – a price support level was set by the President. It is the only time I know of when a President publicly overruled his Secretary of Agriculture."*

The first major farm legislation during the Eisenhower Administration was the Agricultural Act of 1954, which was signed into law on August 28, 1954. It established a flexible price support beginning in 1955 for basic crops (excluding tobacco) at 82.5 percent to 90 percent of parity and authorized a Commodity Credit Corporation reserve for foreign and domestic relief. Included in the bill was the National Wool Act of 1954, which established a new price support program for wool and mohair to encourage domestic production. It was set at 300 million pounds for 1955.

In communication to his constituents during the deliberation on this bill, Young was critical of Benson. In his April 14, 1954, *On Capitol Hill* column, he wrote, "Secretary of Agriculture Benson, by his stubborn, relentless attack on the present farm price support program, has driven a wedge deep into the heart of the Republican Party."

A month later, in a May 19 *On Capitol Hill* column, he wrote:
> I supported the administration's wool bill which passed the Senate recently and which is expected to be approved by Congress before adjournment. This will give the wool growers a support level equivalent to 100 percent of parity or above. The cash price of wool will be allowed to seek any level the supply and demand market will provide. The difference between the support level and the actual price received by the producer on the cash market will be paid to him in the form of a government check, commonly known as a production payment. This will provide a much better price than the present program. Since we import more than two-thirds of our wool requirements, a more simple, direct, and effective approach to the wool price problem would have been through more tariff protection or quotas on foreign imports. I would have much preferred this approach. This was impossible, however, as the present administration's thinking on international matters, including tariffs, is quite similar to that of the previous administration.

In his July 14, 1954, *On Capitol Hill* column he wrote:
> The Senate Agriculture Committee bill on price supports and other farm legislation will be considered by the Senate itself soon. The fight on the Senate floor will be one of the most bitter we have had in years. Unquestionably there will be a considerable difference between the House and Senate bills. These differences will be resolved in conference between the House and the Senate.

Soil Bank Legislation

Two years later, the Agricultural Act of 1956 was signed into law on May 28, 1956. It created the Soil Bank Act and authorized an acreage reserve program for grains, cotton, peanuts, and tobacco. It also provided for a 10-year conservation reserve program.

There was bipartisan support for the Soil Bank legislation, which Young co-sponsored and which Benson also supported. The bill provided for 27,000 North Dakota farmers to receive Soil Bank checks totaling $13.5 million. Young and Senator Langer held 18 meetings across the state in July 1956 to inform farmers about the program. In his September 5, 1956, *On Capitol Hill* column, Young acknowledged that there had been some concerns over the program:

> Most of the confusion and misunderstanding regarding the Soil Bank program can be traced to the efforts of people who, for political reasons, don't want the program to be a success. Some agitators have gone so far as to urge A.S.C. committeemen, and farmers, to disregard soil bank regulations. It would be just as serious to violate these regulations as it would be to violate regulations pertaining to the price support program, and to the collection of income taxes.

Young wrote that the soil bank concept was designed to bring agricultural production in line with present needs and to conserve soil fertility. However, after it was in place for several years, Young believed the program was handled poorly. *"Too much land was taken out in some communities – in fact it ruined some. Some North Dakota communities and little towns were hurt badly by too much land being taken out of production in their trade territory."*

One year while Benson was Secretary of Agriculture, Young heard he was scheduled to speak in Fargo, and it angered him so much he personally went to the White House to have the speech cancelled. A short time later Young was in Langdon when John Scott, a conservative Republican who was active in the John Birch Society and a strong Benson supporter, expressed his displeasure to Young. *"He came to my room just raging mad and asked me if I stopped Benson from coming to North Dakota. I said, 'Yes I did.' We almost got into a fist fight over that."*

Following the death of Senator William Langer on November 8, 1959, Quentin Burdick ran against Governor John Davis to fill his Senate seat. Davis was in a difficult position over whether to support the Eisenhower Administration, which included Benson and his agriculture policies. Burdick knew this and ran a small ad in all state newspapers that simply said, "Beat Benson With Burdick."

Young campaigned for Davis and he remembered attending a gathering of Republicans in Rolla. *"They had a sizable crowd and we were invited to someone's home afterward. I think it was some women's group. Secretary Benson was quite an issue at the time and most conservative Republicans thought he was very good. I spent most of the time at this particular meeting arguing with these women. They were really giving me a hard time about being opposed to Benson and John Davis sort of sided in with them. On the way back to the hotel we were both in the back seat of the car and when we got into a little discussion about it, I said to John: "'Who in the hell are you for, anyway?' Those were the harshest words we ever had."*

Young believed Davis mishandled the issue of Benson in his campaign, which he lost to Burdick. *"About two weeks before the election Davis came out against Benson. That turned some against him and didn't give him much help from others who didn't support Benson. He should have maintained his position or he should have changed it long before."*

Disagreements with farm organizations

One of the prominent Great Plains agriculture publications of the 20th Century was *Capper's Farmer*, founded by Arthur Capper, a Kansas Republican who served five terms in the United States Senate between 1914 and 1951. The magazine ran what it called a "tape recorder interview" in a question-and-answer format with Young in its December 1959 issue titled, "Disunity of Farm Leaders Makes Job Harder for Congress."

In the article, Young expressed the frustration he had with national farm organizations and farm leaders, whose support he didn't enjoy during much of his Senate career.

The first question asked of him was "Senator Young, why didn't we get major farm program changes this year?" He answered:

The big reason is the stubborn and self-righteous attitude of many farm leaders. In this respect they're as guilty of perpetuating the farm program mess as they accuse Benson of being. Many lawmakers in both Houses, particularly the vast majority from farm areas, have little knowledge on how to evolve a farm program. Agricultural legislation is about as technical as any we [the Agriculture Committee] write. To a great extent they rely on the views of farm leaders. But because of the sharply conflicting positions – all claiming to be the real farm spokesman – the nonfarm area lawmakers are understandably confused and have no idea what course to follow. The second way this situation obstructs congressional activity is not so obvious, but it is a hard political fact of life. It is just plain dangerous for a lawmaker to approve anything not supported by the farm leader who is strong in his area. In my own case, I'm being publicly attacked for not going all out for the wheat bill favored by the president of the North Dakota Farmers Union, which, as you know, is the biggest organization there. He [Glenn Talbot] wants his program pushed despite any other considerations. And his is an extremely new approach based on far more production controls than before.

Young said he did not let the pressure influence his Senate decisions.

I brush it off. But then, I'm one of the lucky ones. I know of others who must bow to such pressure. The voters of North Dakota have registered their approval of my approach to the farm problem where it counts – in the ballot box. I was the only Republican senatorial candidate in 1956 who polled more votes in his state than President Eisenhower did – and North Dakota has more farmers in relation to total population than any other state. I have not changed my approach since then. I am first a farmer, second a Republican.

He said he didn't know why farm leaders didn't unite behind one workable program.

As long as they cling to their selfish interests and ignore the big problems, we will continue to drift in farm policy. But, I predict the minute they get together, 90 percent of our farm program difficulty will be licked

. . . In some sections of the Midwest, the three

organizations are running neck and neck on members. Still, the Farm Bureau is in right field with its Benson program, the Farmers Union is in left field with its direct payments and production controls on every farm commodity, and the Grange falls in between with self-help. Also, many state Farm Bureaus disagree sharply with national Farm Bureau leaders. It seems to me that if the leaders really represent farmers from such areas, they'd be a lot closer together than they have indicated to Congress up to the present.

Young also addressed how Congress should approach farm programs in the next year.

There is no doubt that Congress as a whole has let farmers down this year . . . what we must, and can do, is correct some of the defects in the current wheat program. We should have done that this year, and must do it next year if the program is to survive. Considering the lack of agreement among farm leaders, and Benson, many of us are convinced it is impossible to enact any entirely new and beneficial program. But, because of the mounting surpluses and growing antifarmer public opinion, it is imperative that we at least try to get some of the present defects corrected. If we can cut down surplus wheat production, much of the pressure of public opinion will ease off. With an improved public attitude, we'll have a better chance to develop and enact a sound, long-range wheat program.

Kennedy-Freeman Farm Bill

The decade of the 1960s brought three significant farm bills, in 1962, 1964 and 1965.

The Food and Agricultural Act of 1962 was signed into law September 27, 1962. Called the Kennedy-Freeman Farm Bill after the President and his Secretary of Agriculture Orville Freeman, the legislation endured significant opposition, defeats and revisions before it was completed. When done, it authorized an emergency wheat program with voluntary diversion of wheat acreage and continued feed grain support. It also included a marketing certificate program for wheat that was later rejected by the wheat producers who were required to approve its marketing quota.

In a *On Capitol Hill* column of March 7, 1962, Young wrote about the pending farm legislation:

> All of the farm organizations and others who testified recognized that there is a serious surplus problem. All the general farm organizations want continued permanent price supports and also believe in some kind of land retirement program. Beyond this, there is little unanimity as to what should be done. No farm organizations support the Freeman plan in its entirety. The position of the Farmers Union and the Grange is generally favorable, but they too advocate some changes. For wheat they want a two-price rather than a three-price system as presently proposed under the wheat certificates . . . I have long advocated a two-price system for wheat with bushel allotments. My bill would be a far more simple and workable program than the Freeman proposal.

In his April 25, 1962, *On Capitol Hill* column, Young lamented the busy pace of the Senate.

> Springtime in Washington is one of the really splendid periods of the year. Thousands of tourists, including many from North Dakota, pour daily into the Nation's Capital to see the sights and visit their delegations in Congress. This year is no exception, and the number of people coming to Washington as sightseers or on business is higher than ever before.
>
> The Senate and House have been hard at it since Congress reconvened in January, with no time for a breather until now – this short Easter recess. In my case, as a member of two very important committees of the Senate, Agriculture and Appropriations, plus serving on eight different Appropriations subcommittees, there has hardly been time to notice the arrival of spring.
>
> Every day of the past several weeks, from three to five committees and subcommittees on which I serve have held meetings, frequently at the same time. It becomes a case of deciding which is the most important one to attend. All of them are important. Of course, when there is a conflict involving the Agriculture Committee, it is that committee which takes precedence in almost every case.

By the time the bill had passed in September, Young did not support it. He wrote in his September 18, 1962, *On Capitol Hill* column:

> The omnibus farm bill has traveled a rocky road since it was first considered by Congress in January. It has just been approved by the majority of the Senate-House conferees. It now needs final approval of each House of Congress before it can be sent to the President. As one of the Senate Conferees, I refused to give it my approval.
>
> This bill, sponsored by Secretary of Agriculture Freeman, is a strange combination of tough production controls on the one hand and more flexible, much lower supports on the others. The new wheat certificate plan is one of the most complicated farm programs ever written by Congress. The omnibus farm bill, as now written, will draw considerable support from those who believe in now price supports or at best, very low price supports. They will get the low price supports they want for feed grains commencing with 1964. If Congress approves this complicated wheat certificate plan, with its tough production controls, coupled with lower, flexible price supports, it could well fail to get the necessary two-thirds vote in the next wheat referendum. Thus, those who believe in low price supports or none at all could gain most of what they have sought for years.

In 1962, Young was still in favor of price supports, as he indicated at the conclusion of his September 18 column:

> I believe that a good price support program is as necessary now as ever before. It doesn't make sense to drastically lower price supports at a time when everything a farmer has to buy keeps increasing. I believe that farmers would be willing to go it alone if the rest of the economy were willing to do the same. It is not my intention to take part in any program to pull the props out from under any protection farmers may have until others are willing to go it alone, too. I voted for both farm bills when they passed the Senate earlier this year in the hope that they could be improved in conference. This resulted in some rather severe criticism. I did it because I wanted to go the last mile toward trying to write better farm legislation before it was too late. The action of the House-Senate conferees was a deep disappointment to me. If the present trend continues, I can see only more difficult times ahead for

farmers. I refused to vote for lower and more flexible price supports for Secretary Benson and I don't see any reason why I should do it for Secretary Freeman.

Wheat Referendum

In September 1963, Neil Bjornson joined Young's staff as an agricultural assistant. An Arvilla, North Dakota, native, Bjornson had earned a degree in agricultural economics from North Dakota State University in 1958 and was working as a farm manager for First National Bank in Fargo when Young hired him. He had previously worked for the extension service. Art Schultz, who at the time was the State's Extension Director and a good friend of Young's, recommended Bjornson when Young asked for suggestions on who he could hire to handle agriculture issues in his office.

At the time he was hired, he was the only staff member on Capitol Hill with the specific title of agricultural assistant, even though staffers in other offices had similar responsibilities. "This was important to the Senator," Bjornson remembered. "At that time he was a senior Republican on the Senate Agriculture Committee, and he was the ranking member on the Agricultural Appropriations Subcommittee, so he had major responsibilities from the committee's standpoint."

The first large agriculture issue that Bjornson was thrown into was dealing with the failed wheat referendum of a few months earlier in the spring of 1963. This referendum was an annual vote where wheat growers would approve or disapprove the continuation of the price support program, and it was usually approved by an overwhelming majority. All previous referenda had been limited to commercial wheat growers. "Part of that year's price support program was a limitation on acreage, and this vote included the so-called non-commercial wheat growers," recalled Bjornson. "That was anybody who had a wheat allotment, acreage allotment, of 15 acres or less. At the time, they outnumbered the commercial wheat growers by nearly 3 to 1. The American Farm Bureau Federation, the National Chamber of Commerce, and the National Cattlemen's Association, for some reason, jumped into this very actively with a vote no campaign. The Cattlemen's Association's cry was 'Stop cow quotas in the wheat fields!'"

The *Fargo Forum* editorial on May 19, 1963, urged a yes vote on the wheat referendum that week:

We'll Bank on Sen. Young and Advocate 'Yes' Vote

For what it may be worth, we think that the farmers of North Dakota and Minnesota would be well-advised to vote "Yes" on the wheat referendum Tuesday.'

Our main reasons for such a stand do not involve the bitter warfare that is going on between the Farmers Union and the Farm Bureau in the "vote yes – vote no" campaign, nor on any hypothetical study of our own as to which decision would mean more dollars for wheat farmers of this area.

The main reason we are inclined to the "vote yes" viewpoint is that we believe North Dakota has in Washington one man who knows as much about the agricultural situation of the nation as any other individual. He is Sen. Milton R. Young, a member of the Senate Agricultural Committee. He has unequivocally advocated that the farmers support the two-price program that would be adopted for the 1964 wheat crop should the yes vote carry the referendum by a two-thirds margin.

We know how thoroughly Senator Young understands the national agricultural problems and we are convinced that he would not advocate a course of action which would be harmful to North Dakota agriculture, or Minnesota agriculture. He is our No. 1 reason for suggesting a yes vote.

The other reason is a little more complex. A great many of the people who are advocating a no vote are doing so on the plea that it will mean freedom for the American farmers. But in the next breath they say that if the 1964 program is rejected, then Congress won't fail to pass a new law establishing a new program for the wheat farmers. They imply that Congress won't dare sit still and let wheat prices collapse.

In other words, they readily admit that if the "no" campaign wins, then the farmers will need help from Congress.

Just what do they mean by freedom to farm if they are going to rush pell-mell to Washington to get another program passed? If freedom to farm means the abolition of all price supports and all other controls over wheat, that is one thing. If freedom to farm means that all they want from Washington is a different type of assistance, then their campaign is based on a foundation of sand.

It is fundamental that the nation is not going to continue to permit a huge carryover of wheat each year that builds up a tremendous storage bill paid by the government. The wheat surplus must be cut back to manageable size, or there will be no wheat program whatsoever.

The *Forum* has long contended that the farmers have to agree to a cutback in production so that the surplus could be reduced. A two-thirds yes majority is needed to put the farmers on record as striving for such a goal. A no vote of more than one-third, which would kill the 1964 program, would be regarded by many non-farm Congressmen as an invitation to remove all governmental protection and assistance for the wheat farmer.

The referendum was defeated, largely because of the opposition by the non-commercial growers. Developing another program to replace it was the main issue facing the Senate Agriculture Committee during Bjornson's first months in Young's office.

The committee approved a two-year temporary program that Bjornson said was modeled more on how feed grain programs had been designed than on previous wheat programs.

An Alliance With Southern Democrats

Bjornson, who served as Young's agriculture aide through 1972, was immediately aware of the close alliance Young had with Southern Democrats on agriculture issues:

The Democrats controlled the Senate and the Agriculture Committee almost all the time. Allen Ellender of Louisiana was chairman. The ranking Democrat was Jim Eastland of Mississippi, the next Democrat was Spessard Holland of Florida. When I first went there, Herman Talmadge of Georgia was probably sitting fifth or sixth down the table. There were no Western or Midwestern or Northeastern Democrats, they were all Southern Democrats on the Agriculture Committee. The Southern Senators had an interest in agriculture because the Southern states in those days were quite rural. The Senator was always a strong proponent of agricultural research and extensions, so he was always looking for increases in these areas. Funding for the rural electrification program got to be almost an annual battle to keep the REA program strong and maintain the strength of the co-ops. And again, he could remember when we didn't have electricity out in many of the rural areas.

Young acknowledged his alliance with Southern Democrats in a re-election campaign speech on October 20, 1962, in Washburn:

I do work with these Southern Democrats. Senator Ellender of Louisiana is chairman of the Senate Agriculture Committee, and the whole power of this Committee rests in the hands of Southern Democrats. He's also chairman of the Public Works Appropriation subcommittee and he's helped me get many projects for North Dakota this year, such as the Bowman Haley Project for $180,000. Senator Russell is the chairman of Agriculture Appropriations and he helped me get the $2 million research laboratory at NDSU, and the $400,000 laboratory for Mandan. Yes, I plead guilty to working with Southern Democrats.

Supporting Agricultural Research

As his statement illustrated, Young's support of agricultural research brought millions of dollars to North Dakota. The USDA's principal scientific research division, the Agricultural Research Service (ARS), is the largest agricultural research organization in the world today with some 100 different research facilities across the country. ARS research first began in North Dakota in the mid-1930s when Dr. Harold Flor, a plant pathologist for USDA, made a name for himself for his research on flax rust he conducted in the plant pathology department at the North Dakota Agricultural College, now North Dakota State University. By the mid-1960s, the ARS had made its facility at NDSU one of the world's major research centers, and had established the Northern Great Plains Research Laboratory on the other side of the state in Mandan.

Although discussed by the ARS since the 1950s, growing concern about the need for more research on agricultural chemicals that were being introduced into the environment brought a group of ARS scientists into Young's office in the late 1960s. They presented their concerns about this issue to Senator Young and asked for his support of funding to build a new laboratory to study the problem. As retold in a summary of the history of the ARS, Young's reply to them was that he agreed with the need for such a laboratory and, "where in North Dakota would you like to build it?" It was added to the research facilities at NDSU.

In the early 1960s, the ARS was focusing on the need for a national program of human nutrition research. Young addressed this in a report he submitted to Congress in 1963 that had been prepared by the USDA's Agricultural Research Service. The report outlined the need for an expanded national research program in human nutrition and proposed to establish three regional research laboratories, each near a medical school: one each in the North Central, Southeast and Southwest United States.

The only laboratory established under the original concept of that report was located, not surprising considering Young's influence on the Agriculture and Agriculture Appropriations committees, in Grand Forks. A field station of the Vitamins and Minerals Laboratory of the ARS Human Nutrition Division in Beltsville, Maryland, the State of North Dakota provided land adjacent to the University of North Dakota campus for its construction, which began in 1969 and was completed in September 1970. In 1972, it was designated a Human Nutrition Research Laboratory of the ARS North Central Region. Its capabilities were expanded beyond research with experimental animals with the establishment of an active clinical nutrition research program. The laboratory was designated the Grand Forks Human Nutrition Research Center in 1977.

Wheat Marketing Certificates

When Lyndon Johnson became President after the assassination of President Kennedy, Orville Freeman remained as Secretary of

Agriculture. Young personally liked Freeman. *"I thought he was a fair Secretary but he didn't know too much about agriculture. President Johnson knew agriculture quite well and he practically told Freeman what kind of a farm bill he could have."*

The Agricultural Act of 1964, which was signed into law April 11, 1964, authorized a two-year voluntary marketing certificate program for wheat. In his *On Capitol Hill* column of April 1, Young wrote about the wheat legislation after it passed the Senate and before the House vote:

> In the Senate, it had the support of all members, both Republican and Democrat, from the spring wheat-producing states and most members from the other major-wheat-producing states including the two Republican Senators from Kansas, the biggest wheat producer. Unless it receives the same bipartisan support of most House members from the commercial wheat areas, there will be no wheat program. Disapproval of the wheat program would simply mean that farmers would not receive the wheat certificate payments valued at an average of approximately 47 cents a bushel, plus diversion payments. Disapproval would leave farmers with $1.25 price supports, a loss of wheat acreage history to any farmer who over-plants his wheat allotment, and another meaningless wheat referendum that would have to be held this spring. There is no possible chance of further wheat legislation during this session of Congress. The certain drastic drop in income to wheat producers, coupled with the 25 percent drop in beef prices, means hard times for North Dakota, where more than 80 percent of all income is derived from the sale of farm commodities.
>
> Members of Congress, as is usually the case, are being bombarded with all kinds of unreasonable, inaccurate, and vicious propaganda against this wheat legislation. The bakers and other processors are claiming the wheat certificate is a tax on bread and that it would result in much higher consumer bread costs. It is true that the wheat certificates would be a part of the cost of wheat to the processors. However, with lower price supports and lower cash prices, the price paid for flour by the bakers will be no more than it has been, and probably a little less. The cost of wheat in a loaf of bread (2 ½ cents) is

so small that the price of wheat would have to increase 60 cents a bushel to effect a 1 cent increase in the price of a loaf of bread. Consumers can expect no drop in the price of bread if wheat prices should drop from 50 to 75 cents a bushel as will be the case of the wheat program is defeated. This means that the processors of wheat products stand to gain a huge windfall profit of one quarter billion dollars or more. It is small wonder that they are fighting this wheat legislation. (There has been no opposition from North Dakota bakers.)

In his May 13, 1964, *On Capitol Hill* column Young wrote about the future of agriculture:

North Dakota, the nation's most agricultural state, has reason to be concerned about the future. The general decline in farm prices, which commenced shortly after World War II, continues and may be accelerated.

The day may not be far off when all price support programs will be discontinued. Farmers trying to go it alone, with prices of almost everything they must have pretty well rigged against them, would have rough going. What is most disturbing and discouraging is the inaccurate and misleading propaganda leveled against every price support program. As an example, last year during the campaign to defeat the wheat referendum it was claimed, among other things, that there was not a surplus of our kind of wheat. Claims such as this now look rather foolish.

The recently passed two-year wheat program has its shortcomings, but it does give us considerable relief and a little time to write better legislation. Propaganda aimed at discrediting this program is already receiving wide circulation. Much of this emanates, as did the propaganda against the "Yes" vote in last year's referendum, from some Minneapolis grain trade interests. Why any North Dakota people echo such arguments without first carefully ascertaining how it would affect our wheat industry is something I will never understand.

The charge is now being made that wheat certificate payments being made on domestic use are unfair to North Dakota producers. These payments are based on the domestic consumption of all wheat, which is about 45% of total production. It is argued that 80 percent of

North Dakota wheat is consumed domestically and the certificate payment to our producers should be higher than the national figure. This is a persuasive argument unless you look carefully at all the factors involved.

. . . What we need most to enable us to increase our production and acreage in North Dakota is a greatly expanded export market. However, if we are successful in attaining a high level of exports, we would actually lose certificate payments under the formula proposed by the opponents of the present program. Thus we would be penalized for doing something that we ought to do – that of finding more outlets for our wheat.

Little Support for Goldwater

In the 1964 Presidential Election, North Dakota decisively voted for Lyndon Johnson over U.S. Senator Barry Goldwater of Arizona, one of the few times that North Dakota has supported a Democrat Presidential candidate over the Republican nominee.

Even though Young personally liked Goldwater, they did not share common views on agriculture. *"He was against everything that most farm organizations wanted, that most farmers wanted."*

When Goldwater planned a September campaign stop at the 1964 National Plowing Contest at the Elmer and Ramona Fraase farm near Buffalo, North Dakota, he asked Young and Republican Senator Karl Mundt of South Dakota to help him write his speech. *"Senator Mundt was good in agriculture and was an excellent speaker himself and he and I worked hard to write a speech that we thought would have gone over well in North Dakota and wouldn't have gotten him into any trouble. But he had his regular speechwriter write one, too. It was a damn fool speech and this was the one given to the press. I was supposed to ride out to Fargo with him from Washington and he even held the plane for about an hour. I left the office and even left my home and went to another place so they could not get in touch with me. I waited until I was sure he was gone. He never quite forgave me for that.*

"After he got out to Fargo, he had read our speech on the plane, liked it and even quoted from it – quite a lot of it – but the first speech

136

that he gave the press was about all the press carried. I had a lot of Republicans tell me – some very good friends of mine – that they were very disgusted that I wouldn't ride out with him, but I always felt so strongly on farm matters – far stronger than most farmers realize – that I felt that appearing with Candidate Goldwater would lead them to believe I was endorsing his farm policy which was almost exactly opposite of my own."

1965's Four-Year Farm Bill

The Food and Agricultural Act of 1965 was signed into law November 3, 1965. It provided four-year commodity programs for wheat, feed grains, and upland cotton. It authorized a long-term diversion of land under a cropland adjustment program, and it continued payment and diversion programs for feed grains and cotton, and certificate and diversion programs for wheat.

Young wrote in his October 29, 1965, *On Capitol Hill* column about his concern over the lack of interest in farm legislation that year, when deliberation over President Johnson's Great Society programs had commanded the attention of Congress:

> The four-year farm price support program just squeaked through Congress. It is fortunate that it passed as it will be needed more than ever to meet the certain continued and perhaps even more sharply increased costs of all farm operations. An indication of the lack of interest in farm programs and the problems we have in getting them through Congress was experienced with the Sugar Act, which would have soon expired. The enactment of a five-year extension of the program just barely got by Congress. There wasn't sufficient interest in extending this program to even maintain a quorum in the Senate when it was finally approved by the Senate less than an hour before adjournment. It required some urgent pleas by the leadership of the Senate to get enough Senators back to the floor to make the necessary quorum of 51 required for the enactment of any legislation. A great many had already left Washington.

The passage of this four-year omnibus farm bill was a departure from the separate and short-term bills for each crop that had been passed in recent years. Most provisions of this 1965 legislation were actually extended an additional year through 1970 because of the 1968 Presidential Election that brought to office a new administration. This brought an unusually stable five year-period of agricultural policies.

Reconsidering the Brannan Plan

Beginning in the late 1960s when the price of wheat was depressed, the general thought was that a price of two dollars a bushel would be an acceptable price for wheat farmers. Neil Bjornson remembered how during the deliberation of the 1973 Farm Act, Young came to a meeting of the Senate Agriculture Committee and proposed that the government establish two dollars as the price for a bushel of wheat. "He said, 'If the price didn't get there, the government would make a compensatory payment. And everybody who was going to qualify for that had to stay within an allotment, within a base acreage.'"

This two-dollar wheat proposal evolved into what became known as the target price concept. It was similar to the Truman Administration's Brannan Plan, which Young had strongly opposed.

Nixon's Farm Policies

Although Young got along fairly well with President Richard Nixon on a personal basis, Bjornson's recollection was that they did not have a close relationship. Nixon's first Secretary of Agriculture was Clifford Hardin, who had similar views as Ezra Taft Benson in the Eisenhower Administration. Young, however, considered him a better overall administrator than Benson.

Hardin began an extensive review of price support programs. He sought to have a more market-oriented farm policy that would further expand exports, reduce government costs and allow more flexible acreage reduction. The Agricultural Act of 1970 gave Hardin a more flexible approach to supply control, relaxing planting restrictions by replacing acreage diversions on specific crops with a general set aside that called for reduced plantings, but did not designate the crops that had to be cut back. The legislation was in effect for three years, through the 1973 crop year.

This increased production lowered crop prices and Bjornson remembered how farmers began to turn on Nixon and his agriculture programs. "Farmers were receiving less than $1.50 for a bushel of wheat, and Nixon was catching all the hell from farmers. They didn't like him. So Nixon started looking around for another Secretary of Agriculture."

Bjornson remembered Young being very agitated one morning after returning from a White House briefing in 1971. Young said to him, "You might as well know it now, Nixon told me he's going to announce the nomination of Earl Butz as Secretary of Agriculture." Nixon had told him, "Milt, I know you're not going to like this." Young's reply was, "I sure as hell don't like it."

Young knew Butz from when he was an Assistant Secretary of Agriculture in the Eisenhower Administration. At the time of his appointment by Nixon, Butz was a top administrator at Purdue University at West Lafayette, Indiana. *"I believed Butz was committed to moving government out of agriculture to a much greater degree than I felt was necessary or wise."*

Because of disastrous harvests in the Soviet Union in 1972, Butz and National Security Advisor Henry Kissinger brokered a deal for the Soviets to purchase 30 million tons of American grain. China had also begun purchasing American grain. Young supported the 1973 wheat sale to the Soviet Union and defended the Nixon Administration against critics who claimed the Soviet Union received special treatment. Congressional investigations concluded that the Soviets paid the same price for wheat as other countries.

Bjornson remembered Butz being at an Agriculture Committee hearing shortly after the Soviet Union wheat sale was announced. Senator Henry Bellmon of Oklahoma opened the hearing by saying, "Mr. Secretary, if this meeting had been held ten days ago, it would have been a lynching party. But now I don't know what we're going to say. You have to either be the luckiest man in the world, or you go to the right church."

The Soviet Union sale increased the price of wheat from less than $2 a bushel to $5. A strong supporter of increasing exports, Young was pleased with the Nixon Administration's success at commodity sales to foreign countries. However, he heard criticism from some North Dakota farmers about selling food to Communist countries. Other criticism over exports in general came from bakers. *"They convinced the public that if the country didn't stop these exports, the price of wheat would go so high bread would be a dollar a loaf."* Young vehemently disagreed. *"No state gained from that deal more than we did."*

A Seniority Decision

In early 1973, Young had to make a choice between serving as a ranking member of the Senate Agriculture Committee or the Senate Appropriations Committee. New seniority rules of the Senate prohibited any member from serving in a ranking position on more than one major committee. In his *On Capitol Hill* column of January 17, 1973, he announced his choice.

> I chose the Senate Appropriations Committee because it is the most powerful. This committee funds not only all farm programs, but health, education, and all other programs which would be meaningless without adequate funding. I still retain enough seniority on the Senate Agriculture Committee to assure that I will be a member of the all-important Senate-House Conference Committee on farm legislation. I have served on all these conference committees on agriculture since 1948. I am the only member of either the House or the Senate from North Dakota in the last 35 years to serve on this very important conference committee which actually writes the final version of all farm bills.

Bringing Target Prices to the 1973 Farm Bill

When it came time for the Agriculture Committee to begin

considering the 1973 Farm Bill, crop prices were high, thanks to the Russian sale and others large sales. Young wrote in his January 22, 1973, *On Capitol Hill* column:

> Present and favorable farm income is largely due to good crops, farm price support loans, and huge export sales. Unfortunately, higher farm and retail food prices have increased consumer opposition to price support and other farm programs . . . Generally farm prices are good now, but most people seem to have forgotten that wheat prices were as low as $1 per bushel in western North Dakota only a few months ago and farmers were lucky last year to sell good potatoes for $1 per hundred. Consumers would better understand present farm prices if they had realized how low they were only a short while ago.

The Committee was looking for a change in focus, Bjornson remembered:

> With the higher prices, there was renewed talk that there was no need for government farm programs anymore. Senator Young had seen these things happen before. His early involvement in politics went back to the post-World War I era, when agriculture had expanded very rapidly during the war, then all of a sudden the markets that they were satisfying were gone. He'd seen this happen, and he wasn't quite convinced that we had reached the golden era. He said for wheat we need something that will give us a fallback. If we're out of here, we don't need the acreage restraints, we don't need the price support program, that's well and good. But in case we aren't out of the woods, we need a fallback. And that's really what the concept of the target price was, and it made a lot of sense to other members of the Committee. Hence, it was expanded to include other commodities.

Steven Allen, a staff member on the House Agriculture Committee at the time of the consideration of the 1973 Farm Bill, recalled the mindset of the Committee members on both sides of Capitol Hill:

> The old farm legislation that was in place prior to 1973 had fallen into disfavor in many quarters because of its rigidity and high cost. The whole notion of paying farmers not to farm was becoming extremely unpopular. Farmers were locked into rigid base acres and allotments. And year-to-year government programs that established

the national base acreage, the amount of land to be set aside and not farmed, and the support price (otherwise known as the loan rate), were often based on economic assumptions that later were proven to be faulty. It was the classic case of government management that was supposed to be able to outguess markets and rarely, if ever, could.

This affected export programs. Besides the cumbersome nature of government management of a free enterprise activity, the high loan rates (relative to world market clearing prices) often left the United States as the supplier of last resort in export markets. Therefore, farmers would end up forfeiting to the Commodity Credit Corporation (CCC) large amounts of grain that they had put under loan to the government. This meant that the government would find itself in the grain business owning huge stocks at times, which were very expensive to the taxpayers to own and carry and became politically unsustainable in the early '70s.

In 1973, when the old farm legislation was set to expire, the Agriculture Committees of the House and Senate found themselves seemingly at a dead end on how to proceed with a new farm bill. It was at a Senate Ag Committee meeting where Senator Young came forward with the idea of turning to the target price concept as the basis for new farm legislation. He had remembered that back in 1948 then-Secretary of Agriculture Charles Brannan had proposed this type of plan that was bypassed at that time. However, Senator Young felt that this was a plan whose time had come what with the recent Russian grain sales and the much higher world grain prices and would address the problems with the old farm bill. His idea was immediately accepted by a majority of the other Ag Committee members and passed the Senate unanimously shortly thereafter. By August of that year, the target price concept was the new agriculture law of the land.

The main selling point for the target price concept was the fact that it would allow for income support for farmers but did it in a way that didn't interfere nearly so much with the markets. It was set up to work as follows: on wheat the target price was, say, $2.75 per bushel and the loan rate was set at $2.00 per bushel. Therefore, if the average market price for the first five months of the market year was $2.50, a wheat farmer would receive a check from the government for 25 cents per bushel times his established yield times his acres. A farmer could still put his wheat under loan and use it as a marketing tool, but with wheat prices above the loan rate he would pay off the loan and sell his grain on the open market and the government would not be nearly so apt to own huge grain stocks. As a result of all of this, a farmer's income would still be supported by this combination of direct payments and loans and the CCC would not have the expense of carrying the world's grain reserve. This plan had a more market-friendly approach to it, even though it didn't reform all aspects of farm program features such as leaving base acres tied to planted acres.

Bjornson remembered that Young's target price proposal was initially only for wheat. "He wasn't suggesting it for other commodities. But by the time they got through writing that farm bill, there was a target price plan for feed grains, for cotton, for rice. It was pretty much across the board."

Agriculture Committee members spoke on the floor of the Senate about the new farm bill. In those remarks on June 5, 1973, Young called it one of the best farm bills Congress ever considered:

Farm programs in the past have assured abundant supplies of food and fiber at reasonable prices to the great consuming public. It is this kind of legislation that has helped make our farmers the most efficient and productive in the world. There is need for increased production both to meet increased domestic needs and foreign export requirements. This year we will export more than $11 billion worth of farm commodities. If it were not for these huge exports, our balance of payments with the rest of the world would be even more dangerously out of balance. Increased exports offer one of the best means of improving our balance of payment and thus restoring the stability of the American dollar.

This bill gives farmers considerable protection against a drastic drop in prices if the requested increase in production results in price-busting surpluses. By increasing production to meet increased domestic needs and greater foreign exports, this could easily happen and farmers could find themselves in deep financial trouble.

The price for major farm commodities is tied to parity. If operating costs continue to rise, so would this target price. The heart of this provision is that if farm prices stayed as high as they are now there would be no payments to farmers. If farm prices decline below the target price, payments would again be resumed and there would be every justification for them.

Most of the opposition to this bill comes from those who want the farmers to depend entirely on the free market for a good price with little or no price supports at all and no government program that would give even the slightest protection against bankrupt prices. Neither the present Farm Price Support Act of 1970, which is in effect for this year's crop, nor the bill we are now considering interfere in the slightest with the free market.

There is one major difference between farmers and any other segment of our economy. When farmers sell their products, they have to accept what the market will provide. When they buy all the things they need to farm, they pay the going price without any means to control those prices.

On June 5, 1973, three Senate Agriculture Committee members, Chairman Herman Talmadge, a Democrat of Georgia, Republican Carl Curtis of Nebraska, and Democrat Hubert Humphrey of Minnesota delivered floor remarks about the bill.

Talmadge:

This bill gives the Secretary of Agriculture great flexibility in assuring adequate supplies for expanding markets, both at home and abroad. First, it imposes no required controls on agricultural production. It is not restrictive. It is designed to assure consumers of a continuous and abundant supply of food and fiber, and it breaks away from the programs of the past. Second, it eliminates Government payments to farmers when market prices are at established levels and provides for payments only when market prices are below those established levels. And then payments would be only the difference between these two levels of prices.

Curtis:

I join with the distinguished chairman of our committee in mentioning that it was the distinguished

Senator from North Dakota (Mr. Young) who brought forth the idea of the target prices that are incorporated in the bill. I believe that it will work. I believe that it is a new innovation that meets with wide approval. And I believe that not only all those in agriculture, but also everyone else interested in the economy of America is indebted to our chairman and to the distinguished Senator from North Dakota.

Humphrey:

I, too, want to salute an old friend who has been as faithful as any man could ever be to the farm population of the country, the distinguished senior Senator from North Dakota (Mr. Young). I have worked with him for years. He is a friend of American agriculture. And when I say that, I mean that he is a friend of the American people. Before the debate is over, we will find out that the pending legislation is a vital part of our national security. It will have something to do with our leadership in the world. It has a great deal to do with the viability of our economy, our balance of trade, our balance of payments, and our ability to survive as a people and to be a great country.

Known as the Agriculture and Consumer Protection Act of 1973, the four-year bill was signed by President Nixon on August 10, 1973. Butz proclaimed it to be "an historic turning point in the philosophy of farm programs in the United States."

Carter Farm Policy Continues Target Prices

The last major farm bill Young worked on in Congress was the Food and Agriculture Act of 1977, which was signed into law on September 9, 1977. Another omnibus law, it increased price and income supports and established a farmer-owned reserve for grain.

This was President Carter's first year in office, and when differences were being worked out between the House and Senate versions of the bill, Young wrote in his August 4, 1977, *On Capitol Hill* column:

President Carter stated in no uncertain terms that he would veto the bill if it contained the higher supports of the Senate bill. The big change in the new bill over the present program is that much more importance is attached to the target price provision which I originated. This will mean very sizable payments to farmers, especially since future allotments will be based on seeded acres for that year rather than on the 1952-53 crop years. Disaster payments will be much more meaningful too when the new program, based on seeded acres and other provisions, becomes effective for the crop year 1978.

While Young did not agree with many of Carter's agriculture policies, he liked Bob Bergland, Carter's Secretary of Agriculture. Bergland was a Roseau, Minnesota, native who had served in the U.S. House of Representatives from 1971 to 1977. *"He is the first working farmer we had as Secretary of Agriculture for some time. It makes a lot of difference if they understand farming. Bob Bergland will make a good Secretary of Agriculture if he could do as he wanted to. He knows agriculture and is sympathetic and he knows farmers and they like him. He has some influence on President Carter but not too much."*

Young did not approve of how Carter exerted his influence in the Agriculture Committee. *"He had a man sitting right in the committee with a microphone telling us what we could and not put in the bill and constantly warning us that the President would veto the bill if we put in provisions that would mean higher farm price support loans."*

He also objected to the way Carter imposed his human rights programs in foreign agriculture sales. *"President Carter's human rights program didn't help us sell large quantities of wheat to Russia. Communist countries like Russia do not believe in Carter's human rights program. They do not even believe there is a God. It is rather irksome to them to get these lectures and they might have bought more wheat. This emphasis on human rights is rather naïve to a Godless people like Russian Communists."*

Influencing Agriculture Policy in Five Decades

For five decades in the 20th Century, Senator Young, "Mr. Wheat," was a major influence on agriculture policy in the United States Congress. Bjornson believes Young's greatest contribution as a Senator was the importance he put on maintaining a reasonable, realistic government presence in agriculture. "He recognized the need for some type of economic protections for the producer. Not just to keep the producer in business, but to also maintain a productive capacity. He also at the same time recognized that there was a finite limit on this. You couldn't just open the doors to the Treasury. It had to be a two-way street. At some point, the producer was going to have to recognize the need for some limitation on production."

Bjornson believed that Young's philosophy of working within the system on agriculture policy was a large part of his success. "He believed that you had to work within the framework of the system to accomplish anything. You didn't start your crusade attacking the system, you worked within the framework of the Senate, within the framework of the Congress. Partisanship wasn't where you started. He said many times, publicly and privately, that farm policy is not something that is settled on a partisan basis. The Senate Agriculture Committee staff, who were Democrats except for one Republican, had a standing joke: 'Milt Young is the best Democrat we've got here!'"

Young's championing of the target price concept of the 1970s is considered a milestone in the history of United States farm policy. Today referred to as a "counter-cyclical payment," it remains a central feature of present-day farm policy, where when prices go down the payments are increased and when prices go up the payments get smaller or even disappear altogether.

Wars, Weapons and World Issues

The years that Young served in the Senate spanned three major world military conflicts, even though World War II ended less than a year after his arrival in Washington. In addition, the Cold War, which began in the mid-1940s, posed its own defense and diplomatic challenges for the United States. Through these major conflicts, and many others around the world, Young's membership on the Appropriations Committee and its defense and intelligence subcommittees provided him a front-row seat to America's involvement.

During the years from 1925 to early 1945 that Gerald Nye represented North Dakota in the Senate, Young considered himself "a strong Nye supporter" and agreed with his isolationist views that had established Nye as a leading opponent of America's entry into World War II. However, after Pearl Harbor was attacked, Young changed his opposition to the United States entering World War II. *"I went all out to support the war and still managed Nye's 1944 re-election campaign. Nye didn't change his isolationist views, however, Senators Arthur Vandenberg of Michigan and Everett Dirksen of Illinois and quite a few of them who followed were all strong isolationists but later realized that we had to live in a changed world and we couldn't go back to being isolationists."*

Young became less of an isolationist the longer he was in the Senate. He was consistent in vocally opposing the country's involvement in major military conflicts, but when once engaged, he supported requested appropriations and troop levels for the military.

Yet, with only a few exceptions, Young consistently voted against foreign aid. In 1948 and 1949, he favored foreign aid to help Chiang Kai-shek remain in control of mainland China. *"That was a good cause. If he had won, China would not have become Communist."*

At the end of a Congressional session in the early 1970s, Young was forced to handle a foreign aid bill for the Republicans because many Senators had already left town. *"The Democrat chairman was against foreign aid, too. So I said I would handle it if the Democrats on the committee would cut out $500 million more. They said go ahead and handle it because we have to get the bill through some way. So that's what we did."*

Prior to the differences Young had with some of the agriculture policies in the Marshall Plan to rebuild post-war Europe, he disagreed with General George Marshall's handling of the Chinese Civil War in 1945. President Truman had dispatched Marshall to China to be the broker for a coalition government consisting of the Communists under Mao Tse-tung and the Nationalist allies supported by the United States under Chiang Kai-shek. He failed in his attempts and the Communists prevailed in 1949, winning control of mainland China.

"I was not a fan of George Marshall. I was quite sympathetic to the Chinese Nationalists and I got to know Generalissimo Chiang Kai-shek and Madame Chiang and some of their family quite well. Being anti-Communist I naturally felt more sympathy for them, and I believed Marshall was too unsympathetic toward the Nationalist cause. He was sent to China to try to work out some kind of peace agreement between Communist China and Chiang Kai-shek. I don't think he accomplished much. I agreed with Senator Joe McCarthy, who was no fan of Marshall and was sure he sold out Chiang Kai-shek."

Young believed "some terrible mistakes were made" at the close of World War II as the Allies divided several nations, including Korea. He remembered comments by Idaho Republican Senator William Borah, who served in the Senate from 1907 to 1940 and was on the Foreign Relations Committee for 20 years. *"Senator Borah said after World War I, 'When you divide up a people, sooner or later you are going to have another war.' The German people were split up after World War I and there was another war."*

In 1949, Young voted against establishing NATO, the North American Treaty Organization, and in 1954 he voted for SEATO, the South East Asia Treaty Organization. Near the end of his Senate career, Young mused that he voted wrong on the two issues.

"I am at a loss to know why I voted against NATO because I voted for the United Nations Charter in June 1945. NATO has been the answer to combating Soviet influence. I think without it Russia would not only have dominated all of Eastern Europe but probably most of Western Europe. I think it saved them. But I have been disappointed in countries like France and most of the NATO countries with the exception of West Germany. They have greatly decreased their contributions and we haven't. I thought by now we should be able to withdraw most of our troops we have over there. They have plenty of manpower. I favor reducing troops in Korea and Europe to some extent. When we were having trouble with North Korea it probably wasn't the best time to announce it. Congress has made attempts to reduce our Army in Germany and I voted for it on two or three occasions. NATO isn't of much value unless other countries are going to become more involved with troops and money. I see the United States playing a lesser role because to a considerable extent it affects our balance of payments with the rest of the world and it had become a tremendous burden on us. With respect to Germany, they buy much of their military equipment from us. France and England make good fighter planes but the NATO countries buy mostly American fighter planes and other weapons.

"I should have voted against SEATO in the light of experience and even the information available as of that date. SEATO was a mistake because it was trying to control too much of the world and there was no way of winning a war fighting in the jungles."

The Korean War

As tensions boiled over into all-out war in Korea in June 1950, Young remembered how speeches about Korea were given on the floor of the Senate nearly every day. *"Senator Kenneth Wherry of Nebraska was the Republican leader and about every day he would make an anti-Korean War speech. I would often join him in speaking out about not getting into that war. Senator Vandenberg was the ranking Republican on the Foreign Relations Committee at that time and he supported the war. Senator Taft did, too, but he was not as outspoken as Senator Vandenberg."*

The Korean War was an issue during Young's re-election campaign in 1950, and he wrote about the conflict in his *On Capitol Hill With Senator Young* columns that summer.

On July 12, he wrote:

> Whether total war can be averted will depend almost entirely on what decisions the Soviet Government makes in the next few weeks. If we are driven out of Korea, and militarily our position is not very tenable, it doesn't necessarily mean the end of hostilities – in fact it may be just the beginning. In that event, we must face total mobilization and war. Victory in Korea – if the Soviet Government is willing to let matters rest – may mean a prolonged period of uneasy peace.

On July 26, he wrote:

> All-out war with Russia is entirely possible. Whether it be peace or war will depend largely on what a few men in the Russian Kremlin decide . . . If we are to survive in any future great war, we had better be helping arm our allies comparable to the way Russia has armed her satellites . . . Early fighting in the Korean Peninsula has revealed a tragic shortage of military equipment. And it is difficult to understand why. Apparently, our Intelligence Service or the Administration were not fully informed concerning the superbly trained and equipped North Korean Communists.

On August 9, he wrote:

> History may well record Korea as another Pearl Harbor or even worse. Even with the tight censorship imposed, bits of the tragic story are leaking out – a story of heroic fighting on the part of our armed forces against tremendous odds. The story which will be eventually written concerning events leading up to the Communist

attack will be one of sorry lack of statesmanship, second
rate leadership and almost unbelievable stupidity.

Young agreed with many Republicans who were critical of
Truman's Secretary of State Dean Acheson for the speech he made in
January 1950, indicating that Korea was outside America's sphere of
interest or influence. *"They claimed it invited or encouraged the North
Koreans to strike. I was opposed to the war and I kept on speaking
against it all the way through, although after we got in I voted for
the appropriations necessary to carry it on. It was not a popular war
in North Dakota but our people were very loyal. You didn't hear of
desertions and demonstrations. Part of its unpopularity was that it was
a 'no-win' war. We couldn't bomb beyond the Yalu River on the border
between China and North Korea, so we couldn't bomb China's troop
concentrations. Their argument was that it might bring in the Russians.
China was already in the war with a big army. I did not believe that our
bombing beyond the border would bring about World War III. The most
discouraging phase of the war, I believe, was the mistake that General
Douglas MacArthur made when he sent our troops up to the Yalu River
in bitter cold weather against the hordes of Chinese. We didn't have a
chance, especially under such limited warfare. We could not bomb these
Chinese concentrations north of the Yalu. Our troops were all but wiped
out in that engagement."*

MacArthur's Yalu River fiasco aside, Young was disappointed when
on April 11, 1951, President Truman removed him as commander of the
United Nations forces in Korea for publicly disagreeing with Truman's
Korean War policy. Upon his return to Washington, D.C., MacArthur
made his final public appearance before Congress. In the speech, which
was interrupted by 30 standing ovations, MacArthur said, "Old soldiers
never die; they just fade away . . . And like the old soldier of that ballad,
I now close my military career and just fade away – an old soldier who
tried to do his duty as God gave him the light to see that duty."

Young remembered talking to Senator Richard Russell about
MacArthur after he was fired, but before his speech before Congress. *"I
was in the Marble Room which is in the Capitol right off the Senate*

Chamber visiting with Senator Russell. He said he spent an evening with MacArthur during World War II on an island in the South Pacific, and he said that evening MacArthur made the damndest speech he ever heard." Russell told Young, "You wait until he comes back. This will be one of the greatest speeches." It was. *"Listening to that speech I had a feeling of great admiration. It was very dramatic. Almost everyone in the Chamber had tears in their eyes. My colleagues seemed to be sympathetic with MacArthur."*

Young attended the 1952 Republican Convention in Philadelphia, where General Dwight Eisenhower defeated Senator Robert Taft of Ohio for the Party's nomination for President. One of the planks in the Party's platform approved at the convention called for the liberation of the Communist nations. *"I believe one of the reasons Eisenhower was elected President in 1952 was because of his pledge to end the Korean War. Just after Eisenhower's election, his Secretary of State John Foster Dulles began a tough policy of confrontation of Communism around the world – brinksmanship was the word – and he talked about massive retaliation. It heated up the Cold War, and I thought things were going too far. Dulles wanted military bases and he really wanted to encircle Russia completely militarily. This, more than anything else, was what caused us to become involved in a bitter Cold War with them."*

Right after the November 1952 election, Young made his only visit to Korea, as part of President-elect Eisenhower's delegation. *"It was late November and chilly there. I slept in a little old trailer home not far from the front and it was either hotter than hell or colder than hell. I spent quite a bit of time with the military. They took me clear up to the front and fired a few shots over the enemy lines to show me how they were doing. South Korea was badly devastated at that time. When I was in Puchon I was walking down the street and a young kid came up behind me and an officer grabbed him. He said he would have gotten my wallet in a second – that they are regular magicians. They slice a hole in your pocket and out comes your wallet. People were so poor then and the kids would do anything for a living."*

The Domino Theory

The suggestion of a concept that later became known as the "domino theory" was first made by President Eisenhower at an April 1954 news conference. Eisenhower reasoned that if the Communists were successful in taking over the rest of Indochina, momentum would then grow for other Communist insurgencies in places like Burma, Thailand, Cambodia, Laos and Indonesia.

Young did not agree with the theory. *"I didn't believe in it, although most people did. I think a good example of that is Indonesia. The Communists had strong control of that government. Indonesia got rid of its Communists. They murdered as many Communists when they took over as most Communists did when they took over a country. But they did it all on their own and it is a strong anti-Communist country now with very little help from us. We have been giving them some help, although I would not like to elaborate on how we assisted them. The British helped Malaysia take over from the Communists. It is not a strong nation but I think it is a nation that will be capable of staying anti-Communist for the foreseeable future."*

Vietnam

In 1954, Young made the first of three trips to Vietnam. While in Saigon, he observed thousands of people moving into South Vietnam from North Vietnam. He also traveled a considerable distance into the rural areas and visited with the average Vietnamese. *"Agricultural agents I traveled with around the country could go almost any place and the local people were friendly with them because they helped them. They didn't have any problem at all. In fact the Ambassador thought I was crazy driving way out in the rural areas but I felt safe with our agricultural people. This was when Ngo Dinh Diem was President. But I couldn't see how we could fight a war in an almost solid jungle area – and there really wasn't much support for the war. I was leery about this from the beginning."*

When he returned from his trip, Young wrote about his reservations in his April 27, 1954, *On Capitol Hill* column:

There is great concern in Washington over the deteriorating French military situation in Indo-China. As in Korea, the Communists are fighting with great determination and total disregard for human casualties. The French, with their own and Vietnamese forces, outnumber the Communist Viet Minh troops. The French and their local troops, too, have much better equipment. They have planes, other military equipment, and assistance provided under a more than $1 billion United States appropriation for the present year.

There is a sad lack of support on the part of the local people for the French, who have controlled this area for 100 years. The native states want more independence, which the French unwisely have thus far refused. As long as these demands for independence are not met, there will be little enthusiasm for fighting Communists among the local people. Our top military men tell us Indo-China is tremendously important if we are to keep Southeast Asia from being controlled by the Communists. However important that may be in the eyes of military leaders, I have grave doubts that the United States has the military and financial capability of almost single-handedly holding the line against Communism in both the Far East and Europe.

We must count our foreign policy as a failure if nine years after World War II we cannot find enough people among the teeming millions of the Far East willing to fight the battle against Communist aggression. A monumental mistake – for which we are primarily responsible – was made when we joined in the policy calling for total destruction of both Germany and Japan. Communists automatically moved into the vacuum this created. It would seem to me if Indo-China is so important militarily in the Far East, a way could be found to get enough soldiers from this heavily concentrated area without sending American boys into this conflict. I am unalterably opposed to sending our troops to another "Hell hole" on the Continent of Asia.

Young believed one of the reasons President Kennedy increased the nation's involvement in Vietnam so dramatically was because of the 1960 Presidential campaign's rhetoric. *"During the 1960 campaign, Nixon tried to set Kennedy up as being soft on Communism since Nixon was such a hard liner. Most of the leaders of the Democrat Party then were on the dovish side. I remember Kennedy's Secretary of Defense Robert MacNamara thought we could win this war in a short while. He made a speech in the streets of Saigon urging our people to go all out to win this war and our troops would be home by Christmas. This was very naïve."*

Again, as in the past, even though Young opposed this war, he always voted for appropriations to support it. And, he made a conscious effort to not make as many public statements against the war as he had during the Korean War. *"We had enough dissension among our own people and the problems on campuses all over the United States that I thought the more one condemned and criticized it, the more it encouraged young people to demonstrate and cause trouble. We were in the war and I wanted to make the best of it and get out of it in an honorable way, which wasn't easy. We did get out of the war in an honorable way. We didn't retreat but it was a very costly thing. I think that anyone who knew the military situation and the fighting ability and the determination of North Vietnam as compared to South Vietnam could well realize that North Vietnam would attack again and they would probably win."*

Young was surprised when President Johnson announced on March 31, 1968, that he would not seek re-election to a second term, but he understood the difficult situation he was in, especially among his fellow Democrats. He had some advice for the Republican Presidential candidates, too.

In a February 12, 1968, television interview in Bismarck Young said:

> I really believe that the Republican contenders for the Republican nomination for President may change their views somewhat towards election and maybe even during the campaign they will. I notice that some of them now have changed their views a little bit over a couple of months ago. To me this is about the only way you can really settle this war in Vietnam. A good, healthy discussion of this problem during the campaign may bring out the answer. I personally believe that the

election of a new President, whether he be Republican or Democrat, would have a better chance of bringing this to a conclusion.

President Nixon surprised the world when he mined Haiphong Harbor in May 1972 and the Russians and Chinese didn't take any actions to counter that aggressive move. *"Previous to that time, the opposition to Johnson and Nixon in this war was that if we bombed certain targets or mined Haiphong Harbor, it would bring the Chinese and Russians directly into the war. I give Nixon credit for ending the war. It was a costly way of getting out. Billions of dollars worth of equipment was left for the South Vietnamese to fight and win the war, although the South Vietnamese really didn't fight much. It was better for us than walking away or retreating. The peace agreement in 1973 came about because our leadership hated to be in the position of withdrawing, and it would be the first time in our history that we walked away from a war that we were in.*

"Vietnam was a war which we didn't win and we didn't lose. It was a bad venture. It demoralized our people at home. We lost a lot of people in a war that we shouldn't have been involved in the first place."

Defense and Intelligence Appropriations

As part of his work on the Appropriations Committee, Young was a member of the defense subcommittee that dealt with classified information and appropriations for the Central Intelligence Agency, the Defense Intelligence Agency and other intelligence agencies, including the Federal Bureau of Investigation. Many of the projects it funded were top secret, and membership on the subcommittee was based on seniority.

Young wrote about this in his April 25, 1962, *On Capitol Hill* column:

> One of the most interesting Appropriations subcommittees on which I serve is the unit handling funds for the operation of the Central Intelligence Agency. Unfortunately, the CIA's work is super-secret and with the exception of the six members of the Senate subcommittee and a similar group in the House very few,

if any, members of Congress know either the details of its work or its costs of operation. The CIA needs to justify its appropriations only to these two legislative units, and the Bureau of the Budget, because of the need for utmost secrecy in it operations.

This is much like the development of the atomic bomb during World War II, which was one of this country's best kept secrets. The budget for development of the A-bomb was hidden in appropriations so successfully that only a handful of people knew the bomb was being developed and what it cost.

"When funds for the atomic bomb were first approved by Congress in the late 1930s fewer than a dozen members knew about it. I think it must have been the best kept secret of all time. I understand even Truman while he was Vice President didn't know. But it had to be kept secret because the Germans had the know-how to make an atomic bomb. And, had the Germans known about the United States developing the bomb, they might have developed it first and the whole world would have been changed."

Near the end of his career as Senator, Young said he was proud of how closely the subcommittee members guarded the appropriations they considered. *"During this time I have been on it, there has never been a leak from our five-man subcommittee. We were not an oversight committee, but we exercised a certain amount of authority, justifying their appropriations. We have always had to hide their appropriations by adding their funds to various big items in the Defense Appropriations bills. There are certain things that are real top secret which are never disclosed. I think this is necessary. The public knowing about some of these things would weaken our position with the rest of the world. There are even some things that very few members of Congress know about – even those on the Intelligence Committee. It might be military programs or it might be intelligence-gathering operations. But only two of us on the Appropriations Committee and two others – only four members of the Senate – knew about some of the funds that we bury in other appropriations for new projects.*

"The problem with any intelligence is best explained by the attitude of former Senator Margaret Chase Smith [Republican of Maine]. *She*

was on the five-member subcommittee on Intelligence Operations that I served on, but she wouldn't serve on such a committee if it had more than five members. She didn't believe in a big committee and neither did I. With a large committee and a large staff there is just no way to keep highly classified information from becoming public. I know there were some things we knew that these big Intelligence Committees never did find out. The CIA was really supposed to tell them but some things were too sensitive. I found out that they didn't always even tell everyone on our subcommittee of five when Senator Russell was chairman that he knew a few things the rest of us didn't. They were the kind of things I personally didn't care to know and especially if it involved the names of some of our agents in foreign countries. There was some pressure from the press or other people for inside information from me, but they finally found out that I wouldn't talk so they didn't bother me much."

One clandestine CIA operation that Young's subcommittee funded was called Project Jennifer, and is now known as Project Azorian. It became one of the most expensive and deepest secrets of the Cold War. It involved building a ship called the *Glomar Explorer* to secretly raise the Russian submarine K-129 that had sunk to the Pacific Ocean floor in March 1968. The United States Navy located the sunken ship at a depth of 16,000 feet north of Hawaii in August of that year, and the CIA began plans to secretly take from the sunken submarine a Soviet SS-N-5 SERB nuclear missile. The CIA asked the Intelligence Subcommittee for funds to build a ship capable of raising the submarine, which had a price tag of $350,000, which it hid in other defense appropriations for several years until it was completed in 1974.

The *Glomar Explorer* recovered the submarine in August 1974, and at Young's insistence, a burial ceremony was held for the six bodies trapped in the submarine. The ceremony included the playing of the Russian national anthem. *"A film of the burial was made, which I saw, and which I wanted to have available for us to show the Russians sometime when we had good relations with them, to show that we gave the sailors a good burial."*

It was 18 years later when a videotape of the burial was given to Russia by then-CIA Director Robert Gates during a trip to Moscow in October 1992. Several years later, relatives of the crew members were shown the video of the burial at sea.

As a member of the Intelligence Subcommittee, Young became familiar with the operations of the CIA, and especially how it interacted with the State Department. *"The CIA was required to work out of the embassies and would be under the control of the ambassadors. I think they gave most of their information to the ambassador but there were some that the CIA didn't trust and they didn't get along very well. I remember one in Thailand. This CIA agent would go to the prime minister or whoever the head of the government over there was and walk into the backyard and play with the kids and knew the whole family. The ambassador was a bit jealous of that and insisted that he be present when I met with that CIA agent. But we would work it out where the CIA agent and I would meet on the street someplace and have a visit. This also happened when I was over in Austria one time. We had our meeting on the street about two hours before we met the ambassador. The CIA almost invariably knew much more than the ambassador."*

North Dakota's Air Force Bases

In their 1977 book, *North Dakota, A History,* Robert P. Wilkins and Wynona H. Wilkins wrote that Young told Secretary of Defense George C. Marshall in 1951 that "North Dakota was one of two or three of the 48 states that did not have a military installation of any kind. By 1960, the Defense Department responded to his bid for fair play and had built Air Force bases in Minot and Grand Forks." Young said that while he often received credit for where the bases were located in the state, he had nothing to do with it. He was, however, contacted when the locations of Fargo and Bismarck were changed to Minot and Grand Forks. *"The Air Force first picked Fargo and Bismarck as sites for the two big air bases. Their reasoning was that during World War II, they used both Fargo and Bismarck as modification centers and thought they would make good sites for these new bases. The people in Minot and Grand Forks got busy and made good cases for their two cities, and the Air Force itself decided to change the location from Bismarck to Minot and from Fargo to Grand Forks. Then I got hell from the other side. Bismarck and Fargo wanted the bases and they thought I had something to do with their moving. I didn't."*

Evan Lips, who was mayor of Bismarck at the time, was among those who were upset at the final decision. "It had been announced that the bases would be built in Bismarck, Fargo, Duluth, Minnesota, and Miles City, Montana. Then we heard they might be moved. So some of us went out to Washington to see Senator Young," Lips recalled. "We talked to him for awhile and then he took us over to see the Majority Leader, who was Senator Lyndon Johnson. He was sitting in his office with his feet on his desk, and we talked to him awhile. But it didn't change. The bases went to Minot and Grand Forks."

In 1974, President Ford's Secretary of Defense, James Schlesinger, proposed deactivating a fighter interceptor squadron at the Grand Forks Air Force Base. Young didn't object. *"If we didn't need it, that was all right with me. But then he wanted to deactivate the Air National Guard unit in Fargo. This is one of the best in the nation and it operates at about half the cost of a similar regular Air Force base. In competition with the regular Air Force and the Canadians, that Air National Guard has won top honors. I told Secretary Schlesinger he just could not deactivate our National Guard. He finally backed down but he was quite persistent. At that time he needed me more than I needed him."*

Fortuna Air Force Station

In addition to North Dakota's two Air Force bases, Fortuna was the home of a radar station as part of the country's Cold War defense radar program. It was a 33-acre Aircraft Control and Warning facility that from 1952 to 1979 was located west of Fortuna and north of Alkabo in northwestern North Dakota. It then became a long-range radar facility for the military's NavStar satellite navigation program until it was decommissioned in 1984.

Young was involved in the site becoming one of the long-range radar facilities in 1979. An article in the *Washington Post* on August 9, 1979, was critical of Young. *"The* Washington Post *accused me of being able to manipulate this location. I did have something do with it, but this was based on the fact that Fortuna is probably the best location. It is furthest north, there is a radar station there now that houses about the same number of people who would be there if they had this NavStar Station. If I hadn't been there, there are locations like one in Wisconsin which might have been accepted, but it is quite a resort area. There is another in Nebraska, but that wouldn't have been as favorable, or as good a site as the one at Fortuna. Fortuna is the best possible site. Of course, it is a small town and Crosby is about 25 miles away. Many times the generals in the military, Air Force included, liked to have all the bases in a warm climate so they could play golf the year 'round! Certainly my seniority helped in the selection of Fortuna."*

A Minuteman missile in LaMoure

In 1968, Young acquired for LaMoure a deactivated Minuteman I missile from the Grand Forks Air Force Base for display on city property. At the September 8, 1968, dedication ceremony, Young was joined by Governor William Guy and Major General W.P. Wilson, chief of the National Guard Bureau in Washington. Also featured that day was a flyover by the Air National Guard of Fargo and a demonstration by the Army's Golden Knights precision parachute team from Fort Bragg, North Carolina.

In his remarks that day, Young praised the capability of the Minuteman missile. "No one – friend or foe – should underestimate the destructive power of these missiles. If only 10 percent were fired successfully, they could completely destroy every worthwhile military target and city in a nation such as Russia."

He also talked about the need to replace the B-52 bomber:
It is the greatest bomber in the world. I joined with

other members of Congress dealing with military affairs who believe that we should continue the research and development of the high altitude 2,000 mile-an-hour bomber as a replacement for the B-52. We have already spent more than $1.5 billion to develop a high-altitude bomber capable of flying more than 2,000 miles an hour. The Secretary of Defense has refused in the last three years to continue with the development of this plane. He has, I believe, unwisely depended too much on the missile system as our first line of defense. It is apparent that Russia will soon have the capability of having a better inventory of aircraft – both fighters and bombers – than the United States.

The major military issue which will be coming up soon will be whether to proceed to develop even bigger and more powerful missiles than the Minuteman III, or to spend more money on bombers such as I have mentioned. With our limited financial resources we cannot, nor do I believe it is necessary to, embark upon all of the military programs our Defense Department would like, but we do have to maintain a favorable balance of power with Russia.

No one dislikes the spending of huge sums of money on defense more than I, but I see no alternative. The only real deterrent to Russian aggression is the maintaining of a military posture at least as good, or preferably better than theirs. This is the best assurance I know of that we will not be intimidated by such nations as Russia and China, or become involved in a third World War. May we always be able to view this missile we are dedicating today as a symbol of peace rather than war.

LaMoure's Minuteman missile was taken down in 2001 when the land where it was placed was used to expand the city's nursing home. Restoration efforts by some LaMoure citizens, including Young's daughter-in-law, Marcia, raised $10,000 in private donations to repaint and restore it. In July 2005, it was placed on land on Highway 13 that leads into LaMoure, adjacent to the town's Omega Motel.

LaMoure's Omega Coast Guard Navigation Station

In the late 1960s, the United States Navy and Coast Guard began considering sites for establishing the first worldwide radio navigation system. Called the Omega Navigation Systems, eight stations would be built around the world, each one transmitting a very low frequency signal that was repeated every 10 seconds in a pattern of four tones unique to the station.

Sites in North Dakota and Minnesota were among those considered. As a member of the Defense Appropriations subcommittee, Young was upset that he was not told which North Dakota sites were considered, because he wanted to suggest three locations, including his hometown of LaMoure. When he did hear the sites the Coast Guard was considering, he was still upset. *"The sites they looked at were obviously not suitable, and then I heard it was set to go to Roseau, Minnesota. However, the LaMoure site was ideal and the cost was considerably less than the one at Roseau. I proved to the committee that the construction costs at LaMoure were better than at Roseau."*

By securing the project for LaMoure, Young had taken it away from the district of Minnesota Congressman Odin Langen. *"It was difficult, something I wouldn't want to do very often, although I didn't think he was very interested or concerned about it going to Minnesota. It helped that I was a Senator and on the subcommittee dealing with military construction."*

Six stations began operating in 1971, with the Coast Guard staffing the two sites in the United States in LaMoure and Kaneohe, Hawaii, and in partnership with the other sites in Argentina, Norway, Liberia, and France. Japanese and Australian stations became operational several years later. LaMoure's nearly 1,200-foot-high tower remained in operation as part of the Omega program until the end of September 1997. Global Positioning System (GPS) technology had become a more preferred system of navigation guidance, and the cost of the Omega program could no longer be justified. The United States Navy now operates out of the LaMoure station for very low frequency submarine communication purposes.

USS LaMoure County

Two U.S. Naval vessels have borne the name *USS LaMoure County*. The first was an LST-S42-class tank landing ship during World War II. The second *USS LaMoure County* was the 16th of 20 Newport-class tank landing ships built in the late 1960s and early 1970s. With all of the LaMoure County Commissioners and several other LaMoure area residents present for the ceremony, Pat Young christened the ship on May 22, 1970, at the National Steel Shipbuilding Company site in San Diego, California. It was decommissioned in 2000 and sunk as a target in July 2001.

ABM Missile Site

Another component of the Cold War was the development of an anti-ballistic missile system by the United States Army, called the Safeguard Program, in the late 1960s. It was begun by President Johnson and continued by President Nixon. As a member of the Appropriations Committee, Young supported funding for this program.

Plans were to construct several Safeguard sites within the United States, but the only one completed was the Stanley R. Mickelsen Safeguard complex in Nekoma. It defended the Minuteman intercontinental ballistic missile silos near Grand Forks Air Force Base. A separate station north of Nekoma near the town of Concrete that ran a long-range detection radar station supported the Mickelsen complex. Called Perimeter Acquisition Radar (PAR), it detects when an incoming missile is targeted from as far away as the North Pole.

The Mickelsen complex was the only operational anti-ballistic missile system ever deployed by the United States, with one single deployment on October 1, 1975. Less than four months later, on February 10, 1976, the complex was deactivated.

Young was livid over the closing of the complex, which he blamed on Representative Mark Andrews, North Dakota's lone Congressman. *"They started the movement in the House Appropriations Committees about a year before. I should add that the President, the Bureau of the Budget, the Joint Chiefs of Staff and the Pentagon were strongly opposed to closing our ABM site. Senator Burdick voted against the closing. Andrews, in supporting its closing, created some real problems between him and me for awhile. I think we should have kept this as long as the Russians had theirs, or at least until we had some experience after all of the money put into it."*

He was particularly bothered about being unable to stop the closing of the complex in the Senate, which was being led by Senator Edward Kennedy, Democrat of Massachusetts. *"I fought to keep it open on the Senate side and I won over a motion by Senator Kennedy by two votes. I then made a motion to reconsider the vote which, if it had passed, would have made it impossible for Senator Kennedy to get his reconsidered as he would then need a two-thirds vote. This is what is considered a 'clincher' motion. The reason I wanted to tie it down to where it would take a two-thirds vote to reconsider was that we had several Democrat Senators who were candidates for President who I thought Senator Kennedy would have been able to switch their votes in his favor overnight. My losing this clincher motion put Kennedy in a strong position and all I was able to salvage out of the big ABM site the next day was the PAR radar.*

"One of Kennedy's most effective arguments was that he was able to quote Congressman Andrews' statement from the Congressional Record *in which he supported the move on the House side to close the base. That is an important thing in Congress. If one member in the Senate or House from one state is opposed to something, it has to be very important or they will support his position. For example, if either Senator is opposed to some water project in his state, they just are not going to put any money into it. It's a lot easier to keep the money out than get it in.*

"Both economically and militarily, it was a bad move to close this base. We had spent about $6 billion on research and development of the ABM program. This would include ABM sites and several others – one in Montana which was closed after it was about one-fourth completed."

Young was able to keep the PAR radar station in operation following the closing of the Nekoma site, and it continues to be operated by the United States Air Force. When the Air Force acquired it in 1977, it was named the Concrete Missile Early Warning System. In 1983, when the Concrete post office closed, its name changed to the Cavalier Air Force Station, due to its location 11 miles east of the town of Cavalier, North Dakota. The station is home to the 10th Space Warning Squadron of the 21st Space Wing based at Peterson Air Base in Colorado.

In February 1979, Young was honored with the Minuteman of the Year Award from the Reserve Officers Association of the United States. Washington area television news stations covered Young's remarks while accepting the award at the association's National Council banquet. Young shared his perspective on defense issues during his tenure in the Senate, especially as it pertained to the Cold War:

> We have been blessed for the last 100 years with the necessary active and reserve military strength and economic strength to pursue our national interest – that is, from a position of being the strongest nation in the world. The situation in the last 20 years has changed to the point that we are no longer sure that we are the strongest military nation in the world today. Our leaders in the White House and the Joint Chiefs now talk about a "Rough Equivalency" of strength with the Soviets. This weakened position is compounded by the current devaluation of the dollar around the world and the increasingly unfavorable balance of payments.
>
> We must increase our active and reserve military strength. We should place a higher priority for funding such strategic weapons as the replacement of the B-52 bomber with the B-1, a new ICBM, Trident Submarines, Cruise Missiles and the neutron bomb.
>
> It is highly essential that we go forward as rapidly as possible with the development and procurement of new weapons for both of our active and reserve forces. The Defense Department has justified the Total Force concept for years. It has testified to the essential role of the reserves, including the Air and Army National Guard, in any future war. Reserve and Guard units have demonstrated their readiness and capability, even though usually equipped with old weapons and, in some

cases, deficient numbers of weapons. Therefore, modern fighter aircraft, tanks, helicopters, artillery and missiles must be procured for our tactical forces, including the reserve forces.

We must place a very high priority on increasing our naval strength – active and reserve – to ensure that we can control the seas. Control of the seas is a must in time of war and the knowledge that we can control the seas is essential if we are to pursue our peacetime interests.

When I first came to the U.S. Senate in 1945, the defense appropriation for that fiscal year was $44.1 billion. The next fiscal year, 1946, it was just slightly higher. Defense spending declined after 1946 to a low of only $9.9 billion in FY 1948. Since then funds for defense have increased almost every year.

The defense appropriations bill the Congress passed for Fiscal Year 1979 was $117.2 billion. The increase between 1945 and 1979 is large – but much less than for most all other government agencies.

Education, training, employment and social services increased 304 percent; Health increased by 322 percent; Income Security went up 329 percent; Interest rose by 210 percent; and General Government and all other functions increased by 195 percent.

More simply stated, the cost of Defense in the last ten years increased by only 48 percent, while the cost of all other functions of the Federal Government increased by 264 percent during the same ten-year period.

Personnel costs for our defense forces represent one of the sharpest increases in cost. This increase was due largely to the popular but very costly all-volunteer military force. Even with the attractive incentive payments, all four of our active duty services, as well as the Reserves, are failing to meet their military strength requirements.

We have wasted billions of defense dollars by developing weapons systems but when they were ready to go into production or become operational, they were abandoned. Three of the biggest and most dramatic of such cancellations were the B-70, the ABM, and the B-1.

The B-70 was cancelled after two aircraft had been built. This was terminated after $1.7 billion had been spent. The ABM program took years to develop and consisted of the most modern radar and computers our technology could build. It was operational for only a few months when Congress terminated the program after $5.8 billion had been spent. Since then we have spent more than $700 million on continued research for the same kind of defense system.

The B-1 program was cancelled last year after $4.3 billion had been expended to develop four aircraft. These aircraft were very successful in their test program and the Air Force and Defense Department had every expectation that the aircraft would meet all performance requirements. The B-1, or some other strategic bomber, is urgently needed to replace the aging B-52s.

When I visited the Minot Air Force Base in North Dakota last fall, they had a picture taken of a young serviceman and me alongside a B-52 bomber. I asked the young serviceman who was the oldest – he or the B-52 – and he said the B-52. Since it takes 5 to 10 years to develop and start production of a strategic bomber, time is of the essence if we are to maintain the bomber leg of the Strategic Triad.

Abandoning or delaying construction of these and other new weapons systems unilaterally has weakened our position in the SALT II [Strategic Arms Limitation Treaty] negotiations when it could well have increased our bargaining position. This weakened position has been described as the reason U.S. negotiators have given up positions or compromised positions that were favorable to our interests.

Our current SALT Treaty has not caused the Soviets to alter their spending for defense. Today, the Russians are capable of and are building military equipment that may not equal our technology in some categories but it is not far behind. Their ICBM warheads are now MIRV'd. They are far more sophisticated and accurate than before; their Foxbat fighter is one of the fastest in the world; their Ballistic Missile Submarines are improved and more capable; they have modernized and greatly increased their number of tanks; and their Ballistic missile and Air Defense systems are continually being improved.

They now may well be further advanced than we are in laser technology. All of this increased military capability by the Soviets has come during our present SALT Treaty. I question how much, if any, the present

SALT agreement has deterred the Soviets in their determined drive for military supremacy. A good SALT II agreement would be helpful and desirable but, from the information I have been able to obtain so far about the new SALT agreement, and their adventurism around the world, I would have to oppose it.

In another very important area of national defense, that of intelligence gathering, the Soviets have greatly increased the effectiveness of their KGB while our CIA has been severely crippled by the exposure to the whole world of just how the CIA operates. It cannot ever be effective with all of its sensitive procedures constantly becoming public knowledge.

There is just no way that intelligence gathering, especially covert, can be effective when all its procedures and operations and operatives become available to the Soviets through adverse leaks from very large investigating committees of Congress and their big staffs, as well as disgruntled CIA employees in their publications. Even more important, their scope of operations has been far too severely curtailed.

Intelligence gathering through covert operations has been practically wiped out. This lack of cover obtained intelligence was responsible for our total lack of information on the recent disastrous situation in Iran and the developments leading up to it. Spying, especially through covert operations, is a dirty business but a common practice among most nations of the world – and is necessary if we are to continue as a world power. There is just no way for covert spying intelligence to co-exist with our present idealistic and highly publicized human rights policies.

If the Soviets have caught up to our military strength – and if that is what our Defense Department means when they testify that our objective is "Rough Equivalency" – now is the time to re-evaluate our situation. We need to plan ahead – not for five years, but for 25 years. We need to realistically look at our potential enemies and determine what must be done to remain strong and capable of maintaining our way of life and pursuing our national interest. This is essential if we are to maintain our current position of just "Rough Equivalency" with the Soviets.

The cost of maintaining our military strength is high and will be higher is we increase our strength. This cost must also be considered with our domestic needs and our ability to pay for both. In this regard, we must be mindful of the financial situation we find ourselves in today.

There is one development of our beloved country that deeply concerns me. We are fast becoming a welfare state and my great concern is: Can a welfare state compete militarily with a totalitarian nation such as Russia – which has practically no limit on the percent of their national income that can be spent for military supremacy?

We must not forget that all our better way of life would become meaningless if we become a second rate power to any nation whose major goal is world conquest. We must wisely spend every dollar that is available for military and other purposes. Our national debt now estimated for Fiscal Year 1980, which Congress is now considering, is $899 billion and the interest alone is estimated to be $66 billion a year.

The picture I have described for you tonight is not bright and cheerful, but I have not meant to indicate that we are beyond our capabilities. I believe we are capable of increasing our strength both militarily and economically while meeting our necessary domestic needs. It will take hard work, strong leadership, and exceptional wisdom over the next two decades or more if we are to maintain our leadership and capabilities of the world.

Trips abroad

In his early Senate years, Young traveled with committees and in later years he traveled alone with Senate Appropriations Committee staff members. Each had its advantages. *"When I traveled as the only Senator, I didn't get to see the leaders in the countries as much, but felt I saw more of the actual operations in the country."*

On a trip to the Middle East in 1950, the delegation had wired ahead asking that there be no parties, but the ambassador insisted they go to a cocktail party in Damascus with him. *"I said I was traveling hard and not feeling very well and do you mind if I don't go. 'Oh,' he said, "after all, it is given in your honor!' I went to it and the first thing after I got there, the Defense Minister of Syria got me in a corner – a big son of a gun – and according to him you would think I was solely responsible for all the Jews coming into Israel."*

On another trip to the Middle East a couple years later, one of the leaders he met was King Ibn Saud of Saudi Arabia, who served from 1926 until his death in 1953. *"He was a very interesting and intelligent person and a tough fighter. I remember having lunch with him out in the desert and we were trying to find out the results of the off-year elections just held in the United States. None of our people could find out but King Ibn Saud and his people gave us amazingly full and accurate information. He had an elaborate radio set up way out in the desert where they would listen to the news from all over the world and we got all the news we wanted first from him."*

A gold silverware set that was a gift to Young from King Ibn Saud is part of an exhibit about the Senator in the LaMoure County Museum in Grand Rapids.

He met Prime Minister Jawaharlal Nehru during a trip to India. *"He was quite popular at that time and I think an able leader. You have to have a lot on the ball to become the leader of a nation like India with its huge population, poverty and many difficult problems."*

During two different trips to Taiwan, Young had lunch with Chiang Kai-chek, and he became acquainted with Madame Chiang Kai-chek. *"He wasn't a very talkative kind of person but very friendly and intelligent. The thing he talked about mostly was their strong determination to go back and take over China. I think that was the objective that kept his people together. They really believed that, whether it was possible or not."*

Winston Churchill

In the early 1950s, Young met Winston Churchill during a trip to Europe. *"I think he was one of the great men of the world. When you met with him personally, he was a little different than when you saw him in public. One thing I particularly noted, and got some encouragement out of when I visited with him personally, was his tendency to stutter. But that doesn't show up in his public speaking. There were four Senators who visited with him at about 11 in the morning. We visited and had a few drinks until about 1 p.m. – and probably would have gone on longer except that Mrs. Churchill – who was American – found an excuse to break up the meeting. He was having a good time and we were too. I especially enjoyed it as it was a rare privilege to hear him speak so fluently and casually. We talked about international problems of the day and some of the problems that he had with the Labor Party. There was a shortage of potatoes and some farm commodities and I understand the Labor leaders there would blame it onto the weather. Churchill said they had weather, too, when they were in the majority. Churchill is a very down-to-earth type of person. I may say that most of the great men that I meet in public office are down-to-earth people who listen. Churchill was a brilliant man. He had his ups and downs in British history but he came along at just the right time and was just the kind of leader that England needed when they got into World War II. He was the kind who wouldn't give up. He had a brilliant mind and commanded respect from everyone and especially here in America. He seemed to inspire people."*

Meeting Khrushchev in Moscow

Young traveled to Moscow in 1956 after Nikita Khrushchev, who had became First Secretary of the Communist Party of the Soviet Union following the death of Joseph Stalin in March 1953, opened the country to more visitors.

"It had been years since they let anyone in and we had an hour-and 45-minute meeting with Khrushchev and Minister of Defense Nikolai Bulganin. They were concerned about the encirclement of Russia. Khrushchev said, 'you won't sell us machine tools but we can make them, too, even if it will take us some time to do it.' About this time, Chiang Kai-shek was on Formosa and the Chinese Communists began shelling Quemoy and Matsu. We could have become involved in an Asian War. But I think what kept it from happening was the feeling that

the Russians and the Chinese had about Eisenhower – a feeling that if they got into war, it would be an all-out war, it wouldn't be a limited one, I think that is largely the reason they backed off."

Hungarian Revolution

During his trip to the Soviet Union, Young also traveled to Hungary with Senator Henry Dworshak, a Republican from Idaho, a few months before the Hungarian Revolution of 1956. He had earlier visited Hungary at least three other times. *"The Communists were fairly friendly with me. They said they understood that I appeared on Moscow Radio a couple of days before when I was attending an agricultural fair and I said, 'That is true.' And they invited me to see their agricultural fair and take me around. We had our people, too, a CIA agent was along and I know their KGB was along, but I remember one particular fellow who was a top agricultural man a big Hungarian. He spoke pretty good English. Every once in awhile he would call me aside to show me one of their plows and quietly ask me if they got into trouble with Russia, 'do you think that the United States would help us?' I think they were led to believe that we would help but I was careful not to give them any encouragement. That they would run the chance of talking that way with me with the KGB not being far away indicates how anxious they were to know if I thought the United States would help them. I would have liked to see them liberated but we were in no position to do it. We didn't have the military forces there and the NATO countries would have been no help. There was no way of helping them unless we had planned a long ways ahead. And this was quite deep in Communist-dominated territory. At that time you found a lot of anti-Communists becoming very outspoken wherever we went in Hungary and Czechoslovakia."*

Young's traveling partner, Senator Dworshak, had a Czech family background. *"I remember the two of us going to a big state-owned department store. Dworshak was thinking of buying a set of china to take back. The manager of the store called him aside and said, 'Don't buy our china. We don't make it good anymore.'"*

Pat's China diary

On October 21, 1976, when Young was in Bismarck campaigning for the elections of President Gerald Ford and other Republican candidates, he received a call from Max L. Friedersdorf from Ford's staff. Friedersdorf told him that the President wanted him to be a member of a delegation to visit the People's Republic of China, which was leaving in two weeks on November 5. His wife, Pat, who was in LaMoure at the time, remembered getting her husband's call about whether they should accept the invitation. "I replied, 'Yes, I'll go if it kills me!'" Young had declined two previous invitations to go to China after President Nixon opened China to United States visitors because they had been offered during his 1974 re-election campaign. He didn't believe he should decline another one.

A *Bismarck Tribune* article on October 22 announced the trip:

Young Selected for Trip to China

Sen. Milton R. Young of North Dakota said Friday that he will visit mainland China early in November in response to an invitation from the new government of that country.

Young said he had been invited by President Ford to be a member of a six-member delegation the Peking government has asked this government to send on an official mission to Red China.

The delegation will include, in addition to Young, who is dean of Senate Republicans, two other Republican senators and three Democratic senators, accompanied by their wives.

It is the first invitation the Communist Chinese government has extended to this country's government in over a year, Young said.

He cited this as an indication that those now in control in Peking desire to have a friendly relationship with the United States.

Peking's official radio confirmed early Friday that Premier Hua Kuo-feng had been named chairman of the Chinese Communist Party to succeed Mao Tse-tung, who died Sept. 9.

"I was interested in the fact that this invitation was extended so shortly before the Nov. 2 election," Young said. "Peking has a good intelligence system. This would seem to indicate that they believe that President Ford will be re-elected."

Young said the Red Chinese are "more concerned about us becoming a secondary power to Russia than we ourselves seem to be. The Russians maintain an army of about half a million men on their (the Chinese) border constantly."

Young said that the Chinese trip will give him an opportunity to boost U.S. wheat sales there.

"This won't be a wheat selling trip," he said. "but mainland China does import a lot of wheat, mostly from Canada, and I won't pass up any opportunity to extol the quality of our (North Dakota) wheat."

This will be Young's first trip overseas in eight or nine years but his fourth to the Far East. He has never been in mainland China but has visited Hong Kong twice and was three times in Southeast Asia, the last during the Vietnam War, of which he was one of the earliest critics.

Upon their return on November 23, Pat wrote a detailed account of the trip:

We had planned a vacation to Arizona after the November election, so instead found ourselves scrambling to line up passports, shots and warmer clothes. Milt kept his campaign commitments in the state before returning to Washington. On the evening of November 4, Secretary of State Henry Kissinger met us at a reception and a briefing for the trip.

Kissinger told them the only way anyone visited the People's Republic of China was at their specific invitation and as their guests. Chinese officials had asked President Ford to send a delegation of six Senators and their wives. The trip had originally been scheduled for August, but had been delayed because of the great earthquake in July and the rapidly declining health of Chairman Mao that resulted in his death in early September. The Youngs had not planned to go on the earlier trip. The other five Senators and their wives on the journey were Republican Senator and Mrs. Carl Curtis of Nebraska, Democrat Senator and Mrs. Birch Bayh of Indiana, Democrat Senator and Mrs. Ernest Hollings of South Carolina, Republican Senator and Mrs. Ted Stevens of Alaska, and Democrat Senator and Mrs. Bennett Johnston of Louisiana. They were accompanied by Dr. Robert

Wolthuis, Special Assistant to the President, and his wife, who were the White House escort officers, and two representatives from the Department of State, Dick Hart and Terry Howe.

Pat wrote:

> Kissinger told us we really do not know anything about how China operates or reaches decisions. I asked him if it was safe to send so many members of Congress over there and he said, 'No, but what can you do about it?' Most of the people Kissinger had worked with over the years are now purged or have disappeared. He suggested we not mention Taiwan or agree to supply them with any military weapons.

On November 7, the delegation arrived in Tokyo before going on to Shanghai the next day. While there, Pat found a place to change her American Express travelers checks back to U.S. currency because they were told the Chinese would not accept American Express. "They were upset with the president of the company because he had some friendly relations with Taiwan!"

After a day-and-a-half in Shanghai, they took a four-hour train trip to Nanking, staying at what Pat described as "what was once an elegant hotel, but across the street was definitely a military office of some sort. There were beautiful gardens around the hotel and the weather was delightful."

> From there we drove 36 miles in a motorcade to visit a peasant farm commune.
>
> We learned that no one owns a personal car in China. There are some buses, military vehicles of various kinds and some primitive (by our standards) motorized farm equipment – like a walking plow with a small motor. We saw crops of wheat, rice, cotton, lots of cabbage and other vegetables all planted and harvested by hand. It was harvest season when we were there. We also saw many pigs, but few cattle, although water buffalo and cattle were used for farming. The farmers were proud to show the group their new peasant housing. Seven people lived in three rooms, and they were anxious to tell us how much better life was for them now than it had been before Chairman Mao.
>
> The delegation ate in a private room in the hotel by themselves if there was no official dinner. We all liked

the Chinese food and everyone learned to use chopsticks except Milt and Marvella Bayh. We also learned to like the Chinese beer, which they served with every meal except breakfast.

A few days later they arrived by train in Peking, where they toured the Forbidden City in a snowstorm. After all the walking and trips up and down the stairs, her husband's hips stiffened up and he had trouble walking. Their guide took Young to a hospital, where he was given an acupuncture treatment. He had three of these treatments. "He insisted the treatments did not hurt – and they helped considerably," Pat wrote.

On November 15, Young and Senator Curtis visited with the Chinese Agriculture Minister, and following a 10-course dinner of Peking Duck, returned to their room to pack for Canton the next morning. Later that evening there was an earthquake, which measured 6.9 on the Richter scale. Pat wrote:

It gave the room a real jolt and left the chandelier swinging. We were told to dress in warm clothes and go downstairs immediately, but before we left the room we were told we could stay in the room for the time being. We visited with each other in the hallway for a while and waited for the "all clear," which never officially came.

We were glad we didn't have to evacuate, as it was very cold and the 'earthquake prevention' housing, as they insisted on calling the little shacks they had built to live in during the earthquake in July, didn't look the least bit inviting or warm. Milt gave up after about half an hour and put on his pajamas and went back to bed and right to sleep. I tried to rest fully dressed with my mink and snow boots on but it didn't work too well. I finally got ready for bed but no sleep.

Because Pat had come down with a stomach virus, the Youngs left Canton early and went on to Hong Kong so Pat could rest and recover before meeting the delegation there a few days later. On November 22, the Senators held a news conference in Hong Kong and left the following day, stopping in Guam before their 12-hour flight to Arizona. The Youngs stayed at their home there until returning to Washington, D.C., in early January.

The December 6, 1976, *New York Times* carried an Associated Press story about Young's acupuncture treatment:

Senator Undergoes Acupuncture

Sen. Milton R. Young says he underwent three acupuncture treatments on a recent trip to China. The 78-year-old said last week the treatments had been administered to relieve hip joint pain caused by walking and climbing.

Robert Wolthuis wrote in a December 1, 1976, letter to Young on White House stationery, "Wallace Bennett [recently retired Republican Senator from Utah] always told us you were a man of great wisdom but we had never seen that North Dakota wit. You handled the top ranking Chinese better than anyone else. When you got involved, people were very impressed."

"The Chinese were a very friendly people. Law-abiding. They just about have to be because of the type of government they have. They can easily get rid of someone who does not support their type of government. But they are a very intelligent, hard-working people. It is amazing that they can feed that many people. They are almost self-sufficient in food production and they even export a little rice but import some wheat. No other nation in the world could do this – feed and clothe that many people – but they live on very little. They are highly disciplined. I think you are going to hear much more about China in the future."

Young wrote at length about the trip in his *On Capitol Hill* column that was released on November 29, 1976:

My recent two-week visit to the People's Republic of China (PRC) was my first foreign trip in 14 years. It was the result of a special invitation by the Chinese Government to President Ford, who selected six Senators and their wives to go. It was the first such official Chinese invitation in over a year and came shortly after the death of Chairman Mao Tse-tung. All expenses while in China, including transportation, were paid by the Chinese Government.

We visited several major cities and surrounding farm areas, including Shanghai, Nanking, Uangchow, Peking and Canton. We traveled by car, train (overnight from Nanking to Peking with very good accommodations) and in a Russian jet owned by the Chinese, as well as bus and boat. The Chinese food was excellent and almost everyone learned to eat with chopsticks except me! In Shanghai we were met by a high-ranking Chinese Government official, Madam K'ang Tai-sha, Deputy Secretary General of the Chinese People's Institute of Foreign Affairs, and six members of her staff who traveled with us during out entire visit. We met top Communist officials in every area. They run the country.

It appears that China is following more closely the pure Lenin-Marxist doctrine than Russia. Chairman Mao Tse-tung, while savage and ruthless, was very intelligent and had great ability as a leader. People seem to worship him and follow his teaching and directives closely.

Their dislike and fear of Russia is very real and increasing rather than diminishing. Since their break with Russia about 10 years ago they have dedicated themselves to becoming self-sufficient and militarily strong and have made considerable progress. They have developed many new and sophisticated military weapons besides the hydrogen bomb – one of which they detonated while we were in China. They have also developed much new and quite sophisticated industrial equipment.

The major reason for their more friendly relationship recently with the United States is mainly because they fear more than anything else the possibility of Russia becoming the sole superpower in the world. They are even interested in the NATO countries of western Europe, as well as other nations not aligned with Russia, being militarily strong.

They have also made remarkable progress in becoming almost self-sufficient in food production. It is doubtful that any other nation in the world could feed, clothe and educate 800 million people (one-fourth of the world population) as well. They are a very intelligent, industrious, proud and quite honest people. They have practically wiped out the vast illiteracy of only a few years ago. Opium and other drugs, as well as prostitutes and beggars, once common in much of China are practically unheard of now. Most hotel rooms are not locked and, unlike cities in most countries, it is safe to walk their streets day or night.

There is no unemployment in China. It is a

completely regimented state with everything owned by the government. And the government tells each person what kind of job he will have and at what pay. There seems to be little variation in the pay for a top doctor or other professional and a factory worker or peasant who works in the fields. Even most professionals are required to periodically work on the farms. There is much poor housing, but this huge population seems to be quite well-fed and clothed in a simple and inexpensive way. They are putting great emphasis on education of all their young people.

China, where the land has been farmed for over 2,000 years, is still very productive. Most of the land is irrigated and every possible foot of land is being farmed. With the exception of northern China, most of the farms produce from 2 to 3 crops a year. A common practice is 2 crops of rice and 1 of wheat. From my observations, it would appear they are better farmers and produce much more per acre than does Russia.

China is almost entirely a cereal-eating people, which makes it possible for them to feed many more people than we do by feeding much of our grain to livestock. They have practically no beef cattle. They have some dairying, and hogs are produced on practically all communes. It is difficult to get accurate figures, but it appears that China produces at least 1.5 billion bushels of wheat and around 6 billion bushels of rice annually. It is hard to realize how they are able to harvest this huge production with little mechanized harvesting equipment. Rice and wheat, for the most part, are cut and threshed out by hand. Water buffalo, except in the northern provinces, are the main source of power other than the men and women by the millions.

China exports some food products such as rice but mainly to acquire foreign currencies to buy other commodities, which they need to import, such as wheat. At our conference with one of the 3 new top leaders of China, Vice Premier Li Hsien-nien, I got into an interesting discussion with him about wheat. He somehow knew I was a wheat farmer. He has a considerable agricultural background of his own. At one point when he was discussing the problem they have of importing wheat I said, "The next time you need wheat, why don't you call me up?" He got a chuckle out of this, but his response was that the price of our wheat is too high. The opportunity to discuss this further did not arise. I was particularly interested in his comment about the high price of our wheat.

Canada and Australia have been supplying most of China's wheat requirements in recent years. The export price of wheat in Canada is set by the government itself. When grain traders in the export business, or nations which buy wheat directly, have to acquire wheat in the United States, the price is set solely by the free market. The Canadian export system is simpler and may have some advantages. According to reliable information, Canada's wheat export price for the past few months has been about 15 cents a bushel lower than ours. This would account for a least a part of the decline in United States wheat exports and lower prices.

In my many travels to countries all over the world no people have ever been more friendly, from the peasant to the highest ranking official. The Far East is a different world than it was only a few years ago. Most of these nations have advanced culturally and industrially, as well as in military strength. China, with her 800 million people and their intelligence and willingness to work and sacrifice, could well become a much more powerful and more important factor in Far Eastern affairs in the future.

Our more friendly relationship with China is the result of four years of negotiations by President Nixon, President Ford and Secretary Kissinger. The so-called Shanghai Communique signed by both nations is not binding, but it could present some difficult problems in the future. For example, over a period of time the PRC may well continue to insist that we withdraw all of our military forces from both South Korea and Nationalist Chinese-controlled Taiwan. Our complete withdrawal from these two countries could well cause another war and a takeover by the Communists.

Until these problems are resolved, there will be no full recognition by the United States and the PRC. It would be a pity if all the great progress we have made with China in the last four years were lost. Patience and continued negotiations might well resolve these difficult problems peacefully and thus avert future military conflict.

We were all treated well in China and I felt the trip was very interesting, as well as informative and enjoyable. Because of my age, I seemed to get a little special consideration and treatment. By custom they have great respect and a degree of reverence for the elderly. They always opened and closed the car doors for me but not for the women. They even gave me some special consideration such as three acupuncture treatments to relieve a hip joint problem acquired from excessive walking and climbing.

One of the many exciting experiences of our trip occurred in Peking. While talking to my office in Washington on the telephone, an earthquake suddenly caused the room to move violently and the chandelier to swing! We were ordered to dress warmly and go downstairs. Later they decided we could remain in our rooms but to stay dressed. It was a long night and we later learned that the earthquake registered 6.9 on the Richter Scale.

We visited agriculture communes, workers, housing, schools, hospitals, factories, a hydro electric plant, the huge Yangtse River Bridge, and the 2,000-year-old Great Wall. It was a very helpful and worthwhile experience, especially for a Member of Congress who must almost daily deal with world problems which have a direct bearing on our future.

National Issues and North Dakota

In addition to agriculture and defense, Young was involved in legislation on a number of other national issues that had a direct impact on North Dakota and its future. This chapter covers water development, civil rights, ethics investigations, voting decisions, working with his staff, and his relationship with civic leaders in the state.

Water Projects and Garrison Diversion

Water development was an emerging national interest and, in addition to Garrison Diversion, North Dakota had many other water development needs. In 1948, Young announced in a news release that more North Dakota water projects would be funded by Congress that year than had previously been funded throughout the entire history of the state. This appropriation of more than $60 million was for projects that included Garrison Dam, Pembina Dam, Tongue River Dam, Jamestown Dam, Park River Dam, Baldhill Dam and flood control for Mandan and Beulah.

The year before Young was appointed to the Senate, Congress had passed the 1944 Flood Control Act to develop and manage the water and natural resources of the Missouri River Basin. The act authorized the Missouri River Basin Project, which was later renamed the Pick-Sloan Missouri Basin Program to recognize its founders, U.S. Army Corps of Engineers Missouri River Division Engineer, Colonel Lewis A. Pick, and Assistant Regional Director of the Bureau's Upper Missouri Region William G. Sloan.

One of the most comprehensive plans ever created for developing and managing a basin's water resources, the Pick-Sloan Program was developed in response to devastating Missouri River floods in 1942 and 1943. It was initially designed to construct 95 dams with 17 hydroelectric power plants, along with facilities for irrigating some five million acres of land. The benefits to the Missouri River Basin would be municipal and industrial water supply, irrigation, hydroelectric power, flood control, navigation, sediment abatement, fish and wildlife enhancement, recreation, and pollution control.

The original intent of the Flood Control Act was to bring irrigation water to North Dakota by pipeline from the Fort Peck Dam in eastern Montana, which had been completed in 1940. When this proved to be unfeasible, construction began on the Garrison Dam in western North Dakota in 1947. The fifth largest earthen dam in the world, it was completed at a cost of $294 million in April 1953.

President Eisenhower joined Young and other state and national dignitaries at the dam's dedication ceremony June 11 of that year. The Dam's west embankment was filled with thousands of spectators who heard Eisenhower say, "The dam was built with the people's money. Its benefits must go to the people."

After Garrison Dam was completed, the Garrison Diversion Project was proposed to construct a water system to deliver water for irrigation through canals to north-central and eastern North Dakota.

Throughout Young's tenure in the Senate, the politics of Garrison Diversion and related water projects were among the most contentious and exasperating legislation he would champion.

"There is always some local opposition to almost any kind of project and especially water projects. The Garrison Dam was authorized the year before I went to Washington and it involved drowning out the Three Affiliated Tribes and a lot of white farmers and I got right in the middle of that. It involved taking two towns – Van Hook and Sanish – and many acres of good farm land. I don't know how I was ever re-elected as I had to fight for the appropriations and there was a difficult, controversial

question as to whether there would be a pool level of 1,830 or 1,850 feet. The people in Williston and Usher Burdick wanted the 1,830 feet level because at that lower level, it wouldn't back water up to Williston. But in order for Garrison Diversion to be feasible, you had to have 1,850 feet level, otherwise you would have to pump the water up too high. There would have been far less water available. I stayed with the 1,830 feet level for three or four years as I kept thinking the problems would go away. But the time came when we either had to go to 1,850 feet or there would be no Garrison Diversion so I asked the Appropriations Committee to put language into the report requiring it be 1,850 feet. By that time General Pick had left as Chief of the Corps of Engineers and he had a lot of influence with Congress. I thought all I had to do when I wanted it to go 1,850 feet was to keep still and they would put it up there. But when I proposed the 1,850 feet level, the Committee gave me a hard time and even my best friend, Senator Russell, said, "Milt, you have been on both sides of this problem.' He made me work pretty hard to get the pool elevation raised to 1,850 feet which we had to have."

The Garrison Diversion Conservancy District was established by the North Dakota Legislature in 1955. Attempts to pass federal authorization to begin construction of the project were unsuccessful in 1957, 1960, 1963 and 1964.

Young wrote about trying to pass the legislation in his April 25, 1962, *On Capitol Hill* column.

> There has been no perceptible progress in recent weeks on Garrison Diversion legislation. This is presently in the Senate Democrat Policy Committee, which controls the order in which legislation is called up before the full Senate. I believe this policy committee will schedule the Garrison Diversion measure some time soon, or at least before adjournment.

Congress approved the construction authorization in 1965. The groundbreaking for the Snake Creek Pumping Plant, the first Garrison Diversion project, was held July 14, 1968, during the heat of Young's re-election campaign against Fargo Mayor Herschel Lashkowitz. Like the 1953 dedication of Garrison Dam, another crowd numbering in the thousands brought national and state dignitaries to participate in the groundbreaking ceremonies.

Vice President Hubert Humphrey was scheduled to give the main address at the groundbreaking, but was unable to attend because he was ill. Speaking on his behalf was Secretary of Interior Stewart Udall. "The Garrison Diversion Project not only makes agriculture more stable and profitable but also makes North Dakota a more desirable place to live because of the vast increase in recreational facilities it brings," he said. "It will transform North Dakota's economic base and the lives of its citizens far more than any of you know."

In his remarks, Young called the project "the greatest thing that ever happened to North Dakota."

The McClusky Canal was later authorized and built between the years of 1969 and 1976.

Young used his influence on the Appropriations Committee to get the initial construction funding for the Jamestown Dam in 1952, which had been authorized as part of the Missouri-Souris Unit of the Pick-Sloan Missouri River Basin Program in 1944, but had not been funded. He held this up as an example on how to get legislation passed to benefit North Dakota.

"First, whatever you want must be meritorious. Then you have to make a case for your project and get the support of the local people. You have to have strong local interest. With the Jamestown Dam, local interests had appeared three or four times for it. On the next to the last day of the session, a supplemental bill came over from the House late the day before adjournment. Five Senators, including myself, handled that bill and then sent it back to conference with the House. Other Senators had a couple of projects they wanted and I told the committee I would like to add one project, too, if they were going to put other projects in. They said there had been no hearing on the one I wanted in Jamestown. I said I could have the hearing right away but they said, 'No, we haven't got time for that.' They decided to put the money in for it.

"That is how that project got started. It required a lot of work with

others. You can't vote against everything everyone else wants when they are good projects and expect to get something of your own. In order to accomplish things and get projects or anything else, you have to make contacts with your colleagues and do a good job of salesmanship. And its very important that when other Senators have something they want and need, if it has merit, you can't be looking the other way. It's not like you make agreements with other Senators – I'll support this project if you will support mine – I can't think of a single incident of that kind but I think that most Senators are quite considerate. If you help them – some of them forget about it entirely – but others don't. You always have to present a good case."

In an October 11, 1971, *On Capitol Hill* column, Young wrote about the environmental controversies generated by water projects:

From the beginning of my service in the Senate I have either sponsored, co-sponsored, or played a major role in securing the necessary appropriations for every major dam and water project in North Dakota. They include Garrison, Dickinson, Heart Butte, Bald Hill, Jamestown, Pipestem and Bowman-Haley dams and the flood protective works within such cities as Fargo, Grand Forks, Mandan and Minot.

These dams and flood control projects have made great contributions toward alleviating flood losses, providing cheap electrical power, irrigation, recreation and downstream navigation. Practically all of these, and even smaller dams, were opposed by some environmentalists. Invariably there was very strong opposition from some good friends of mine living in the areas adversely affected. There was always the difficult and unhappy task of deciding whether to support or oppose these projects. I supported them when I felt that the good that would come from them, especially in alleviating severe flood conditions, would far outweigh any adverse effects. Over the years I have been in the middle of many of these bitter controversies.

The proposed Burlington Dam near Minot would prevent devastating floods such as the City of Minot has experienced in recent years. This, too, is opposed by some responsible environmentalists and other well-meaning and sincere people who will be adversely affected. Because I believe the benefits far outweigh the adverse effects, I feel it is incumbent upon me to support this project.

One of the more controversial projects has been the river bank stabilization below Garrison Dam. This saved the sewer and water systems at Bismarck and Mandan, two of the big R.E.A. generating plants upstream, and much valuable farm land. The objections have been so severe and wide-ranking that several months ago I advised interested people I would no longer sponsor further authorizing legislation and would prefer to have it handled by other members of the North Dakota Congressional delegation. I would continue to secure the necessary appropriations.

Environmentalists and people living upstream on the Sheyenne River make a strong and appealing case against the construction of the Kindred Dam. I will not be supporting the construction of this dam, and will leave others the sponsoring of this project. I will not stand in their way.

Moderate environmentalists are making a worthwhile contribution in stopping some dams that shouldn't be constructed and recommending new environmental features for those that are being constructed.

As the North Dakota delegation worked to move these water projects through Congress with their colleagues, national environmental organizations and supporters and opponents in the state, and the policy of the incumbent President also tempered their success. This was especially true with President Carter, who cut 19 water projects from his 1978 fiscal budget, including Garrison Diversion. Although Secretary of Interior Cecil Andrus spoke out against the project, Carter indicated he opposed the water projects because of his campaign pledge to reduce government waste. As can be expected, this did not sit well with Young.

"It was difficult to understand. I was really shocked. I had no advance warning that this would happen, but I was one of the first members of Congress, either Republican or Democrat, to be informed of it.

"I notified the Associated Press in Bismarck and they got it on the

wire and then the AP in Washington started digging into it and found that there was a whole list of projects on Carter's 'hit list.' But it was a day or two before all of them were known. President Carter really had no legal right to impound funds which had been authorized and appropriated for this project by Congress. A recent Supreme Court decision required that any impoundment of funds would have to be specifically approved by Congress. Garrison Diversion was authorized under laws passed by Congress and signed by the President. If the President wanted to change a project, about his only recourse would be to ask Congress for new and different authorizations or he could veto an entire appropriations bill, even though such a bill would involved literally hundreds of projects which would all go down the drain.

"The idea of diverting water eastward from the Missouri River – such as the Garrison Diversion project – originated about the time we became a state. North Dakota has spent a lot of time and money on the project ever since. It has had bipartisan support through all these years and no opposition at all until recently, when the Audubon Society became active. As you know, the Audubon Society took legal action against Garrison Diversion through Secretary of Interior Andrus. The Audubon Society and the Secretary of Interior reached an agreement concerning the future of Garrison Diversion, which was approved by Federal District Judge Charles Richey. The State of North Dakota had no part in the agreement made. Secretary Andrus did not have any right to do what he did and neither did the judge who made the deal with the Audubon Society and the Interior Department working with environmentalists to drastically change the project. Judge Richey could order that all construction on the project be stopped but such action could be appealed by the State of North Dakota. The action he took in approving the unreasonable agreement between the Interior Department and the Audubon Society, as I understand it, will cause some real problems as it may not be appealable. This was strictly illegal.

"When we appropriated the money for this project this year [1979], the Senate Appropriations Committee wrote strong language into

our report criticizing the Court and the Interior Department for their actions and directed them to proceed with the construction of the project as authorized by Congress. The President, under Presidential orders, does have considerable power but I can't see any way now that they can avoid going ahead with Garrison Diversion. They can slow it up by throwing roadblocks in the way, and they probably will because Carter, in appointing Andrus as Secretary of the Interior, got some of the toughest environmentalists in the United States as his assistants in the Interior Department. The Bureau of Reclamation, which used to be proud of this project, doesn't even dare speak of it anymore. So the problem of Garrison Diversion becomes very complicated.

"Carter's opposition against Western water projects brought more support than ever for them. People who didn't support them very much came out in favor of them. There is more support now than there ever was. We spent, if you include Jamestown Dam, which is also a part of the Pick-Sloan Plan, about $171 million. Without Jamestown Dam, about $150 million. I got these figures from the Interior Department. I asked what it would cost to terminate the contracts and restore the North Dakota environment to the same as it was before the construction project started and they gave me a figure of $92.3 million. Carter's stand on these Western water projects seemed political – like a way to get back at people who hadn't supported him. But some of the environmental sentiment is changing now because water means so much to the West and I don't think President Carter realized that we wouldn't have 100 million people in the Western part of the United States if it hadn't been for reclamation and water projects. There wouldn't have been that opportunity for them."

Although some water projects were cut, Garrison Diversion was eventually saved in the 1978 budget. And despite the best efforts by North Dakota's Congressional delegation, during Young's tenure in the Senate the project did not receive the federal funds it needed to be completed as originally designed in the 1940s.

Civil Rights

Philosophically, Young was opposed to most civil rights legislation, and voted against two Civil Rights Acts during the Eisenhower Administration, in 1957 and 1960. *"I was opposed to most civil rights legislation. The Supreme Court had pretty well legislated on this subject – probably more than was necessary or they had a right to do. This is one case where I thought the Court did get into legislation. Eisenhower wanted to follow the direction of the Court decision and did call out our troops two or three times at Little Rock and other places. The Southerners made speeches saying that the time would come when we would have a whole lot more trouble with the blacks in the North than they have in the South."*

Many of his closest colleagues were very vocal in their opposition to civil rights legislation, especially the Civil Rights Act of 1964, the most significant civil rights legislation that passed Congress. Young's good friend, Senator Richard Russell of Georgia, led the opposition to the bill when it was considered by the Senate on March 30, 1964, including a 54-day filibuster to prevent its passage. Young voted for all the amendments that were introduced by the Southern Senators, mostly to soften the Act. On June 10, the filibuster ended when Senator Robert Byrd, Democrat from West Virginia, completed a 14-hour, 30-minute speech, and the vote was taken later that day. Young voted for it, and it passed by a vote of 73 to 27. Most of the 27 who voted against it represented the solid Southern block.

"Part of my voting with the Southern Senators had to do with their support for agriculture and measures I thought were important for North Dakota. I am sure my friends Senator Russell and other Southern friends would have preferred that I continue to vote with them all the way through but they understood my feelings on it. I wanted to help them but I thought that the bill had merit even with some shortcomings."

The legislation outlawed racial segregation in schools, public places and employment, and created the Equal Employment Opportunity

Commission to implement the law. It was signed into law by President Johnson on July 2, 1964.

Ethics and Investigations

For a few years in the 1960s Young served on the Senate Ethics Committee, an assignment he didn't enjoy. *"It meant a lot of extra work and a great many charges were made against members of the Senate. Most had little or no substance – but they still wanted an investigation and often demanded public hearings on the charges. The charges were often made against people who were entirely innocent and could have been badly hurt if we had public hearings. I became very disgusted with all the problems of serving on this committee and finally went to the Majority Leader, Mike Mansfield from Montana, and asked to be relieved of my assignment there. He strongly urged me to stay on and I resigned at the end of that year."*

Young did not personally observe many unethical attempts to influence voting. He did, however, become involved in three issues that were investigated. The first happened in 1956. Young brought up an issue with the Senate's Select Committee on Investigations which, true to its name, looked into charges relating to political activities, lobbying and campaign contributions. He asked for an investigation about an article that was written about him by K.W. Simon and R.C. Nathan, who were editor and an officer of *The Leader* newspaper, respectively, which was published by the Democrat-NPL Party. Young believed the article that ran with a headline of "Young Sells Out Again," had made a "completely untruthful smear attack against me by claiming I received a contribution of $5,000 from Henry Grunewald." The investigation found that Grunewald, a Washington influence peddler who had been tied to some previous political scandals, had delivered a campaign contribution check to Young's campaign manager but on behalf of the Republican Senatorial Campaign Committee, not himself.

A June 6, 1956, news release from Young's office about the unanimous decision by the committee said Simon and Nathan testified under oath that they did not mean to say Young had accepted a bribe from anyone; that they had no evidence to prove any of their charges; that they had no evidence to prove Young was guilty of any improper conduct during his 11 years in the Senate; that the newspaper article was meant to embarrass him politically, even if it had meant destroying his character and reputation; and they admitted that the newspaper had made some unwarranted charges but excused this by saying *The Leader* had always been a "hell raising" newspaper.

Chairing the Investigations Committee was Senator John McClellan, a Democrat from Arkansas, who was quoted in the news release as describing the article as "that sordid and irresponsible type of journalism that resorts to the poison pen to contaminate the news and pollute the stream of public information through the media of a free press."

Another investigation involving Young occurred when he was a member of the Senate Ethics and Conduct Committee. *"A reporter called me and said he 'believed' that I had gotten some $3,500 in illegal campaign funds from the Ashland Oil Company. He just said he 'believed' that. He had no evidence but he tried to use it against me. I made a special request for the committee to have our investigators thoroughly investigate this charge because I knew I hadn't received any money from that company. I would have remembered it because the most I ever spent in a campaign before my last was $50,000. The investigation found that the president and the chairman of the board of directors of Ashland Oil Company, and, I think, two others said they knew of no such donation and if there had been one I would have had no way of knowing about it."*

In 1976, Young's love of karate brought questions about his ties to Tongsun Park, a South Korean businessman who was accused of giving illegal campaign funds to members of Congress. Park was charged with using money from the South Korean government in an unsuccessful effort to convince the United States government to keep troops in Vietnam. In 1977, Park was indicted by a U.S. District Court on 36 counts, including bribery, illegal campaign contributions, mail fraud, racketeering, and failure to register as an agent of the Korean Central Intelligence Agency. He avoided a federal trial by testifying to the court in exchange for immunity.

"A reporter for the Christian Science Monitor *called me and said my name had come up as one of those who possibly had some connection with Park. I told him that I had never even met him but I had been president of the Tae Kwon Do Karate Association run by Jhoon Rhee, an American citizen of Korean descent, and had been a very honest person in my dealings with him. He never contributed to my campaign and I never asked him to. I never received any compensation for any kind as president of his Tae Kwon Do Association."*

The investigation by the Ethics Committee completely exonerated Young. *"I was on the Ethics Committee at the time they made these accusations and some of these press people were really on a 'fishing' expedition. The press wanted us to hold open hearings on hearsay evidence that could really ruin some very decent person who was accused of such charges. We didn't hold open hearings as often was demanded because the committee wanted to know for sure we had a case and not just an opportunity to make headlines and ruin some decent person."*

Voting Decisions

Young called half of the roll call votes in the Senate meaningless. *"But an opponent can publish your attendance record and if it is only 60 percent or less it can hurt you some. If I am busy in an important committee meeting with the House and I know the vote is unimportant, I will miss one occasionally. And, quite often a Senator is gone for a couple of weeks – on a foreign trip or something – and will miss a lot of votes while gone. So later he will bring up a lot of amendments – meaningless amendments – and ask for Ayes and Nayes to improve his voting record. We can sometimes get 10 or 15 extra votes in a day that way.*

"Sometimes if it is an important issue that I am not familiar with – and I spend so much of my time on appropriations – from morning until night – and I see some Senator I have a lot of confidence in voting

opposite to the way I intended to vote, I will ask him why and he will usually tell me. And sometimes you will feel they are right and sometimes not. But it does have some effect. Tax matters are a good example. They are very complicated and even the best of lawyers, after they get through writing a tax bill, will disagree on what it means. So I go to two or three and ask them how they are voting and why. Sometimes you will feel they are right and sometimes not. But it does have some effect.

"The same is true on agricultural bills. I was a seatmate of Senator Leverett Saltonstall when he was the ranking Republican on Appropriations. Agriculture didn't mean much in Massachusetts, although they have a little there. In fact, he lives on a little farm now. But when a farm bill would come up, he would usually as me, "Milt, what is my vote?" And I would usually tell him to vote the opposite of me because I knew his thinking on farm matters and I would tell him, your vote is "NO" and mine is "YES." He often mentions that yet. I don't think I ever told him wrong. I wasn't even tempted to, but it would have been nice to. Once in awhile I thought his vote should be the same as mine and that would take a little explanation."

Young was influenced by the mail he received from constituents, which totaled as many as 60,000 letters a year toward the end of his Senate career. *"Alexander Hamilton believed that you should always vote your convictions regardless of the people's thinking. Abraham Lincoln thought much differently. He believed you should pay more attention to what people's views were. But determining the people's thinking often isn't easy. Your mail is always helpful, but sometimes you get a lot of mail on a subject and find out when you get out to the state the sentiment is just the opposite."*

An example of this was the transfer of the operation and defense of the Panama Canal from the United States to Panama in 1977. At the time Young did not base his support for it from the mail he received. *"I don't think all Hell could persuade the majority of people to vote to give away the Panama Canal. This is a good example of where you may not have to vote against the thinking of the majority of the people but I have always had one thing I have stuck by quite closely. If I feel I know more about a subject which involves the security of the United States, I vote the way I think is right, regardless of what public opinion is."*

Young also relied on input from others close to him on voting decisions. *My wife, Pat, has some strong convictions and she gives me a little lecture once in a while. I don't always heed her advice, but sometimes her judgment is better than mine. One key advisor was Chris Sylvester, my administrative assistant. He is a very sharp person and has a good legal mind. He follows legislation quite closely and is very helpful – although there are a lot of amendments that come up that are not even printed and you have to pay close attention during the debate to even know what they are about. He has some strong feelings and sometimes he does influence me. Fortunately, we think quite a bit alike on most things. I do listen to him and his analysis and judgment is good on difficult legal questions. One good example only this year* [1979] *was when I voted for the establishment of a Department of Education. He was strongly opposed to this. Most people thought the House would not approve it, and some Senators often vote for something because they think the House might not approve it, especially toward the end of the session. When they know a bill isn't going to go anywhere they might vote that way. But in the case of the bill to establish a Department of Education, I had committed myself a month or more before."*

Sylvester had been on Young's staff since 1955 and had served on his staff until his retirement. Born on a Red River Valley farm near the town of Thompson, he was raised in nearby Hatton by his grandparents. Following graduation from the University of North Dakota School of Law in 1954, he worked briefly for North Dakota Attorney General Paul Benson, who had worked for Young while he was in law school and eventually became a federal judge. Benson approached Sylvester about moving to Washington to become Young's administrative assistant, more commonly known as "AA." In an August 1979 interview with Dr. D. Jerome Tweton, Sylvester described his job responsibilities during his tenure in Young's office that ran from 1955 to 1975 as "researcher, sounding board, driver, press secretary, just about any role."

Another longtime employee was Louise Christopher, who began working in Young's office in June 1958. A Williston native, she had been a legal secretary for Williston attorney Arley Bjella before moving to Washington in early 1957 to take a stenotype court reporting course. She had planned to return to her home state to become a court reporter. Instead, at the request of Bjella, who was active in state Republican politics, Young and Pat Byrne took her out for dinner when she arrived in the city. This resulted in a close friendship with Pat, and Christopher was hired in the office later that year. Christopher described her work as Young's personal secretary as "taking dictation, paying personal bills, coordinating vacation schedules and travel vouchers for the entire staff, typing and updating his daily schedule of committee assignments, and social engagements."

She described Young's working style: "He kept in close touch with his constituents and made frequent trips back to North Dakota. He had a reputation for being a very conscientious legislator and insisted every single letter from a constituent be promptly acknowledged and answered. At times this seemed to his staff to be a bit of overkill, especially when he wrote 'thank you for your thank you' letters.' He was very generous to his staff with promotions and salaries. The one thing he could not tolerate was tardiness in reporting to work, and accordingly most of the staff members made every effort to be on time each day. He also firmly insisted on loyalty from all his employees."

Upon Young's retirement, Christopher described herself as "the last person on deck who personally closed and locked his office for the final time in January 1981."

Working with state civic leaders

Chester Reiten was mayor of Minot during the 14 years from 1970 to 1984. During those years he had frequent meetings with Young both in Minot and in Washington. He joined Young for lunch on a few occasions in the Senate Dining Room at the Capitol. "Only Senators and their guests could eat there. One time we were there and we met John Stennis, a Southern Democrat, [from Mississippi]. All of a sudden it dawned on me that they were very good friends, they talked, they kidded, just like buddies. So then I figured out, that's why he's so effective. It's because he had a network of people. Then we'd go sit down and eat and the other Senators would come over and they would chit chat with him, and go on. Some of them were Democrat. He was effective because he had a network of friends who helped him out. It wasn't just what the bill had to say. They trusted him and they respected him."

Reiten also observed his effectiveness when it came to flood control legislation. "By 1972, Minot had had four serious floods. Several times I went to see Senator Young about flood control and I testified in front of a committee. He asked me good questions, and when it got done, he would say, 'This is important to the people of Minot and we will want to pass it.' And it always passed."

During another visit, Reiten was in Young's office when the White House called. "The person calling from the White House said to him, "Senator Young, we want you to come over here to have some discussions on a bill.' The Senator said, 'I'm sorry, I'm very busy and can't come.' Well, the only one in there was me, and if he had said, 'out you go,' I would have gone on. Instead, he said to me, 'Never allow them to think they have you in the palm of their hand. Never allow them to think that they can be assured of your vote or else they will forget about you. Always have it so they're not too sure about what you will do.' I thought that was great insight to how he worked there. He wasn't a pawn of anybody."

Among the buildings and projects in the state that bear Young's names is Minot's Milton R. Young Towers public housing project. Built in 1972, these 220-unit public housing towers are located near Minot's downtown area.

Longtime Jamestown engineer and civic leader Johnny Klingenberg recalled Young's efforts to bring more industry to North Dakota in the early 1960s. Following an address Young gave to the 1961 Legislative

Assembly about the need for more industrial expansion, Jamestown leaders hosted a meeting in their city. "A number of people from all over the state came, to meet businesses from out of state. Senator Young told us to pay extra attention to the people from Western Gear, which built equipment for aircraft and military vehicles," Klingenberg remembered, because Young thought Jamestown could be a good relocation site for Western Gear.

"Getting Western Gear to relocate here from Washington state was a big boost to the Jamestown area," Klingenberg said. "The company hired 100 people right off the bat. Our city industrial development committee raised money and was able to get industrial development revenue bonds to lease land near the airport to build the plant." The business continues to operate in Jamestown, now under the name of Lucas Aerospace.

Klingenberg said of Young: "People around here loved him. Whenever he was in the area, he would stop and meet some of us for a cup of coffee. He wanted to know what our concerns were. He was always looking out for the town."

Young used his influence to bring other industrial manufacturers with ties to the military to the state, including Lockheed to Minot in 1970, Northrop, now Northrop Grumman, to New Town in 1971, and Brunswick, now Sioux Manufacturing Corporation, to Fort Totten in 1974.

Restoring Ford's Theatre

One of the first historic places Young visited when he arrived in Washington, D.C., in 1945 was Ford's Theatre. Built in 1863, it closed as a theater two years later following the assassination of President Abraham Lincoln by John Wilkes Booth on April 14, 1865. The building was leased and later purchased by the federal government for office space and storage beginning in August 1865, and it housed an Army Medical Museum for a decade beginning in 1867. The interior collapsed in 1893, and a Lincoln museum opened in the facility in 1932.

A longtime admirer of Lincoln, Young talked to some staff of the National Park Service during that first visit who told him they regretted its poor condition and that it hadn't been restored. *"They explained how weak the walls were getting, and that planes were forbidden from flying over it in certain kinds of weather."*

The staff didn't know at the time that Young and another North Dakotan would be instrumental in seeing the theater restored. Fargo native Melvin D. Hildreth, Jr., was a Washington attorney whose clients included the Ringling Brothers Barnum and Bailey Circus, and who was active in Democrat politics in the District of Columbia. So well-connected to Washington politics was he that President Truman appointed him to be general chairman of his 1949 inauguration ceremony, directing the activities of some 30 committees working on inauguration plans. He also handled grandstand arrangements for three Franklin Roosevelt inaugurations. Hildreth had an interest in seeing some improvements to Ford's Theatre, and sent Young a letter during his first year in the Senate asking him to introduce legislation to restore it. This was the beginning of an effort that Young and Hildreth would pursue for years. In February 1946, Young introduced Joint Resolution 139, which directed the Secretary of the Interior to estimate the cost of restoring it.

Young and Hildreth attended several Senate and House Interior Committee hearings on that resolution, and when that was unsuccessful, on similar resolutions he introduced in future sessions. *"The committee members were always friendly, but somehow the Southerners, many of them good friends of mine, like Richard Russell, didn't like the idea of restoring Ford's Theatre. They seemed to think in doing so they would be idolizing Lincoln, so very quietly the bill would be killed. Some people in the city of Washington also opposed it, with some of them fearing the competition of another live theater. The question always came up with the Committee members as to whether it would be another live theater. I always said no, because there was other live theater in the city."*

In the early 1950s, Young brought Senator Willis Smith, a Democrat who had been Governor of North Carolina before being elected to the Senate, over to the theater. *"He fell in love with the idea and he would have been a great help had he not died of a heart attack in 1953."*

Throughout the years, the area's daily newspapers were supportive of the effort, but it took eight years of continued work on the part of Young and Hildreth before any legislative progress was made.

Their first victory came in 1954, when a resolution passed that required the Park Service and an architect to come up with plans and costs of restoring the theater. On the House side, Republican Congressman George A. Dondero of Michigan introduced identical legislation to Young's in the Senate, and President Eisenhower signed the legislation May 28, 1954.

The battle then moved to securing funding for the restoration. *"I would try every year. I would get the money in the Senate bill but when we went to conference with the House, they said if you come back next year and appear before our committee for it, we will probably approve it. I did that several times and finally the House conferees approved my bill. The first procedure involved getting funds to investigate the feasibility and cost estimates of the restoration. Once I got that through, getting the appropriations was much easier."*

Finally, in 1964, 18 years after Young introduced the first resolution, Congress authorized $2 million to restore Ford's Theatre.

When it was complete, *Washington Post* reporter Richard L. Coe wrote in his January 12, 1968, *One on the Aisle* column about Young's role in the Ford's Theatre restoration:

> There are at least two requisites for getting anything done in Washington: patience and bipartisanship. The approaching opening of the restored Ford's Theatre highlights this trimly. In 1945, Sen. Milton R. Young (R-N.D.) was serving an appointive term which North Dakota voters have been extending ever since.
>
> Because he was a North Dakotan but, as a Washington resident had no vote, Democrat Melvin D. Hildreth confided an idea to the Republican Senator: Why not, as an aid to historians and tourists, restore Ford's Theatre as closely as possible to how it looked the night of April 14, 1865? By the following February (1946), Sen. Young had introduced a Senate resolution to that effect. Gradually fellow legislators began to get approval from the grassroots. President Eisenhower finally signed the bill in 1954. By then Mr. Hildreth was Washington's Mr. Democrat.
>
> Research work on ways and means then was taken up by Interior's National Park Service. In 1955 it estimated $2 million would be needed to plan such reconstruction. It took some years to get an appropriation for a bit over two million to carry out the project. In mid-1964 this was settled through the active interest of Interior Secretary Udall.
>
> Thus, it will be 22 years and some months between the birth of an idea and its fruition when, on Jan. 20, a special telecast inaugurates the restored building. For the young men in Vietnam that was a lifetime, for the White House it was four Presidents, and for all concerned it was bipartisan down the line.

Sen. Young has observed, "A great many people played major roles in making this restoration possible, almost too many to name because oversights would be unintentional. But, there was one great soul who was largely responsible for encouraging me to undertake this project, the late Melvin Hildreth. His enthusiasm and dedication were always a source of inspiration to me," said Young.

Democrat Hildreth died in 1959, but it's good to know that his Republican friend remembers him as that dream is becoming a happening.

Although usually content to remain on the sidelines, Young was in the limelight at the dedication of the restored Fort's Theatre and Lincoln Museum on January 21, 1968. Secretary of the Interior Stewart Udall presided at the dedication and introduced guests. Young gave a history of the reconstruction, which restored the theater to the way it was the night Lincoln was assassinated. Senator Charles Percy, the junior Senator from Illinois, stood in for Senator Everett Dirksen, the senior Senator from Illinois, who was scheduled to give readings from Lincoln. Dirksen was ill.

The U.S. Army Chorus and National Gallery each performed music of the period, and the actor Jason Robards gave a poetic reading.

On January 30, CBS television broadcast live nationally an all-star "gala" from the theater, giving the general public the first look at the newly restored site. The long-time director of the theater was Frankie Hewitt, the wife of CBS Television executive Don Hewitt, creator of the flagship CBS News program, *60 Minutes,* which premiered that fall.

On February 12, legendary actress Helen Hayes became the first actress to appear on the theater's stage since Laura Keene starred in the performance of "Our American Cousin" the night Lincoln was shot April 14, 1865. This 1968 performance – on Lincoln's 159th birthday – was a theatrical version of Stephen Vincent Benet's epic poem, "John Brown's Body."

Despite the original intent of the legislation that the theater would not stage live performances in order to not compete with other similar venues in the city, Secretary Udall insisted that it feature live performances in honor Lincoln, who enjoyed attending the theater.

On February 18, 1974, Senator Hubert Humphrey of Minnesota delivered the following remarks on the Senate floor that explained how Ford's Theatre came to host live performances:

"Some think I do wrong to go to the opera and the theater; but it rests me. I love to be alone, and yet to be with people. A hearty laugh relieves me; and I seem better able after it to bear my cross." Quote by Abraham Lincoln.

President Lincoln knew well the charm and beauty of another great theater – Ford's Theatre. He attended perhaps a dozen performances at Ford's during his four years as President.

In light of his great love for the performing arts, it is a tragic irony that the fact of his assassination at the theater provoked an attitude of hate toward the very thing he valued so highly. In the aftermath of Lincoln's assassination at Ford's, actors were stoned in the streets and theaters were closed all over America. Secretary of War Edwin Stanton ordered Ford's Theatre permanently closed, its beautiful interior gutted and for more than 100 years it stood as a bleak reminder of the tragedy brought on by the act of a madman.

No small part of the tragedy was that Abraham Lincoln's humanistic involvement with the performing arts was all but forgotten. And perhaps it would have remained so but for the dogged perseverance of two quite dissimilar but both extraordinary people.

One is a Member of this body – Senator Milton Young, whose persistent efforts to have Ford's Theatre reconstructed to reflect the beauty and elegance it enjoyed in 1865 spanned some 15 years. Year after year Senator Young made his appeal for restoration of this beautiful building and slowly but surely he lined up the support for its eventual reconstruction.

During those early years Senator Young conceived of the restoration as a museum project. He wanted the theater to look as it did in 1865 so that when visitors came from all over the world they would see a national historic site worthy of the name. It was midway in the planning for this museum that the meeting took place which altered this concept.

Frankie Hewitt, an energetic, intelligent, dynamic and beautiful woman, whose own life of dedication to bettering the lot of mankind is not unlike that of President Lincoln, ran into an old acquaintance at the theater in New York City one evening in 1965. He was then-Secretary of the Interior Stewart Udall, under whose direction the reconstruction of Ford's Theatre was about to begin.

In casual conversation about the restoration project, Frankie asked if plans were included to use it as a theater, and was told they were not. She suggested that restoring the site of an assassination as such was akin to building a monument to a murder, and suggested, instead, that restoring it as an active theater would make it a living memorial to a great President's love for humanity and the performing arts.

Fortunately, she found a ready ally in Secretary Udall, who shared her love for the performing arts. His only question was how such a theater program could be financed and run in a National Historic Site. The government could not and should not undertake such a program directly, he felt, and he did not know if alternatives were available.

Mrs. Hewitt assured him that the theatrical community would enthusiastically support a program at Ford's and she felt equally sure that sufficient private funds could be found to support such an undertaking. At that time, she was merely expressing an opinion, in no way expecting that almost the whole burden of making it all come true would eventually fall to her.

And so began what must seem like a lifetime of weekly commuting from her home in New York City, where her husband, Don Hewitt, producer of the immensely successful CBS-TV news show, *60 Minutes,* and her two children live, to Washington. She called on Senator Young and found an ally; she got Mrs. Lyndon Johnson and the White House involved; she explained her idea to interested Members of Congress; she worked long and hard trying to win over a reluctant bureaucracy. And then, once the political decisions had been made, she undertook to find a theatrical producer and the private funds necessary to launch Ford's as a national theater.

In a July 22, 1970, *Washington Post* article about the theater, Young was quoted about his first restoration efforts in the Senate in 1946. "I really had very little faith in the bill at the time, because a bill to build a bridge across the Missouri River had been batting around for 40 years and nothing ever came of it."

Ford's Theatre is administered by the National Park Service, and a plaque stood in the theater's museum for many years recognizing Young's efforts. It read, "In commemoration of the dedicated efforts of the Honorable Milton R. Young, Senator from North Dakota, whose single-minded devotion enabled the restoration of this historic building, January 21, 1968."

"When it first opened, they asked me to be a member of the Ford's Theatre Society Board of Trustees and I was for a couple of years. I usually could not attend all their meetings so they took me off and put my wife, Pat, on the Board. She enjoyed this and I always suspected one of the reasons they wanted my participation was that they could be quite sure it would be continued as a live theater."

Three months after his retirement from the Senate, the Youngs were recognized during a March 21, 1981, "A Festival at Ford's" performance at the theater. An ornate festival program ran full-page photographs of the featured performers, who included Tony Bennett, George Benson, Lynda Carter, Johnny Cash, David Copperfield, Rodney Dangerfield, Dom DeLuise, Andy Gibb, Lena Horne, Marilyn Horne, Loretta Lynn, Natalia Makarova, Luciano Pavarotti, Itzhak Perlman, Juliet Prowse, Dame Joan Sutherland, Twyla Tharp and Andy Williams. Along with these performers, the program also included a full-page photograph of the Youngs, who were unable to attend the event.

In the program, Hewitt wrote:

> Ford's Theatre was restored to its present elegance because of the perseverance and dedication of one man, the Honorable Milton R. Young, who came to Washington 35 years ago as a Republican Senator from North Dakota. It was in his very first year here that the freshman Senator launched the bipartisan collaboration which became Ford's hallmark.
>
> . . . Senator Young's perseverance finally paid off

in 1964 when $2 million was voted by Congress and the restoration work was begun. Back in those days, it was thought that Ford's would be restored primarily as a national historic site, a museum housing an important collection of Lincoln memorabilia. Many people in the theatrical world, however, felt that it should once again serve as a living theatre, a place of joy and laughter, a living testament to President Lincoln's oft-demonstrated love for the performing arts. I was among those people.

There was a considerable body of thought opposed to the live theatre concept, and it included people in positions of authority over Ford's. So it was that in mid-1967 I decided to pay a call on Senator Young to try and win his support for our budding live theatre program. To my complete and utter delight, I found an enthusiastic ally.

Ford's Board of Trustees recently ordered a special medallion with an engraving of President Lincoln on one side and Ford's Theatre on the other. A limited edition of numbered silver medallions had been ordered and they, along with a bronze version, will be sold to raise money for the theatre program. At its last meeting the trustees expressed the feeling that Medallion Number One rightfully belonged to Senator Milton R. Young. And so, we close this gala evening to pay tribute to one who could truly be called the "Patron Saint of Ford's Theatre."

In going back over the records in preparation for this message, I was tickled to run across a quote by Senator Young regarding Ford's, in which he said, "this is one of the few projects with which I have been involved for which I have received no criticism at all." Tonight we can only offer more praise and a deeply-felt thank you.

In 2004, Eva Reffell, a University of Michigan graduate student, wrote a research paper on the efforts between 1865 and 1958 to reconstruct the theater. Among her conclusions on why Young and Hildreth were successful in reopening it when others were not was because they represented the first generation of Americans "who had no connection to the upheaval of the Civil War." She wrote, "Despite its effacement, Ford's Theatre was remembered throughout the 19th century, and in the 1920s aging Union soldiers and their descendents worked to designate the building as the Lincoln Museum. In doing so, they tried to perpetuate the memory of their own war, identities and political priorities."

Reffell added, "The reopening of the theater in 1968 as both a cultural institution and a memorial to Lincoln seems to have ended its controversial status. Few people are invested in how Lincoln's assassination is represented now that he, his contemporaries and their children are dead."

In his remarks at the dedication in 1968, Young reflected on the years he spent on the theater's reconstruction. His thoughts were also expressed in an article in the February 2, 1968, issue of *Time* Magazine:

"A visit to the Nation's Capitol is a great experience for many families. Long-planned and expectantly awaited, it is undertaken with great enthusiasm. Here is a city that belongs to every American, the seat of our national government, the scene hallowed by the great names in the drama of American history. Now for those who revere Lincoln, a visit to the restored Ford's Theatre will be an unforgettable experience. To me, it is a dream come true."

Eight Presidents

Young considered himself an independent politician who wasn't afraid to be a maverick, and his political decisions reflected this throughout the years in public service. He spoke frequently of his admiration for President Abraham Lincoln, and thought highly of President Thomas Jefferson. In the Senate, he served with John Kennedy, Lyndon Johnson and Richard Nixon before they became President. During his years in the Senate, eight presidents occupied the Oval Office.

What follows are Young's remembrances of each:

Franklin D. Roosevelt (1882-1945; President March 4, 1933 - April 12, 1945): Young began serving in the Senate during the final month of Franklin Roosevelt's 12-year Presidency. Although Roosevelt's popularity was strong, it was Young's observation that the Democratic Party in later years did not invoke FDR's name as often and seemed to want to distance itself from him. *"For a while after Roosevelt died, no Democrat would make a speech unless he lauded Franklin Roosevelt, but they soon dropped that."*

Harry S. Truman (1884-1972; President April 12, 1945 - January 20, 1953): Young considered Truman to be one of the best friends the farmers had in the White House. *"He strongly favored a farm program."*

Young observed that Truman started out very popular, with much support as the man who assumed the Presidency following the sudden death of Roosevelt. Young called him a "middle-of-the-roader." But he watched as Truman became more liberal and his policies more controversial, to the point that he was the underdog in his 1948 election bid.

In August 1948, Truman called a special session of Congress, which displeased Young. *"There was a lot of politics involved in it and I believe it re-elected President Truman. I attended a joint session of the 80th Congress just before Congress adjourned but before the special session was called, and President Truman didn't get much applause at all. It looked like he was all done for. Shortly afterwards he called the special session, and he campaigned hard against Congress, calling it a 'do-nothing Congress' on his whistle stop campaigns by train across the country."*

Just before the election, he was so unpopular most people thought this was the end of Truman. He came back with a tough campaign and beat Dewey. I met and talked to Dewey quite a few times.

Young had several personal conversations with Truman when he was President. *"Once at a luncheon over at the White House, Truman invited about a dozen Democrats and me – I was the only Republican. I never quite understood why and I had a lot of questions from Republicans wanting to know why I happened to be at that luncheon. He also wouldn't use the power of the Presidency too much for support on legislation. He would always ask in a nice way."*

When delegations from North Dakota's Indian reservations came to Washington, they asked to meet the President. At Young's request, Truman agreed to see four or five groups of state Indians.

Truman was one of the friendliest Presidents to me of any of them. I don't know as if I ever helped him very much either. He had a lot of good qualities. He took the responsibility for things that had to be done. He understood agriculture and was friendly toward it. And I think he understood the average businessman's problems. I think he will go down in history regarded as a stronger President than he was when he left the Presidency, and that isn't true of all of them."

Dwight D. Eisenhower (1890-1969, President January 20, 1953 - January 20, 1961): Although he supported Senator Robert Taft of Ohio for President over Eisenhower at the 1952 Republican Convention, Young campaigned for Eisenhower once he received the Party's nomination. One of Young's favorite photographs shows him with Eisenhower shortly before the general election of 1952, which appears on the back cover of this book. It was taken October 4, 1952, as part of a statewide campaign swing that also took them to Bismarck. *"The photograph was taken outside the North Dakota State University Field House in Fargo when Eisenhower was making campaign stops through the state on the Northern Pacific Railroad. A Grand Forks photographer covering the event told me he would like to have a picture of me with my arms around Eisenhower, like what Senator Langer often did with visiting dignitaries to the state. Milt Rue of Bismarck and George Longmire of Grand Forks, two of the state's prominent Republicans, thought it was an excellent idea and could be done.*

"So on this cold, windy night, the photographer opened the car door where Eisenhower was sitting prior to returning to the train station and he explained to him about the photograph he wanted. In a typical expression for Eisenhower, he said, 'By golly, I'll go for that.' So he got out of the car and the photographer took the one snap that turned out to be a good picture of us."

During the 1952 Presidential campaign, Eisenhower promised that if he were elected he would go to Korea to inspect the military situation first-hand. In November, shortly after defeating Democrat Adlai Stevenson in a landslide, Eisenhower kept his promise. Young was one of the Senators asked to travel with Eisenhower's delegation to Korea.

"On international matters, Eisenhower was far more capable than most of our Presidents. For one thing, he never gave any indication of what he might or might not do, like whether he would use a nuclear bomb or not. Tough characters like Stalin knew he was a general and they knew if there were any trouble, he would go all out to win."

Young got along well with him. *"My relations with Eisenhower were very good but typical of a general. He had good staff and some of them were military men. He had a staff you could trust and his word was always good."*

Eisenhower would call Young for support on legislation. *"In 1953, I helped make arrangements for President Eisenhower to attend the big state celebration for completing Garrison Dam. He called and said, 'Milt, I am coming out for the closing ceremony and I am going to stay at Minot and go to that dinner that you suggested.' Then he said, 'Now I would like to have you vote so and so on this bill.' And I told him that I would do almost anything for him but I had already committed myself on this bill and I didn't see how I could change it. But I often thought afterwards it didn't amount to that much. I could have gone with him and written to the people who contacted me and made a public statement apologizing for having voted differently than I had indicated."*

Young supported the 1956 Federal Highway Act. *"It is one of the best things Eisenhower ever did, and he didn't get enough credit for it. I often thought they should name the interstate systems the 'Ike Highway' or the 'Eisenhower System.' He tied it into national defense – the ability to move a lot of traffic. It was something that was needed and it made it easier to sell to Congress."*

Following Eisenhower's heart attack in September 1955, Young was impressed at how he carefully followed his doctor's instructions. *"I remember eating with him at the White House. If he had roast beef, he'd look carefully to see of there was a little strain of fat in it and if there was, he'd send it back."*

Although they never played golf together, Young played at Burning Tree Golf Course in Bethesda, Maryland, several times at the same time as Eisenhower did. *"It was interesting with the Secret Servicemen all over – some of them with machine guns in golf bags."*

Young said about Eisenhower: *"In later years, Eisenhower wasn't one of the more brilliant Presidents, but I think he was a good President for the time."*

In 1956, when both Young and Eisenhower were up for re-election, Young received the highest percentage of votes of any Republican candidate for the U.S. Senate. Eisenhower received 57.4 percent in winning a second term in his rematch with Democrat challenger Adlai Stevenson. Young won 63.9 percent of the votes in his victory over Quentin Burdick.

John F. Kennedy (1917-1963; President January 20, 1961 - November 22, 1963): *"I always thought that he had more personality than either of his brothers, Teddy or Bobby, but many of the members of the Senate wouldn't agree with me on that. I got to be a pretty close friend of John Kennedy and liked him personally. I don't think he was quite as liberal as the other Kennedy brothers."*

Young and Kennedy co-sponsored a bill together. *"That was a bit unusual. The textile mills, which use a lot of wool, were mostly located in Massachusetts and the New England states, and they were always fighting with the wool growers. Finally they got together on a bill and the wool growers wanted me to sponsor it and the textile people wanted John Kennedy. So he and I sponsored the legislation that was part of the 1954 Farm Bill. It is practically the same wool legislation we have now. It worked out well. There has been no problem renewing it every time it expired."*

When President Carter nominated Theodore Sorensen in late 1976 to be the head of the Central Intelligence Agency, Sorensen came to Young's office and reminded him that he had been the administrative assistant for then-Senator John Kennedy and had helped write that wool bill.

"Kennedy had a brilliant mind and I could discuss farm policies with him. I remember when he was campaigning in North Dakota (for President in 1960), *he spoke at the airport in Fargo and he said he was for the same farm program that Milt Young is for. Kennedy then teased, 'I don't know how he can oppose me in this election.'*

"He tried to establish the Alliance for Progress in building Latin American relations. I remember the trip he made down there. This is a good example of where I think a President has too much authority on foreign matters. While he was down there he promised many billions of

dollars worth of assistance – something he could never sell to Congress."

During the Cuban Missile Crisis in October of 1962, Young recalled, *"I learned through intelligence sources a week or two before this broke that the Russians had missiles there and I am sure President Kennedy learned about it about the same time or before. I was up for election then and I mentioned the fact that the Russians had missiles there. I thought Khrushchev would back down. If we had had ambitious military people, it could have easily escalated into a war. They could have claimed that we had a destroyer shot at or something like that and we could have been off to the races. I think President Kennedy handled the Cuban situation very well. I was pleasantly surprised because of his age and not being tested.*

"The Bay of Pigs was an unfortunate thing. But one of the decent things about President Kennedy was that he assumed full responsibility for it. I think he was persuaded by the people who escaped from Cuba that it would be easy for the CIA project to succeed because once the invaders got into Cuba, the local people were so anti-Castro that they would all flock to them. Here is one case where I don't think the CIA was well informed about Castro's Cuba. Of course, the CIA was told to organize troops for the invasion of Cuba. It wasn't their idea but they were told to do so by President Kennedy and the Security Council. They should have known how difficult such an operation would be. Of course one thing that was promised was that we were going to give them air support but Kennedy changed his mind on that the day of the invasion and stopped the air support. But I don't think it would have succeeded anyway."

Young thought Kennedy was a good President. *"He was the same person in the White House as he was in the Senate. He probably won't go down in history as one of the greatest but I think he would have gone down in history as a good President if he could have kept on serving. One of President Kennedy's greatest assets was that he had the support and confidence of the younger people. The younger generation would have helped him become a great President. One of the problems today is that most of the candidates for President don't have the following of the younger people. A lot of young people don't even vote because they just aren't that much interested. But if you had a Kennedy – like John – they would be voting."*

Lyndon B. Johnson (1908-1973; President November 22, 1963 - January 20, 1969): *"Johnson was the ablest majority floor leader in my time in the Senate. He was really cut out for that kind of thing. He was always a friendly person. Every once in awhile I would have lunch with him in the office of the Secretary of the Senate, along with half a dozen other Senators. They would be all Republicans and he would tell us some things about his problems with his Democrat colleagues. He was quite outspoken about it."*

One time when he was running for President in 1960 before his selection as Kennedy's running mate, Johnson called Young over to his desk. *"He said, 'I want you to get some delegates for me in North Dakota.' I said, 'How in the hell can I get any delegates for you in North Dakota, I am a Republican.' He said, 'That doesn't make any difference. I want you to get some delegates for me.' I think I did get him at least one."*

Young and Johnson shared common interests, such as agriculture and oil. *"He loved politics. I think one of the reasons why he was so influential was his sense of humor and his method of approach to people. He had a unique way of saying things that I think is in a way common to a lot of Texas people. They have more humorous ways of asking and answering questions."*

In 1953, when Johnson was elected Majority Leader, the numerical balance was so close between the Republicans and the Democrats in the Senate, that any defections one way or the other could make the difference on a partisan vote. *"Senator Johnson was sometimes called a 'wheeler and dealer.' If you had some problem he might help you out by bringing it up out of order to have it considered a little earlier than otherwise. This was something he was good at, something that most any good party leader often does. They don't have to trade with you, but if you have some important legislation you want considered they can either bring it up next week or maybe two or three months later. Consideration of that kind is perfectly legitimate. They can help you. Senator Johnson was that way. He was, as I said before, very personable and likeable. You couldn't dislike him."*

As a floor leader, Young said Johnson was different from any other. *"He'd argue with a lot of his own Democrats. He'd get a little tough with them at times, but with the sense of humor he had he would usually bring them around."*

If Johnson wanted Young's support on something, he'd try to persuade him on the merit of the issue. *"He never suggested a trade or anything with me. He was a very persuasive fellow. Of course, he and I naturally thought about alike on so many things. My major interest – of course as a farmer all my life – was farm matters. And, I just always believed, long before I came to the Senate, in the need for having the most modern equipment possible for the military forces."*

After suffering a heart attack in 1955, Young thought Johnson *"slowed up some for quite awhile, but he wound up smoking and drinking again. He was still a good operator; it didn't bother him in that way. I think he restricted his working hours a little more and the public functions that he would go to. He was still very effective."*

Young didn't believe Johnson was happy as Vice President under Kennedy. *"He wanted to operate more on his own. The Vice Presidency wasn't his cup of tea. A Vice President is supposed to listen to the President all the time and do what he wants him to do, run errands for him, speak for him, what not. Vice President Johnson was a little bit too independent as to be parroting ideas that the President wanted. I think they got along all right, but there was some cleavage."* North Dakota voted for Johnson over Goldwater in 1964, one of the few times – and to date the last time – that North Dakota has been carried by the Democratic Presidential candidate in the general election.

Young attended two meetings at the White House in a month's time when the Vietnam War was beginning to escalate. *"There was a question about what we would do about Vietnam – go all out to win or get out. President Johnson asked each of us for our views. At both meetings, I told him that unless we could get a lot of help from our allies, we had better keep out of a war like that.*

"*He was a ruthless politician in a way, but one of the most friendly of all. I went over to see him several times alone when he was President – perhaps more than all of the other Presidents put together. We would talk about farm matters and he asked my views on a lot of other things. I remember that one time I was there when a farm bill was pending. It had passed the Senate and was pending in the House. He was quite interested in it and said, 'I want you to go back and make a speech in the Senate on it.' I said, 'Mr. President, it passed the Senate and is over in the House.' And he said, 'It doesn't make a damn bit of difference, I want you to go and make a speech.' So I went back and did quite a lot of work on about a 20-minute speech.*"

He believed Johnson to be the most down-to-earth President he knew. "*He was a real friendly person. A likable person but, as I said before, I think he was more cut out as a leader of the Senate than as a President. He was very good at arm twisting on Capitol Hill and he had a good memory – especially when some of his own people voted against him after they had promised to vote with him!*

"*He was a good listener. He studied people. He made a point of understanding every Senator, their peculiarities and their thinking. He knew them very well. He knew about you and how you were going to vote or about how you planned to vote. For me it was agriculture and military things, as well as anything affecting the oil industry and foreign matters. I supported him in the Vietnam War. I was opposed to getting into it in the first place, but I felt that it was something we couldn't run away from. I didn't think cutting off appropriations or crippling our military effort was the way to end the war. It was a war that I don't think he was responsible for. He inherited it. I think it broke his heart to leave the Presidency that way, because it was probably the sole reason he decided not to run again.*"

Neil Bjornson, Young's agricultural aide during the Johnson Presidency, remembered one of the few times he saw Young "sweat" over an issue was when Johnson nominated Abe Fortas to the Supreme Court. "He had committed to Johnson that he would support the nomination," Bjornson recalled. "And as things developed, and as new information came to light, he came to the conclusion that he just couldn't support him." Young told Bjornson, "You don't just walk to the floor and cast your vote. I told the President I would support Fortas, and now I've got to tell him I can't." If it wasn't the toughest decision he ever made, Bjornson believed it was one of the most difficult. "Making that call to the White House to tell Johnson wasn't easy. Lyndon Johnson wasn't an easy man to say no to."

"He initiated too many new social programs that we are paying for now. Even the liberals didn't give him much credit. He should have had all the credit in the world from them but he got involved in the Vietnam War and sent our first troops over there. They never did forgive him for that.

"One incident I will never forget was when Senator Carl Hayden of Arizona died in January of 1969, President Johnson gave one of the eulogies for him, and Senator Barry Goldwater the other. Both were very touching tributes. Goldwater had grown up with Senator Hayden and was very close to him. Later, Johnson attended a reception in the home of a nephew of Senator Hayden and there was a long line waiting to shake hands with the President. When I got to him, he gave me the darndest bear hug you have ever seen. This was typical of him. He was a loving person – especially to those he liked. This was the last time I ever saw him."

Johnson died on January 22, 1973, at the age of 64.

Richard M. Nixon (1913-1994; President January 20, 1969 - August 9, 1974): Young believed that in many respects Nixon was a great President.

He thought Nixon's long record as an anti-Communist while in Congress and as Vice President and President was helpful in dealing with the Russians. *"The Russians especially seemed to trust a man like that more than they do some of the liberals who publicly give them some support. They knew exactly where he stood. The Russian leaders grew up in rough and tough politics and as a result they seemed to understand and trust that kind of person, and Nixon was that kind of person. We have a difficult problem appropriating enough money for defense now. I never had too much enthusiasm that they would ever accomplish much with détente. I never thought that Communist Russia would keep its word. It might do some good. We have to try to limit arms, and I hope it works, but I have never been a great enthusiast about this kind of disarmament."*

Nixon was more liberal on domestic issues, Young believed. *"One example is revenue sharing, which he sponsored and I opposed. It has been very costly but very popular with all the political subdivisions, even though it costs a lot of money. I remember when a delegation of North Dakota legislators was in Washington and wanted to see Nixon. I didn't think it would be possible but I called and he said, 'Fine, come on over.' He used them as an audience to get on his soapbox and tell all the good things about revenue sharing and all these legislators agreed with him – and I still voted against it. I still feel that way about revenue sharing, but we have it now and the federal government just borrows the money to finance it."*

Visits to the White House and private conversations with Nixon were not as frequent as with Johnson. *"On several occasions when I would go to the White House with the Republican leadership or with the joint Democrat-Republican leadership, he would ask me to wait and we would have a few words about pending difficult issues. I didn't make special trips over there to visit alone with him as I did with Johnson. Sometimes he would call me for support on certain bills.*

Nixon did have some good people and I think Kissinger will go down in history as the ablest Secretary of State we ever had and probably one of the best. Nixon was a hard worker, he didn't relax much, except he played a little golf. He loved golf and he would have been far better off if he had played more golf. Nixon was under a terrific strain most of the time."

Young voted for Harold Carswell and Clement Haynesworth, both rejected as Nixon's nominees to the U.S. Supreme Court in 1970. *"The main reason I think the Senate rejected them is because they were too conservative, especially on civil rights issues."*

Young didn't like Nixon's Vice President Spiro T. Agnew. *"I didn't feel too sorry for him when he got into trouble and had to eventually leave office. He wasn't my choice in the first place and he was never the friendly type – more the hard-boiled type. I always suspected he had been mixed up in some bad deals in Baltimore and Maryland."*

A large dinner for Young in Fargo in 1970 commemorating Young's 25 years in the Senate drew a crowd of some 2,000 people, and Vice President Agnew was the speaker. *"He was quite popular at that time but I remember he stayed at the Town House [Hotel] and neither I nor anyone else could get up to see him. He wouldn't come down to visit with the people that he should. Even at the airport, for example, the high school band from LaMoure had come to Fargo and played at the airport when we arrived. I wanted him to go over and say hello to the band and I had quite a hard time getting him to do that. The Secret Service was always giving instructions, and, of course, the more they stay away from people, the better they like it. There were several others I thought would be better to be Nixon's Vice President, including Congressman Gerald Ford."*

Nixon's lessening of tensions with China and the Soviet Union and his handling of the Middle East situation were what Young believed were his greatest accomplishments as President. *"His greatest contribution was foreign policy because we couldn't keep on with that Cold War forever. Directly as a result of this, we sold the Russians a lot of wheat and our farmers got $5 wheat for the first time. This $5 wheat, however, did cause some problems such as inflated land prices. I remember one time being over in the Soviet Union right after they opened it to visits. I was with the four Senators and one of them was Senator Molly Malone* *of Nevada. He would argue rough and tough politics with them and almost swear at them but when we went to leave, they had their arms around him like a long lost brother. He was the one they liked the best and talked with the most.*

" I don't know if they can ever resolve the Middle East problems, but he and Kissinger went about as far and effectively as anyone could. It is amazing that a man like Nixon could become friends with President Sadat of Egypt and President Hafez al-Assad of Syria when these two countries were bitter enemies. I remember one comment that Kissinger made about Sadat. Shortly after a meeting with him, he said he is a far more intelligent man than most people give him credit for. "

Young believed limiting a President to two elected terms might have contributed to Nixon's Watergate crisis. *"I often thought that a limitation on the terms that a President can serve isn't as good as it appears. I voted for it but I am not sure it wasn't a mistake. If Nixon thought there was a possibility he might run again, for example, I think he might have conducted himself a little differently. "*

His initial reaction when the Watergate scandal began to burgeon in early 1973 was that he believed the allegations of White House involvement. *"I never did trust H.R. Haldeman, John Ehrlichman or Chuck Colson, and I never doubted that they had a lot to do with it. "*

At a Senate Republican Conference meeting during Watergate, Young said he believed Nixon was going to drag the Republican Party down with him. Shortly after, the same day or the next day, the Republican leadership sent a delegation over to the White House to tell Nixon what two or three others – including Young – had said.

"In spite of all of this, Nixon had the guts to invite members of Congress over there in groups and let them ask him any kind of question they wanted. In the group I was with, I was the senior member, so he asked me first if I had any question that I wanted to ask him. I said, 'Mr. President, you belong to the Columbia Country Club and used to play out there. I was out there Sunday after your press conference, the first one you had for a long while, and I was playing with a fellow that was

taking a poll around the course to find out what they thought of your press conference. These were mostly all conservative, wealthy people and most of them thought you did a good job. When we got around to the Snack Bar by the seventh hole, Mrs. Mateo was working there and he asked her what she thought of your press conference. She said, 'I think he is too smart a man not to know what was going on.'"

Nixon made no comment and went on to the next Senator. *"It wasn't really a question, he didn't really have to answer but this lady did say exactly what a lot of people were thinking. He was too smart a man not to know much of what was going on. I passed it on to the President because I thought she made a good point."*

The rough language in Nixon's Watergate transcripts didn't surprise Young. *"That wasn't so typical of the meetings I had been in with him, but all the Presidents I knew swore quite a bit. I don't think anyone used tougher language than Truman, but it was so natural for him, like when he called that music critic of his daughter a S.O.B."*

Throughout his Presidency, Nixon was close to Reverend Billy Graham, and he went to some of the services he conducted in the White House. *"I often wondered what Reverend Graham thought about Watergate. I don't know if there will ever be a scandal on the scale of Watergate again. There will always be some crooks and dishonesty in government. But I think with public awareness and safeguards we have now, there will never be anything like Watergate. I believe Nixon would have been found guilty in an impeachment trial."*

Watergate was worse than Young first thought it would be. *"But through it all, the government didn't lose any money and nobody got killed. I didn't worry as much about Watergate as I prepared for the 1974 re-election as I should have. If I had known that it would turn out as bad as it did, I am sure that I wouldn't have been a candidate. I am lucky as hell to have won."*

Gerald R. Ford (1913-2006; President August 9, 1974 - January 20, 1977): Young believed President Ford's pardon of Nixon was right for the nation. *"It took a lot of guts to pardon Nixon. If he hadn't, the trials would have gone on and the country would have been torn apart and the wounds wouldn't have been healed for a long while. We would have been weakened greatly in dealing with foreign nations."*

On Capitol Hill, Young heard a great deal of criticism about Ford after the pardon. *"All I heard about was his pardon of Nixon. In some respects it wasn't justified but in retrospect I think it was the right thing to do. The country did get back together. Watergate is a thing of the past. It has hurt the party and it probably will for years to come yet. And we need a strong two-party system – more now than ever before. "*

Burning Tree Golf Course in Bethesda, Maryland, was the location of a golf game with Young and Ford not long before the Presidential election in 1976. In the golf cart was the President, his partner John Rhodes, the Republican Minority Leader in the House of Representatives, along with Young and his partner, Frank Jamison, who was married to actress Eva Gabor.

"I wasn't playing worth a darn then and neither was Frank but he kept on raising the bets! I lost $24 and Frank lost $56. Ford hits a long ball and played very well. He would been a good player if he played very much. He had seven pars. On the last par 5 hole, he hit an 8 wood out of the rough over 200 yards. His caddy gave him a 3 iron for his shot to the green and that really was the wrong club. President Ford doesn't hit the 3 iron very well. He went into the woods with that shot but still parred the hole. When the ball went into the woods he swore a little bit. The interesting thing was that after he finished the hole, he said to the caddy: 'I shouldn't have sworn, should I?' The caddy said, 'No, you shouldn't have.' It was typical of the President after he got through to stop at the clubhouse and have a couple of drinks – just like any one else would do. I suppose it was about 6 p.m. We just sat and had a good visit."

Young's assessment of Ford was that although he was not a brilliant man, *"he is an honest conservative, and while he may not go down in history as a great President, I think he will be a respected one."*

Jimmy Carter (1924- ; President January 20, 1977 - January 20, 1981): During Carter's 1976 Presidential campaign, Young observed that the Georgian was a master organizer. *"I remember being at a checkup at the Mayo Clinic and a doctor asking me who I thought was going to win the Democrat nomination. I said, 'Carter.' I gave as an example what he did in Iowa. He got the delegates in Iowa just because of his organization. He probably was the best organizer of all the Democrat candidates. And I think that was largely responsible for his victory, as well as the weakness of other candidates."*

In 1980, Young was critical of the slow pace Carter was taking with making appointments to his administration, and his poor handling of Cabinet changes. *"What it boils down to, I think, is that he hasn't picked good staff members to work with him – especially in the White House. He never had much experience in business and industry and dealing with foreign governments. He lacks in many ways."*

He also was skeptical of Carter's plans to reduce the federal government. *"It would take a very good leader as President, a strong Cabinet, and strong people in the Administration. One of Carter's problems is that his aides in the White House are not too savvy about the federal government. They know a little about it but they aren't the kind of people who could be successful at something like the reorganization of the government."*

Young described Carter as having *"a rather sharp, different approach than other Presidents when he wants something. He's very persistent. The last issue was on the Panama Canal and I told him I didn't see how you can sell that to the people of North Dakota, but I told him that I would consider it. He asked, 'Why don't you come over and see me?'"*

On another occasion, Carter called Young looking for support on the nomination of Paul Warnke to head the Arms Control and Disarmament Agency. *"Again he asked, 'Why don't you come over and see me sometime?' Both times I happened to be in such a position that it made it difficult to accept. I am a little reluctant to go over there because I am afraid he would be a hard dealer and it is possible he might even approve Garrison Diversion if I did. But I think the price could be very high!"*

Recalling in 1948 when President Truman called the 80th Congress the "Do-Nothing" Congress, Young believed that description would much better fit the 95th Congress as he described it in 1980: *"President Carter is stopping water projects and other regular public works projects and spending huge amounts of money to provide temporary government jobs."*

Four Re-Election Campaigns

Young's 1946 election victory established him as a politician who could win in a statewide vote for a federal office. Four years later, in 1950, he was back on the ballot to secure his first full six-year Senate term.

This was the first of five campaigns over the next 24 years where Young fought to stay in the Senate. Regardless of his opponent, Young took each campaign seriously, "always running scared," as he admitted in a November 23, 1962, interview in the *Fargo Forum*. "There are no cinches in politics. It's always the confident guy who gets beat." It was perhaps one of the keys to his success as a campaigner.

His hands-on style of directing his own campaigns was consistent with his personality throughout his political life. *"The source of some of my trouble was that I insisted on running my campaigns completely myself. I made all of the decisions. I listened to other people but I did all the planning and decided the kind of campaign we would conduct, where I would go and the advertising."*

He kept a close watch on his campaign contributions. *"I turned down some smaller ones from people who I thought couldn't afford to contribute – or when I thought I had enough money and didn't want to accept anymore. I always made a practice of writing thank you letters to those who contributed. Also, I never believed in carrying over funds from one election to another. I never had a special account in the office – like many that have been turned up recently. I didn't know that many* *in the House and Senate had these special accounts. When I had any money left over – one year I had about $700 – I gave it to the state organization so I never carried any over."*

Each of his last four campaigns produced a half-hour documentary film to air on statewide television a few days before the election. All but the last were made by North Dakota's premier filmmaker of the time, Bill Snyder of Fargo. The Flint Agency of Fargo produced the 1974 film. *"These films dealt with my accomplishments, the kind of office I ran, the kind of friends I had around the state and interesting details about developments in North Dakota that I had something to do with and few people knew anything about. These were far more effective than most of my opponents realized."*

Young also insisted that all his campaign printing be done by state companies and that everything carry the "Union Bug" mark, indicating it had been produced in a union shop.

The following is a summary of Young's four re-election campaigns, in 1950, 1956, 1962 and 1968.

1950

Opponent: Harry O'Brien, Democrat, Park River
Final vote total: November 7, 1950
            Young 126,209 (68 percent)
            O'Brien 60,507

By January 1950, Young had risen in seniority in the Senate. He was on the Senate Appropriations Committee, and its subcommittees on Agriculture, Deficiencies and Army Civil Functions, the District of Columbia, Interior, Labor-Federal Security, State, Justice, Commerce and the Judiciary. He was the ranking Republican on Agriculture Appropriations.

Young also was on the Agriculture and Forestry Committee and its subcommittee on Price Support Legislation. As the second-ranking Republican on Agriculture, he was an automatic Senate conferee with a similar committee appointed by the House on all agriculture legislation. In an April 19, 1950, letter Young wrote to W.M. Smart, the executive secretary of the Republican Organizing Committee (ROC) in Bismarck, he explained that the conference committees had 14 members, seven each from the House and the Senate. "We address the difference between both houses and oftentimes completely re-write this legislation. Acceptance by both houses afterward is usually automatic."

He also was on the 11-member Senate Republican Policy Committee headed by Senate Majority Leader Robert Taft of Ohio, and was the Secretary of the Senate Republican Conference, composed of all Republican Senators.

As he was gearing up for another re-election campaign, Young spent much of his time in LaMoure during the last days of his mother's life. She died March 1, 1950, at the age of 83. His father would die a year later on March 25, 1951, at the age of 89. In a response to a letter written by Mrs. Alfred Zuger of Bismarck, Young wrote, "Thank you so much for your kind expression of sympathy on the death of my mother. This was very kind of you, Mrs. Zuger. Mother meant a great deal to the entire family, as she does in all families. I will miss her tremendously."

A bad winter storm and Mrs. Young's funeral caused a four-day delay in the start of the ROC state convention. When it met in Bismarck on March 13 and 14, the LaMoure County delegation consisting of A.J. Sandness, C.J. Robideau, both of LaMoure, Ingvald Musland of Edgeley, Ed Reed of Grand Rapids, and Martin Gackle of Kulm, nominated Young for re-election. Young then fought off a primary challenge by NPL candidate Tom (T.H.H.) Thoreson, a lawyer from Grand Forks, to be on the Republican ballot. The vote totals from the June 27 primary election were Young 98,458 and Thoreson, 39,805.

Harry O'Brien, a state senator and Park River newspaper publisher, was endorsed by the Democrats to run against Young. *"Harry was a good state senator and was a good friend of mine. But he was not too well known around the state."*

One of the major agriculture issues in the campaign was the Brannan

Plan for Agriculture, named for Charles Brannan, President Truman's Secretary of Agriculture. *"The big objection to it then was the set price of 100 percent parity and then paying farmers the difference between the market price and 100 percent parity. The Farm Bureau was strongly opposed to it and I was too. Much of the League favored it."*

In an October 21, 1950, letter to Ray Schnell, a state representative from Dickinson, who would be elected lieutenant governor in that election, Young wrote about agriculture:

> The thing I am most proud of, Ray, is the fight I put up for 90 percent of parity for the basic commodities (wheat, cotton, corn, rice, peanuts and tobacco) at all time when they were under either acreage allotments or quotas. This resulted in the improvement of the Anderson Act, which we were able to force them to use the old parity formula for basics, which, at the time was $2.15 at 100 percent for wheat as compared to $1.90 under Anderson Act and even less under the Aiken Act. You will note [Bill] Thatcher's statement that my amendment "means $150 million saved for farmers in these four states on wheat and corn."

Schnell used some of this information for his segment in a live 15-minute radio broadcast across North Dakota produced by the Young campaign that aired on November 3. He covered farm matters like price supports and rural electrification. Fargo lawyer Herb Nilles spoke about general issues, including Young's belief in the free enterprise system, and Ernest Livingston of Minot addressed Young's work for appropriations for state water projects.

The Korean War was also an issue. *"Most Republicans blamed President Truman's Secretary of State Dean Acheson for the speech he made indicating that Korea was outside of the United States' sphere of interest or influence,"* referring to the January 12, 1950, speech Acheson made at the National Press Club in Washington, D.C., which seemed to indicate that South Korea was not considered part of the United States defense perimeter in Asia. It was interpreted by the Communists as signaling that the United States might stay out of any conflict in Korea, which was not Acheson's intent. *"They claimed that invited or encouraged the North Koreans to strike. I was opposed to it and I kept on speaking against it some all the way through, although after we got in I voted for the appropriations necessary to carry it on. It was not a popular war in North Dakota but our people were very loyal."*

In his campaign, Young touted the funds that he had helped secure during the past four years for the Rural Electrification Administration (REA), especially through his work on the Appropriations Committee. He had secured $14 million for an REA transmission line for east-central North Dakota, which occurred because of an amendment Young handled on the interior appropriations bills. He also helped secure additional appropriations for many dam projects in North Dakota, including $4.9 million to build the Missouri-Souris Dam.

On October 21, Young answered a letter from John Knauf of Jamestown, who was concerned about Young's opponent distributing literature in foreign languages to North Dakotans, especially the state's large German population. Young answered that he believed sending campaign material written in German was effective and he had done it in the past with literature and advertisements in Norwegian and German. "But, I won't have time to do it this campaign. We will just have to let it go."

North Dakota Republicans prevailed in the November 7 election. Young's 126,209 votes were more than double O'Brien's 60,507 vote total. Norman Brunsdale became governor, succeeding Fred Aandahl, who replaced William Lemke in the House. Aandahl joined Usher Burdick in the House, and Langer remained in the Senate with Young.

Even though this was Young's second statewide campaign for his Senate seat, he realized the difficulty of achieving widespread name recognition. Young and Paul Benson, his administrative assistant who would later become a longtime federal judge, discussed this when driving back to LaMoure after a campaign stop in Williston.

"I said that after being in office five or six years I believed that not more than 75 or 80 percent of the voters had ever heard of me. Paul couldn't believe that, so we decided we would stop at various places along the way and I would introduce myself and see how many people

had ever heard of me. Our last stop was a filling station about a mile or two east of Bismarck, which was run by an old German-Russian. I introduced myself to him as one of North Dakota's Senators and he looked at me and he said, 'I thought we only had one Senator – Langer! He should be President!' I had made my point that name identification is not easy to come by. And most candidates are not half as well known as they think they are."

1956

General Election Opponents: Quentin Burdick (D), Fargo

A.C. Townley, Independent

Vote Totals: November 6, 1956

Young, 155,305 (64 percent)

Burdick, 87,919

Townley, 937

North Dakota's political scene was dominated by the Nonpartisan League for much of the 20th Century. 1956 was the year the state's political landscape began to change, and that change attracted national attention.

In his *Politics and People* column in the March 21, 1956, issue of the *Baltimore Sun* Thomas O'Neil wrote:

> A rare political migration is about to take place in North Dakota involving the wholesale transfer of some 60,000 voters from Republican allegiance to Democratic. With its completion the Democrats will achieve major-party status in North Dakota for the first time, public policy will be settled at general elections rather than in Republican primaries, and one name will disappear from the roster of single-party states in the American political scheme.
>
> It is an abrupt change for even a state so volatile politically as North Dakota, where the populist heritage has many evidences, including the only state-owned and operated banking institution in the United States. The instrument of impending change is the Nonpartisan League of North Dakota which sprang up 40 years ago

as an expression of agrarian unrest and almost ever since has operated politically as a Republican faction. It has decided to sever the association, a decision which its leaders attribute to dissatisfaction with Republican farm policy in Washington.

Both the League and the regular Republicans are in agreement on the probable number of voters to be affected. Mr. Oscar Zetter, executive director of the Nonpartisan League, and Gov. Norman Brunsdale, leader of the regular Republicans, made separate estimates that, of roughly 100,000 followers of the Nonpartisan League, 60,000 will become Democrats and the homeless 40,000 will move toward regular Republicanism.

The realignment of NPL members occurred at state conventions in 1956. Those known as "old guard Leaguers" remained in the Republican Party, along with Republican Organizing Committee members. The others, known as the "insurgent Leaguers," merged with the Democrats.

A vote to accept the NPL into the North Dakota Democratic Party was one of the first orders of business at the Democratic Party Convention held March 28 and 29 in Bismarck. Fargo attorney Quentin Burdick, who was endorsed for the U.S. Senate seat to run against Young, referred to the NPL's shift in allegiance to the Democratic ballot as "a second political prairie fire" in a March 14, 1956, Associated Press news story. (The first was the formation of the NPL in 1915.)

On April 6, a "Republican Unity Convention" was the first convention at which Old Guard NPL and ROC members joined forces to select a single slate of candidates to support in the Republican primary. Delegates endorsed State Senator John Davis for Governor over Lieutenant Governor C.P. Dahl.

As O'Neil had written in his *Baltimore Sun* column, the 1956 campaign began a change in North Dakota politics that resulted in the emergence of the Democratic Party. It also became the first time when the fall election became all-important in North Dakota. Prior to that the significant battle had been in the primary election in the Republican Party between the NPL candidates and those opposing the NPL, like the ROC.

Quentin Burdick was the son of Congressman Usher Burdick, who had always run as an NPL candidate in the Republican column. Young first came into contact with Quentin in Langer campaigns when he was an active Republican in Cass County. Quentin was closely aligned with the Farmers Union, and he was the organization's attorney. *"His views at that time of the campaign were much in accord with Glenn Talbot and the Farmers Union. Politically I always ran scared, and in this election Burdick had especially strong support from the Farmers Union and labor."*

Young believed having Usher Burdick still a Republican and running for re-election to the House, and his son running as a Democrat for the Senate, was confusing to voters. *"It made it a complicated campaign for me. Usher often thumped out on his typewriter speeches and statements for Quentin to make."* One of the very sensitive issues in the campaign came when Young talked about Quentin Burdick's involvement in 1948 as a delegate to the Progressive Citizens Convention in Philadelphia that nominated former Vice President Henry Wallace for President. *"Communists pretty well controlled that convention. I made some mention about that Progressive Citizens Convention at a political meeting during the campaign. Usher didn't come to me personally but he told some others that if I mention that again he would leave any meeting I was at. So I had to be quite careful about it afterwards."*

In 1956 Bill Wright was editor of the *Jamestown Sun* before leaving newspaper work to become a political aide to Young, Representative and Senator Mark Andrews and Governor Allen Olson over the next three decades. In his September 22, 1956, *Wright Angles* column, he wrote about a Republican rally in Valley City earlier that week:

> Rep. Usher Burdick's talk at Valley City was of somewhat more significance than the mere words he spoke. He had decided to sever his Nonpartisan League connections earlier, despite the fact that his son, Quentin, is a candidate on that side of the fence.
>
> It must have been somewhat of an inner battle for the old boy to stand up and urge re-election of Senator Young when Young's re-election means defeat for his son. The Burdick family political differences are one of the oddest in politics. We don't think it will happen, but picture, if you will, the situation if Quentin should defeat

Sen. Young. There'd be Usher on the Republican side of the House and Quentin on the Democratic side of the Senate.

In addition to Burdick, A.C. Townley was also seeking the Senate seat. Young referred to him as a "nuisance candidate." Townley, one of the founders of the Nonpartisan League 40 years earlier, had declined dramatically in influence and regard as a political figure by 1956. Townley injected the Farmers Union into the campaign.

"Townley said about me, 'Milton Young is the candidate of the Farmers Union.' That was because I was always for farm programs and higher price supports and the Farmers Union stood for the same thing. Many of them thought that I was close to the Farmers Union and that was far from being a fact. In fact, Glenn Talbot was the president of the Farmers Union during most of that time and he despised me. In his speeches around the state he often had a lot of mean things to say about me. But we believed in many of the same farm programs. Some of the programs I originally sponsored myself. Often times before an election if Talbot didn't take after me, I would go out of my way to stir him up. I would make some statement and give it to the press, which was critical of Talbot and the Farmers Union. It was good campaign strategy because there were so many in the Republican Party who seemed to be sold on the fact that I was owned by the Farmers Union when actually we didn't get along at all. Now that was Glenn Talbot. Bill Thatcher was a little different story. He was much more friendly and he was head of the Farmers Union Grain Terminal Association. Incidentally, he and Glenn Talbot didn't get along too well either. In fact, I remember one time Thatcher told me I wouldn't be bothered with Glenn Talbot much longer. He didn't say why but it was only about a year or two later in 1961 that Talbot was transferred to their national headquarters in Denver."

During the campaign, Young recalled that he and Burdick *"didn't get into farm issues very much, even though Burdick was closely tied in with the Farmers Union. Burdick constantly attacked my record, sometimes a little viciously, especially the parts of it, of course, that were conservative. All the time and he was very aggressive. I can't remember specific voting issues that we disagreed over the most. It was mostly my conservative voting record."*

One of Young's favorite campaign stories happened in October when he was invited to be in Bottineau for an evening meeting the same day he had planned to be in Watford City.

"Buck Worthington from Bottineau urged me to come to this meeting. I said, 'Buck, I can't make it, my schedule is too full and I have to go to an REA meeting in Watford City – they always drew big crowds – and speak at 4 p.m. It would be too far to drive to Bottineau in time.' He said, 'We'll send a plane to bring you up.' I said it would be after dark but he said they would have cars at the field to light the runway. I finally agreed to go and hurried through my speech at Watford City. I guess we started close to 5 p.m. and it was dark soon afterwards.

"This was one of the few times I went to sleep in the back seat of a small single engine plane. In fact, I only dozed off for a short while. When I woke up we were circling around. Fortunately, he had a landing light on the plane, which enabled us to read the sign on a country elevator. The name of the town was Delaraine. He didn't know much about North Dakota and I didn't know of any place name Delaraine. I asked where we were and he said, 'In Canada!'

"Bottineau was only about 30 or 40 miles due south but there was a stiff southeast wind which probably made navigation on this very dark night a bit difficult. He started out for Bottineau but after awhile he started circling and I said, 'What's the matter?' And he said, 'I don't know where we are but if worse comes to worse, we can always go and land in Minot.' I said, 'How's the gas?' and he said, 'It is all right for awhile yet.'

"At that point I wasn't sure whether we were near Minot or Winnipeg. Soon he started circling again and finally said, 'I think I'll stop at a farmhouse and find out where we are.' It was pitch dark but I didn't say a word because I thought he would do a better job if I kept still. He landed in a cornfield – where part of it had been cut and put in bundles – but with that stiff wind, he only went about 75 feet before he stopped.

We walked up to a farmhouse – which was only about a quarter of a mile away. The farmer said we were three and a half miles north of Bottineau.

"The pilot wanted me to go back and get in the plane and fly to Bottineau, but I said, 'No, I will have this farmer drive me in.' The farmer told me that the field was about the only place he could have landed because there were a lot of rock piles, ditches, haystacks and whatnot all around. I sure didn't want to fly in to Bottineau after hearing that!"

In an Associated Press profile on Young that ran in state newspapers in late October, reporter Russ Greenlee wrote:

> Young regards agriculture and its problems second only to world peace in importance to his country, and if you can talk with him five minutes without getting into agriculture and its pros and cons, why you're a magician.
>
> . . . Young believes his biggest and best recommendation for re-election is his record on farm legislation, coupled with his seniority on the agriculture and appropriations committees and his membership on the Senate's conference committees on agricultural and money bills. The farm price problems notwithstanding, Young says, 'the most important issue of all' is that of world peace, and to his way of thinking, the only way to achieve world peace is for the United States to retain its military strength, stressing air strength above that of all other branches.
>
> "We'd better spend on our air forces," he says, "than to throw our money around the world. I do believe, however, we should help those countries, which in event of war would fight on our side." He lists such countries as Britain, Germany, Greece, Spain, Turkey and "even Japan," and includes Chiang Kai-shek of the Chinese Nationalist government.
>
> "The United States made the mistake of almost completely disarming after World War II," Young says. "It should not make that mistake again. Since the Korean War, we have the strongest military force in our peacetime history. Let's keep it that way."

President Eisenhower was running for a second term, opposed by the Democratic nominee, Adlai Stevenson of Illinois. On September 21,

Vice President Richard Nixon spent two hours in Fargo campaigning for Eisenhower and the other Republican candidates.

Nixon was quoted in the *Fargo Forum* on September 22, "I don't know if you understand the esteem with which Senator Young is held in Washington. You probably accept him out here as just another fellow. He's a straight talker, a square shooter, a man of integrity and a man who brings a great deal of confidence. We need him in Congress and the Senate and I urge you to support him for re-election."

Four days later Estes Kefauver, the Democratic nominee for Vice President, visited Jamestown, campaigning for Stevenson and the statewide Democratic candidates.

Townley ran large newspaper ads at the end of the campaign that featured a headline half way down the page, asking, "Is Quentin Burdick a Communist?" and addressed his participation at the 1948 Progressive Citizens Convention, which Young had brought up once before being rebuked by Usher Burdick. Quentin Burdick demanded an apology from Townley and the newspapers that ran the ad, and following the election, the Farmers Union announced on November 14 it was filing a lawsuit against Townley for attacks against Burdick and the Farmers Union.

One of the newspaper apologies appeared in the *Golden Valley News* on November 15:

> Quentin Burdick, the unsuccessful candidate for nomination to the U.S. Senate, is requesting that all North Dakota newspapers who carried an advertisement sponsored and paid for by A.C. Townley and his supporters apologize for printing the ad because of the slanderous and defamatory remarks that it carried. We were elk hunting in Montana when the advertisement arrived accompanied by a check to pay the cost of insertion. The help, not knowing what to do, inserted the ad as did many other papers in the state. We still can't figure out where Townley got the money to sponsor the campaign or the nine votes he received in our county. As everybody here knows, this was Townley's stomping grounds in the early days and it was here in Beach that he started his long political career, but we still didn't think he would poll nine votes in Golden Valley County.

Anyway, we not only want to apologize to Mr. Burdick but also to Senator Milton Young and the Farmers Union organization for the insertion of the ad and for the slanderous remarks it contained.

In spite of the party realignment by the NPL that defined this election, and the unpopularity of Eisenhower's farm programs, North Dakota voters still swept into office state and federal Republican candidates. Eisenhower polled 62 percent of the vote, and Young's tally was 155,305 votes, to Burdick's 87,919 and Townley's 937. Although Young won decisively, the vote was closer than in any of his other Senate campaigns, except 1974. *"Burdick took after me every day in that election."*

Despite Burdick's loss, the 1956 election helped bring about the emergence of the Democratic Party in North Dakota. *"The 1956 election was important to Quentin Burdick because he gained name identification that helped him get elected to the House in 1958. But in all the elections since that time, he conducted an entirely different campaign. He rarely, if ever, attacked his opponents after his campaign against me when he spent that whole campaign attacking. He changed his tactics and I think this had much to do with his later vote-getting ability."*

Burdick went on to win the U.S. House seat in 1958, and defeated John Davis for the U.S. Senate seat by some 1,000 votes in a special election in 1960 after the death of Senator Langer in November 1959. *"When Quentin was first elected, that was really the start of the Democrat Party being strong here. Bill Guy claims most of the credit, but if Quentin Burdick hadn't been elected to the House, I doubt if Guy would even have been elected Governor."*

Following the breakup of the League, Young observed how the complexion of the future campaigns changed. *"Usually for years the issues were Langer/Anti-Langer, League/Anti-League. But after the League broke up and part of them went with the state Republicans and the others turned Democrat, our Party then was so strong we could elect almost any candidate we endorsed. And we did for two or three elections. I think one of the mistakes was that the Party didn't keep on endorsing some old-type Leaguers. They got so they endorsed mostly straight Republicans so we lost much League support. By this time Langerism as an issue was mostly gone."*

1962

General Election Opponents: William Lanier, Jr. (D), Fargo
Vote Totals: November 6, 1962
                                    Young 135,705 (61 percent)
                                    Lanier 88,032

One of the opening salvos of this campaign came in November 1961, when North Dakota Democratic Party leaders charged that the John Birch Society, an extreme conservative group that had as one of its goals fighting Communism, had taken over the North Dakota Republican Party. *Fargo Forum* state editor Gifford Herron wrote about the charges in his November 5, 1961, *North Dakota Whirligig* column:

> Some leaders in the North Dakota Democratic party have been warming up their guns for the 1962 election campaigns by concentrating on their contention that the John Birch Society has taken over the Republican party in the state. Republican leaders are vigorous in their denials.

William Lanier, Jr., of Fargo, the state Democratic Chairman, and National Committeeman Dr. S.B. Hocking of Devils Lake, made the charges at meetings across the state, citing a resolution passed in the Republican-controlled North Dakota House of Representatives in the 1961 session that was later killed in the Republican-controlled Senate. The resolution, supported by the John Birch Society, called for Congress to put before voters a constitutional amendment to prohibit the government from engaging in any enterprise that competes with citizens, and to repeal the federal income tax amendment to the U.S. Constitution. They also charged that some Republicans chairing recent party fundraisers were members of the John Birch Society and that Young (although he had denounced it on many occasions) had reached a truce with the Society.

Young denied any change of opinion about the group, and state Republican officials called the other claims false.

Later in November, Young and Governor Bill Guy received standing ovations when they spoke at the state convention of the North Dakota Farmers Union. Young spoke about the recent omnibus farm bill adopted by Congress, and told the group some of the amendments he helped get passed would help state farmers, including a 30 percent increase in durum acreage and a 10 percent increase in malting barley acreage.

In his November 12 *North Dakota Whirligig* column, Herron wrote:
> The talk at the state Farmers Union convention included that "U.S. Senator Milton R. Young, a Republican, cannot be beaten for re-election next year." Some volunteered the remark, "And there's no reason to beat him, either."

Among the people Herron mentioned who were being considered to challenge Young were Norris Bakke of Mayville; State Supreme Court Justice Thomas Burke of Bismarck; State Senator Walter Fiedler of McLean County; John Lord, a Bismarck lawyer who had been the unsuccessful Democratic nominee for governor in 1958; Bismarck attorney Charles Tighe; former State Senator Ray Vendsel of Carpio; and Lanier, who had challenged Young in the 1946 election.

Young spoke at the state convention of the North Dakota Farm Bureau the following week, and answered questions from delegates that were largely critical of the 1962 wheat stabilization program.

A poll taken by Democrats at a dinner honoring Senator Quentin Burdick on December 1 chose Guy and Lanier as the top two candidates to challenge Young for the Senate.

An editorial in the *Fargo Forum* on December 10, 1961, addressed Young's seniority:
> **Senator Young's Seniority Becoming Important Factor**
> Senator Young is outranked by only 17 Senators in length of service, and only five of the 17 are Republican. In the U.S. Senate, length of service is a dominant factor

in establishing a member's committee assignments
and his influence within his own party . . . The North
Dakotan has a chance of becoming one of the most
important figures in the U.S. Senate, providing, first of
all, that the Republicans regain control of the Senate
during his period of service . . . Senate seniority is a
very poor basis on which to campaign for re-election.
It seldom has much appeal to the voters. They are more
interested in determining the outcome of any election
on the basis of the stands the candidates take on current
issues. Therefore, what the man had done in his years
of service for his home state and for his party is a much
more important factor in determining his chances than
his number of years in the Senate. Senator Young need
apologize to no one for the record he has established
since his original appointment in 1945, and he stands a
good chance of extending his seniority in the Senate for
several more years.

Unanimous endorsements for re-electing Young, and Representatives
Hjalmer Nygaard of Enderlin and Don Short of Medora to the U.S.
House were approved by the North Dakota Republican Convention
in Bismarck at the end of March. Overshadowing these re-election
endorsements was the six-way Republican race for governor. The top
two contenders for governor going into the convention appeared to
be GOP National Committeeman Mark Andrews from Mapleton, and
Bismarck businessman Harold Schafer. The other contenders were
three state legislators, Senator Donald Holand of Lisbon, Senator
George Longmire of Grand Forks, and Representative Don Halcrow of
Drayton, as well as Fargo attorney Harold Bullis.

It took 10 hours and seven ballots on Friday, March 30 for the
Party nominee to emerge with the needed 257 votes for endorsement.
Andrews' vote total was 273 1/2 to Halcrow's 236 1/2 votes. Schafer
had the lead in the first three ballots, but dropped out after falling behind
Halcrow in later ballots. With Andrews as the Republican to challenge
Governor Bill Guy, Cass County was certain to remain the home of the
next North Dakota governor.

A week later, state Democrats were in Bismarck for their convention.

With Guy well positioned to receive endorsement for a second term as governor, the attention was on the candidates seeking endorsement for the federal seats. The announced candidates for the Senate endorsement were three attorneys, Lanier, State Representative Leonell Fraase of Tioga and Norris Bakke of Mayville. When the voting began, the name of State Senator and attorney William Reichert of Dickinson was also on the ballot, but the endorsement went to Lanier on the first round.

In addition to being state party chairman, Lanier was one of the Democrats who had shepherded the NPL to its alliance with the Democratic Party in 1956. The April 13 *Fargo Forum* coverage of the convention reported that Lanier said in his acceptance speech, "I will spend five months covering the entire state. I will spend, if elected, 16 hours a day 365 days a year representing all interests of North Dakota," and "I will never compromise a principle."

The campaign issues over the summer centered on Young's and Lanier's often opposing views on the traditional topics of interest to North Dakota voters, such as farm programs, Garrison Diversion and foreign policy.

Newspaper profiles of the candidates that ran in late October 1962 highlighted their differences in style and political philosophy. Don Reeder of the Associated Press wrote:

> Young cannot be described as a dashing figure. Neatly clad in dark suit and homburg, he still looks nothing more than a prosperous farmer. He's hardly a thrilling speaker and has a personality that is warm but not overpowering. When he gets excited he's apt to stutter a bit . . . Young supporters credit his success to hard work and a radiation of sincere honesty. He knows his state and knows his voters. Maybe it's not very exciting, but it sure has paid off on election days.
>
> The lean figure of the 64-year-old lawmaker ordinarily is recognized everywhere he goes. "Hello there, Milt" is the usual greeting from old friends. When Young meets a voter new to him, he eases up to him with what must rate as a new high in modest introductions: "Hello, I'm Milt Young, one of your Senators." He behaves like he was only elected yesterday and seems pleased and even

a bit surprised when people recognize the name.

Young almost invariably manages to work the talk around to farming – admittedly not a difficult feat in North Dakota. That's when his ruddy face fairly lights up with interest, and it's obvious the Senator is batting in his own ballpark. He often asks voters if they understand the new farm bill and nods his head sympathetically when they confess they can't figure it out. The Senator confides some of the top experts in Washington don't fully understand it either.

Young has a habit of gazing intently at anyone he talks to, giving the impression he is tremendously interested in their every word. Farmers, grain elevator operators and store clerks find themselves gabbing away at their Senator like they were chatting with a neighbor.

Young does not follow voting lines laid down by either the Farmers Union or Farm Bureau, and he has never been endorsed by either for election. "I believe in farm programs," he asserted. "Anybody who farmed in the '20s and '30s believes in them. But I think they should be the right kind of programs."

In the 16 years since Young had defeated Lanier in their first face-off in the 1946 Senate campaign, Lanier had remained active in North Dakota politics. *Fargo Forum* writer Jim Meeker noted in his profile of Lanier that ran on October 28, 1962, his work behind the scenes to strengthen the North Dakota Democratic Party over the past decade, especially the alignment of the Nonpartisan League with the Democrats.

He helped organize a Democratic-Farmer-Labor Association, which is credited with providing a vehicle for the NPL merger. In response to the charge that he was organizing this group only to serve as a launch to run against Young in 1956, Lanier pledged that he would not run for office until there were North Dakota Democrats elected from the top to bottom of the ballot.

"Lanier traveled 30,000 miles in 1955 and 1956 in promoting the amalgamation of the two groups," Meeker wrote. In 1956 he was vice chairman of the Democrat Party, stepping up as chairman five years later and resigning before the state convention that endorsed him for the Senate race.

Lanier supporters called his five-month campaign against Young his "Twelfth Marine assault." By the end of October he had campaigned in 471 North Dakota communities, nearing his goal of visits to 500 by Election Day.

The article described his campaign style. "Lanier campaigned with a big booming voice and a big right hand. He can go door to door in his good humored fashion, and he keeps his audiences rollicking with humor as he delivers one stab after another. For these five months he has campaigned 14 hours a day, covering tens of thousands of miles. On the basis of literature distributed, he estimates he has shaken 45,000 hands."

The last weeks of the campaign turned the world's attention to an international crisis that derailed the campaigns of candidates across the country. North Dakota was no exception. On October 22, President Kennedy announced a naval blockade against Cuba, in response to a buildup of nuclear weapons by the Soviet Union on that Communist island, which became known as the Cuban Missile Crisis.

Because Young was a member of Senate committees that dealt with sensitive defense and national security issues, he had been aware of the situation in Cuba for several weeks. Prior to October 22, many Republicans in Washington were critical of what they claimed was President Kennedy's inaction on this issue, including Republican Senator Kenneth Keating of New York, who on October 10, claimed he had "100 percent reliable" information that the Russians were building intermediate range missile sites in Cuba capable of launching nuclear warheads. The Kennedy Administration had responded by saying there was no evidence of such a buildup, noting the Soviets had never put missiles in other countries, not even their satellites in Eastern Europe.

Lanier criticized Young at a campaign stop in Grand Forks October 21. He said Young's assertion that action against Cuba was inevitable was "irresponsible and dangerous for the security of this country and the world." He also claimed that Young "has always been an obstructionist, a negative on foreign policy." Young's claim that Cuba had offensive missiles, Lanier said, was a positive "misstatement," that was unsupported by the President, the State Department or the Central Intelligence Agency.

"The next day President Kennedy called all the members of Congress to meetings in different places. I went to the one in Chicago where they advised us there would be a showdown the next day with Russia over missiles in Cuba. I had advance information about the missiles from intelligence sources before the Chicago meeting."

After Kennedy acknowledged the missiles on October 22, Young said in a statement he issued the following day, "I approved of the President's statement of the blockade and felt it was long overdue. I had known of the buildup of medium range missiles. I support the action of the President and would support any action necessary to protect the security of the United States."

Following his announcement of the blockade of Cuba, Kennedy cancelled his campaign appearances for Democratic candidates and asked members of Congress campaigning for re-election to remain in Washington for consultations on the developing crisis. Young was already in North Dakota making campaign stops.

On October 23, Lanier and Scott Anderson, the Democratic-NPL candidate for the state's Eastern District Congressional seat, issued a joint statement reversing their earlier stand that Young incorrectly claimed offensive missiles were in Cuba. "The presence of Russian offensive weapons of destruction in Cuba has made it necessary that our President take direct action. We support this action and feel it will effectively and peacefully deter further Russian aggression in this hemisphere."

Young's reply to Lanier's statement was, "His own President contradicted him in a nationwide broadcast last night. We are in deep trouble, not only in Cuba, but throughout the world. I for one am, of course, supporting the President in whatever action he deems necessary."

The Cuban Missile Crisis ended on October 28, when Kennedy and United Nations Secretary General U Thant reached an agreement with the Soviets to dismantle the missiles.

On October 31, a week before the election, Young was quoted in the *Fargo Forum* about the campaign:

> This is the toughest I have experienced in 30 years of public life. The tactics being used by my opponent seemed to be the general tone of the other top candidates on the Democratic ticket. In almost every instance these attacks have been complete misrepresentations or distortion of the true facts. I have never been involved in this kind of a campaign before and I have some doubts whether Lanier's tactics will pay off for him.

Despite his concerns, Young won re-election handily, with 135,705 votes to Lanier's 88,032. Nygaard and Short were also returned to Congress. Guy was the only Democrat elected on the state ticket, defeating Andrews by some 2,000 votes to gain a second term, although it was the smallest majority in a North Dakota governor's race in 30 years. In newspaper comments the following week, Guy said, "I can't help but admire the Republican efforts. Their organization certainly did a good job of turning out their votes." He credited Young's vote-pulling power for some of the success.

1968

General Election Opponents: Hershel Lashkowitz,
Democrat, Fargo
Duane Mutch, TRT Taxpayers
Reform Ticket, Larimore
Vote Totals: November 5, 1968
Young 154,968 (65 percent)
Lashkowitz 80,815
Duane Mutch 3,393

Every election cycle is preceded by speculation about candidates challenging each other. A wave of excitement spread through the state in early 1967 when the name of a possible challenger to Young surfaced. News reports said longtime CBS Television newscaster Eric Sevareid, a native of Velva, might be interested in returning to his home state to seek the nomination.

While this news of a potential high-profile matchup in a state race caught the attention of many political observers, it did not ruffle Young. When asked about it, his terse answer was, "What does Eric Sevareid know about wheat?"

This re-election campaign could be considered Young's easiest. Ironically, on the national scene, 1968 was one of the most politically tumultuous. The assassination of the Reverend Martin Luther King, Jr., on April 4 in Memphis was followed two months later with the murder of Senator Robert F. Kennedy in Los Angeles. Riots and anti-war demonstrations occurred nationwide, and on June 23, the Vietnam War officially became the longest war in American history.

In his *On Capitol Hill* newsletter mailed in February, Young warned about the risk of America becoming the world's policeman:

> Our role of trying to police the entire world is getting us more deeply and seriously involved, particularly in Southeast Asia and Korea. We are stumbling from one crisis to another and are on a collision course with disaster. We are in no position to fight a new land war on another front in the Far East unless we resort to nuclear arms.
>
> The United States is no closer to winning the war in Vietnam than it was three years ago. The enemy has been able to counter our every effort to escalate the war. North Vietnam now has an army of more than 500,000 of the toughest guerilla fighters in the world, compared to 350,000 a year ago. The infiltration of troops into South Vietnam is continuing to increase and the enemy has the capability of increasing this infiltration from the present 75,000 to at least 100,000 a year. Our peace offensive has not been as aggressive or as effective as our military efforts. They are doing a superb job under impossible circumstances.
>
> I supported bombing but I am certain the war will have to be won on the ground in the jungles of South Vietnam. President Johnson was wrong to divert large sums of money and equipment provided by Congress for overall defense needs, in order to make the Vietnam War costs appear less than they actually are.

With all the unsettling events of the year that were to unfold, 1968 began with a rare moment in the spotlight for Young. While usually content to remain in the background, especially at social events, Young was an honored guest at the January 21 dedication ceremony and the January 30 gala reopening ceremony for Ford's Theatre. Young delivered remarks at both events, sharing in the history of the theatre and about his repeated attempts to pass legislation to restore it.

Two months later on March 31, President Johnson announced he would not seek re-election. Johnson's decision increased interest in the contest for the Democratic Presidential nomination, which had featured Senator Eugene McCarthy and Senator Robert Kennedy, before Kennedy was assassinated in early June.

Young issued a statement shortly after Kennedy was shot following his primary victories in California and South Dakota:

> It is just impossible to realize that this terrible tragedy has visited upon a second Kennedy brother. There is nothing about the late President Kennedy or his brother, Robert, to invite hatred or violence. I have served in the Senate with all three of the Kennedy brothers and never knew any of them to do anything that would cause anyone to hate them, much less want to do violence to them. The campaign between Senator Kennedy and Senator McCarthy was on a most friendly basis and could hardly have been the cause of this tragedy. Far too much hatred and violence is being encouraged throughout our country today. Crime and violence cannot help but be a major concern to everyone. As is usually the case, it strikes down some of the most respected people. I hope and pray that Senator Kennedy can completely recover.

Kennedy died on June 6, and his funeral was on Saturday, June 8. This was just five days before North Dakota Republicans opened their largest state convention in history in Fargo, with 930 delegates. Nationally, the Republican contest drawing the greatest attention was for the Presidential nomination, which included top contenders former Vice President Richard Nixon and Governor Nelson Rockefeller of New York. In the state, the biggest contest was among five men who were vying to topple William Guy in his bid for a fourth term. They were Ed Doherty of New Rockford, Robert Reimers of Melville, Richard Elkin of

Bismarck, Robert McCarney of Bismarck, and Earl Redlin of Ellendale.

A constitutional amendment adopted June 30, 1964, lengthened the two-year gubernatorial term to four years, which put the seat up for re-election in 1968 for its first four-year term. Were he to win, Guy would become the first person elected to a fourth term as North Dakota Governor. There was speculation that Guy would challenge Young for his Senate seat, but that would not be resolved until the Democrats convened a few weeks later.

Doherty won the gubernatorial nomination on the fourth ballot, but he would be unsuccessful in fending off a primary election challenge by McCarney on September 3. Incumbents Young and U.S. Representatives Mark Andrews and Thomas Kleppe won their nominations by acclamation. Andrews was seeking his third term, after having been first elected October 22, 1963, to fill the vacancy caused by the death of Representative Hjalmer Nygaard that July. Kleppe was seeking his second two-year term in the U.S. House.

As he accepted the nomination, Young was critical of the outgoing Johnson Administration:

> The prestige of the United States throughout the world has deteriorated almost beyond comprehension. Our nation is being humiliated by acts of piracy and arrogance on the part of even some of the smallest Communist countries. We have very few real allies left. We are no longer the admired and respected nation we once were.

New York Mayor John Lindsay addressed convention delegates on behalf of Rockefeller's Presidential bid. State Republicans were still at odds with the John Birch Society, which tried to seat a group of its members as District 19 delegates at the convention. These Grand Forks County delegates, who were led by John Scott of Gilby, were replaced by what the credentials committee called "regular Republicans."

"You haven't heard the last of this," Scott announced after the rebuff. It nominated its own candidate for Senate to challenge Young, Duane Mutch of Larimore. Young had never backed down from wrangling with the John Birch Society, which had continued to generate support throughout the 1960s.

"Late in the campaign during a stop in Bismarck, two women approached me and offered to help my campaign. 'We want to help clear your name,' they told me. 'They're saying you're a Communist.' I had become used to those charges from John Birch Society members, who did not agree with many of my views, including price supports for farmers."

The days leading up to the opening of the Democratic convention June 27 in Bismarck continued to bring speculation about whether Guy would challenge Young for the Senate seat. A statewide poll conducted by the *Minot Daily News* in April 1968 showed that Guy would be a formidable opponent. Young polled 46 percent with Guy only four points behind at 42 percent.

One Democrat had announced in March he was seeking the nomination for Young's Senate seat. He was Robert Moses, 40, son of the late John Moses, who had been Governor from 1939 to 1945 and died shortly after being elected to U.S. Senate. It was his seat to which Young had been appointed in March 1945.

Moses listed his home as Bismarck, but for the past two years had been working on agriculture programs in Africa with the U.S. Foreign Assistance Agency. In 1952, Moses ran for Secretary of State as a Democrat and had worked for the North Dakota Farmers Union and owned a public relations firm in Bismarck.

A week before the convention Fargo Mayor Herschel Lashkowitz announced he would seek the Democratic-NPL endorsement for the Senate. A World War II veteran of the U.S. Army, Lashkowitz had been a writer for the motion picture industry for two years. He returned closer to home where he earned a law degree from the University of Minnesota and joined his father's law practice. The 50-year-old Lashkowitz had been mayor of his hometown since 1954. He had run as an Independent candidate for Governor in 1960, and later sued Governor Guy for libel on the basis of some of his campaign statements against him. The lawsuit was dismissed. Lashkowitz served a term in the North Dakota Senate beginning in 1964 and instead of seeking re-election, he unsuccessfully ran for the Democratic-NPL endorsement for East District Congressman. He would end his political career, following 20 years as mayor of Fargo, by returning to the North Dakota Senate for another 15 years, from 1975 to 1990.

At the news conference announcing his candidacy, Lashkowitz said the major issues on which he would base his campaign were international affairs and bringing peace to Vietnam. When asked if he thought the Democrats had a chance to win state or local elections because of the Johnson Administration's unpopularity, Lashkowitz replied, "I have never entered a campaign without seeking and intending to win. Victory, after all, is within the grasp of those who seek it."

Before the convention, State Senator Herbert Meschke of Minot and former State Senator George Sinner of Casselton announced the formation of a committee to support former State Tax Commissioner Lloyd Omdahl for Governor in the event that Guy would seek the Senate nomination. In their announcement, Meschke and Sinner said, "We believe Governor William L. Guy is the finest statesman in North Dakota history and we would support him for re-election. However, should Guy and the Party decide the Governor should run for the U.S. Senate, we think the most outstanding man with the widest experience to succeed him is Lloyd Omdahl."

Two days before the convention began, bowing to party pressure, Guy made the announcement that he would run for re-election for Governor, and that he was backing Walter Hjelle for the party's endorsement for the Senate. Hjelle at the time was the state highway commissioner.

The convention brought to Bismarck both of the Party's leading Presidential candidates, Vice President Hubert Humphrey and Senator Eugene McCarthy. Neither were strangers to the state. Humphrey was born in Wallace, South Dakota, in the far northeastern part of the state close to the North Dakota border. He had been a Senator from Minnesota before becoming Lyndon Johnson's Vice President. McCarthy, a native of Watkins, Minnesota, began his teaching career in North Dakota at

Mandan High School 30 years earlier. While teaching English, geography and history, McCarthy also met his future wife, another Mandan High School teacher, Abigail Quigley, a native of Wabasha, Minnesota. In his speech to the delegates, he made reference to having been in the Bismarck Municipal Auditorium to watch Mandan High School win the 1940 state basketball tournament.

The vote on the Senate endorsement came down to Lashkowitz, Moses, Hjelle, and Meshke, who entered the race at the convention. Lashkowitz prevailed, despite Hjelle's support from Guy. Following the endorsement, Lashkowitz said his campaign would focus on both foreign and domestic affairs, especially seeking an honorable peace abroad, that would "quiet the turbulence in the cities and give farmers a fair share of the wealth."

The state campaign over the next few months was relatively quiet, with the front pages of state newspapers leading with such national stories as the Nixon-Humphrey-Wallace Presidential campaign, the Apollo 7 space flight marking the return of America's manned space program after the January 1967 tragic Apollo 1 fire that killed three astronauts, and the marriage of former First Lady Jacqueline Kennedy to Greek billionaire Aristotle Onassis on October 20.

Another reason for the campaign's low profile was the late adjournment of Congress in the middle of October that kept Young and other members of Congress from hitting the campaign trail full time. In campaign appearances, Lashkowitz accused Young of "selling out" the nation's family farmer by voting against a $20,000 ceiling on farm payments and for the failure by Congress to enact a four-year farm program extension. He also charged Young with using for political purposes the postage-free franking privilege given members of Congress for communicating with constituents.

And he criticized Young for his lack of action when the Gulf of Tonkin Resolution was passed by the Senate August 7, 1964. This resolution increased President Johnson's authority to wage war in Vietnam, including the power to commit troops for as long as he deemed necessary, as well as take any other steps he considered necessary to protect the nation's interest. At a mid-October news conference, Lashkowitz said Young "should justify to the people of North Dakota his role in getting the United States into its no-win, no-lose, no-peace situation in Vietnam. My opponent did not raise his voice once during the three-day debate on the Gulf of Tonkin Resolution. By this action, the Senate, which should be a full partner and advisor to the President on foreign policy, abdicated its responsibility. Senator Young's record is one of blind occurrence in this sad picture. What North Dakota needs is a stand-up, speak-out Senator in Washington."

In response to the Gulf of Tonkin charge, Young said Senator Burdick did not participate in the Resolution's debate either. He described as "disastrous" the Johnson-Humphrey Administration's foreign policy in a speech in Minot on October 22. And, he said he sometimes got "a bit lonely" as the only grain farmer left in the United States Senate at an October 26 campaign stop in Hope. "It isn't easy to get Senators with no actual farm experience to understand the problems of farmers."

Young refused Lashkowitz's requests to debate him, and three weeks before the election, Young said at a news conference that it was a "highly unlikely possibility" that Lashkowitz would win.

While in the state, Young spent time with his wife, Malinda, who had been a resident of a Fargo nursing home. A November 1 profile about Young in the *Fargo Forum* wrote that his wife "has been ill for three years and needs around-the-clock care. Although he has three sons, 11 grandchildren and one great-grandson whose companionship give him much happiness, they cannot fill the void of a partner who has played a role in the ups and downs of his farm and public life."

Like other elections, the Young campaign inserted fliers in statewide newspapers. The six-page, full-color piece highlighted his accomplishments, including farm programs, and featured letters of praise from farmers. It included a photo of Young attending a White House briefing on the Vietnam War, along with other members of the Senate Appropriations Committee, conducted by President Johnson,

Secretary of State Dean Rusk, Secretary of Defense Clark Clifford and CIA Director Richard Helms.

Other flier highlights touted his success in bringing a jewel bearing plant to Rolla which employed workers from the Turtle Mountain Indian Reservation. It also recognized Young's success in getting Ford's Theatre reconstructed, which had been completed earlier in the year.

Young's prediction of victory in the election held true. He received 154,968 votes to Lashkowitz's 80,815, and Mutch's 3,393. At 65 percent, Young's vote total was the largest percentage of any Republican Senator in the nation with opposition. Kleppe and Andrews were returned to Congress, and Guy defeated McCarney to win an unprecedented fourth term as Governor, to this date the only person to do so in the history of the state.

Richard Nixon was elected President, giving the nation a Republican Administration. The makeup of the Senate going into the 91st Congress, which convened in January 1969, would be 57 Democrats and 43 Republicans. With the Democrats still controlling the Senate, majority party leadership positions and committee chairmanships would elude Young once again.

The 1974 Election:
North Dakota's Perfect Political Storm

On June 3, 1969, six months after Young began his fourth term in the Senate, his wife, Malinda, died in a Fargo nursing home at the age of 73. Young had spent time with her two days before her death before leaving for Washington. He immediately returned to the state and her funeral was June 6 at Zoar Lutheran Church in LaMoure.

Six months later, on December 27, Young married his longtime secretary, Pat Byrne. Having been on the staff for 24 years, there was no question that she would continue to work in his office. But he cut her pay in half to thwart any criticism about having his wife on his office payroll. Pat was not happy about it, but Young didn't change his mind. Cutting her pay didn't quell all the critics, however, and Young received letters from constituents criticizing him for doing that. *"Many of the letters said, 'Why in the hell don't you cut your own pay in place of Pat's?' Later, I tried to raise her pay, but she wouldn't let me."*

Now in his seventies, Young considered whether he should serve out his full six-year term or resign mid-term. As long as his annual checkups at Mayo Clinic in Rochester, Minnesota, gave him a clean bill of health, he believed he should continue in his job. *"If Pat had her way, she would have liked to see me resign mid-term. But she left it up to me to decide."* Politically, with Governor Guy remaining in office until January 1973, Young would not resign and allow a Democrat Governor to appoint his successor. Young kept open the option of resigning, however, if North

Dakota would elect a Republican Governor in 1972.

On January 5, 1972, Guy announced that he would not seek re-election to a fifth term as Governor. He also indicated that he would leave office, seek work in the private sector and consider a run for the Senate in 1974. That set in motion the beginning of what had the potential to become the perfect storm in North Dakota's political history. If Young were to seek re-election and Guy become his challenger, two of the most prominent political figures in the state would at last face each other in what could become the "race of the century." As the events of the next three years unfolded, few political observers would challenge the belief that it far exceeded its potential.

What follows is a summary of the campaign, including Young's personal recollections. A more detailed analysis of this race begins later in this book in Allan C. Young's *Race of the Century: Guy vs. Young 1974 North Dakota U.S. Senate.*

The decision to seek a final term

The 1972 general election closed the door on whether Young could resign and his successor be appointed by a Republican Governor. Democrat Arthur Link, who was elected West District Congressman in 1970 but did not seek re-election in 1972, defeated Republican gubernatorial nominee Richard Larsen, who had been the unsuccessful candidate for lieutenant governor four years earlier. Nationally, Richard Nixon was easily re-elected, defeating Senator George S. McGovern in a landslide.

Link was sworn in as the new Governor on January 2, 1973. Speculation had begun even before then about the 1974 election, especially about a Guy-Young contest. Age would certainly be an issue in this campaign, with Guy being 53 years old when he left the Governor's Office.

The December 30, 1972, *Grand Forks Herald* editorialized:
> Guy's chances of election to the Senate, of course, depend in large measure on whether Sen. Milton R. Young decides to run again. There has been no better vote getter in North Dakota political history than Young.

He probably is at the height of his career right now. But both the elections in November and the earlier primaries showed that age is becoming an important factor in the voters' decisions. Young will be 76 years old at the time of the next election, would be 77 by the time he could be sworn in for another term and 83 by the time it ended.

It is not certain that he will seek another six years in the Senate. He has said he will make his decision known sometime next year. Guy probably won't wait for Young's decision. He will start campaigning as soon as he has moved out of the governor's mansion. Republicans, stung by the gubernatorial loss, will probably do everything they can to blunt Guy's campaign.

Should Young's decision be not to run for re-election, there would be heavy pressure on Rep. Mark Andrews to move into the Senate race and stop Guy. But Andrews likes it where he is and might not be willing to move.

A *Fargo Forum* editorial on January 2, 1973, opined:

The surprise election of Congressman Link as Governor and of Democratic State Sen. Wayne Sanstead of Minot as Lieutenant Governor keeps the Democratic Party in a position of prominence, a prominence that has been won largely by Gov. Guy's performance in his 12 years in office . . . If the Republicans had taken over, considering their overwhelming majorities in both the House and Senate, Gov. Guy would have been effectively sidelined as a factor in state government. With the Democrats continuing to hold the governorship, though, citizen Guy should remain quite visible in North Dakota government and politics.

Dick Dobson, in his January 13, 1973, *Inside North Dakota* column in the *Minot Daily News,* wrote:

Young has privately expressed confidence that he could defeat Guy and he has commented that nothing would suit him better than a hard-fought campaign.

Young's political assets include his seniority, his key position on the Senate Appropriations Committee and his record of bringing home federal projects and grants of every description for North Dakota.

But many political observers and oddsmakers, including some prominent and knowledgeable Republicans, believe that Guy could parlay his own popularity and "the age issue" into an election victory.

Two significant events followed the inauguration of President Nixon that January. On January 23, Nixon announced that after 12 long years, the Vietnam War would end on January 27, 1973, with the signing of a peace treaty in Paris. The day before the announcement, former President Lyndon Johnson died of a heart attack at his ranch in Texas at the age of 64.

Young attended a three-hour briefing at the White House the day of the announcement about the end of the war that detailed the cease-fire arrangements. He then issued a statement:

> I am satisfied that the best possible solution was obtained . . . Our involvement in this unfortunate and unpopular war is definitely being ended, and all of our prisoners will be released within 60 days and a full accounting will be made of those missing in action. We have already withdrawn all our combat forces. All our other military personnel, including military advisers, will be withdrawn within the time frame of the release of our prisoners. We have paid a terrific price in lives and money. I hope and feel sure that we learned a lesson and we will not be drawn into any more unnecessary wars all over the world.

In a tribute to Johnson, Young said:

> He was the easiest to contact and visit with of the presidents who served during his time in Washington. He was the closest to agriculture and rural America of any of the presidents I have known. Probably no president ever was responsible for getting enacted more domestic programs – not all which I agreed. Lyndon Johnson succeeded to the presidency at a most difficult time, when we were already halfway into the war in Vietnam. He inherited many top government officials who were very war-minded. I cannot help but feel that history will be kind to this most personable of all presidents.

In early February, a poll conducted by 11 weekly newspapers in a hypothetical Senatorial contest showed Guy with a slim lead over Young. The percentage was 46.4 for Guy and 44.6 for Young.

Young knew that if he were to announce for re-election he should do it early to help with fundraising and discourage challengers. The opportunity to make an announcement arose during a Lincoln Day Dinner in Bismarck February 12, which would bring in Senator Robert Griffin from Michigan as the featured speaker. Young told his son, Scoop, that he had two speeches in his coat pocket, one announcing his retirement and another that he was seeking re-election, and that he would decide before the dinner which one he would use. He was leaning toward announcing he would run again, when a few hours before the dinner, three of his closest political friends, John Rouzie of Bismarck, National Committeeman Dr. Ben Clayburgh of Grand Forks, and Roland Meidinger of Jamestown called him into one of their hotel rooms. *"They told me, 'Don't run again. You can't win.'"*

Young didn't like being told he couldn't win. It angered him to the point that he considered it a challenge he wanted to take on. He continued with his plans to announce his re-election. To a standing ovation at the $15-a-plate-dinner at the Grand Pacific Hotel, Young said, "I will be a candidate for re-election."

At the dinner Young told the crowd:

> I had always expected to retire by the time I reached my present age. I am finding that this isn't so easy, especially when my health is good. The Mayo Clinic only recently found me to be in excellent condition. Seniority, experience and friendships attained through many years in the Senate do make it much easier to get things done. Age can be an asset in a legislative body, and particularly in the United States Senate where seniority and experience can put you in a position of power and influence. Acquiring the necessary knowledge and a good working relationship with other members of the Senate and throughout the government is important if you are to be an effective legislator.

Although not referring to Guy as his opponent, Young did address the issue of age head-on, saying the best time for someone to go to the Senate is between the ages of 30 and 40, allowing time to attain seniority on committees. "I went to the Senate when I was 47," he said. "That was a little too old. Fifty-five is much too old!" This was the age Guy would be if elected in 1974.

Dobson wrote in his February 17 *Minot Daily News* column:

It appears that North Dakota will witness another historic fight between political giants in 1974. Young is officially off and running and his probable opponent, former Gov. William L. Guy, indicated his interest in the race a year ago. It will be the longest campaign in the state's election annals and it will undoubtedly be one of the most exciting.

It wasn't until 11 months later in January 1974 that Guy made his intentions to run for the Senate official. He did it at two news conferences on January 18, one at his home in Casselton and the other at the Bismarck Holiday Inn. In his announcement Guy said:

I have long believed that the seniority system is one of the grave problems in Congress. It places too much responsibility on people who are neither willing nor able to carry it out. It lacks courage and ambition to tackle problems facing the country. Under the seniority system, Congressional committee leaders are not selected on the basis of ability or willingness to work but because they outlived their peers.

That same day, Young issued a statement addressing Guy's comments on seniority.

It will be a big issue in the campaign. It has its faults but the biggest beneficiaries of the seniority system are the smaller population states. The seniority system is not going to be changed and it does give power and influence to those who earn it by years of service. I'm pleased he's finally made his announcement. It's been a long wait. He's been a candidate for the Senate for 10 or 12 years.

During his announcement, Guy also referred to the Watergate scandal in Washington, which by then had escalated to impeachment inquiries by Congress. "These events have seemed incredible and, I think, dangerous for the nation. I do not intend to use Watergate as a campaign issue. Any effect it has in the election will be in the mind of voters."

In early 1974 it was clear that Garrison Diversion would continue to be the contentious issue it had been during the past decade. Richard Madson of Jamestown, chairman of the anti-Garrison Diversion group, known as the Committee to Save North Dakota, Inc., challenged Young to debate the project so the people of North Dakota could "hear both sides of the issues presented in formal debate so they can determine once and for all if a moratorium and independent analysis on the Garrison project are necessary."

Young had earlier called Madson "an environmental-ecology extremist," and had expressed concern that funding for the project may not be included in the 1974-75 federal budget because of opposition from groups such as Madson's.

On January 22, however, Young announced he had received assurances from the White House that the present budget would include at least $10 million for Garrison Diversion. "I fully expect to get the Senate to appropriate far more than the amount requested in the new budget," he said, adding that opposition to the project by the Canadian government was one of the major obstacles preventing Garrison Diversion from moving ahead.

Another issue in January 1974 that concerned Young was the Nixon Administration's consideration of lifting wheat import quotas. Since 1937, the United States had restricted wheat import quotas to about one million bushels per year. He expressed confidence that American farmers could produce all of the wheat needed for both domestic consumption and foreign exports.

Despite Young's announcement a year earlier, political observers like Dobson wondered if he would remain in the race. In his January 26 *Minot Daily News* column, Dobson wrote, "Speculation continues in some quarters that Young may yet decide to retire, albeit very reluctantly, and hand over the Senate seat he has held for 29 years to the winner of a Guy-Andrews battle."

Dobson referenced a recent article in the *Chicago Tribune* that noted that both Young and 81-year-old George Aiken, Republican from Vermont, were considering retirement. The article said, "Republicans hope Aiken won't retire and that Young will. Aiken is considered unbeatable, while Young is considered very beatable." Aiken did decide to retire, which would mean that during the next session of Congress, if Young were to be re-elected, he would be elevated to the position of top-ranking Senate Republican.

Amidst the retirement speculation that Young consistently denied, Dobson reported Young's campaign continued to move forward. His re-election chairman, State Representative A.G. Bunker of Fargo, appointed Williston and Dickinson radio station manager Ray David as his full-time campaign coordinator. A 16-member "Farmers for Milt Young" committee was also formed, naming State Representative Howard Bier of Hazelton its chair. "Bushels for Mr. Wheat" was the fund-raising campaign they began, asking state farmers to send in a check equal to the price of whatever number of wheat bushels they were able to contribute to Young's campaign.

Early 1974 found Robert McCarney continuing to talk about his role in the upcoming election. He had been unsuccessful in his Republican campaigns for Governor in 1964, 1968 and 1972, and for West District Congressman in 1970. Although successful in wresting the Republican nomination for Governor and the U.S. House in primary elections in 1968 and 1970, McCarney had been defeated in both general elections.

He seemed interested in challenging Guy for the Democratic nomination for the Senate, despite the fact that Guy had defeated him for Governor in 1968.

By March, Young was comparing this campaign with his previous ones and finding some challenges. He was quoted in an Associated Press story on March 23, 1974, that the Watergate scandal and new federal regulations on reporting campaign contributions were making fundraising more difficult. "Now, anything over $100 has to be reported, and a lot of people just don't want to have their names publicized," he said.

But he reported that overall his fundraising was going well, and he was hoping to watch his campaign expenses. "I'll have to be careful in my spending because I don't want to go into debt."

He also reported that he had not found much sentiment in North Dakota for impeaching President Nixon. "If you vote impeachment, you are going to alienate that 25 percent of the Republicans who think Nixon can do no wrong. However, if you vote against impeachment, you are going to alienate a great many other people."

In mid-June, both Guy and Young released their financial assets. Guy listed his net worth at $234,000. Young was quoted in an Associated Press article that it was more difficult to assess his net worth because of the 1,300 acres of farmland he owned in LaMoure County when he became a Senator in 1945. "It would be difficult to appraise because it has never been for sale as there have been no offers to purchase it." He added that he owned one share of stock in the Farmers Union Cooperative Elevator in Berlin.

The North Dakota Democratic-Nonpartisan League and Republican conventions were scheduled in Minot three weeks apart. The Democrats opened their convention June 21. By then, McCarney had announced his intentions to challenge Guy for the Democratic nomination for the Senate in the September 3 primary. When asked if he planned to attend the Democrats' convention, he was quoted in state newspaper accounts as saying, "Are you kidding? They'd kill me!"

McCarney did, however, present the differences he had with Guy in a televised program on June 20, especially his charges alleging Guy's involvement in a political scandal at Minot's First Western State Bank some five years earlier that was investigated by the U.S. Justice Department, the FBI, the Federal Deposit Insurance Corporation and the U.S. district attorney for alleged political violations. In the indictment against the bank, Guy's name was not mentioned.

Guy responded in a statement following McCarney's program, "Nothing he said in that TV advertisement regarding me was true. Nothing! It was just one lie or crude innuendo after another."

Guy received the Senate endorsement at the convention by acclamation, and pledged to run an "open, issue-oriented campaign."

A week later, Guy asked Young to publicly discuss with him the charges that McCarney had leveled against Guy when the two appeared together at a legislators' golf tournament in Carrington. The charges were related to the First Western State Bank scandal that McCarney had made in his television show before the Democratic convention. Guy's telegram to Young wrote, "Most people recognize the sabotage role McCarney is playing in the campaign against me, but because you are creating the impression that there may be substance to his charges, I invite you to sit down with me to quietly discuss those charges in the presence of a few newsmen." Guy called the charges "false, frivolous and shopworn."

Young declined in a return telegram dated June 28. He wrote:

This legislative golf tournament has always been a sociable, fun affair. I have no intention of using that gathering as a place for you to get me involved in a political debate over a problem that is entirely your own.

Your problem with Robert McCarney and the First Western Bank of Minot is your mess, not mine. I don't intend to get involved in it and I resent your trying to use me as a tool to help you in your difficulty. I wrote to you in March that I would like very much to make this campaign a clean and honorable one. I plan to campaign entirely on my record. Since that time, I have never mentioned your name in the campaign once until yesterday and then only in reply to questions raised by the Associated Press. In your more than 60 appearances around the state since this March 8 letter you have constantly attacked me personally and by your customary innuendo.

As the state Republicans were gathering for the opening of their convention July 12, Dobson wrote in his July 5 *Minot Daily News* column:

Perhaps the only and therefore the biggest problem facing officials of the Republican state convention in Minot's Municipal Auditorium next weekend will be to keep the delegates in their seats. There are no contests for party endorsements, the proposed platform is not expected to provoke much debate, the convention hall is not air-conditioned and the weather probably will be hot. Given these factors, the challenge will be to keep a quorum.

The keynote speaker at the convention was George H.W. Bush of Texas, the National Chairman of the Republican Party. He acknowledged, "many political observers along with the Democrats were predicting the Watergate scandals would spell political disaster for the Republican's 1974 election effort. However, Republicans are fighting hard and will exert the maximum effort to keep the Democrats from gaining a majority in Congress sufficient to override a Presidential veto."

State Senator and Minot Mayor Chester Reiten nominated Young. "It is a compliment to the man that I must review his record, for most politicians spend most of their time talking about their record," Reiten told the convention. "With Milt Young this is not true – he gets things done quietly. Yes, quietly he gets much done. The many people who know him, know that this great concern is to help others – not to recite his past deeds. Milt Young is a warm and compassionate man, yet a man who has the guts and the fortitude to fight for the people of North Dakota. He delivers for North Dakota – he can deliver more in the U.S. Senate for North Dakota in six weeks than a newcomer could do in six years. There are show horses and there are work horses. North Dakota wants a work horse in the U.S. Senate."

Young held a sheaf of wheat presented to him by Reuben Metz of Alfred, chairman of Young's District 28, when he accepted the nomination. "This will be my last campaign for any office," he told the convention. "I had given considerable thought to retiring, but disliked surrendering the Senatorial seniority I have gained."

He acknowledged the early concerns about him running. "A few months ago there was some pessimism about my chances for re-election. That seems to have changed almost completely," he said. "Never in all the years I have been a candidate for the Senate have people been so friendly as I travel around the state. If I am to be defeated this year, they are certainly going to do it with kindness."

He said he intended to campaign on his record. "North Dakota still has many problems that will require experience, seniority, and all the influence that goes with it. If I can't prove during this campaign that I have accomplished much for our state, I don't deserve to win."

In his own account of the events leading up to his nomination at the convention, Young said: *"I was giving a lot of thought of retiring. I think though that my opponents used the wrong approach. They – the opposition – said I couldn't be re-elected and that was a real challenge. There was some of it in my own Party and they probably had good reason for it because actually I hadn't realized that I was as damn old as I was. I was so busy and my health was good. I had always wanted to serve in such a way that when the time came to quit I could still be elected. I didn't think of quitting because I thought I couldn't be re-elected.*

"Guy had been Governor for 12 years, and he used the argument all over the state that I couldn't be elected again. The Democrats tried to discourage me from running as well as some in my own Party. A lot of them thought I couldn't win. That became a real challenge. I thought I could and I did win, but not by very much.

"I was making a speech at a Lincoln Day Dinner meeting in Bismarck with then-Senator Bob Griffin as the keynote speaker. This would have been in February of 1973. Not too long before the election and at a time when I either had to announce as a candidate or stay out of it. If I tried to stay out of it and remained undecided there would have been other candidates doing some work and spending money to get the endorsement. Then if I back into it later I would have made a lot of enemies and been a lot weaker – so I thought that I should announce then and if I had to, I could get out of it later. But three of my friends – Dr. Ben Clayburgh of Grand Forks, who was the National Committeeman, John Rouzie of Bismarck, and Roland Meidinger of Jamestown, called me over to their room about an hour before the speech and begged me not to announce my candidacy. I had already planned to do it, though, and I did. Apparently they thought I had no chance of winning.

"Bill Wright, who had worked for me off and on for quite a long time, came back to Washington and said he wanted to visit with me about the situation in North Dakota. But he wanted to do it over a couple of drinks so it would be easier for him to talk about it. The opportunity didn't arise, so one day he came into the office and stood across from

me looking rather starry-eyed and said: 'Senator, you can't win.' I said, 'Well, tell me why. Who thinks I can't win?' He said he didn't want to name names but I said, 'What you tell me is meaningless unless you tell me who thinks I can't win.' Then he mentioned a few such as John Rouzie, who is a close friend and raised much of the money for my campaign. These fellows were convinced by that poll and with what the National Committee had to say and really thought I could not win. Bill was even convinced I couldn't win. That was one of the most difficult decisions I ever made. Bill Guy was at his peak. He had been Governor for 12 years and during the two years he was out he was campaigning all the time. He was an able person but he spent most of the time he was Governor, and afterwards, trying to discredit me – and he did a fair job. He was an antagonist of mine from the time he became Governor because he wanted to be a United States Senator and I was the one he thought he had to beat.

"I had a problem at first with the Republican Senatorial Campaign Committee because there was a poll taken by Central Surveys, an Iowa concern, that showed that Guy would beat me by about some 50 percent to 30 some or about 20 points and I think that Congressman Andrews was willing to run if I would step aside. Some Republicans wanted him to run so it was a little hard to raise money at first.

"The National Committee or the national structure wanted me to step aside and let somebody else run, but there were some political writers who were boosting Congressman Andrews' stock as a candidate, claiming that I could not win. Many in North Dakota believed that, too. The big "IF" in political history is how an Andrews-Guy campaign would have turned out. Well, Bill Lanier and I never agreed too much – we were opponents twice – he once said that Guy and Andrews deserved each other. I could not help but believe he was right.

"Those pollsters didn't always ask the right questions. They would ask people: 'Who do you think is going to be elected?' I was getting to be an old man and Guy was very popular. But I conducted a poll myself and I did it as honestly as I knew how because I wanted the true

feeling. I put it the other way around and asked: 'Who do you plan to vote for?' rather than 'who do you think will be elected?' That poll came out about even. In an effort to get the broadest representation, I had the people who conducted the poll for me send a questionnaire to about 3,000 people and I paid for it myself. We took the names out of telephone directories. It wasn't a scientific poll but I think it was more accurate than a scientific one.

"As for the argument that I was getting too old, I started to counter it when Senator Bob Griffin spoke at the big Lincoln Day dinner in Bismarck when I announced I would be a candidate. Senator Griffin at that time was, I think, 42 years old. He had been in the House for about six or eight years and six years in the Senate. I said, 'Bob Griffin is just the right age to go to Congress and by the time he gets seniority, he still can be very active and it will be his best years.' I said that Bill Guy was too old to start. That kind of took hold too, with many people."

National controversy drives the final months

The last five months of the campaign were dominated as much by the national news related to the Watergate scandal as it was the state issues.

The resignation of President Nixon on August 9 made the campaign more difficult for Young and all Republicans running for office that year. Young did not defend Nixon, which drew criticism from staunch Nixon supporters in the state.

History was made on September 3 when more votes were cast for Democratic candidates than for Republicans in a North Dakota primary election for the first time since they began in 1908. Guy handily defeated McCarney for the Democratic nomination for the Senate by a more than five-to-one margin of 55,269 to 11,286. Young polled 51,705 votes.

Two independents, James Jungroth of Jamestown and Kenneth Gardner, Jr., of Drayton, also would oppose Young and Guy in the general election.

Guy's assessment of the primary vote was that the Democrats were

North Dakota's majority party. Young opined that all of the 11,000-plus votes that went to McCarney were votes against Guy, and they were votes he expected to receive in the November election to win a sixth Senate campaign.

The week following the primary brought more controversy from the Watergate scandal when on September 8 President Ford surprised the country with his announcement of a "free, full and absolute" pardon for former President Nixon for any criminal conduct during his Presidency. Young's reaction was that the pardon may have been premature.

In early October, state Democrats released a poll taken by the Peter Hart polling firm of Washington, D.C., showing Guy with a wide lead over Young in the Senate race. The percentages showed Guy with 53 and Young with 35, with 10 percent undecided. The poll, however, had been conducted in April, and many political observers, including Democrats, believed the race had tightened up and didn't take into account the Independent challenges of Jungroth and Gardner.

In the final months of the campaign, Young and Guy exchanged barbs about farm policy, defense, and campaign contributions. An Associated Press article on October 11 quoted Young as saying the campaign was the toughest race he had ever been in. "I'm doing things in this race I have never done before," he said, such as distributing campaign buttons and purchasing campaign billboards.

He also predicted that Jungroth's presence on the ballot as an Independent could likely decide the election. He predicted Jungroth would get some 20,000 votes, with about two-thirds of them being votes that would have gone to Guy and one third of them that would have gone to him.

A mid-October poll conducted by 11 North Dakota weekly newspapers showed Guy and Young running a virtual dead heat, with Guy at 46.2 and Young at 45.9 percent. Jungroth's percentage was 2.1 percent. Only five percent were undecided.

A national Associated Press story on October 22 noted that Democrats were looking for many election victories in the Midwest. It singled out

Republicans in North Dakota and Kansas as being "seriously threatened with losing U.S. Senate seats. In North Dakota, Sen. Milton Young, a Republican, is in a nip-and-tuck battle with former Gov. William Guy. Guy's camp said the former Governor was running far ahead of Young in the spring but the gap has narrowed."

On October 23, in an Associated Press article out of Bismarck, Young blamed the Watergate scandal and related incidents for making this campaign so difficult. "Guy is not a big vote getter," Young said. "The reason why he is tough for me is Watergate, Agnew, Nixon and the pardon."

He said he discouraged President Ford from coming to North Dakota to campaign, not wanting to be too closely identified with the administration. "I have the reputation of being independent," he explained.

Guy, in an Associated Press article that ran the next day, agreed that Watergate was working to his and other Democrats' advantage. "Since Watergate, the public has become disenchanted with the federal government, including the Presidency and Congress. It is a factor on the minds of the people that would not help incumbents and Republicans."

He said that in his campaign travels he has "found that most North Dakotans think it is time now to retire the senior Senator."

In the last week of the campaign, the traditional television show and statewide news inserts touted Young's seniority. These campaign materials included a memorable television advertisement that showed him breaking a board with a Tai Kwan Do karate chop. He had been practicing the martial art for several years.

A final poll taken the week before the election by the University of North Dakota Bureau of Governmental Affairs showed the Senate race to be a virtual tossup, with Young polling 46 percent to Guy's 44.3 percent. Jungroth and Gardner's totals were small, 2.8 percent and .8 percent respectively. The undecided percentage of 6.5 percent was shown as the key to who would win the election.

"I called Guy a 'phoney liberal' during the campaign because he

would come out and advocate something real conservative. I remember that one time he came out with a farm program that the Farm Bureau endorsed. He didn't say enough about what it was so you really didn't know what type of program it was. This caused me to question both Bill Guy and the Farm Bureau to tell the people what kind of program they were talking about. Neither of them answered. On the whole, Bill Guy I think could be characterized as quite liberal. Sometimes on some things he was very liberal but he was quite clever in coming out occasionally for something that was a bit conservative which did tend to confuse people.

"I didn't get along with Guy on a personal basis like other opponents because I didn't feel he was completely honest and he certainly had no sense of humor and was not the kind of person that you could visit with – at least I couldn't. I believe this was because during all the years he was in politics his major objective was to defeat me. The election results did indicate that in his own area and a few others he did a pretty good job of destroying my credibility with a big majority of voters. That probably became the biggest issue of all in the state. In western North Dakota I did well.

"I didn't get down in the [Red River] Valley much at all but often when I would be at a meeting people would say, 'Gee, you look good.' They had gotten the idea that I was old and feeble. If I could have had the time to get around a little more, I think I could have changed a lot more votes. I only had about three weeks to campaign after the adjournment of Congress. I did do a little campaigning – mostly weekends – about a year before the election.

"For the first time my stuttering came up in a campaign. Some people would tell me that Bill Guy was using it. I heard that several times and I had never heard it before. Bill Guy was a very articulate speaker. In fact the press was greatly impressed with his speaking ability when he was first endorsed for Governor and this continued all the time he was Governor.

"Guy said I was in the hip pocket of the Pentagon several times. One of his weaknesses was that he was too strongly antimilitary. He was strongly opposed to the Anti-Ballistic Missile (ABM) program. At one time when

they thought they might have some trouble or rioting at the ABM site, he said he would not call out the National Guard or do anything to protect it. As I recall, he was critical or some of my votes on projects like that.

"Watergate was an issue because when I criticized Nixon, I antagonized many Republicans. I remember one of them, for example, a doctor from Jamestown wrote me a tough letter. He said that was the worst thing I had ever done in all the years that I had been in politics. In denouncing Nixon, I alienated at least 5,000 or 10,000 strong Nixon supporters. I get letters yet that say, 'Give us back Nixon and the $5 wheat.' Guy didn't have to say much about Watergate. The news was full of it – all bad – and it hurt every Republican.

"It was a bitter, tense campaign. It is the first time that an opponent had a strong political machine backing him since League days. Some Democrats became very bitter. Some of them, even some in LaMoure that I grew up with who were always friendly, became quite bitter and outspoken. Much of it was usually the age thing, as well as Watergate and the pardon of Nixon.

"It was much harder to get newspaper support during this campaign than others. Bill Guy was a master at getting publicity. Then, of course, he liked to talk about himself quite a lot. His being a great leader and with his age, he could bring new leadership – young leadership, progressive leadership for North Dakota in the United States Senate.

"The Los Angeles Times *had a fellow here most of the time during the last days of the campaign. I'll always remember when I first met him. He saw me after seeing Guy and he said, 'I gather that your opponent doesn't like you!' I said, 'That's right and I don't like him either.'*

Election night and beyond

Like he did every election night, Young stayed at home on November 5 with only a few close friends and family to watch the returns in LaMoure. He had prepared himself for the worst, and by the time he went to bed, it looked like he had lost. *"The Associated Press called at 7 the next morning for a concession statement. Pat answered the telephone and said they were not up yet and would call them back after they got to the office. The election results from some of the western counties had begun to come in, and I was gaining votes. I told the news reporters covering the election, including several from out of state, that I would not have a statement until all the votes were in."*

The first election totals reported on November 6, with all but 37 of the state's 1,649 precincts reporting, gave Guy a 56-vote lead. When all precincts were in, Young had a 46-vote lead. Jungroth received 6,739 votes and Gardner polled 810.

After hearing the close election results the next day, Young told his longtime LaMoure friend Claire Sandness, "Well, we're back to where I started in 1932, when I won by only 37 votes."

While most elections are decided soon after Election Day, the razor-thin vote difference in this race signaled the beginning of a long process of agonizing counting, canvassing and recounting.

These headlines from the next two months on the front pages of the *Minot Daily News* succinctly summarize the story:

Thursday, November 7, 1974:
Young Leads by 96 Votes; Recount Said 'Inevitable'

Friday, November 8, 1974:
Race Still Very Nip and Tuck; Guy Cutting Into Young's Tiny Lead as Canvasses Report

Saturday, November 9, 1974:
Errors Increase Young Lead; Seven Counties Left in Canvass Work

Dick Dobson's *Prairie Perspective* column that day carried the headline:
Guy Carried East, Young Took West

Monday, November 11, 1974:
Jungroth Feels He Helped Cause

Tuesday, November 12, 1974:
Young's Lead Drops With New Reports

Wednesday November 13, 1974:
Young-Guy Winner Still ???

Thursday, November 14, 1974:
Cass Dragging Its Canvass Feet

Friday, November 15, 1974:
Young Confident He's Won Senator's Lead 176 With All Canvass Reports Finished

Saturday, November 16, 1974:
This was the first day since the election that a story did not appear on the front page. The page 2 headline:
Any Appeal In Recount Would Go To Senate
The headline on Dobson's *Prairie Perspective* column:
Young's Lead in Paper Ballots

Monday, November 18, 1974:
Recount Decision By Guy

Tuesday, November 19, 1974:
'FINAL' – Young By 177 Votes State Canvass Ended; Election Recount Comes Next

The final general election totals in the Senate race, as reported by Secretary of State Ben Meier, were: Young, 114,852; Guy, 114,675; Jungroth, 6,679; Gardner, 853. *(Author note: These totals differ slightly from those listed on page 437, which were drawn from an earlier source than the final official report issued by the North Dakota Secretary of State's Office).*

Friday, November 22, 1974:

Link Fires Salvo At Senator And Young Fires One At Link

Regarding the recount, Young had questioned the fairness of the state law that permitted his opponent to select the six district judges to conduct the recount, while he had an equal interest but no voice in their selection. Governor Link charged that Young was questioning the integrity of North Dakota's district judges.

Monday, November 25, 1974:

Young and Guy Choose Their Lawyers;
Judges Gather to Discuss Procedure

Young's challenger in two of his Senate campaigns, William Lanier, Jr., emerged as a prominent figure in this contest as well, when Guy selected him to be his chief counsel in the recount. Young chose attorney Kenneth Moran from Jamestown.

Tuesday, November 26, 1974:

Recount Ground Rules Set; Judges Will Request Help From Canvassing Boards

The six district judges overseeing the recount were Ralph B. Maxwell of Fargo, Douglas B. Heen of Devils Lake, Larry M. Hatch of Linton, Alfred A. Thompson of Bismarck, Roy A. Ilvedson of Minot, and Norbert J. Muggli of Dickinson.

Wednesday, November 27, 1974:

Guy Recount Requests Filed; Verdict Must Be Reached Within 15 Days

Thursday, November 28, 1974:
Six Judges Will Check Recount

Friday, November 29, 1974:
Senator Recount Started

Monday, December 2, 1974:
Ilvedson Denies Motion of Young Forces Over Recount
Minot Attorney Walfrid B. Hankla, representing the Young campaign, made a motion in District Court to stop the recount, claiming North Dakota's recount law was unconstitutional. Hankla argued that the law enacted by the 1971 Legislature denied due process under the Fifth and 14th Amendments to the U.S. Constitution. District Judge Roy Ilvedson denied the motion.

Tuesday, December 3, 1974:
Young's Lead Cut To 169 With Recount Done In Two Counties – 51 Remain

Wednesday, December 4, 1974:
Five Counties Completed With Young by 180

Friday, December 6, 1974:
Guy Closes to 129 Votes; Mott Ballots Voided For Not Having Proper Marks
These ballots, which changed the votes for both Young and Guy, showed two votes marked for the Senate race, apparently because of confusion caused by having the names of four candidates on the ballot.

Saturday, December 7, 1974:

Young Leads Guy By 134 In Recount

Dobson's *Prairie Perspective* column:

Vague Laws Add to Drama

Monday, December 9, 1974:

Recount Like Yo-Yo As Young Goes Up, Then Down, Now Up Again

Two-thirds of the state's 53 counties had completed their recounts, with Young holding a 168-vote lead.

Tuesday, December 10, 1974:

Young's Lead at 200 With 45 Counties Finished

Wednesday, December 11, 1974:

Young Heads for Victory; Has 185-Vote Lead With But Two Counties Left

Thursday, December 12, 1974:

Canvassing Board Is Being Called – Final Young Recount Margin 186 Votes

The recount officially ended at 6 p.m. December 10. Young issued the following statement upon hearing the vote total:

> I am most grateful to the people of North Dakota for re-electing me to the United States Senate. My razor-edge majority is not like the more than 60 percent margins I have received in every election in the last 30 years. This was the worst possible year for an incumbent Republican to be seeking re-election – and especially when I had a formidable opponent. This was the longest and most difficult campaign I have ever been involved in and I am happy that it is over. I plan to continue to working hard in the Senate the same as I always have, using my position of seniority to help people with their problems, as well as the State of North Dakota and its communities.

Friday, December 13, 1974:

Is It Over Or Not? Challenge Possibility Hinted By Ista

State Democratic-NPL Party Chairman Richard Ista said the Party had not closed the door on a further challenge to the Senate election. "The ultimate decision will be made by Bill Guy and I hope he won't make a decision until after the weekend," Ista was quoted as saying in an Associated Press story. "The only option that is open now is an appeal to the U.S. Senate. This is a bitter pill to swallow."

Saturday, December 14, 1974:

Senate Battle Now 'History' In Guy's View

In a news conference in Fargo on Friday, Guy said the Senatorial race was "history." In an Associated Press story, Guy was quoted as saying "I wanted to win that election and it would be dishonest of me if I said I was not deeply disappointed to lose. Our plans for the future are indefinite. What activities I go into in private life will depend upon the challenge offered. I hope I can find that challenge in North Dakota." Guy did not rule out being a candidate in a future election or accepting a federal position. Guy said he did not plan to challenge the recount. He said ballots with "double votes," where voters marked the names of two candidates instead of one, were the reason Young won. "By voter preference, I won the election, but by the technicality of the election law, I lost it." He blamed the double voting on "ineptness of ballot construction." He also was critical of Jungroth, who was a former state Democratic-NPL Chairman. "He turned against his Party and added to the confusion."

Tuesday, December 17, 1974:

Governor Certifies Winner

Governor Link certified on Monday the winner of the U.S. Senate race, after he received the official report from the State Canvassing Board.

Wednesday, December 18, 1974:

Guy's Counsel Calls For Election Reform

Fargo attorney William Lanier, Jr., who was the chief counsel for Guy's Senate election recount, called for legislation reforming state law to "assure a fool-proof and fair election system," according to an Associated Press story. "We can no longer afford the danger of paper ballots where hundreds of people are losing their votes to double voting, and where more will be disenfranchised by either careless or tired election officials who do not stamp and initial their ballots."

Friday, December 20, 1974:

Dobson's *Minot Daily News Prairie Perspective* column:

Burdick Blamed For Guy's Defeat

"Some Democrats are grumbling in the aftermath of the November election which saw Sen. Milton R. Young defeat former Gov. William L. Guy by 186 votes, that Burdick didn't do as much as he should have for the party ticket," Dobson wrote. "It is not secret, either in North Dakota or in Washington, D.C., that Burdick was not wildly enthusiastic about Guy's candidacy. Burdick and Guy have had many differences over the years. Nonetheless, Burdick did his duty as a party soldier. He delivered a seconding speech for Guy at the state Democratic-NPL Convention and he campaigned extensively for the party ticket in late October."

Monday, December 30, 1974:

Senate Contest Voted Top News Story of 1974

This is an annual vote taken by North Dakota newspaper editors and broadcast news directors at the end of every year, and the selection of the Young-Guy race as the state's top news story of 1974 underscored its significance.

In all of his other Senate campaigns, Young spent about $50,000 each time. This campaign carried a price tag of $300,000. Some $57,000 of that was for lawyers hired for the recount. The Republican Senatorial Campaign Committee put up about two-thirds of this money, and Young raised some from a few other sources. He paid the last $7,000 himself.

"I think where Bill Guy probably made his biggest mistake was in the overconfidence he had. He was so sure that he was going to win. Even after the recount started, he expressed confidence in winning. Somehow or other he had it all figured out that he would win.

"I felt the judges were completely honest but they held somewhat different views on their interpretation of which ballots were valid and which ones weren't. This was a problem because the present law is not too clear. But they were fair about it.

"Guy became very bitter and it is no wonder he never has conceded the election. He was so sure that he was going to win. This is another indication of the strong dislike Guy had for me over the years. He might have won the election if he had conducted his campaign in another way. He had a lot going his way – Watergate alone should have won the election for him. No candidate that I know of ever campaigned so many years for the Senate – all during the time he was Governor and two years after he retired as Governor. Many Republicans lost and others barely won like Dole in Kansas and Bellmon in Oklahoma.

"Quentin Burdick did not openly campaign for Guy in this election. There is some gentlemen's agreement about that. It is seldom one Senator will oppose another Senator from either Party when he goes into that Senator's state, but in my case Senator Mondale did come to

North Dakota to make a couple of speeches in the Red River Valley in support of Guy. Humphrey told me that he was often asked by North Dakota Democrats to come to the state and campaign against me, but he never did. He always refused and many of them are still mad at him.

"Burdick didn't make any major speeches against me. But his top aide from his Fargo office – Tom Stallman – who is a very effective staff member and a former legislator from Richland County, worked hard for Guy. Burdick himself did some – especially on the Indian Reservation. I lost the big Reservations by about a 2-1 vote.

" I think one of the reasons why I did so poorly in the [Red River] Valley and that area in my last election was that in several instances I was quite critical of Bill Guy because he was constantly attacking me – but he did most of it in meetings where the press was not present or through some of his political stooges. I told a member of the press at a press conference shortly before the election that Bill Guy was 'one of the most sanctimonious liars that I ever dealt with.' That was a pretty strong statement which may have hurt me. Even though it was the truth, I think the statement was the kind that hurt me.

"Guy never yet has conceded defeat. From the time he was elected Governor until that election – 14 years afterwards – including the two years he was out of office, he campaigned constantly against me. His whole strategy was to discredit my record. Oftentimes I thought it was dishonest and I even said so at the time. But, he was popular in those years. He got great press. When he left office almost every newspaper had a full page feature story. One wonders how he got that far and that popular – not having much of a sense of humor, if any. But he did have a lot of ability as a speaker. He worked hard at politics. I don't know if he worked so hard at his job as Governor as he might have. I admit to being prejudiced. He really should have been elected to the Senate with all that tremendous publicity – with all the polls predicting that I would lose.

"Really, he worked for 14 years to win this election. Guy had much in his favor. There was Watergate, for example. I couldn't defend Nixon *even though he did many good things such as getting us $5 wheat. I still get some mean letters from Republicans for not defending him. Some of the international relations he handled well. But, Watergate was a horrible mess and I was quite critical but in doing so I made enemies of quite a few dyed-in-the-wool Republicans. Nixon could do no wrong with them, so I alienated maybe 5,000 or more Republicans who probably didn't vote at all. Watergate confused many good Republicans all over the United States and I will always feel that if it had not been for Watergate, I would have won by a big majority. But the one thing – the age issue – helped Guy the most. The charge was that I had been a good Senator but was 'too damn old' and you couldn't argue with that very much!"*

In the Arena

Milt Young held one of North Dakota's seats in the United States Senate for all or part of five decades, which provided him an unrivaled arena for rubbing shoulders with some of the most powerful and influential people in the state, nation and world. His years in the Senate were also a time when the collegial traditions of the Upper Chamber of the United States Congress encouraged civility and respect, with less of the strident partisanship so prevalent today.

Young's personality was well suited for this environment. "He didn't approach things on a partisan basis," said longtime aide Neil Bjornson. "Another strength he had, particularly when you look at the long tenure he had in the Senate, was his magic with the voters. The first question he had on anything was, 'how does it affect the folks back home?' His primary belief was that he was there as a representative of North Dakota and North Dakotans. He was very down-to-earth, an easy man to like. He wasn't the type that was given to airs. I think, quite frankly, you had an awful lot of people who admired him because here was a fellow who had problems. He had the stutter. He never did cover it up. I think there was some admiration for that. That he was willing to do that, and that he could overcome that. And too, his approach to things, it was a common sense approach."

As he approached the end of his Senate career, Young had amassed a large collection of stories about his colleagues, both in Washington and North Dakota. Some have been shared in other chapters. More are here.

Washington Colleagues

Young often aligned himself with Southern Democrats, sharing with them similar views on agriculture and defense, among other issues. *"Southerners, because of having little industry, and being a very poor part of the nation for years after the Civil War, paid more attention to agriculture. If the Republicans had been as close to agriculture as the Southern Democrats, we would have been in control a lot more of the time. Sometimes people ask me why I work with Southern Democrats so much, and I joke with them and say, 'I come from the southern part of North Dakota.'"*

The Southern Senators were strong supporters of defense issues, as well. In his book, *Lyndon Johnson: Master of the Senate,* Robert A. Caro writes about an exchange Young had with Georgia Senator Richard Russell on defense:

> Once, Senator Milton Young of North Dakota said to him, "You people in the South are much more militarily minded than in the North." "Milt," Russell replied, "you'd be more militarily minded, too, if Sherman had crossed North Dakota."

Senator Richard Russell (1897-1971), Georgia, Democrat: In almost every reference to Senator Richard Russell, Young referred to him as his closest friend in the Senate. This Democrat, known to many as the "Georgia Giant," served in the Senate for nearly 40 years, from 1933 to 1971. *"From the beginning, Senator Russell sort of took me under his wing, so to speak. I made many trips with him to Latin America and Europe and various places. He was chairman of the Subcommittee on Agriculture Appropriations and I was the ranking Republican most of the time except [in 1947-49 and 1953-55] when the Republicans controlled the Senate and I was chairman of that Subcommittee.*

"Senator Russell's views were much the same as mine. We jointly sponsored the continuation of 90 percent supports for basic farm commodities, which was very popular then. He was always very helpful

to me on appropriations. If I had a good case, he helped me out on many things – half a dozen projects in North Dakota. On Garrison Dam itself we had all kinds of problems and he was always able to help me. If I had two-thirds of the Appropriations Committee against me, if he wanted he could turn them around – and he would.

"He was always such a decent fellow. Such a brilliant mind. A good example of that was the last three or four years he served. He would come to work late but he would read half the night and I think he could read a page while I read a paragraph. Sometimes we would be discussing some subject which had been debated the day before in the Senate and he knew more about it than anyone on the committee. I think he is recognized as one of the real gentlemen, real statesmen of my time. He was more help to me than any other Senator.

"Once in awhile I would have some difference with the Southern Senators and then I would have to scold them a little and remind them that they might give us a little more cooperation. One thing about the Southerners is that they were very close to agriculture, much closer than the Eastern Senators were. That is one of the reasons I worked so closely with them. Senator Russell always apologized when he was in disagreement with me, saying something like, 'I regret very much to find myself in disagreement with my good friend.' He was a true friend."

Young believed Russell would have been an excellent President. *"If he hadn't been a Southerner, he would have been nominated and elected. In fact early in 1952, I met some of the press as I was leaving the Senate Agriculture Committee. This was on a Friday afternoon. There were three or four newsmen and I didn't even know who they were. They wanted to know if I didn't have a good story for them for the weekend. I said yes, I had a damn good one. I said 'If the Democrats have sense enough to nominate Dick Russell for President, I'd support him.' It wasn't so much of a story until some of the Republican Party officials in North Dakota started reading me out of the Party."*

Senator Robert A. Taft (1889-1953), and Senator Robert A. Taft, Jr. (1917-1993), Ohio, Republicans: Senator Robert A. Taft,

Republican from Ohio, ranked right after Russell as Young's favorite colleague in the Senate. *"Taft took a liking to me when I first came to the Senate and we became very close."*

Young served with the elder Taft, who began his Senate career in 1939, until Taft's death in 1953. His son, Robert Taft, Jr., also an Ohio Republican, was in the House of Representatives from 1963 to 1971 and one term in the Senate from 1971 through 1976.

"The father was more brilliant, more aggressive and more of a fighter. Young Bob is a very fine person but he was too easy going. He is a very fine and honest person but he wasn't the fighter or the aggressive person that his father was."

Early in Young's Senate career, the elder Taft taught him a political technique that he adopted and used to his advantage during his years in Washington. *"One day he called me and said he wanted to discuss the Taft-Hartley Bill with me. I said, 'I'll be right over.' 'No,' he said, 'I want to come to your office.' 'No,' I said, 'you are busier than I am and I will come over there.' But he insisted on coming to my office. This was a case when someone hadn't fully made up his mind, and a top leader comes to see you. We discussed the Taft-Hartley Bill in considerable detail and I think I made a commitment to vote for it then. I have followed that practice ever since. If I want something from a top official, I don't ask him to come to my office, I go to his office."*

Young shared a desk with Taft for much of the time they both served in the Senate. *"When he spoke, I noticed sitting next to him that he had a tendency to lean against his desk and keep pulling away on his pants leg. Sometimes that pants leg would be up to his knee by the time he got through speaking. He had a brilliant mind and was a very down to earth fellow. I sometimes would hand him a bill and say, 'Bob, what is this about?' and he would go through it in about a minute and tell me about what it sought to accomplish. We had adjoining parking spaces in our Senate office building garage. He drove an old Plymouth and his wife drove an old Dodge. This was just at the end of World War II. One morning he came in with a new Olds 88 and he waited for me to* drive in. He said, 'Milt, don't you think that is the prettiest car in the garage?' He was a wealthy man and could have had a Cadillac like many others did – but he was just as proud of that Olds 88 as if it had been a Cadillac."

Taft was responsible for Young becoming the Secretary of the Republican Senate Conference Committee – a position he held for 24 years, longer than anyone else in the history of the Senate. *"I went to all leadership meetings at the White House, sat in on important conferences and was one of the leaders. I had the opportunity to speak up and express my opinions when I wanted to and I kept the records of the meetings."*

Young originally voted against federal aid to higher education, but changed his position in part because of Taft's view on the issue. *"I thought this could better be financed locally without any government interference. But one of the early supporters of aid to education was Senator Taft. He may have had some influence on me on this issue. I always had a lot of confidence in what he said. Here was a fellow who was supposed to be real conservative and he supported aid to education and other programs thought to be liberal at the time. He also supported the co-ops in the Senate, when the average businessman really hated them, and he got into a lot of trouble doing what he thought was right. Federal assistance to housing was another issue where he took a fairly liberal position."*

When Taft sought the nomination for President in 1952, Young supported him at the Republican Convention in Philadelphia that ultimately chose General Dwight Eisenhower over Taft. *"I didn't think Eisenhower, who had spent his lifetime in the military, was as well qualified. I talked with Senator Taft one day at our Senate desk. I said, 'You will have all the businessmen on your side on account of this Taft-Hartley Act and many other reasons.' He said, 'No, Milt, the big political power is in the New York area and I don't have that.' Easterners helped General Eisenhower get the nomination. They made him President of Columbia University and thus he got acquainted with the people who really had the power."*

Young recalled how disappointed Taft was at being denied the nomination. *"He had worked hard for it and I think he deserved it in a lot of respects. He was a different person than many people thought he was. He lived in the White House when his father* [William Howard Taft] *was President, and was a great lawyer – one of the best. He wasn't as conservative as a lot of people thought he was. At that time the anti-co-op issue was really a hot one. I remember when Taft campaigned in North Dakota for state delegates, Minneapolis business interests placed a full page ad in the* Fargo Forum *and the* Grand Forks Herald. *Both ads just tore the shirt off Taft when he was probably the best friend the businessmen ever had.*

"He felt badly about this attack. He recognized that there was a need for co-ops as well as federal aid to education. He was one of the strongest sponsors of this legislation. It probably would have been years before Congress would have passed any federal aid to education had it not been for his support. To some extent I had influence on him as far as farm policies. Being a farmer and knowing farm problems he thought I could be helpful to him."

Joseph McCarthy (1908-1957), Wisconsin, Republican: McCarthy was raised on a Wisconsin farm and Young appreciated the support he gave to farm legislation. McCarthy came to the Senate in 1947, just after World War II had ended, and Young initially believed there was some merit to the investigations he launched on alleged Communist infiltration of the federal government, especially the State Department. *"During the war, we were partners with Russia and there were some people who carried that partnership a little too far. When he began his investigations concerning Communist infiltration in government, there probably was a need for someone to look into it. But an investigation like that needed someone who was a little more rational than he was. He was tremendously popular for awhile, but then he got so he wasn't accurate with his statements."*

McCarthy began his investigation hearings in February 1950. *"I think most of the Senate, or at least half of them, supported McCarthy at first but as he went too far his support dwindled. McCarthy got started in all of this because the anti-Communists here, and especially the Taiwan-Chinese Nationalists, were greatly concerned about the Communists and they tried to influence many to get involved, including me. I was interested to some extent, but I thought it was not a job for me. It was a lawyer's job. But we were partners of Russia in this war and for awhile afterwards some of our people carried that partnership a little too far. And, of course, Stalin's actions after the war changed things. He wanted to grab all the power he could and he was very ruthless in the negotiations after the war. We withdrew most of our troops from Europe after the war at the same time that he was keeping huge military forces in Europe.*

When Young lived at the Wardman Park Hotel in Washington, he saw McCarthy when he came there to deliver radio broadcasts to his constituents in Wisconsin. *"They had a studio there and he would come up to my room before doing some of these broadcasts – which was a question-and-answer format. He would take a tumbler about two-thirds full of bourbon and drink it down straight and then take about one-half box of baking soda for his bad stomach. He would then do the broadcast and you would never know he had a drink."*

Later in 1950, Young helped McCarthy find a place to visit in North Dakota during the Congressional recess. *"That summer he told me he wanted to go out on a farm during the recess to get away from everything and work hard and get back in shape physically. He told me one noon that he and a newspaperman – I have forgotten his name – were going out to make the harvest and they were going to North Dakota. I said, 'Joe, you had better let me pick out a place you can go where you get good food and good people to work for' 'No,' he said, 'I don't want anyone to know where I am going.' But finally one day he said, 'Well, if you will pick out a place that you think is all right and swear you won't tell anybody who I am, go ahead and do it.'"*

Young called several of his friends from the state legislature and made arrangements with State Senator Mike Raschko of Dickinson for McCarthy to go to the farm of Joe Lefor south of Dickinson, who was a relative of Raschko's. *"The newspaperman didn't stay very long but Joe was there two or three weeks. I was going to put on a party for him before he left but about that time Lefor's son came back from Oregon. He was active in the Young Republicans and he recognized him right away. McCarthy left the same day. But they said he was a hard worker. He was a husky man. He could shovel grain with the best of them. Later, Joe Lefor made a special trip to Washington to see him. He liked McCarthy very much."*

As chairman of the Senate Committee on Operations, McCarthy held many hearings investigating Communism infiltration in government through the committee's Subcommittee on Investigations. McCarthy's investigations into the U.S. Army began in 1953, and evolved into investigations of McCarthy himself the following year. In April 1954, 36 days of the Army-McCarthy Hearings were broadcast on live television, drawing an estimated 20 million viewers. McCarthy's charges and tactics were highly controversial, and at the end of August, a Select Committee opened hearings to consider a Senate resolution to censure the Wisconsin Republican.

"I remember when they were about to try him by the Select Committee. I attended a meeting at his house with some other Senators. McCarthy had hired Edward Bennett Williams, now a famous lawyer, but who was just starting then. I had hired him for a previous case so I knew Williams quite well. He called me later and said, 'Can't you keep Joe McCarthy still, keep him from talking?' And I said, 'No, I can't do a thing with him.' But I don't think Joe would have been censured if he hadn't taken after and been so abusive of many of the members of the Select Committee."

When the entire Senate considered McCarthy's censure in December 1954, Young was among the 22 Senators to vote against it. The resolution passed with 67 votes. The only Senator not voting was John F. Kennedy of Massachusetts, who was hospitalized for back surgery. *"It probably wasn't the right vote. The worst thing Joe did was to attack quite viciously the committee that was set up to investigate him and his charges. The Senate selected eight or 10 of the most highly respected members of the Senate – the most fair and honest – for this committee and when Joe attacked them he assured himself of being censured. In retrospect, I think I probably should have voted to censure him but the major reason I didn't was that I thought, at least at first, that he served a good purpose in investigating Communism in government. After all, this was shortly after the war and we were partners with Russia and some people carried that partnership a little too far. Another reason was that Senator McCarthy was always very good on farm matters. I believed so strongly in farm programs that I couldn't help but feel sympathetic toward him. In retrospect, though, I think it was the wrong vote. He probably deserved censure."*

Hubert Humphrey (1911-1978), Minnesota, Democrat: Young believed his colleagues' respect and admiration for Humphrey grew the longer he served in the Senate. *"This goes back to his reputation as a happy warrior. He fought hard for the good of his Party. He was always friendly. There was nothing mean about him. He was intelligent and influential, one of the more influential ones. He was one that members of the Senate listened to, very good on farm matters. I think on international questions, especially when he was Vice President, he was always involved and close to the so-called intellectuals. As Vice President, he had access to all the CIA information and thus was better informed on difficult international questions and, as a result, took a somewhat different position than some of his liberal friends."*

Eugene McCarthy (1916-2005), Minnesota, Democrat: Young described McCarthy as *"the most delightful person I ever knew. Everyone liked him. There is one interesting thing he would do. I would be sitting among a bunch of real tough conservatives. He would come over there and sit down and say, "Milt, don't you think it is time that we Socialists have a caucus?" It was typical of his sense of humor as they were tough conservatives and he was very liberal."*

Karl Mundt (1900-1974), South Dakota, Republican: *"Senator Mundt was an especially good friend. He campaigned in North Dakota* *for me and I campaigned in South Dakota for him. We were both on the Agriculture and Appropriations Committees and we thought much alike. Sometimes we differed, like on wheat sales to Russia. He was strongly anti-Communist and was opposed to those wheat sales."*

In November 1969, Mundt suffered a severe stroke that prevented him from taking part in any day-to-day work in the Senate. Instead of resigning, Mundt's wife, Mary, ran his office until his term ended in January 1973. During this time, Young and his staff were among Mundt's Senate colleagues who assisted in keeping the South Dakota Senator's office operating.

George McGovern (1922-), South Dakota, Democrat: Young and McGovern, the Democratic Party's 1972 Presidential nominee, were longtime members of the Senate Agriculture Committee. Young did not have specific comments about McGovern during his 1979-80 interviews with Dr. D. Jerome Tweton, but McGovern described Young as "one of the steadiest men I ever knew. There were never any surprises, at least in my experience with Milt Young. He was a steady advocate of agriculture and the farm families in his state. On the Senate Agriculture Committee, I remember that on almost every issue that came up, there were no surprises with Milt. He emerged as a chief spokesman on our committee of anything that had to do with wheat, and of anything that had to do with farm families and their welfare. I don't know of a time when he reversed himself on an expected position on agriculture's issues. That seemed to be his major interest. If anyone in the Senate was Mr. Agriculture, it would be Milt Young."

McGovern said he and Young "had very similar interests, we had very similar constituencies, and he was consistent about that. He wasn't erratic. You pretty much knew where he was going to come down as far as issues that affected the rural populations of both of our states. I can't recall Milt taking a position on the fundamental interests of farmers where he and I differed. And that was helpful, because it meant support from across the aisle, from the Republican side, so he and I always presented a bipartisan position on rural matters and rural interests."

However, McGovern said he and Young hardly ever agreed on defense issues. "He was always strong for whatever was proposed by the Armed Services Committee, headed all those years by Senator Russell. I was not. From the day I entered Congress until the day I left, I thought we were spending too much on the military. I don't think Milt ever agreed with any of my proposals to reduce military spending and the size of the military budget."

Allen Ellender (1890-1972), Louisiana, Democrat: He and Young played golf and went on several foreign trips together. Ellender was chairman of the Public Works Appropriations Subcommittee and later chairman of the full Appropriations Committee. *"One time when I was out in North Dakota, he made a statement at a hearing severely condemning reclamation projects, including Garrison Diversion. When I got back, I had a visit with him and I told him how North Dakota had sacrificed 500,000 acres of land for that project, and how badly we needed irrigation in our semi-arid area. 'Oh,' he said, 'well, that's different.' He never took after Garrison Diversion again."*

Norris Cotton (1900-1989), New Hampshire, Republican: *"We voted fairly closely on many issues. He was a very able person, who spent much of his life, more than 30 years, in Congress and first went there as an employee. I would say he was on the conservative side, but on some things like Health, Education and Welfare, where he was the ranking Republican on the Committee, he was a little on the liberal side. I think he was a good legislator. If you are going to be liberal, those are the programs where you should be on the liberal side. He was a very good friend of mine. I had breakfast with him nearly every day, and I ordered the same thing every morning – orange juice, bacon and eggs. It got so the waitresses at the Senate Dining Room never asked me what I wanted, they just brought it to me. I got a bad habit from him during these breakfasts. He would insist on tipping the waitress $1 for a breakfast that cost only $2 or $2.50. I thought I should do that, too, and I am still tipping $1 for breakfast."*

John Kennedy (1917-1963) and Edward Kennedy (1932-2009),

Massachusetts, Democrats; Robert Kennedy (1925-1968), New York, Democrat: Young believed that of the three Kennedy brothers with whom he served in the Senate, *"John was the most sincere and personable one. Robert was pretty good that way, too. Ted Kennedy can be real friendly – more for a purpose – if he thinks it may be important in the future. He can be very friendly but John, I think, was naturally more friendly with everyone. They are all very intelligent. They could all be great leaders."*

George Aiken, (1892-1984) Vermont, Republican: *"I remember when Senator Aiken sat next to me in the Senate, and on farm legislation he was strongly in favor of flexible price supports. I always wanted higher and more rigid supports, and he and I argued about this issue. Once I made a speech about it on the Senate floor and I was very serious about what I was saying. During the speech, he slipped a card on the desk on top of my manuscript which read, 'Don't confuse me with the facts, my mind is made up!!' That eased all the difficulties."*

Robert Byrd, Jr., (1917-) West Virginia, Democrat: Byrd was Majority Leader during Young's last years of the Senate, being first elected to that position in 1977. *"He is a very able leader, a stern leader and he is a master at persuading other Senators. When you can even beat Ted Kennedy out of the Majority Leadership position like he did, you are pretty good."*

North Dakota politicians

John Baer (1886-1970) Republican: He was from Beach, and represented the state in the U.S. House of Representatives for two terms from 1917 to 1921. *"He was the cartoonist for the Nonpartisan League and later for labor publications and became exceptionally good. He lived in Washington all his life after he left North Dakota, and I got to be quite well acquainted with him. He was a Democrat but ran as a Leaguer on the Republican ticket. He loved to come to the Senate restaurant and I would sometimes invite him when I had North Dakota guests and he would come and visit and do some cartoons for them. He* *did hundreds of cartoons for North Dakota people.*

"He was a very likable person. He was soft spoken and a very decent fellow. You wouldn't get any political argument visiting with him about labor or anything else. We didn't talk politics and issues much. I knew he did cartoons for some League candidates in North Dakota while I was in the Senate. That was quite a long while ago but I never asked him to do any for me, even though I saw him quite often. He remained quite liberal politically. He was close to labor. He talked about his days in North Dakota, and knew everyone who was involved in politics. We often had visits about them, and I learned as much about the League from him as I did from Langer. He talked like the average Leaguer about their issues and problems but he wasn't argumentative at all. He told some very interesting stories about what happened within the League in those early years. He also got along with Langer."

A.C. Townley (1880-1959) Nonpartisan League: A Minnesota native, he farmed in the Beach area before founding the Nonpartisan League in 1915. His influence with the NPL, however, did not last beyond its first early years. Young had contact with him when he visited Washington in the 1950s, and when he ran as an Independent in 1956 for Young's Senate seat. He ran again for the Senate in 1958, losing to Langer, whose first state office was as Attorney General on Townley's original Nonpartisan League slate of candidates in 1916. *"Many people often wondered why he didn't run for the Senate or Governor when the League was strong. At one time he could have been elected to any office including the Senate. But I believe at first he was really sold on the cause of farmers and their problems.*

"I never heard him speak in his early League days but he had the reputation of being a silver-tongued orator and, I understand, he was real good. Townley only came to Washington for a period of about four or five years before he died. I don't think he was the kind of person that he was earlier. By the 1950s he became more the isolationist type or Birch Society type. He was anti-Communist. Almost everyone that he didn't like he called a Communist. That was the strange thing about

some of those early Leaguers. They were real liberal when they started out but when they turned, they never stopped in the middle at all. They went clear to the right of me.

"I don't think Townley went to see Langer in Washington at all in those years. He spent more time in my office and usually arguing because he got to be much more conservative than I was. He wasn't very friendly with me. I don't know why he kept coming to see me except that he probably considered me the most conservative of the North Dakota delegation. He had a very sharp tongue. He practically told me that I was not good as a Senator. In his opinion, I wasn't conservative enough. I think he was bitter in those later years. Even the Leaguers ignored him. He was no longer an idol of most Leaguers. I don't suppose he spoke at a NPL Convention for maybe the last 20 years of his life.

"On his anti-Communist platform he got quite a few followers around the state. He would hold meetings and get 50 to 100 there. It was mostly playing these recordings and I think he sold some and he would speak some. For awhile, he promoted the sale of oil stock in a well at Robinson, North Dakota. It was an ordinary well but they pumped out almost pure gasoline and he had a lot of farmers and other people believing that there was gasoline down there or oil, and he sold a considerable amount of stock in it. In my hometown of Berlin, at least half a dozen people went to Robinson and bought stock – and they actually believed it had great possibilities."

Townley was killed in a car-truck collision near Makoti, North Dakota, on November 7, 1959, one day before Langer died in Washington, D.C.

Lynn Frazier, (1874-1947), Republican: Frazier represented North Dakota in the U. S. Senate from 1923 to 1941, and was Governor from 1917 until being recalled in 1921. The following year he was elected to the Senate, running as the NPL candidate on the Republican ticket. Langer defeated Frazier for re-election in the 1940 Republican primary after Frazier had left the NPL.

"I didn't know him well. I remember when he and William Lemke left the League in 1940. Lemke came with us in the ROC and was elected

to the House of Representatives, but Frazier ran independently and lost. He wouldn't come with us to the ROC but I don't know if he would have helped us or not. I think Lemke did and I think that Gerald Nye did in the early years because we needed what were then called the 'Rumper Leaguers.' The League was quite badly split. Those who disliked the League leadership such as Langer were called 'Rumpers.' In LaMoure County, I don't think I would have been elected to the Senate in this strong League County if it hadn't been for the 'Rumper Leaguer' support."

Charles Robertson (1889-1951), Republican: He served in the U.S. House of Representatives from 1941 to 1943, and again from 1945 to 1949. *"I liked Charlie. He was a lot of fun to be around. Charlie ran as a Leaguer but in his heart, he was very conservative. Through the influence of Langer, he was endorsed by the NPL Convention. Many Leaguers were never quite satisfied with him but then he switched to the ROC and was defeated. I think that was a mistake. He probably couldn't have been elected again either as a Leaguer because the Leaguers thought he was too conservative. His problem was not so much his conservative voting record and Langer not supporting that. It was more with Leaguers throughout the state. Charlie was a businessman and quite conservative, much more so than I was."*

Gerald P. Nye (1892-1971), Republican, was appointed to the U.S. Senate in 1925 to fill the vacancy caused by Senator Edwin Ladd's death. He was re-elected to three terms until being defeated for re-election by Senator Moses in 1944. By then, Nye had made a national name for himself as an isolationist, but during his third term Young observed how he fell out of favor with North Dakota voters. *"A good example is when he spoke at Watford City right during the depth of the Depression not so long before he was up for election the last time. The people were desperate, there were no crops and they were very hard up and he hardly mentioned their problems at all. He just went on and gave that isolationist speech. That hurt him badly."*

Otto Krueger (1890-1963), Republican: Following 20 years as the Wells County Auditor in Fessenden, North Dakota, Krueger was North

Dakota's Insurance Commissioner and State Treasurer in the 1940s before he was elected to three terms in the U.S. House, serving from 1953 to 1959. *"Otto was kind of a strong-headed old-German type, one of the Germans from Russia. Very conservative. Very anti-Langer. But he was elected County Auditor in Wells County for years and years right when the League was strong. He was not flashy but people liked and respected him."*

Three Governors: Young was in the Senate during the terms of the state's three ROC Republican governors between the years of 1945 to 1960. However, he said he did not manage the ROC from Washington, like he observed Langer doing with the NPL. *"I had a surprisingly little role as far as the strategy and picking of ROC candidates. Langer practically ran the Nonpartisan League from Washington but we had a Republican Governor and he was the leader of the Party. In fact, it is difficult to have a very strong party unless you have the Governor."*

The three governors were **Fred Aandahl (1897-1966),** who served from 1945 to 1951; **Norman Brunsdale (1891-1978),** who served from 1951 to 1957, and **John Davis (1913-1990),** who served from 1957 to 1961. Young's observations of the three:

"I believe that Aandahl was the strongest leader of the three ROC governors. He was maybe a little bit dictatorial. He had strong opinions and strong views. Brunsdale was a very shrewd, intelligent fellow, a good politician, but he was more easy-going. Davis was a good governor but he didn't exert the strong leadership of the two previous governors."

Two of these governors, Aandahl and Brunsdale, also represented their state briefly in the U.S. Congress, and Davis narrowly lost an election bid to the Senate.

In 1950, Aandahl was elected to the U.S. House, replacing William Lemke, who died in 1950 during the campaign. Because of pressure from ROC leaders to run for Langer's Senate seat, he did not seek re-election to the House. *"Most of the leadership in the ROC thought that he was the only one who had a chance and it was his responsibility to be the candidate. Being the loyal Republican that Aandahl was, he agreed to this, even though it was against his own better judgment, and especially that of Mrs. Aandahl, and I believe his daughters, too. Early in the primary campaign, especially before the campaign got started, I think a lot of people thought he would win. But after the campaign got going Fred really wasn't a match for Langer. Fred made the same kind of speeches most of the time about free enterprise."*

Aandahl received 10 percent of the vote in that election, with Langer and Democrat Harold Morrison out-polling him. From 1953 to 1961, Aandahl was the Assistant Secretary of the Interior in the Eisenhower Administration, and instrumental in sending to Congress the first approval of Garrison Diversion.

When Langer died on November 8, 1959, Governor Davis appointed Brunsdale to fill his seat. *"He told John Davis that he had no interest in running and wouldn't be a candidate. I think Brunsdale deserved consideration for a long and great political career. But politically it was perhaps a mistake as far as Davis is concerned. I don't think he should have had himself appointed but he should have appointed some young person who could later have been a candidate – perhaps not for the Senate again but for some other office in the next election such as Governor. Then that would have made a good team – Davis running with the one who was in the Senate. I think Davis must have wanted to go to the Senate himself, and I think he was a little afraid that if he appointed some young fellow who did a great job and became very popular, he might have a problem. A lot of people would think: "Why take this young fellow out after he has been there and done a good job?"'*

Brunsdale held the U.S. Senate seat from November 19, 1959, to August 7, 1960. Davis was the Republican candidate for the seat, which was won by Quentin Burdick in the June 28, 1960, special election. He defeated Davis by 1,100 votes, and took office 40 days later.

"If John Davis had worked half as hard and had gone for publicity as much as he did afterwards when he was a candidate for Commander of the American Legion, he would have been elected to the Senate. Secretary of Agriculture Benson was a problem for Davis during the

1960 election. I had fought Benson from the start and Davis was kind of for him and he didn't have too much to say about him until about two weeks before the election. At that late date, he came out against Benson, and Benson was more of an issue than anything else in the campaign. That was too late to come out against Benson. I often thought that he would have been better off to have stayed with his old position than to change right before the election. I wasn't consulted by candidates too much on how to run campaigns. Most candidates wanted me to help them but they didn't listen to my advice very much. I went around the state for John Davis as I have for Republicans in all other campaigns. Davis never made a point of asking for my support. I had the feeling he was quite sure he was going to win the election."

Davis was elected to a one-year term as national commander of the American Legion in 1967. He was appointed director of the Office of Civil Defense by President Nixon in 1969, a position he held until 1976.

Among the many North Dakotans Young knew during his years in politics, Young especially liked his North Dakota Senate colleague, Devils Lake lawyer and Republican activist **Clyde Duffy (1890–1977), Republican.** *"Clyde Duffy was very popular and a great personality. In politics, a lot of good people never get the breaks and sometimes the good people get the breaks and don't take advantage of them. Clyde Duffy is, as you say, a very intelligent person, a very decent person. He served in the North Dakota Senate for 10 years before running against Langer in 1958. He would have made one of the best members of the Senate that we ever sent there. But he didn't get the breaks and was unfortunate in not coming along at quite the right time. In the early years, he was not as active in the ROC. He was a loyal worker within the ROC but had a good law practice and was very busy. In later years he was very active in the ROC."*

William Langer (1886-1959), Republican: For 25 years, from the mid-1930s through the end of the 1950s, Langer's and Young's political paths were intertwined. They never ran against each other for a political office, and Young was realistic in his assessment of the outcome of such a contest. *"Well, some people said that I could beat him but I don't think so. Langer was a genius when it came to politics. He would work hard at it and he could come out here and see more people in a week than I could in three weeks. He would work half the night. He had almost a hypnotic personality. No, I don't think I could have beaten him. I knew much more about farm problems, and farm legislation was very important then. He didn't have a good grasp of farm legislation and he didn't pay much attention to it. He voted for farm legislation but would even ask me to go to North Dakota and hold farm meetings. I could have beaten him with the farm vote. But he was really clever politically.*

"Langer loved a fight and wasn't happy when things were going smoothly. He seemed to enjoy it most when he had some trouble. He even indicated that to me at times."

In Washington, Langer was known for multi-hour filibusters on the Senate floor. *"There were times when Langer, about once or twice a week, would talk for four or five hours and Glen Taylor of Idaho established a Senate record, I think, of 21 hours. Later* [in 1957] *Senator Strom Thurmond of South Carolina broke it with 24 hours and 18 minutes of continuous talk against the Civil Rights Act. There were many Senators during that period who would talk for several hours at a time. The purposes for filibusters vary, but in the case of Langer, he liked to do it just to throw his weight around and make the leadership pay a little more attention to him. During one filibuster in 1950,* [11:30 a.m. September 22 to 5:23 p.m. September 23] *we were meeting in the old Senate chamber while they were repairing our present Senate chamber. It was very small and I was in the chamber until about 11:30 that night, after Senator Langer had started to speak about 6 p.m. The Republicans, like the Democrats, always tried to have one or two on the floor at all times and I recall they decided Senator Saltonstall and I should take over at 7 in the morning. So I went to the doctor's office to get something to help me sleep and then to my office.*

"I wasn't in my office more than a half hour or so, when the Quorum Call bells rang and I went over to the Senate right away. Langer had

collapsed and they had taken him to the office of the Secretary of the Senate. Dr. George Calver, the Senate doctor, was there. When I looked at Langer he was very pale and looked just like a dead man. He didn't show any sign of life at all. He wasn't even breathing. I didn't know one could stay alive that long and look that way. But I remember Dr. Calver saying, 'He has started to breathe now, he will be all right.' Langer had a bad case of diabetes and he didn't keep it under control and went into a coma. This filibuster was something he wasn't supposed to do – especially speak all night. As I recall it was around midnight and he had already spoken about six hours – maybe seven.

"A lot of people would get pretty disturbed with Langer during these filibusters, and we had a few others at that time who did the same thing. Quite often about 5 or 6 o'clock in the evening when the Senate was about to have its last vote, he would get the floor and start speaking and give no indication as to how long he was going to speak. Then the leadership would keep us around sometimes for many hours. I stayed up all night many times trying to help break a filibuster. Sometimes he would speak four or five hours and let the Senate vote and go home. This was very disturbing to people when they wanted to get home and have dinner. I believe the Senate is so reluctant to limit filibustering because years ago it was the Southerners who were doing it on the civil rights issues and now it is the liberals who want unlimited debate."

Langer was also known for introducing bills to keep people from being deported. *"For example, a lot of Chinese are ship jumpers – once they get here – and it has been practiced for as long as I have been there. If a Senator introduces a bill to give them citizenship, they won't be deported as long as that bill is pending. If such a bill is killed by the Committee the one it is introduced for is usually deported. Some of them have a lot of merit – sometimes they would have their problems straightened out in six months or a year – but some of these bills have become sort of a racket. Senator Langer introduced a great many of them. It was always difficult for me to understand why he introduced so many except that he was on the Judiciary Committee to which such* bills were referred. Why he did it? He could have gained financially. He introduced them for all kinds of people.

"Many I knew were meritorious. He did one for a hockey player at the University of North Dakota who was from Czechoslovakia. I do some of that myself. Sometimes if a good doctor gets to the United States, I am always ready to introduce a bill to keep him here. Very few of these bills get out of Committee and are approved by both Houses of Congress so that the person the bill is introduced for becomes a citizen. So long as the bill is pending they do not have to be deported. Sometimes the Judiciary Committee will take action on such a bill and if this action is adverse, the person faces deportation. And during my time I have gotten a few through that way. But recent legislation is much more workable now and you can work through the Immigration Service and if you have a good case, you can get straightened out and they can get citizenship."

Young remembered how Langer used to boast about some of the things he would do, ". . . How he would even fix a jury when he was practicing law and things like that, and it didn't bother him at all. I remember many times businessmen would come to Washington hating Langer and he would invite them to have lunch. He would often spend about two hours at lunch with them and when they would come back to my office, the usual thing they would say was, 'He isn't such a bad sort of fellow.' He could exert a lot of influence over them. He had a brilliant mind. If it wasn't for the few fool things that he did, he would have gone a whole lot further politically.

"Langer was a frank sort of person. He bragged about being independent and changing his positions. I remember once he made two speeches in the Senate one day – one on one side of the subject and another one on the other. One of the Senators questioned him about it, and he said, 'You will find out I am the most independent son of a bitch in the Senate.' He was a fighter and I think he was a liberal at heart. I never knew anyone who enjoyed politics more than he did – even when things were rough and he had problems. In the Senate, we were always on good terms personally."

However, it was different back home during campaigns. Langer worked against Young in almost every election that he was a candidate. *"Sometimes I got pretty mad at him. I remember one particular time he gave a speech at Linton. Lydia, his wife, was along – a very fine person – and she was trying to help Bill. She brought a picture of mine that I had given him. Senators don't usually use such pictures since you usually say nice things. She showed the picture to the audience and she read what I had said, 'This is what Milt Young thought about Bill Langer before the election.' When I found out about it, I took the picture he had autographed for me off the wall and threw it on the floor and broke the glass. But it wasn't long afterwards that I put it back together again and have it on the wall yet."*

During the 1952 campaign, Langer accompanied President Truman when he made a "whistle stop" campaign by train across the state, campaigning for Adlai Stevenson, the Democratic Presidential nominee. The President and his daughter, Margaret, took the train, called the *Ferdinand Magellan*, on an 8,000-mile trip through 24 northern and western states. It made its first stop in North Dakota in Fargo at 8:45 a.m. on September 29, and proceeded to stop in Grand Forks at 11 a.m., Larimore at 12:10 p.m., Lakota at 1:30 p.m., Devils Lake at 2:30 p.m., Minot at 5:10 p.m., Berthold at 6:22 p.m., Stanley at 7:20 p.m., Tioga at 8:10 p.m., and Williston at 9:15 p.m. before crossing into Montana for a stop in Wolf Point at 11:50 p.m. On each stop, Truman spoke from the rear platform of the train with Langer close at hand.

In Williston, the President was introduced by Congressman Usher Burdick. "On my trip across the state today, I have had a chance to get acquainted with the candidates for office," Truman said. "Some of them are Republicans and some of them are Democrats. If I was in North Dakota – of course, having been raised a Democrat, I would vote for the Democratic ticket. But I want to say to you that these two Republicans that are friends of mine here in North Dakota are mighty fine men, and I like them both very much. I would hate to vote against them. In fact, I don't – I don't have to make a decision. I told Bill Langer today, if I had known how well the people of North Dakota felt about me, I would have come out here and filed for Governor."

A campaign report in the October 6, 1952, issue of *Time* Magazine noted that "Truman praised North Dakota's nominally Republican Senator William ('Wild Bill') Langer, who was traveling on the Truman train. Langer has stood ace high with Truman ever since 1947 when he cast the deciding vote in committee against Senate investigation of the Kansas City vote fraud."

This was in reference to Langer's vote in the Judiciary Committee on July 9, 1947, that prevented an investigation of allegations of vote fraud in Kansas City. Republicans had pushed the investigation because they believed it would turn up evidence that the Democratic Party machine in Kansas City had falsified election returns in the August 1946 primary. That machine had helped elect Truman to the U.S. Senate in 1934 and 1940. Langer opposed his Republican colleagues and his vote helped keep the investigation from going forward. Had the investigation proceeded, it could have proved embarrassing to the Truman Administration.

Young was active in the 1952 campaign, as well. *"When Fred Aandahl ran against Langer for Senate in 1952, I got more involved in the campaign than did Aandahl. I took after Langer pretty tough and we got into some pretty strong arguments. Usually a couple of weeks after an election he would forget about it and we could visit again. This time it was about five or six weeks after the election he still wasn't speaking to me.*

"Later there was a big rural telephone meeting in the basement of the Powers Hotel in Fargo and Jim Coleman, [longtime Nodak Rural Electric Manager and rural telephone pioneer from Grand Forks], *was master of ceremonies. He called on me before he did Langer. In his election against Aandahl, Langer carried every county except but three. I told the people there that Senator Langer was the most ungrateful person in North Dakota. I said I campaigned against him in every county of North Dakota but three, and those three were the only ones he*

lost. He had a good sense of humor and got a kick out of it and we were back visiting again."

Regarding Langer's relationship with William Lemke, Young observed, *"Langer never said much about William Lemke, but Lemke hated Langer with a passion. There were two things that Lemke wanted to do before he finished his political career, and not many people knew this. He wanted to be Governor of North Dakota before he retired. He wanted to end his political career as Governor, and write a book about Langer. That would have been a good one because it would have concerned a long and bitter relationship. Langer had a bad case of diabetes. Most people, when they came to Washington, would ask all of us in the North Dakota delegation: 'How is Langer's health?' Once, when someone asked Lemke that question, he said, 'Oh, Langer has diabetes but the trouble with diabetes is that it works too God-damned slow!'"*

In 1956, during the Eisenhower-Stevenson Presidential campaign, he made a speech that became quite notorious and greatly angered the Democrats, depicting them as a Party apt to lead the country to war. *"It was called the 'Carloads of Coffins' speech. In that speech, which Senator Langer mailed all over North Dakota, he said, 'If you elect another Democrat President, you will have carloads of coffins coming back to North Dakota.'"*

When North Dakota's political factions realigned in 1956, the ROC become the official Republican Party and the NPL merged with the Democrat Party. Langer stayed with the Republicans. *"After being a NPLer all his life, there was something deep-seated about the Democrat Party that he didn't like. They were more internationalist and we were involved in more wars in their time. And I think, it was to his advantage, as long as the League filed in the Republican column, to elect a Republican President rather than a Democrat. It was a political move. Since he had always been in the Republican column, he stayed there. And a lot of his strongest supporters, like the Germans from Russia, gave him his strongest support. They were strong Republicans then and they are now. That is where I get my biggest vote, too. I think things like that influenced him. Then he was of German-Austrian descent himself. He spoke German quite well."*

In his last campaign in 1958, Langer ran for the first time as the Republican candidate without the endorsement of the NPL. It was the first and only time in the political careers of both Langer and Young that they were not representing opposing political factions in the Republican Party. Langer's opponent was State Senator Raymond Vendsel, a Democrat from Carpio. A.C. Townley and Custer Solem ran as Independent candidates. In this new political landscape, Young anguished over how much support he wanted to give Langer in this election. Among those weighing in on this were Pat Byrne and Chris Sylvester from his staff, both who opposed Young's involvement in the campaign. He compromised, supporting him, but not campaigning for Langer. *"As far back as December before his last election, I made a statement and worded it very carefully. I said, 'The right thing to do is to re-elect Langer.'"*

In the end, he did not need the support of any other state political figure. Langer, whose health had declined significantly, handily won the election by 57 percent of the vote, without making a single campaign appearance in the state.

Usher Burdick (1879-1960), Republican: Burdick served in the U.S. House of Representatives two different times, from 1935 to 1945, and from 1949 to 1959. Young's observation was that he was well liked in Congress. *"He was very humorous but he wasn't the aggressive type – not a leader in the House. He seemed to have a greater emphasis and interest on international issues like the United Nations. He remained an isolationist all the way through his career."*

"I think that one of the most unkind things that happened to Usher Burdick was at the last Republican Convention he attended in 1958 when they didn't give him an opportunity to speak. He had some trouble with his marriage at that time and that may be one of the reasons why. Usher took this very hard and became very bitter about it, left the convention,

went to Fargo and talked his son, Quentin, into running for the House as a Democrat. Had they recognized Burdick at the convention, it could have been a different story entirely."

There was another event involving Burdick father and son that Young wondered, if he had handled differently, would have changed the state's political history. *"One day Langer brought Usher Burdick over to the Senate's Republican cloakroom. Langer wanted to know if I would approve of Quentin being appointed a federal district judge, and I said, 'No, but I would approve his brother, Gene,'* [a district judge from Williston.] *Quentin was very liberal then and Gene was more conservative. I am not sure whether Langer was really sincere about it, but if he had become a federal district judge, he wouldn't have been a member of Congress."*

Young got along well with Usher Burdick until shortly before he retired. *"During the last year he served, we got into a rather bitter exchange of letters. To some extent, I may have been to blame, motivated by my strong belief in farm price support programs. In our exchange of letters I was critical of Usher because of his constant publicity claiming there was no shortage of our kind of wheat. The farm program then, as has been the case since, had one purpose of holding down surpluses as a means of getting a better price. What disturbed me was that farmers naturally liked to hear someone say that there were not any surpluses of our kind of wheat. We have always raised good quality wheat but there was a surplus and I felt Usher Burdick's position tended to turn farmers against a program I believed was necessary."*

Quentin Burdick (1908-1992), Democrat: From 1960, when Burdick was elected to complete Langer's unexpired term, until Young's retirement from the Senate in 1981, these two men represented North Dakota in the U.S. Senate. *"We get along well. He has a different political philosophy than I have. He is much more liberal than I am, but he goes his way and I go my way so we really didn't have any problems. On Garrison Diversion, most water projects and farm programs, Senator Burdick and I vote pretty much the same. I, of course, have served on* *the Senate Agriculture Committee ever since I came to the Senate and helped write most farm programs. On the floor of the Senate, Senator Burdick invariably votes the same as I do on farm matters.*

"He has been very considerate and we have a good relationship. [In 1980], the North Dakota National Guard and the North Dakota State Society in Washington held a reception for me. About 15 Senators came – even Edmund Muskie, who was then Secretary of State. I understand Senator Burdick had invited all of them to come and he introduced them. He even mentioned at this meeting that I had defeated him once. That has never come out in the press much. I am the only one who has defeated both Guy and Burdick."

Hjalmer Nygaard (1906-1963), Republican: Nygaard served in the U.S. House from 1961 until he died of a heart attack while in office on July 18, 1963. *"Hjalmer was probably the best-liked of anyone who served in Congress from North Dakota in my time. He was very highly respected. A very fine person, and he had much to do with Garrison Diversion being authorized. He was on the Interior Committee that handled the authorization."*

Don Short (1903-1982), Republican: A Billings County rancher, Short represented the state's West Congressional District from 1959 to 1965. *"Don is a very honorable person and probably the most conservative, real honest conservative of anyone I have served with. He is very conservative and set in his ways. We had many exchanges of letters but through it all they were friendly. But I think that to some extent, he blamed me for his defeat* [in 1964] *because we did take different views on farm legislation."*

Rolland Redlin (1920-), Democrat: Redlin represented North Dakota's West Congressional District for one term, from 1965 to 1967. *"He was on the House Agriculture Committee. He was a good person to work with, and like me, was very interested in agricultural legislation."*

Tom Kleppe (1919-2007), Republican: Kleppe served two terms in the U.S. House, from the West District, from 1967 to 1971. Kleppe unsuccessfully tried to take Quentin Burdick's Senate seat in 1964, and again in 1970. *"Tom was a very confident fellow. He is made that way. Everything he has been involved in has been a success, including business and athletics. He was a good baseball player and he had a chance to play with the St. Louis Browns. He was the only one I ever knew who made money on horse races."*

However, Young did not approve of how Kleppe ran his 1970 campaign against Burdick. *"I think Tom meant well but I didn't like the kind of campaign he was putting on. He was overly confident and had some poor political advisers. I called him one time when he was in Fargo and talked to him about it. I said, 'Tom, things aren't going good, you ought to change some things or do this or that.' 'No, Milt,' he said, 'it is going so good I wouldn't change a thing.' North Dakotans were turned off by his slick campaign ads. But Tom's biggest problem was his campaign manager, who was trained at the Republican National Headquarters – who was not from North Dakota and did not study North Dakota politics."* After his defeat, Kleppe served as Administrator of the Small Business Administration from 1971 to 1975 in the Nixon-Ford Administrations, and was Secretary of Interior in the Ford Administration from 1975 to 1977.

Mark Andrews (1926-   ), Republican: Mark Andrews and Milt Young represented North Dakota together in Congress for 18 years, beginning in 1963. Of all the colleagues with whom Young served at both the state and national levels, Young was harshest in his assessment of Andrews in his interviews with Dr. D. Jerome Tweton near the end of his career.

Young said he campaigned more for Andrews' election to the House in 1963 than he did for most candidates, except Fred Aandahl. But by 1979, his opinion of Andrews had soured. *"I have had more of a problem getting along with Mark Andrews than with anyone I ever served. He has a tremendous personality and, if he wants to be nice to someone, no one could be nicer. He is smart and he works hard and is a natural politician. When he is real nice to you is when you have to watch him closely. He can be very dirty, treacherous and underhanded. He is not a trustworthy or sincere person to deal with – is always very selfish and seems to be jealous of anything I am able to accomplish."*

One example Young cited was during the vote on the Water Bank Program in the late 1970s. *"I wanted to hold down the money for the Water Bank Program where the federal government leases pothole land and pays on 10-year leases. I thought the $10 million in the bill would be plenty, especially for now. Then Andrews came out not only for the full $10 million against my position but he want further. He said, 'I am for a $30 million program.' Rather than just oppose me, as he usually does, he said: 'I am for three times as much as Milt Young is for.' He didn't have to go that far when he knew I had such strong feelings about it."*

Young also described him as *"money hungry with campaign funds . . . Andrews has gotten much worse in later years. He sorely lacks honesty and humility. Some of his closest associates often refer to him as 'God.' Andrews almost always runs by himself . . . But he can fool many people. He has a lot of good qualities and a tremendous personality. You can be with him for a short while and be completely sold on him. One of Congressman Andrews' assets politically is that he has a reputation of being able to discern the thinking of the audience he is speaking to. He can look at the audience and tell almost exactly what they are thinking about. He speaks in a way that appeals to their thinking . . . He isn't so careful about what he says. He might take one position one place and a somewhat different position another place – and that is one of the things that has made it very difficult to work with him."*

Young told Tweton that he did not want Andrews to run for his Senate seat when he retired. *"I would like to see Congressman Andrews stay in the House. He has become quite effective in the last two or three years. He is acquainted with the House – and that is a problem for a new member – with the House as big as it is. Andrew's 17 years of seniority in the House is crucial, especially if you get to be a ranking member of a committee. If you are ranking or chairman you have a great advantage over someone else who has little or no seniority."*

Andrews said he first met Young when he was chairman of the North

Dakota Young Republicans in the early 1950s. When in the area, Young would stop by the Andrews farm near Mapleton and they would talk farming. During one of those early visits, Andrews remembered, "He was riding on the back end of my Marbeet sugar beet harvester and a beet flew off a little high and hit him in on the side of the head. He just smiled – he knew that's what happens on farms."

When Andrews was considering running for Republican National Committeeman in 1958, he sought the advice of the older generation of state politicians, including Young, Norman Brunsdale, Fred Aandahl and Bill Langer, who all encouraged him. "I remember driving out to former Governor Aandahl's farm near Litchville, and he and I actually sat down on a wagon tongue. In the center of his farmyard he had this wagon and if you needed a place to sit and talk, it was there. I asked him, 'Governor, what should I be thinking about and why should I get involved in politics? I'd like to visit with you and others like you I respect in public office.' He glanced over at the barn, and he said, 'Mark, you've got a barn, I've got a barn. We insure it. I've got a car and a tractor over there, we insure it. Why? Well, because we couldn't afford to lose them. You know, the best insurance policy to keep not only your barn and your house and your car, but your whole darn farm is sound government. And if you don't participate in government, everything is going to go to dust.' That's the result of a 20-minute conversation on a wagon tongue with somebody who I respected."

Langer was a friend of Andrews' father and their families had been close. "I went down to his office, which was dark because he had diabetes and his eyesight was bad. We talked about old times with Dad and all that. And I said, 'Senator Langer, I came to visit with you, as I've been visiting with other leaders in our political life in North Dakota, because I'm thinking about getting actively involved in politics.' He put his big hand on my knee and he clamped down and he says, 'Mark,' he says, 'you'll be great.' I said, 'what makes you think that, Senator?' He says, 'Because you're mean enough to be a damn good politician.' And then he laughed. Maybe I had a reputation for meanness way back before even Milt was perceiving it. I don't believe Langer thought of meanness as being bad, instead he meant being steadfast and standing up for the state, which he always did, certainly."

Andrews did not remember Young as someone who sought out people to run for political office. But that changed once they became candidates. "Once you were nominated by the convention, he would work like the dickens for you."

Andrews said he liked and admired Young. "He was a very likable individual, friendly certainly, to me as a lifelong farmer. There weren't too many farmers as far along in politics as Milt."

As well, they shared similar views on farm policy. "We both felt that we had to keep the opportunities open for exporting our crops. Half of the wheat we produced in North Dakota had to be sold overseas simply because we grew more than we consumed in the United States. We believed the organizations and people who were against open trade were no friends of the farmers."

After Andrews was elected to the House of Representatives in 1963, his wife, Mary, and their three children would leave Washington to spend the summer at their farm. While he was alone in Washington, Andrews often spent time with Young. "Milt and I would meet for dinner a couple times a week and just talk over farming and all that. We used to laugh because he said his sons wouldn't let him come back and run a tractor because he wouldn't understand what tractors were like after the steamers left. He and I were about in the same boat because I know all about two-cylinder John Deeres, but today's tractors, I've forgotten more than I ever knew about them. So we had those things in common, and we felt the same on farm issues and issues that are extremely important, such as exports, because they are important to a state like North Dakota."

Andrews said they worked together on farm legislation. "It depended on whether the House or the Senate was originating the bill. For all the time I was a colleague of Milt, he would give me a number of suggestions and I'd tell him what parts of the bill or what could be added to the bill and still have support from the conferees when it came back to the House."

Beginning with his second term, Andrews sat on the House Appropriations Committee, and he became the ranking Republican on the House Agriculture Committee. He also served on the Budget Committee.

There were a few issues on which they didn't agree. "I voted early on in my House career for open housing, which was not a particularly Republican-supported thing, but I felt it was a grave injustice to force minority families in big cities like Washington or New York or Brooklyn to have to live in the inner city, where they had to pay three times as much for a home as they could pay out in the suburbs," Andrews said. "So I voted for open housing, which I felt opened up a lot of additional opportunities for those families to find affordable housing in the suburbs that they couldn't find in the inner city areas. I don't think Milt supported it. But he didn't say, 'Hey, Mark, you shouldn't do that.' On key things for North Dakota, like Garrison Diversion, for instance, he and I were on the same side of the street, working to do everything we could to get it done."

Andrews believed Young's hard feelings evolved over the years. "When you've been in politics for awhile, people have feelings like that. Milt was sensitive." He thought the issue that most damaged their relationship was their clash over the dismantling of the Anti-Ballistic Missile site near Langdon. As detailed in Chapter 7, Young was upset with Andrews for supporting Senator Edward M. Kennedy in his successful efforts to close the Langdon site. Andrews was aware of this. "Ted Kennedy came to the Senate in 1963, the same year I came to the House, and over the years we supported many of the same issues. It was not a usual thing for a member from an area to say what I did, 'OK, we've scientifically proved this isn't a good deal.' The Republicans in the Defense Department, as a matter of fact, were the ones who brought that out. And I said 'Fine, I'm not going to fly in the face of that.' I felt, when you're talking about national defense, you're trying to get the best information you can, and when the defense experts who were Republican were saying this, I thought I was better off agreeing with it and standing up and saying, 'OK,' and then start the ball rolling towards a better procedure. Frankly, I got an awful lot of support for some other things because I was honest about that.

"It was an outdated technology and even more so, as I recall, the Defense Department said the science behind it was such that we were not cost-competitive with the Soviet Union when we deployed it. As a matter of fact, our missile launching facility was limited to 100 defensive missiles. That was by treaty that the Senate agreed to, and it turned out that it cost the Soviets about one-third as much to send two missiles for each one of our defensive missiles. So the statement was made by the Defense Department at that time, back when the Republicans controlled the Defense Department, that hey, we are going to have to shut this thing down. Milt came to me and talked to me and said, 'What do you think? You're on the Appropriations Committee.' I said, 'Well, I don't think we've got a leg to stand on when science tells us that what we've got is a system that isn't cost-competitive.' He said, 'Well, they want to shut it down,' and I said, 'That's OK with me.' Well, Milt just got wild about that because he had gotten them to start it. That was one of the things that kind of spurred his dissatisfaction with me way back then."

In reflecting on their relationship, Andrews said, "Sometimes he could be very pleasant, other times I would get a letter from Milt about some slight that he perceived that I had done toward him that would damn near burn the pages of the paper it was written on. But particularly after that shutdown of the ABM site, his attitude toward me changed for the worse. In his mind, I was betraying North Dakota. In my mind, I was trying to stand up for the country to get a better ABM site. There was nothing I could really do about that.

"I certainly didn't want to antagonize somebody in my Congressional delegation, particularly somebody who helped me as much as he did that first time that I was running for the House. But our last couple or three years together in Congress were not exactly harmonious. I didn't want to say anything about it. What good did that do? You don't dwell on it, or remember too much the bad things. You remember more the pleasant things that happened, and there were a lot of pleasant things."

Some of Young's staff members believed the Senator's disdain for Andrews grew over the years and had begun even before the ABM issue in the mid-1970s. Some of it, they believed was the natural "young bull – old bull" jealousy that so often occurs with political colleagues. Others suspected that Young thought Andrews had been behind the visit Ben Clayburgh, John Rouzie and Roland Meidinger had with him in February 1973 when they discouraged Young from running for re-election.

Andrews was easily elected to Young's Senate seat in 1980, receiving 70 percent of the vote. Staff members recalled how Young remained bitter about Andrews to his last day in the Senate, adamantly refusing to consider resigning before his term ended so Andrews could enter the Senate early with more seniority than the incoming freshmen Senators.

The hard feelings continued as Andrews' staff moved over to the Senate. "When you're a new Senator, you temporarily move into the office of your preceding Senator," said Andrews. "Milt cleaned out the office of all the typewriters, all the pencils, all the mechanical equipment and everything else. Bill Wright [Young's administrative assistant who later worked for Andrews] later told me – that 'he did that because he was just mad at you and he didn't want you to have any of the pencils or pens or paper or whatever.' But because that happened, my office got everything new. It was a problem and life would have been a heckuva lot easier for me, and I think for him too, if he hadn't gotten that feeling about me."

The last time Andrews saw Young was about a year after the 1980 election. "He and Pat were at the Capitol, and they were going in to visit some of the staff of the Senate Appropriations Committee. We talked in the hallway for all of 10 or 15 minutes."

Andrews served one term in the Senate and was defeated for re-election in 1986 by then-North Dakota Tax Commissioner Kent Conrad. Andrews then established a lobbying firm and divided his time between Washington, D.C., and his Mapleton farm.

Reflecting on their years together as Washington colleagues, Andrews said, "I like to remember the good memories of Milt instead of the ones where he decided I wasn't so good to work with. I think his greatest contribution was always being a stalwart supporter of agriculture. That manifested itself in a number of different ways. The key one was he was always 100 percent for free and open trade."

John and Rachel Young stand on the porch of their home on their Berlin, North Dakota, farm in the early 1900s. *(Family Collection)*

Milton Young stands behind a horse-drawn seed drill, circa 1915, on the family farm. *(Institute for Regional Studies, NDSU, Fargo)*

Harvest on the Young farm with a TC 27-44 tractor. *(Family Collection)*

A panoramic view of Berlin, North Dakota, in the early 1900s. *(Family Collection)*

Milt in the field circa 1930, and Malinda Young in 1940. *(Family Collection)*

Milt and Malinda's sons, from left Duane (Toad), Wendell (Mix) and John (Scoop) in the late 1920s.*(Family Collection)*

Milt and Malinda Young in 1945. *(Family Collection)*

Son Duane and his dog, a neighbor named Pederson, and Young in the 1940s. *(Family Collection)*

The Young farm in the foreground in the1950s, with the town of Berlin shown in the distance. *(Institute for Regional Studies, NDSU, Fargo)*

Wendell (Mix), John (Scoop) and Duane (Toad) Young in 1966. *(Family Collection)*

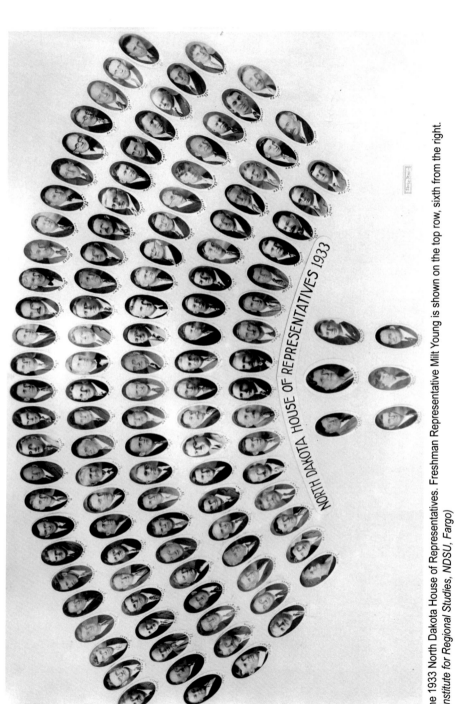

The 1933 North Dakota House of Representatives. Freshman Representative Milt Young is shown on the top row, sixth from the right.
(*Institute for Regional Studies, NDSU, Fargo*)

The 1943 North Dakota Senate. Milt Young, shown on the second row from the top, third from the right, was a State Senator from 1935 to 1945. *(Institute for Regional Studies, NDSU, Fargo)*

This photograph of John and Rachel Young appeared in a May 1941, issue of the *Fargo Forum* marking their 50th wedding anniversary. *(State Historical Society of North Dakota)*

Four generations of the Young family pose in 1946. They are, from left, John Young, Wendell (Mix) and his infant son, James, held by Milt. *(Family Collection)*

Milt and Pat Young hold the two youngest of their 13 grandchildren in December 1970. Than, three-and a-half years, and Anh Lee, three months, were adopted that year by Marcia and John Young. At the request of Senator Jacob Javits (R-NY), Senator Young joined the board of directors of the An Loc orphanage in Vietnam, and he and Javits' office helped Marcia and John work through the details to adopt the children from the orphanage. *(Family Collection)*

THE
REPUBLICAN
R. O. C. TICKET
PRIMARY AND SPECIAL ELECTION—JUNE 25, 1946

V O T E   R E P U B L I C A N

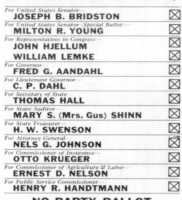

For United States Senator—
JOSEPH B. BRIDSTON ☒
For United States Senator (Special Ballot)—
MILTON R. YOUNG ☒
For Representatives in Congress—
JOHN HJELLUM ☒
WILLIAM LEMKE ☒
For Governor—
FRED G. AANDAHL ☒
For Lieutenant Governor—
C. P. DAHL ☒
For Secretary of State—
THOMAS HALL ☒
For State Auditor—
MARY S. (Mrs. Gus) SHINN ☒
For State Treasurer—
H. W. SWENSON ☒
For Attorney General—
NELS G. JOHNSON ☒
For Commissioner of Insurance—
OTTO KRUEGER ☒
For Commissioner of Agriculture & Labor—
ERNEST D. NELSON ☒
For Public Service Commissioner—
HENRY R. HANDTMANN ☒

NO-PARTY BALLOT

For Supt. of Public Instruction—
ARTHUR E. THOMPSON ☒

IMPORTANT
THE LAW PROVIDES THAT VOTING IN MORE THAN ONE PARTY
COLUMN AT PRIMARY VOIDS YOUR BALLOT.
"Don't Spoil Your Ballot"

JOSEPH B. BRIDSTON

MILTON R. YOUNG

JOHN HJELLUM

FRED G. AANDAHL

NELS G. JOHNSON

ERNEST D. NELSON

WILLIAM LEMKE   THOMAS HALL   OTTO KRUEGER   H. W. SWENSON

C. P. DAHL   ARTHUR E. THOMPSON   HENRY R. HANDTMANN   MARY S. (Mrs. Gus) SHINN

"LET'S FINISH THE JOB"
SPONSORED AND PAID FOR BY THE REPUBLICAN ORGANIZING COMMITTEE.

This ROC campaign poster promotes the candidates for the 1946 election, including Young, who is second from the top on the left. *(Author's Collection)*

Top left, Governor Fred Aandahl presents Milton Young the official papers appointing him to the U.S. Senate, March 12, 1945. Top right, Vice President Harry S. Truman swears in Young to the U.S. Senate March 19, 1945. Truman became President three weeks later, after the death of Franklin D. Roosevelt. At left, President Pro Tempore of the Senate Kenneth McKeller (D-TN) swears in Young following the June 1946 special election. Looking on from left are Senate Minority Leader Wallace White, Jr., (R-ME), Young, National Republican Chairman and U.S. Representative Carroll Reece (R-TN), and Senator WIlliam Langer, (R-ND).
(Institute for Regional Studies, NDSU, Fargo)

Shown here at a U.S. Senate Agriculture Committee hearing in Bismarck, circa 1954, are, from left, P. J. Donnelly, president of the North Dakota Farm Bureau; Glenn Talbott, president of the North Dakota Farmers Union; U.S. Senator Olin Johnston (D-SC), Senator Young, and Agriculture Committee Chairman George Aiken (R-VT). *(Institute for Regional Studies, NDSU, Fargo)*

Young's Washington staff in 1960, back row from left, Cheryl Green, Lou Christopher, Mel Christopher, Shari Vlahovich, Jeanne Ruth, Chris Sylvester, Kay Jensen, Natalie Kuehn; front row, Jeanne Vlahovich, Senator Young, Pat Byrne. *(Family Collection)*

The staff working out of the LaMoure, North Dakota, office in 1959; from left, Mel Christopher, Cheryl Green, Chris Sylvester, Audrey Vikan and Senator Young. *(Family Collection)*

A Senate Agriculture Committee meeting in Washington, D.C., in January 1954. Young is seated at the far left corner of the table. *(Institute for Regional Studies, NDSU, Fargo)*

In October 1947 the Senate Appropriations Committee traveled to Europe to inspect operations funded by the U.S. The Committee visited much of Europe, except the Soviet Union and its satellites. At left, shown boarding the oceanliner *SS America* to sail are, from left, Senators Young, Richard Russell (D-GA), Guy Cordon (R-OR), Wayland Brocks (R-IL), Leverett Saltonstall (R-MA) and Syles Bridges (R-NH).

In center photograph, Committee members are shown following an audience with Pope Pius XII in Castel Gandolfo, at the Vatican in Rome, with Swiss Guards at right. From left, Senators Theodore Green (D-RI), Cordon, Young and William Knowland (R-CA).

At lower left, the Senators review a financial report in the Louvre in Paris October 17, 1947. From left, standing, a man identified as Mr. Yates, Senators Young and Saltonstall, men identified as Mr. Peurifoy and Merrick, two embassy interpreters, and U.S. Army Major General George Richards. Seated from left are Senators Green and Bridges, French Minister of Finance Robert Schuman, and Senator Russell.

At lower right, the Senators attend the October 22 session of the War Crimes Trials at the Palace of Justice in Nuremberg, Germany. From left is an unidentified U.S. Army Officer Guide, Senators Young, Green, Russell and Henry Dworshak (R-ID),*(Institute for Regional Studies, NDSU, Fargo)*

Following audience with Pope Pius XII in Castel Gandolfo

The Senate Appropriations Committee at the airport in Baghdad, Iraq, during its October 1947 trip to Europe. Senator Young is fifth from left. *(Institute for Regional Studies, NDSU, Fargo)*

President Ramón Grau of Cuba speaks in front of a monument with a Congressional delegation commemorating the 50th anniversary of the sinking of the *USS Maine* battleship in Havana Harbor, February 15, 1948. Senator Young is third from left in the front row. *(Institute for Regional Studies, NDSU, Fargo)*

Senator Young visits constituents in Korea November 23, 1952, serving with the 3rd Infantry Division during the Korean War. Front row, from left, Pvt. Phalen Sem, Powers Lake; SFC Leo Ressler, Mandan; SFC Henry Dockter, Linton; PFC Floyd Helm, Denhoff; Cpl. Wallace Olsen, Minot; PFC David Duin, Wahpeton; Cpl. Harold Meske, Zap; PFC Orvin Gust, Embden, and two unidentified soldiers. Standing from left, PFC Wallace Olson, Donnybrook; Cpl. Edward Neiss, Silva; SFC Donald Nelson, Sutton; PFC Wilfred Larsen, Juanita; PFC Gordon Helland, Hannaford; Senator Young; Col. James Hanley, Bismarck; Pvt. Elmer Kluck, Denhoff; Cpl. Walter Steinwand, Ellendale; Pvt. Delbert Alwin, Lakota; PFC Wayne Gebur, Rock Lake, and PFC Thomas Bjerke, Page. *(Institute for Regional Studies, NDSU, Fargo)*

Senator Young joins others on an inspection tour of Panama Canal Zone activities February 11, 1954. Pictured from left at the Pedro Miguel Boat Landing in the Canal Zone are Senators Allen Ellender (D-LA), John McClellan (D-AR), and Henry Dworshak, along with Panama Canal Zone Governor John Seybold, Captain Frank Munroe, Kenneth Bosquet and Colonel C.J. Hauck. *(Institute for Regional Studies, NDSU, Fargo)*

Senator Young, wearing the dark suit, reviews the U.S. Caribbean Command's Joint Honor Guard during ceremonies February 12, 1954, at the Panama Canal Zone with other members of the Senate Appropriations Committee. *(Institute for Regional Studies, NDSU, Fargo)*

Senate Appropriations Committee members meet with Panama Canal Zone Governor John Seybold, at left, February 12, 1954. Others from left, are Senator Allen Ellender, Senator Young, Kenneth Bosquet, Senator John McClellan and Senator Henry Dworshak. *(Institute for Regional Studies, NDSU, Fargo)*

Senator Young, wearing sunglasses, stands in front of a gate house prior to touring the U.S. Naval Base in Guantanamo Bay, Cuba, December 17, 1962. *(Institute for Regional Studies, NDSU, Fargo)*

Senator Young, third from left, tours the construction progress of the Aswan High Dam in Egypt in 1964. *(Institute for Regional Studies, NDSU, Fargo)*

Senator Young is met by Major General George Power and an honor guard in Italy composed of Italian and U.S. troops during a tour visiting elements of the U.S. Army's Southern European Task Force November 11, 1964. *(Institute for Regional Studies, NDSU, Fargo)*

Senator Young meets with Secretary of Defense Robert McNamara and Chairman of the Joint Chiefs of Staff General Earle K. Wheeler at a defense appropriations committee hearing August 4, 1965. *(Institute for Regional Studies, NDSU, Fargo)*

At left, Senator Young aboard the *USS Coral Sea* aircraft carrier during Vietnam War operations in the Gulf of Tonkin November 26, 1966. At right, he visits with PFC Lane Martinson of Devils Lake, who was stationed with the 561st Engineering Company in Thailand on Thanksgiving Day 1966. The other two soldiers are unidentified. *(Institute for Regional Studies, NDSU, Fargo)*

The Youngs pose in front of a portion of the Great Wall of China during an official visit to the People's Republic of China in November 1976. *(Institute for Regional Studies, NDSU, Fargo)*

The 1955 U.S. Senate Appropriations Committee. Senator Young is shown in the top row, far right. *(Institute for Regional Studies, NDSU, Fargo)*

Senator Young stands before the door of the Senate Appropriations Committee meeting room, reviewing a 1963 appropriations bill during the 88th Congress. *(Institute for Regional Studies, NDSU, Fargo)*

Senator Robert Taft (R-OH) and Young were close political allies. Here, Taft drives a tractor during a parade outside the Gardner Hotel in Fargo, North Dakota during his bid for the Republican Presidential nomination in 1952. (*Institute for Regional Studies, NDSU, Fargo*)

North Dakota's Senators William Langer and Milton Young prepare to cut a large loaf of bread at the Fargo Airport January 31, 1957, in front of a Northwest Airlines airplane, as part of a wheat industry promotion. Standing between them is stewardess Joyce Robideau. The loaf contained 365 pounds of flour. (*Institute for Regional Studies, NDSU, Fargo*)

Six North Dakotans who served in the U.S. Congress pose during a North Dakota State Society picnic at the home of former Senator Gerald P. Nye in Chevy Chase, Maryland, circa 1957. They are, back row from left, Representatives Otto Krueger and Usher Burdick, Senators William Langer and Milton Young; front row from left, Nye, and U.S. Undersecretary of the Interior and former Governor and Representative Fred Aandahl. *(Institute for Regional Studies, NDSU, Fargo)*

Former Congress-man Tom Kleppe stands between Senators Quentin Burdick and Milton Young during a break in his September 1975 confirmation hearings to become Secretary of the Interior.*(Institute for Regional Studies, NDSU, Fargo)*

William Lemke, left, served North Dakota in the U.S. House from 1933-41 and 1943-50. Norway native John Moses was North Dakota's Governor from 1939 to 1945 and was elected to the U.S. Senate in 1944, serving only two months before his death March 3, 1945. Nine days later, Governor Aandahl appointed Milton Young to fill the Senate seat vacated by Moses. *(Institute for Regional Studies, NDSU, Fargo)*

Senator Young congratulates former Governor John Davis, the new U.S. Director of Civil Defense, following his swearing in ceremony May 20, 1969. *(Institute for Regional Studies, NDSU, Fargo)*

Senator Young and Representative Hjalmar Nygaard pose with Darryl Eastvold of Mayville at a Capitol Hill luncheon January 30, 1962. Eastvold was national vice president of the Future Farmers of America. *(Institute for Regional Studies, NDSU, Fargo)*

Senator Young and North Dakota native and longtime Washington, D.C., Democratic lawyer Melvin D. Hildreth, Jr., worked together for many years to pass legislation to restore Ford's Theatre. They are shown in the top photograph at the theatre in 1955. Above, Young speaks at a ceremony at Ford's Theatre in 1970, with Secretary of the Interior Walter Hickel looking on. In the background is the flag-draped box where President Abraham Lincoln was shot April 14, 1865. *(Institute for Regional Studies, NDSU, Fargo)*

Senator Young visits with President John F. Kennedy in the early 1960s. *(Institute for Regional Studies, NDSU, Fargo)*

Senators watch news reports of the assassination of President Kennedy November 22, 1963, in a U.S. Capitol office. Seated are Senators Margaret Chase Smith (R-ME), and Everett Dirksen (R-IL). Standing from left are Senators Winston Prouty (R-VT), Frank Carlson (R-KS), Young, Leverett Saltonstall (R-MA), Bourke Hickenlooper (R-IA), Kenneth Keating (R-NY) and Tom Kuchel (R-CA). *(Institute for Regional Studies, NDSU, Fargo)*

Young had the most contact with Lyndon Johnson of any of the eight Presidents in office during his Senate years. In the top picture, they visit in the Oval Office March 25, 1964. In the middle, they share a laugh, after the September 27, 1967, signing of a bill extending the 1964 Food Stamp Act. In the bottom, he attends the March 25 signing of the Supplemental Defense Appropriations Act of 1966. Among those pictured are, front row from left, Senators Young, Richard Russell (D-GA), John Pastore (D-RI) and Carl Hayden (R-AZ), and Rep. Frank Bow (R-OH), the House Appropriations Committee ranking Republican. In the back from left are Rep. Otto Passman (D-LA) directly behind Johnson, Presidential aide Mike Manatos, and Rep. George Mahon, (D-TX) House Appropriations Committee chairman. *(Institute for Regional Studies, NDSU, Fargo)*

Senator Young and Vice President Richard Nixon visit with Washington Senators baseball player Harmon Killebrew in 1959. It was a breakout year for the young star, who hit 42 homeruns. Two years later, the Senators team moved to Minnesota and was renamed the Minnesota Twins. *(Institute for Regional Studies, NDSU, Fargo)*

Senator Young sits at the far left of the head table at a White House dinner hosted by President Nixon December 22, 1969. Also seated at the head table on either side of the Nixons are House Minority Leader Gerald Ford and Betty Ford, and Vice President Spiro Agnew and Judy Agnew. *(Institute for Regional Studies, NDSU, Fargo)*

Senator Young sits at the far right end of the table in front of the fireplace in the White House Cabinet Room May 19, 1972. President Nixon and House Minority Leader Gerald Ford are seated at the center of the right hand side of the table. *(Institute for Regional Studies, NDSU, Fargo)*

Senator Young meets with Secretary of Agriculture Earl Butz, at left, and other committee members Senators James Allen (D-AL) and Robert Dole (R-KS) at a June 1973 meeting of the Senate Agriculture Committee. *(Institute for Regional Studies, NDSU, Fargo)*

Senator Young shakes hands with President Carter as he and fellow Senators, from left, Robert Byrd (D-WVA), Howard Baker (R-TN), Ted Stevens (R-AK) and Alan Cranston (D-CA) prepare to escort him to a June 1979 joint session of Congress, where Carter discussed the SALT II Treaty he signed in Vienna with Soviet Union General Secretary Leonid Brezhnev. *(Institute for Regional Studies, NDSU, Fargo)*

U.S. Republican Senators pose for this photograph in the U.S. Capitol January 15, 1979. Senator Young is standing third from the left at the end of the table . *(Institute for Regional Studies, NDSU, Fargo)*

Senator Young visits with Ronald Reagan in the 1970s. At right, he greets George H.W. Bush at a July 29, 1980, banquet, shortly before Bush was selected by Reagan to be his Vice Presidential running mate in the 1980 campaign against incumbents President Jimmy Carter and Vice President Walter Mondale. In the background is Senator Rudy Boschwitz (R-MN). *(Institute for Regional Studies, NDSU, Fargo)*

U.S. Secretary of State Henry Kissinger waves to the crowd in Grand Forks during a July 25, 1974, campaign stop for Senator Young in his re-election campaign against former Governor William Guy. *(Institute for Regional Studies, NDSU, Fargo)*

Governor William Guy is shown here in 1961, the first of his 12 years as North Dakota's 26th chief executive. The 1974 race for the U.S. Senate between him and Senator Young was an epic clash of political titans in the state's history. *(State Historical Society of North Dakota)*

Senator Young visits with astronaut Walter Schirra at the John F. Kennedy Space Center in Florida January 9, 1968. As a longtime member of the Senate Appropriations Committee, Young was a strong supporter of the U.S. space program and its funding requests. *(Institute for Regional Studies, NDSU, Fargo)*

Senator Young and Senator Karl Mundt (R-SD), shown here in the 1960s, were close colleagues for many years. At right, he unveils a sign designating Young Boulevard at the Earth Resources Observation and Science (EROS) Data Center in Sioux Falls, South Dakota, August 13, 1975. The street was named in Young's honor in appreciation for his assistance in securing funds for the Center, which opened in the early 1970s. It conducts remote sensing and research for the U.S. Geological Survey and Department of the Interior. *(Institute for Regional Studies, NDSU, Fargo)*

Always looking for a golf game, Senator Young, at right, joins legendary North Dakota entertainer Lawrence Welk, second from left, and others for a round at the Linton, North Dakota, golf course in the 1970s. *(Institute for Regional Studies, NDSU, Fargo)*

Wearing his black belt, Senator Young breaks a board in two with his hand with his Tae Kwon Do trainer Jhoon Rhee in his Senate office in the early 1970s. *(Institute for Regional Studies, NDSU, Fargo)*

Visitors to his Washington office July 18, 1979, were Jamestown native and well-known western fiction writer Louis L'Amour and his wife, Kathy, and daughter, Angelique.*(Institute for Regional Studies, NDSU, Fargo)*

Above, Senator Young, second from left, stands next to Senator Walter Mondale (D-MN), who is presenting to REA Administrator Norman Clapp the July 1966 legislation authorizing funding for the Milton R. Young electrical generating station for Minnkota Power Cooperative. The other members of the North Dakota Congressional Delegation are, at far left, Representative Rolland Redlin, at far right, Senator Quentin Burdick and behind him Representative Mark Andrews. PIctured at left are Deputy REA Administrator Everett Weitzell, Young and Minnkota Power Chairman Andrew Freeman at the 1971 dedication of the Milton R. Young Station near Stanton, North Dakota. *(Institute for Regional Studies, NDSU, Fargo)*

Senator Young participates in the ground breaking of the Western Gear Plant in Jamestown June 9, 1974. Also holding shovels are, left, Jamestown Mayor George Burchill and Western Gear President Phil Gomez. *(Institute for Regional Studies, NDSU, Fargo)*

At left, President Truman receives a good omen necklace at the White House from Thunderbolt Lefthand, a Crow Indian from Lodge Grass, Montana, January 19, 1948. With Senator Young are Martin Old Dog Cross and James Driver from North Dakota's Fort Berthold Reservation. In the center photograph, K.B. Abernathy, left, president and chief operating officer of Brunswick Corporation in Skokie, Illinois, visits with young dancers from the Fort Totten Indian Reservation at the dedication of the Devils Lake Sioux Manufacturing Corporation June 8, 1974. Joining in the conversation is Brigadier General John Sterling, Deputy Commanding General, U.S. Army Troop Support Command, St. Louis. *(Institute for Regional Studies, NDSU, Fargo)*

Senator Young visits with Colonel Kenneth Holden, Commander of the 91st Combat Support Group at the MInot Air Force Base, June 1978. Pictured at center is Brigadier General Clyde Garner, Commander of the 57th Air Division, Strategic Air Command, and an unidentified colonel. *(Institute for Regional Studies, NDSU, Fargo)*

Senator Young with North Dakota Girls Nation delegates in Washington, D.C., July 29, 1964. From left are Meredith Hawkins of Jamestown and JoEllen Tanke of Grafton. *(Institute for Regional Studies, NDSU, Fargo)*

North Dakota 4-H Group with the Senator in his Washington office, April 5, 1978. From left, Dave Seilstad, Fordville; Daniel Ray, Grand Forks; Randi Josephson, Washburn (seated); Lewis Shaw, Mandan; Sue Clark, Bottineau; Young; and Ray Wagner, Fargo. *(Institute for Regional Studies, NDSU, Fargo)*

Jim Ramstad of Jamestown, second from right, who represented Minnesota's Third District in the U.S. House of Representatives from 1991 to 2009, was one of the interns in Senator Young's office in 1967. Also pictured from left are Carol Zurcher, Glenn Meidinger, Laura Senechal, Young and Santal Benson. *(Institute for Regional Studies, NDSU, Fargo)*

Senators Young, Burdick, and Representative Kleppe with a North Dakota 4-H group on the steps of the U.S. Capitol in June 1968. *(Institute for Regional Studies, NDSU, Fargo)*

Senators Young, Burdick and Representative Andrews with a group of North Dakota 4-H youth at the U.S. Capitol, June 15, 1976. *(Institute for Regional Studies, NDSU, Fargo)*

Milt and Pat Young stand before a large portrait of the Senator during a March 1970 dinner in Fargo sponsored by the Greater North Dakota Association honoring his 25 years in the Senate. *(Institute for Regional Studies, NDSU, Fargo)*

Some of Senator Young's Washington staff in December 1979, front row, from left, Karen Steidl, Marge Kraning, Fay Weisz, Santal Manos, Diane Hoag and Margie Nicholson; middle row, Lou Christopher, Eileen Wilson, Terry Olson, Senator Young, Pat Young, Chris Sylvester, Jeanne Stoll, Standing from left, Bob Christman, Sharon Shields and Pete Bonner. *(Institute for Regional Studies, NDSU, Fargo)*

This exhibit of memorabilia from Senator Young's life is on display at the LaMoure County Museum in Grand Rapids, North Dakota. *(Author's Collection)*

Senator Young and his daughter-in-law, Marcia Young, greet delegates at the North Dakota Republican Convention in Minot, July 1976. Between them is Dr. Ben Clayburgh, Republican National Committeeman, of Grand Forks. *(Institute for Regional Studies, NDSU, Fargo)*

Milt and Pat Young in the Washington, D.C., office in September 1979, marking Pat's 34th anniversary as a member of the Senator's staff. At right, Senator Young makes remarks accepting the Minuteman of the Year Award at the Reserve Officers Association of the United States banquet in Washington, D.C., February 23, 1979. *(Institute for Regional Studies, NDSU, Fargo)*

This sketch of Senator Young appeared in the June 1, 1983, edition of the *Fargo Forum*, the day after he died at the age of 85 in Arizona. In its editorial about the state's longest tenured U.S. Senator, the *Forum* wrote, "Sen. Young did stay close to the people. He never bothered to polish a Washington image. He was a plain-spoken man, a man who was loved. He served North Dakota so very, very well." *(Fargo Forum)*

A Final Term

Entering his final term in the Senate in January 1975, Young had become his party's Dean of the Senate – the longest-serving Republican in that chamber. He had already made it to the Senate record books serving as Secretary to the Senate Republican Committee from 1946 to 1971 – the longest tenure of any Senator in a Senate leadership position in the 20th Century.

Shortly into his final term, Young began to think about whether he should serve out the entire six years or leave before it ended. He spoke about this publicly at the 1976 North Dakota Republican Convention. In an emotional speech to the delegates, the 78-year-old Young told them he would resign early from the Senate if a Republican Governor was elected in the November general election. If this were to happen, Young said he could leave office, knowing the new Republican Governor would appoint another Republican to his seat. If it didn't happen, he said he would try to finish out his term.

It didn't happen. Governor Arthur Link was elected to a second term, defeating Richard Elkin. Young continued to drop occasional hints about not completing his term. One of the dates he considered was March 12, 1980, the 35th anniversary of his arrival to the Senate. Pat was supportive of her husband retiring early as well.

In 1979, he considered the problems of agriculture and Garrison Diversion and decided he should stay around for a while longer. *"We have written the new farm program and there won't be any more written during the balance of my term. But I would like to see Garrison Diversion through and I think I can be of some help, even though it is in deep trouble. Whether we ever get much of a project or not is a good question."*

He also worried about his staff. *"I have a very good staff – a sizeable staff of about 20 – and it would be hard for them if I quit in the middle of a term. If I finish the term there are a lot of new members of Congress coming in, and most of them could get good jobs. They are very good and very capable. Too, it would complicate matters if I quit early for both the Republicans and Democrats."*

In a December 30, 1979, article in the *Fargo Forum*, Young told staff writer Hal Simons, that although he "might be tempted" to retire in a few months on March 12, his 35th anniversary in the Senate, he "definitely plans to serve out his full term."

Young's final months in the Senate did not go unnoticed by his many colleagues and constituents. On March 12, 1980, many Senators paid tribute to him on the Senate floor, congratulating him on his 35 years of service.

On April 18, 1980, Young spoke to the delegates gathered at the Bismarck Civic Center at his last North Dakota Republican Convention as a U.S. Senator. Newspaper accounts noted his slowness of walking to the podium to speak, caused by peripheral neuritis, a nerve disease. His remarks covered national defense and farm prices, and he criticized "environmental extremists" who he said had halted development of synthetic fuels, nuclear power and the Garrison Diversion project.

He said his combined 48 years in the North Dakota Legislature and U.S. Senate had left him with "many pleasant memories. There were times, though, when I tasted the bitter wine of betrayal by political friends."

He closed by saying to the delegates, "May our paths cross often."

The November 4, 1980, general election was the first one since 1924 that Young wasn't in public office or on the ballot for election or re-election. Ronald Reagan was elected President and, to Young's surprise, the Republicans took control of the U.S. Senate for the first time in 26 years.

He left office with more seniority than any Republican in the history of the Senate. Senator Francis Warren of Wyoming served about a year and three months longer between 1889 and 1930, but he had a break in service, giving Young more seniority. Young had also served longer than any Senator without becoming chairman of a standing committee. And, he had served longer on the Senate Agriculture Committee than anyone in the history of that committee.

During only two sessions of Congress did the Republicans control the Senate while Young was in that chamber – in the 80th Congress of 1947-49 and the 83rd Congress of 1953-55. Had he returned to the Senate in 1981, he would have been Chairman of the Appropriations Committee and President Pro Tempore of the Senate.

The 1980 election that swept Republicans into office with Reagan's landslide saw the defeat of some of Young's longtime Senate colleagues – Democrats George McGovern of South Dakota, Frank Church of Idaho, John Culver of Iowa, Birch Bayh of Indiana and Warren Magnuson of Washington. *"I think the main reason for their defeat was that they were extreme liberals. They weren't the ordinary liberals, but the extreme ones. We have a habit in the Senate of going from one extreme to the other. Some of those elected in place of these liberals will be, I am afraid, extreme conservatives, and that isn't good either. But I think people were just fed up with these real liberal politics."*

Magnuson especially was a close friend of Young's and he didn't think Magnuson believed his re-election was in jeopardy. *"I worked closely with him. 'Maggie' kind of half considered himself to be a North Dakotan. His parents at one time lived near Fort Ransom. He had always been good to me. But 'Maggie' had gotten a little crusty, and, of course, he had a little bit of a health problem. His legs were very bad. He walked awfully slowly and he got a little too independent. I could see where he could have a problem."*

Reflecting on Seniority

In his November 7, 1980, oral interview with Dr. Jerome Tweton, Young was two months from leaving the Senate. He reflected on his Senate career, his last term in the Senate he was just completing, and the importance of seniority.

"I certainly have some mixed feelings about leaving. I will be happy to get away from all the hard work – and the longer you stay the more work they pile on you. It has been very difficult and you get in a lot of political fights. If you fight for the things you believe in you can't avoid fights. I will really miss the busy life that I have enjoyed and especially being able to help people. Every place I go people come up to me and say: 'You have helped me' with this or that. Some of them I have long since forgotten. After serving for nearly 36 years I have helped a lot of people. And that is the part of my work I have enjoyed the most . . . I will be moving into a new life and one I probably don't know much about anymore. I'll really enjoy playing golf. I think I will study ancient history and travel, too."

Young also reflected on changes in campaigning and politics over four decades. *"Politics has changed a lot, especially from the old League days. It was more of a person-to-person thing and often times one person would control most of the votes in a whole township. That is no longer true. There are influential people but not the kind that there were, especially during Bill Langer's days. Campaigning has gone more to television and publicity. Langer was different than any candidate I ever knew. He had an almost hypnotic personality and his speeches were humorous and witty, which made him a great drawing card and helped him get good crowds for political meetings. Campaigning has gone more to television now and I notice in the Senate most of the new Senators are good looking, intelligent young men who made a good appearance on television.*

"My speech defectiveness always was a handicap but probably a worse handicap for a candidate is to do a lot of talking and really say nothing. This speech problem tends to keep me more humble. The big

problem with a speech defect is that I have to concentrate on trying to do a good job of speaking while at the same time thinking about what I am saying. Fred Aandahl once said, 'Milt, you are no orator but you always give them something to think about.' There is an old saying in politics that no one was ever defeated by a speech he didn't make. I think it was when Nye was a candidate and he was among the best speakers, but he depended too much on his ability to influence people by his oratory and he became overconfident."

Despite what his detractors predicted during the final campaign, Young believed *"my last six years were really the most productive."* The examples he cited included securing a \$3.5 million project for a central depot in Fargo for all city buses and cabs, \$16.5 million for a bridge across the Missouri, and \$2.5 million for improvements to the Grand Forks airport.

"Seniority in the Senate is still important. When you are elected to the Senate and go to Washington, the office space you get is based on seniority. When you go to the Senate Chamber, the seat you get is based on seniority. Your committee assignments are based on seniority. When a witness appears before a committee the right to question the witness, whoever he is, is based on seniority. Sometimes when you don't have seniority, you have to wait a couple of hours or maybe until the next day before you can even ask any questions. The chairmanship of all committees is on the basis of seniority and the ranking Republican spot on a committee like Appropriations, such as I have, is based on seniority.

"I got many projects for North Dakota because of seniority, including the Nutrition Laboratory, aid for the Aviation Department and coal research in the millions, all at the University of North Dakota; four other major research laboratories in the state, and two fish hatcheries – one near Garrison Dam and one at Valley City. I obtained the Metabolism Research Laboratory, the Spring Wheat Quality Laboratory and increased funds for the extension service year after year, all at North Dakota State University.

"I also played a major role in securing several dams such as Baldhill, Jamestown and Dickinson. Because of my ranking position on the Appropriations Committee, North Dakota received many other projects and I helped write much farm and other legislation. I was largely responsible for getting the flood protective works on the Red River.

"During the period I have served in the Senate I believe we witnessed the greatest development of any period in our history. Most of our trees had been lost because of the drought. After the drought ended and prices became better we were involved with World War II so little was done to change things. The period I am speaking of since World War II saw great development – hundreds of millions of trees were planted, watershed projects and soil conservation programs made great progress and made North Dakota into a beautiful state. There was little rural electrification development before the war but rural electric and rural telephone services, which now almost completely cover North Dakota, were constructed during this period.

"There was the Pick-Sloan Plan, which authorized Garrison Dam and a few others, which was passed in 1944 but the construction of Garrison Dam started the year I went to the Senate in 1945. This was the period which saw great modernization of agriculture and more beautiful buildings on the farms and in the cities. In the last 15 years we witnessed sizable industrial development in the state and a few larger companies established plants in North Dakota. I don't claim credit for all of this but I did have some part in almost every phase of it. I was handling all of the appropriations for federal projects in North Dakota and secured much legislation necessary for the construction of Garrison Dam.

"I was co-author of the authorizing legislation for the Soil Conservation Service program in the State Senate while I was still in the State Legislature. I was co-author of the authorizing legislation in Congress for rural telephone services. As a member of both the Agriculture and Appropriations Committees, there was hardly a project

I did not have a part in making possible.

"*I persuaded three major industries to put plants in North Dakota
– Western Gear, Brunswick and Lockheed. This development in North
Dakota, along with all the farm legislation and other legislation I co-
sponsored, represented my greatest accomplishments. My being tagged
"Mr. Wheat" both in and out of Congress was the result of my intense
interest in the problems of wheat and wheat farmers and my part in the
writing of farm legislation during my more than 30 years in the Senate.*

"*Another example is important language accompanying the Public
Works Appropriations Bill in which we severely criticized the Court and
directed the Department of the Interior to proceed with the construction
of the Garrison Diversion project as authorized. We couldn't have had
tougher language. Senator John Stennis suggested that I write a good
report for it and they only changed about three or four words at the end
of it. Then when it came to conference with the House, I thought the
House would put up a big argument against it but the Chairman, who
is a Southerner and a good friend, said: "The House concurs in the
Senate language." Seniority was very helpful in this situation. Seniority
is important in a state like North Dakota. A state like California has 40
or more Congressmen who often get together as a block and they have
a lot of influence individually. Seniority is far more important to a state
with a small population than big, populous states.*

"*I do not sponsor a lot of legislation myself but I co-sponsor many
bills with other Senators. Sometimes I think more than I should but
the Senate has gotten into the practice of getting more co-sponsors
than they used to. I remember when Senator Barkley was the Majority
Leader. He wouldn't allow co-sponsors because some Senator might
get over 50 co-sponsors. If all of them voted for it, it would pass – but
quite often a bill will have 53 or 57 co-sponsors and still lose. They go
on as a co-sponsor without knowing too much about the bill or in the
meantime it has been changed by amendments. A few times I have wound
up voting against a bill I introduced myself because it was completely
changed by amendments. I have co-sponsored quite a lot of legislation*

affecting veterans, Vietnam servicemen, amnesty, health programs, and regional programs affecting the West – like reclamation. I only agree to co-sponsor about half the bills I am asked to. Some are really just resolutions that don't mean much but if you went on all that you were requested to go on, you would have a hard time remembering what you sponsored, much less trying to explain them. From time to time I have introduced a complete farm bill, but the committee, with few exceptions, took parts of my bill and made them part of a bill sponsored by the whole committee.

"I spend a lot of time at making serving the people of the state a high priority in my office. I personally handle a lot of things. I sign practically every letter. Just by signing them I can pick up things that we hadn't handled too well. But the major problem is that there are so many you couldn't possibly read them all – they are read three times by staff members to check for errors. Three different staff members read every letter and if one of them finds something that looks wrong or it doesn't represent my thinking, they will hold it out. Or sometimes if I am faced with a real tough letter and I dictate a reply right away – I always feel better if I get it off my chest – I find out the next morning that the staff has held that letter out to see if I still want to send it. Usually I change the letter."

Final Tributes

The final tribute paid to Young by his Senate colleagues came on December 4, 1980. Young and three other retiring Senators were recognized: Richard Schweiker from Pennsylvania, Henry Bellmon from Oklahoma and Jacob Javits from New York, all Republicans.

The tributes were led by Senator Howard Baker of Tennessee, Minority Leader of the Senate, who said of Young:

> I dare say that no man in the long history of the Senate has been more thoughtful, more compassionate, more dedicated, more patriotic or more decent than Milton Young. On this coming Saturday [December 6], Senator Young will celebrate his 83rd birthday and I

know we all wish him many happy returns on that day. It is my understanding, by the way Mr. President, that to commemorate that 83-year-'young', Milt Young plans to unsheathe his karate-trained hand to break board for firewood.

Milt Young grew up a farmer, Mr. President. In fact, if one were to ask him his occupation this very day, after 35 years in the Senate, I imagine Milt would say he is still a farmer, although the soil on Capitol Hill is no doubt less fertile than in his LaMoure, North Dakota, home. During his six terms in this chamber, Milt Young has done more for the people of North Dakota than there is time or space to recount. Suffice it to say, he is fondly referred to in North Dakota as 'Mr. Wheat' and referred to here as 'our most distinguished colleague.'

. . . Senator Young is the only member of the Reorganized Church of Jesus Christ of the Latter Day Saints to have served in the Senate. Throughout that service, he has been the paragon of the humility, hard work and virtue his faith inspires. It was my privilege, Mr. President, once to attend the graduation ceremonies of his alma mater [Graceland College in Limoni, Iowa] and to deliver a commencement address there in his presence. I remember that occasion with great pleasure, Mr. President, because not only was it an honor for me, but it was also an opportunity to see firsthand the extraordinary respect, even reverence, with which his fellow citizens viewed him and in which he was held.

Senator John Tower, Texas:

Milton Young is one of the hardest working legislators I have ever known. I think he is a quite essential public servant because he only seeks to accomplish; he does not seek self-aggrandizement. He is self-effacing, almost to a fault. But with all this, he is certainly one of the most effective legislators I have known . . . He is an unselfish man. He has given of himself without seeking credit or fame for what he has done. I am particularly grateful to him for the stalwart way in which he has supported our efforts to build a defense capability of the United States that will at once enable us to maintain our national security and at the same time support our foreign policy objectives based on a clear perception of our vital national interests throughout the world. Those of us who believe we can ultimately achieve peace through strength will agree to that concerning Milt Young. I have been privileged to serve with him now for 20 years. I have learned from him. I have benefited enormously both personally and professionally by my association with him, and I offer him now my profound thanks.

Senator Thad Cochran, Mississippi:

Senator Young and I have had the opportunity, from time to time, to talk about his early recollections of coming to the Senate and the way things were then. When I was a very small boy, he was already serving in the United States Senate. He has told me of the close friendship with Senators from my region of the country, such as the late Senator Richard Russell. His stories have helped me to appreciate, in a deeper and more meaningful way, what the Senate really is, what it has been and what it should be as an institution. I observe the irony that were it not for Senator Young's decision to retire at this particular time, when the Republicans are gaining a majority in control of this body, he would be our President Pro Tempore, and may not have that honor, in spite of the fact that he has decided to retire. I certainly hope that this comes true.

Senator Richard Schweiker, Pennsylvania:

There was never any question of your having to worry about Milt Young letting you pursue a line of activity or work that you were interested in because it conflicted with him. There never was any question that, if you wanted to take the active leadership in some field in which he has done some work before, he would yield to you.

There always was an opportunity for the newer and younger members of the committee to play very satisfying and fulfilling roles because of his broad leadership, because of his willingness to bring people in, to include them, and to give them responsible roles ... I think also that something should be said about his work on the Defense Appropriations Subcommittee on which we serve. Senator Young is an acknowledged expert in this field because of his service here. Because it is defense, a lot of the work is dealt with in closed meetings, in closed markups, due to this security label and its classified nature. Thus, not all people are aware of the great amount of time, the detail and effort that he has put into this effort. He was one to be there and to take an active and vital role in the closed hearing when the TV cameras were not there. When there was no recognition whatsoever, Milt Young was there minding the store and making sure, from his perspective, that this nation got the kind of defense appropriations he felt were needed, and he was there to listen, to hear and to assess whether such appropriations were appropriate.

Senator Larry Pressler, South Dakota:

Senator Young has represented my neighboring state of North Dakota for nearly all my lifetime. Before I entered grade school I was well familiar with Senator Young's name, and his name and career have been one of the lights upon which I have attempted to chart my course. Senator Young has always been pointed out to me as the finest example of Midwestern integrity and hard-working indomitable Dakota spirit. I am, therefore, extremely proud to be able to serve in the same body and become personally acquainted with the man who is known as Mr. Republican in my part of the country and who was one of my boyhood heroes.

Since I came to Congress in January 1975, Senator Young, the dean of Senate Republicans, has always been extremely generous with his time and assistance for me and other younger members. His friendliness and desire to help others has been a hallmark of his public service. The work ethic that Senator Young learned growing up on a farm has served him well in the Senate. Rising early and staying past the time many Senators have departed for home, Senator Young has always well represented the people of North Dakota. He has never neglected the primary interest of our part of the world, having served on the Agriculture Committee. Milt Young was a farmer before coming to Washington, and with this experience has been primarily involved in the writing of all major farm legislation in the last several decades. He is known nationally as "Mr. Wheat."

Following other tributes, Senator Baker rose to offer a resolution electing Young President Pro Tempore of the Senate:

A resolution (S. Res. 551) to amend S. Res 4 of the 96th Congress, First Session, to provide for the election of Milton R. Young of the State of North Dakota to be President pro tempore: "Resolved, that the Honorable Milton R. Young, a Senator from the State of North Dakota, be, and he is hereby elected President of the Senate Pro tempore, to hold office for the calendar day of Friday, December 5, 1980, vice the Honorable Warren G. Magnuson (excused).

After the resolution was read, Magnuson made the following comments:

Mr. President. As long as I am the object of this resolution, I reserve the right to object. But I shall not object, I want to say that I have known Milt Young for so long. I met him when he got off the train coming from Fargo as a new Senator, and he had a cardboard box with him. He did not know where he was going to stay or anything else, and that was a long time ago. We have been good friends ever since, and I am very privileged to accede to him this one day. Now we have a chauffeur and a car, and I am going to let him use that car tomorrow – only tomorrow."

The following day, Senator Young addressed the Senate as the President Pro Tempore:

This is indeed a great honor and privilege for me . . . I really never thought this day would come. And it would not have except for the thoughtfulness and kindness and consideration of the majority leader Senator Robert C. Byrd, and the minority leader Senator Baker and one of my longtime friends, Senator Magnuson, for relinquishing his important assignment of President Pro Tempore for this one day.

This one day will live a long time in my life and always a most pleasant memory. There is something unusual, too, that I would like to mention. I was the last Senator sworn in by the late Vice President Truman before he became President. I was greatly honored that Vice President Mondale administered this oath of office to me yesterday. He is a great Vice President, very popular and a long-time good friend of mine. So this is a great honor and one of the best days of my lifetime. I thank the leadership and all of the members of the Senate for making this possible.

Senator Baker then said, "Mr. President, I rise only to acknowledge that the distinguished occupant of the chair, the President Pro Tempore, looks and appears to this body as if he had occupied it for many years and graces that position to the great benefit of this body."

The honor the Senate had given to Young was precedent setting. It was the first time in the history of the United States Senate that a minority member presided over the majority party.

In his last *On Capitol Hill* newsletter he mailed out to all North Dakota newspapers, radio and television in December, 1980, Young wrote:

> On January 3, my time in the United States Senate . . . will come to an end. It will be a rather difficult transition from a busy, tense life to one of very little public activity. This will be after having served longer continuously than any Republican in the history of the Senate.
>
> The people of North Dakota have been very good to me. My public career began with election as Township Supervisor in 1924 and I have continuously held elective office all the years since, without ever having been defeated for re-election. Forty-eight of these years have been as a legislator, 12 in our State Legislature and almost 36 in the United States Senate. Fortunately, I have had unusually good health for one my age, and am very proud that my greatest accomplishments and recognition came during this last six years.
>
> My interest in politics began during the Depression and drought years of the late 1920s and 1930s. I felt strongly then that much of the terrible poverty farmers and others suffered in those years could have been averted by good farm legislation. At that time the controversial McNary-Haugen Farm Bill was being considered in Congress. It was because of this deep interest, born of personal experience, that I sought membership on the Senate Agriculture and Forestry Committee, where I soon became deeply involved in all farm legislation. This interest continued for all these years. This committee recently adopted a resolution signed by all its members in recognition of my having served longer on the Senate Agriculture and Forestry Committee than anyone since

the committee was first established 148 years ago.

Of the more than 160 awards I have received, one was received just last month at Atlanta, Georgia. This one was especially treasured. It was given to me by the National Association of State Universities and Land Grant Colleges, with their Extension Services and Experiment Stations, for outstanding service in the field of agriculture.

My other major committee assignment has been Appropriations, where in recent years I served as ranking Republican of the Full Committee, as well as ranking Republican of the Subcommittee on Defense Appropriations. This is an area that took considerable time and effort, largely because of my deep concern that our nation not become a second-rate military power to Russia. I have always felt strongly that we should have the most modern weapons possible.

It was very gratifying to achieve top recognition for these efforts. Each year, the Reserve Officers Association, which includes officers in all the services, including the National Guard, and which has members in every state, gives their Minuteman of the Year Award to the one Member of Congress whom they feel has done the most for national defense. For 1979, they honored me by giving me this Minuteman Award.

I am most appreciative to have been honored by having my name identified with many public service projects of various kinds. It is very gratifying that North Dakota State University at Fargo will have these awards and the rest of my memorabilia in a special place in their new library. The bronze bust in the State Capitol, too, is a wonderful recognition.

I will always be grateful to the people of North Dakota for making possible these many years in the Senate, which have been interesting, hectic, exciting and rewarding. It is the kind of career that I sought and enjoyed. I can't help but leave this office with mixed feelings. Greatly missed will be the close association with so many people over these years and the enjoyment in being able to help them with their personal problems, as well as our beloved state.

In our retirement we will be spending the winters at our home in Sun City, Arizona, and the summers in

North Dakota. The pleasant memories of the years I was
privileged to serve you in the United States Senate will
be cherished always.

The nostalgia surrounding his final weeks in the Senate was interrupted by the practical considerations of closing his office and moving out of his longtime Rock Creek Park apartment home. The Senate had expected to adjourn on Friday, December 5, so the Youngs had completely cleared out their apartment and made arrangements to fly to their winter home in Arizona the next day. A week later, the session still had not ended and work on the Senate floor was continuing until late each evening. This required them to reschedule their plane reservations and to make do in a near-empty apartment.

When asked how he felt about ending his Senate career after adjournment had been delayed by a week, Young replied in a December 12 Associated Press news story that "days like this make it easier."

Milton Young served in the Senate 35 years, 9 months and 22 days. When he retired on January 3, 1981, his length of service was the 14th longest in the history of the U.S. Senate. He also remains the longest serving U.S. Senator in the history of North Dakota.

A Leader Laid to Rest

In September 1981, eight months after leaving the Senate, Young spoke to political science students at the University of North Dakota in his new role as a visiting professor of history and political science, which he held for one semester. As reported in the September 9, 1981, *Grand Forks Herald*, Young encouraged the students to have an interest in politics, despite recent political scandals. "Politics can affect whether you are drafted to fight in another war," he told them.

The article reported how Young downplayed his value as a college professor, telling a group of students the university had "over-rated" him as the instructor and over-promoted the course, and that he wouldn't have accepted the appointment without an understanding that "if it gets too tough, I could run like a rabbit."

In that class, Young reflected on how the increased pace in Congress found busy Senators racing to their desks to cast important votes while staff members told them how to vote. The result of this faster pace, Young lamented, was losing human contact with constituents. "I lost connections. I got so busy. A lot of young people grew up who I never knew."

He also mused on how politics had changed during his Senate career and that people "seemed to take politics more seriously" early in his career. "In an election year, there was hardly a small town where there wasn't a fistfight."

Shortly before his retirement, Young considered himself to be in good health for his age. *"I had and still have a hernia of the diaphragm but I live with it pretty well by using Maalox by the case. Otherwise my health is pretty good except I have some arthritis in my hips. The worst thing about that is it is hard on my golf score. I can't drive as far. I had eye surgery in February 1976, with the new surgery where the cataract is removed and a plastic lens is implanted in the eye. This is rather new surgery and I found that neither the Mayo Clinic, Walter Reed or the Naval Hospital were doing it. Fortunately, we found Dr. A. Edward Maumenee, Chief of the Wilmer Eye Clinic at the Johns Hopkins Hospital in Baltimore, who did it for me. He is one of the top eye specialists in the United States. He removed the cataract and inserted the plastic lens using over 30 stitches and now that eye has 20-20 vision. I will have the other eye done soon."*

Other health concerns arose, however, a little more than a year into his retirement from the Senate. Young underwent surgery in Rochester, Minnesota, in June 1982, to remove a malignant tumor from his prostate. Later that summer, at the Senator's request, Dakota Monument Company of Fargo erected a monument at the Young family cemetery north of his hometown of Berlin.

Young told of his search for a monument to place at the family cemetery in an August 5, 1982, article in the *Fargo Forum*. He said he had been considering different ideas as far back as eight years. He had seen three obelisk style monuments, one at the gravesite of an uncle in Wabasha, Minnesota, another at the gravesite of former Alabama U.S. Senator James B. Allen, and another at the Winder, Georgia, gravesite of Richard Russell, his best friend in the Senate, who died in 1971.

While the obelisk style interested him, Young was concerned that it not be too large or showy in the small Berlin cemetery. He chose one that was ten and one-half feet high, to be made out of Georgia granite, in honor of Russell. There were several sizes of the U.S. Senate seal which could be engraved on the monument; he chose one of the smaller ones. At the time the monument was erected, Young told the *Fargo Forum* that he was "feeling as good as can be expected" following his surgery a few months earlier. Although using a cane to steady himself, the 84-year-old Young told about being honored earlier in the week at the Bismarck Country Club, and "damned if I didn't play one" hole of golf.

By February 1983, Pat Young reported that her husband's health had begun to fail noticeably. At 10:25 a.m. on May 31, 1983, the last person to serve in the U.S. Congress who was born in the 19th Century died peacefully at his Sun City, Arizona, retirement home from prostrate cancer, just 29 months after leaving office.

His body was flown from Phoenix to Fargo two days before his funeral June 4 at the LaMoure High School Auditorium. Attending were between 600 and 700 people, including the state's Congressional delegation of Senator Quentin Burdick, Senator Mark Andrews and Congressman Byron Dorgan. State officials attending included Governor Allen Olson, Lieutenant Governor Ernie Sands, former Governors Arthur Link and John Davis, Agriculture Commissioner Kent Jones, Tax Commissioner Kent Conrad and a number of state legislators.

Presiding at the funeral were Presiding Bishop Francis E. Hansen of Independence, Missouri, and Karl Schiebold of Fargo, an elder of the Reorganized Church of Jesus Christ of Latter Day Saints. Father Jon Wanzek of the LaMoure Catholic Church read a statement from Bishop Justin Driscoll of the Fargo Diocese.

Pallbearers were Robert Christman, Young's agriculture aide at the end of his Senate career; Lester Paulson, a friend from LaMoure; Claire Sandness, lifelong friend from LaMoure and former state senator; Harold Bullis from Wahpeton, a former staff member and state representative; Donald Holand, from Lisbon and Fargo, a former state senate majority leader; U.S. District Judge Paul Benson; Glenn Ellingson, a friend from Berlin; and Art Weber, a friend from LaMoure.

Honorary pallbearers included former staff members Chris Sylvester, Mel Christopher, Ed Hartung, William Block, and Neil Bjornson; North Dakota Republican colleagues Arley Bjella, Brooks Keogh, John Rouzie, Evan Lips, Sr., Earl Strinden, Harold Schafer, Governor Allen Olson, and Ben Clayburgh; *Fargo Forum* publisher William Marcil, rural electric leader Andrew Freeman; M.S. Byrne, Pat Young's father;

and Dick Stoudt Jr., Jamestown; LaMoure Mayor George Kaftan; Henry Hoffman, Berlin, and Oscar Sorlie, Buxton.

Also in attendance at the services were plain-clothed U.S. Marshals who had been detached to guard pallbearer Judge Benson. He had received a death threat in Fargo a few days prior to the funeral, stemming from his presiding over the trial of four persons charged in connection with the February 1983 shootout in Medina, North Dakota, with tax protester Gordon Kahl that resulted in the deaths of two U.S. Marshals.

The colors were presented by servicemen stationed at the U.S. Coast Guard Omega station at LaMoure. Family friend Gayle Kaftan brought her organ to the school to play the music, and another family friend, Emmett Haugen, sang "O, God, How Wonderful Thou Art" and "The Old, Old Path."

Senator Howard Baker of Tennessee, a close Senate colleague, had planned to give the eulogy at the funeral, but was unable to attend due to a last-minute conflict. The eulogy was instead given by Elder Karl Schiebold, who said, "No one in the Senate ever had to guess where Milton Young stood on an issue. He would oppose the President in power if he believed it necessary to gain just legislation for his state. This, I believe, is one of the qualities that determine the difference between a politician and a statesman. Milton was indeed the latter."

He likened Young's stature and the state's affection for him to John Burke, former Governor, Treasurer of the United States and Chief Justice of the North Dakota Supreme Court. "Milton was not to be compared with Daniel Webster or Hubert Humphrey in his ability as an orator or in the use of rhetoric," Schiebold said, "but he had a strong sense of honor and of duty comparable to Burke. Milton Young is known as 'Mr. Wheat,' John Burke is remembered as 'Honest John.'"

Following the service, a mile-long processional of cars made their way to the family cemetery one mile north of Berlin for the burial. Standing in waiting was Young's 7,500 pound obelisk monument, which was erected on a seven-foot deep concrete foundation. The four sides of the tombstone read:

north side

Friend of Farmers. Mr. Wheat

east side

Milton R. Young, United States Senator,
March 12, 1945 to January 3, 1981,
The longest continuous service attained
by any Republican U.S. Senator

south side

Served with honor and distinction.
'He made his mark,' by Jamestown friends

west side

Milton R. Young, born December 6, 1897,
died May 31, 1983.

In the many tributes honoring Young when he died, colleagues, friends and journalists remembered him for his personal and political traits and his contributions to his local community, state and nation.

Richard Pearson wrote in the June 1, 1983, *Washington Post* obituary about Young:

> If Sen. Young's career seemed to lack glamour and diversity, it was because he wanted it that way. As he said, "I have always tried to stay close to the people. In North Dakota to be elected and to stay on, you have to know the farmers and stay close to them. They are loyal to a fault." . . . A tall, laconic man with a leathery face, he was a picture of dignity. He was quiet and even at the peak of his powers on his committees was more listener than talker. One committee assistant remembered him as a tenacious fighter for what he believed in who was devoted to his state and attended committee hearings faithfully.

The June 3, 1983, editorial in the *Bismarck Tribune* wrote:

> Perhaps we in North Dakota stood by Senator Young so long because we saw him as we wanted the nation to

see us. He never was one to seek attention for himself, he rarely made headlines except back home. Despite the trappings of power and the pomp and ceremony of Washington, he remained a North Dakotan, one of us.

North Dakota columnist Wayne Lubenow wrote in his weekly column shortly after Young's death:

He was one of the most open, frank guys I ever met . . . Most Senators and Congressmen from agricultural states refer to themselves as 'dirt farmers.' It is a ploy to get votes. Well, Milt Young was a real 'dirt farmer.' He came up the hard way and he never forgot it.

. . . But Milt Young and I had something else in common. He stuttered and so do I. When we met, it would take 10 minutes for us to say hello to each other. It was worth it. It let me know that a stutterer can become a United States Senator. It let me know that a stutterer can also get interviews for stories.

The eulogies have poured out for Milt Young and rightly so. Let one small voice say that he was the most honest and the most approachable United States Senator I've seen in a long time."

In 1979, Young mused about how he wanted to be remembered in history. *"First of all, I want to be remembered as an honest, hard worker and a man of integrity. I also would like to be remembered as one who enjoyed helping people and the many communities in the state of North Dakota with their problems. Above all, I want to be remembered as being honest."*

Two decades before comparisons would be made between him and John Burke at Young's funeral, Young was among the speakers during a June 27, 1963, ceremony dedicating a statue of Burke in Statuary Hall of the U.S. Capitol. "John Burke," said Young, "might be considered one of those who, through ability and perseverance, is caught by a surge of history, and who moves among the great."

Reflecting on the remarkable political career of Milton R. Young, the same could be said of him.

Chapter Notes

Unless otherwise cited, information in this biography comes from oral interviews conducted with U.S. Senator Milton R. Young by then-University of North Dakota history professor Dr. D. Jerome Tweton in August 1979 and November 1980.

Direct quotations by Senator Young from the oral interviews are shown throughout the text in italics. They have been edited for syntax and sentence form.

Chapter 1
A Dakota Pioneer Family Since 1880

Additional material from family interviews, the North Dakota State Data Center, and the *Berlin Record* and *LaMoure County Chronicle* newspapers.

Chapter 2
A Dirt Farmer During the Depression

Additional material from family interviews; the May 27, 2005, interview with longtime friend Claire Sandness; the *Berlin Record, LaMoure Chronicle, Bismarck Tribune,* and *Bismarck Capital* newspapers. Correspondence is from files in the Milton R. Young papers in the Orin G. Libby Manuscript Collection at the University of North Dakota Elwyn B. Robinson Department of Special Collections.

Chapter 3
An Emerging Political Figure

Additional material from family interviews; the May 27, 2005, interview with longtime friend Claire Sandness; the *LaMoure Chronicle, Bismarck Capital* and *Bismarck Tribune* newspapers; *The Dakota Maverick* by Agnes Geelan and *History of North Dakota* by Elwyn B. Robinson, books; the North Dakota Legislative Council. Correspondence is from files in the Milton R. Young papers in the Orin G. Libby Manuscript Collection at the University of North Dakota Elwyn B. Robinson Department of Special Collections.

Chapter 4
From One Senate to Another

Additional material from family interviews; the May 27, 2005, interview with longtime friend Claire Sandness; and the *LaMoure Chronicle,* and *Bismarck Tribune* newspapers; *The Dakota Maverick* by Agnes Geelan, *The Battle Against Intervention, 1939-1941* by Justus Doenecke, books; the North Dakota Legislative Council.

Chapter 5
A Washington Newcomer
Additional material from family interviews; the *LaMoure Chronicle, Fargo Forum* and *Bismarck Tribune*; the March 11, 1946, *Life* Magazine; and *The Dakota Maverick* by Agnes Geelan, book. Correspondence is from files in the Milton R. Young papers in the Orin G. Libby Manuscript Collection at the University of North Dakota Elwyn B. Robinson Department of Special Collections.

Chapter 6
'First A Farmer'
Additional material from family interviews; the February 24, 2004, interview with Neil Bjornson, and the October 28, 2003, interview with Robert Christman; the *LaMoure Chronicle, Fargo Forum* and *Bismarck Tribune* newspapers; *Calvin Coolidge* by David Greenburg, book; the *Congressional Record*, and the Agricultural Law Center at the University of Arkansas. Correspondence is from files in the Milton R. Young papers in the Orin G. Libby Manuscript Collection at the University of North Dakota Elwyn B. Robinson Department of Special Collections.

Chapter 7
Wars, Weapons and World Issues
Additional material from family papers; the March 17, 2004, interview with Evan Lips; the *LaMoure Chronicle, Fargo Forum, New York Times* and *Bismarck Tribune* newspapers; *North Dakota, A History* by Robert P. Wilkins and Wynona H. Wilkins, book. Correspondence, speeches and *On Capitol Hill* columns from files in the Milton R. Young papers in the Orin G. Libby Manuscript Collection at the University of North Dakota Elwyn B. Robinson Department of Special Collections.

Chapter 8
National Issues and North Dakota
Additional material from the March 17, 2004, interview with Evan Lips; the December 10, 2003, interview with Louise Christopher, the March 24, 2004, interview with Chester Reiten; the February 24, 2004, interview with Neil Bjornson; the October 5, 2009, interview with Johnny Klingenberg; the *LaMoure Chronicle, Fargo Forum, Minot Daily News* and *Bismarck Tribune* newspapers; *The Promise of Water: The Garrison Diversion Project,* by Wayne Gudmundson and Robert Silberman, book. Correspondence, speeches and *On Capitol Hill* columns from files in the Milton R. Young papers in the Orin G. Libby Manuscript Collection at the University of North Dakota Elwyn B. Robinson Department of Special Collections.

Chapter 9
Restoring Ford's Theatre
Additional material from family interviews and papers; the *Washington Post, Fargo Forum* and *Bismarck Tribune* newspapers; the *Congressional Record*; *Ford's Theatre's Reconstruction: Warehouse, Museum, Pilgrimage Site (1865-1968),* by Eva Reffell, paper. Correspondence, speeches, news releases and *On Capitol Hill* columns from files in the Milton R. Young papers in the Orin G. Libby Manuscript Collection at the University of North Dakota Elwyn B. Robinson Department of Special Collections.

Chapter 10
Eight Presidents
Additional material from family interviews and papers; the February 24, 2004, interview with Neil Bjornson; July 18, 1978, oral interview of Milton R.Young by the Lyndon Baines Johnson Library; the *Fargo Forum* and *Grand Forks Herald* newspapers. Correspondence, news releases and *On Capitol Hill* columns from files in the Milton R. Young papers in the Orin G. Libby Manuscript Collection at the University of North Dakota Elwyn B. Robinson Department of Special Collections.

Chapter 11
Four Re-Election Campaigns
Additional material from family interviews and papers; the *LaMoure Chronicle, Fargo Forum, Minot Daily News, Bismarck Tribune, Jamestown Sun, Golden Valley News, Grand Forks Herald* and *Baltimore Sun* newspapers. Correspondence, news releases and *On Capitol Hill* columns from files in the Milton R. Young papers in the Orin G. Libby Manuscript Collection at the University of North Dakota Elwyn B. Robinson Department of Special Collections.

Chapter 12
The 1974 Election: North Dakota's Perfect Political Storm
Additional material from family interviews and papers; the May 27, 2005, interview with longtime friend Claire Sandness; the *LaMoure Chronicle, Fargo Forum, Minot Daily News, Bismarck Tribune, Jamestown Sun,* and *Grand Forks Herald* newspapers. Correspondence, news releases and *On Capitol Hill* columns from files in the Milton R. Young papers in the Orin G. Libby Manuscript Collection at the University of North Dakota Elwyn B. Robinson Department of Special Collections.

Chapter 13
In the Arena
Additional material from family interviews and papers; the September 21, 2009, interview with former U.S. Senator George McGovern, the December 12, 2009,

interview with former U.S. Senator Mark Andrews; the January 4, 2010, interview with Robert Christman; November 16, 2009, email correspondence with U.S. Senate Historian Donald A. Ritchie; October 6, 1952, *Time* Magazine.

Chapter 14
A Final Term

Additional material from family interviews and papers; the *LaMoure Chronicle, Fargo Forum, Bismarck Tribune,* and *Washington Post* newspapers; the *Congressional Record.* Correspondence, news releases and *On Capitol Hill* columns from files in the Milton R. Young papers in the Orin G. Libby Manuscript Collection at the University of North Dakota Elwyn B. Robinson Department of Special Collections.

Chapter 15
A Leader Laid to Rest

Additional material from family interviews and papers; the *LaMoure Chronicle, Grand Forks Herald, Fargo Forum, Bismarck Tribune,* and *Washington Post* newspapers.

Bibliography

Government Documents

Biographical Directory of the United States Congress, 1774-1949. United States Government Printing Office, Washington, D.C., 1950.

Biographical Directory of the United States Congress, 1774-1989, Bicentennial Edition. United States Government Printing Office, Washington, D.C., 1989.

Congressional Quarterly Almanac, 84th Congress, Second Session, 1956. Volume XII, Congressional Quarterly News Features, Washington, D.C., 1956.

Guide to Records of the United States Senate at the National Archives, 1789-1989, Bicentennial Edition. National Archives and Records Administration, Washington, D.C., 1989.

Historic Structures Report: Restoration of Ford's Theatre. By George J. Olszewski, Ph.D., Historian, National Capital Region. United States Department of the Interior, National Park Service, 1963.

Oral History Interview July 18, 1978, of Milton R. Young, Lyndon Baines Johnson Library, National Archives and Records Service, General Services Administration, Washington, D.C., 1980.

Oral History Interview April 5, 1978, of Francis J. Attig, Official Reporter of Debates, 1952-1974, p. 48. United States Senate Historical Office, Washington, D.C.

Oral History Interviews, March 20 – May 6, 1985, of William F. Hildenbrand, Secretary of the Senate, pp. 111-113. United States Senate Historical Office, Washington, D.C.

Oral History Interviews, July 22 – October 22, 1987, of Howard E. Shuman, Legislative and Administrative Assistant to Senators Paul Douglas and William Proxmire, 1955-1982, pp. 482-486. United States Senate Historical Office, Washington, D.C.

Memorial Services Held in the Senate and House of Representatives of the United States, Together with Remarks Presented in Eulogy of William Langer, Late a Senator from North Dakota. Eighty-Sixth Congress, Second Session. United States Government Printing Office, Washington, D.C., 1960.

Memorial Addresses and Other Tributes in the Congress of the United States on the Life and Contributions of Milton R. Young. Ninety-Eighth Congress, First Session. United States Government Printing Office, Washington, D.C., 1983.

Dissertations

Sylvester, Stephen Grant, "Milton R. Young: Dirt Farmer to United States Senator, 1932-1945," M.A. thesis, The University of North Dakota, Grand Forks, 1977.

Young, Allan C., "Race of the Century: Guy vs. Young 1974 North Dakota U.S. Senate Election," M.A. thesis, The University of North Dakota, Grand Forks, 1989.

Interviews

Mark Andrews – December 12, 2009
Neil R. Bjornson – February 24, 2004
Robert Christman – October 28, 2003, January 4, 2010
Louise Christopher – December 10, 2003
Gregory C. Harness – October 14, 2003
Johnny Klingenberg – October 5, 2009
Evan E. Lips – March 17, 2004
George S. McGovern – September 21, 2009
Chester Reiten – March 24, 2004
Donald A. Ritchie – January 22, 2004
Louise Aandahl Stockman – November 22, 2009
D. Jerome Tweton – May 13, 2004
John M. Young – November 12-13, 2003, May 27, 2005
Marcia Young – November 12-13, 2003, May 27, 2005

Residents of LaMoure, North Dakota interviewed May 27, 2005

Al Dohm
Irene Dohm
Janet Hind
Gayle Kaftan
George Kaftan
Maxine Lapham
Onis Poehls
Claire Sandness
Delores Sandness
Vern Sandness

Resident of Edgeley, North Dakota interviewed May 27, 2005

Dorothy Van Ornum

Articles

Harvey, Mark T. "North Dakota, the Northern Plains, and the Missouri Valley Authority," *North Dakota History: Journal of the Northern Plains,* Volume 59, Number 3, Summer 1992, pp. 28-39.

Remele, Larry. "Equal Time for Townley: Media Politics in North Dakota, 1956-1959," *North Dakota History: Journal of the Northern Plains,* Volume 52, Number 1, Winter 1985, pp. 24-34.

Sprunk, Larry J. "North Dakota Oral History Project Issue #2: Senator Milton R. Young – Berlin," *North Dakota History: Journal of the Northern Plains,* Volume

44, Number 4, Fall 1977, pp. 44-46.

"Senators Face Election: An Estimation of Their Intelligence and Capacity," *Life* Magazine, March 11, 1946, pp. 97-103.

"The Congress: The First Seven Months," *Time* Magazine, August 4, 1947.

"Look Out, Neighbor," *Time* Magazine, October 6, 1952.

Young, Anh and Lyle Lere. "Mr. Wheat," 3rd Annual North Dakota Farm Toy Show Official Souvenir Program, June 17-19, 1988, pp. 19-20.

Books

Blackorby, Edward C. *Prairie Rebel: The Public Life of William Lemke.* The University of Nebraska Press, Lincoln, 1963.

Blackorby, Edward C., editor, Janet Daley. *Prairie Populist: The Life and Times of Usher L. Burdick.* The State Historical Society of North Dakota and the North Dakota Institute for Regional Studies, North Dakota State University, Fargo, 2001.

Byrd, Robert C., edited by Wendy Wolff, U.S. Senate Historical Office. *The Senate, 1789-1989. Addresses on the History of the United States Senate, Volume Two, Bicentennial Edition.* United States Government Printing Office, Washington, D.C., 1991.

Byrd, Robert C., edited by Wendy Wolff, U.S. Senate Historical Office. *The Senate, 1789-1989. Historical Statistics, 1789-1992, Volume Four, Bicentennial Edition.* United States Government Printing Office, Washington, D.C., 1993.

Caro, Robert A. *The Years of Lyndon Johnson: Master of the Senate.* Alfred A. Knopf, New York, 2002.

Doenecke, Justus D. *The Battle Against Intervention, 1939-1941.* Krieger Publishing Company, Malabas, Florida, 1996.

Dole, Robert J. *Historical Almanac of the U.S. Senate.* United States Government Printing Office, Washington, D.C., 1989.

Fite, Gilbert C. *Richard B. Russell, Jr., Senator from Georgia.* The University of North Carolina Press, Chapel Hill and London, 1991.

Garraty, John A., and Mark C. Carnes, general editors. *American National Biography, Volume 24.* Oxford University Press, New York, Oxford, 1999.

Geelan, Agnes. *The Dakota Maverick: The Political Life of William Langer, Also Known as 'Wild Bill' Langer.* Kaye's Printing Company, Fargo, North Dakota, 1975.

Greenburg, David. *Calvin Coolidge.* The American Presidents, Times Books, Henry Holt and Company, New York, 2006.

Gudmundson, Wayne, photographs by, Robert Silberman, essay by. *The Promise of Water: The Garrison Diversion Project.* The North Dakota Institute for Regional Studies, North Dakota State University, Fargo, 2002.

Hagel, Jerry and Mary. *Talking Wires: The Story of North Dakota's Telephone Cooperatives*. North Plains Press, Aberdeen, South Dakota, 1979.

Howard, Thomas W., editor. *The North Dakota Political Tradition*. Iowa State University Press, Ames, 1981.

Hurst, Louis, as told to Frances Spatz Leighton. *The Sweetest Little Club in the World: The U.S. Senate*. Prentice-Hall, Inc., Englewood Cliffs, New Jersey, 1980.

Jackson, Kenneth T., editor in chief, Karen E. Markoe, general editor, Arnold Markoe, associate editor. *Dictionary of American Biography, Supplement Nine, 1971-1975*. Charles Scribner's Sons, New York, 1994.

LaMoure Centennial Book Committee. *A History of LaMoure, North Dakota, 1882-1982*. Associated Printers, Grafton, North Dakota, 1982.

Mann, Robert. *The Walls of Jericho: Lyndon Johnson, Hubert Humphrey, Richard Russell and the Struggle for Civil Rights*. Harcourt Brace and Company, New York, San Diego, London, 1996.

Mellichamp, Josephine. *Senators from Georgia*. The Strode Publishers, Inc., Huntsville, Alabama, 1976.

Omdahl, Lloyd B. *Insurgents*. Lakeland Color Press, Brainerd, Minnesota, 1961.

Patterson, James T. *Mr. Republican: A Biography of Robert A. Taft*. Houghton Mifflin Company, Boston, 1972.

Pence, Richard A., and Patrick Dahl, editors. *The Next Greatest Thing: Fifty Years of Rural Electrification*. National Rural Electric Cooperative Association, 1984.

Robinson, Elwyn B. *History of North Dakota*. The University of Nebraska Press, Lincoln, 1966.

Robinson, Sheila, compiled by. *The Story of Garrison Dam - Taming the Big Muddy: Construction of Rolled Earth Dam on the Missouri River, North Dakota*. BHG, Inc., Garrison, North Dakota, 1997.

Rylance, Dan. *Quentin Burdick: The Gentle Warrior*. The North Dakota Institute for Regional Studies, North Dakota State University, Fargo, 2007.

Wilkins, Robert P., and Wynona H. Wilkins. *North Dakota: A Bicentennial History*. W.W. Norton and Company, Inc., New York, 1977.

Who's Who in America, 1954-55, Volume 28. Marquis Publications Building, Chicago, Illinois.

Newspapers

The Baltimore Sun

The Berlin Record

The Bismarck Capital

The Bismarck Tribune

The Forum, Fargo

The Golden Valley News, Beach

The Grand Forks Herald
The Jamestown Sun
The LaMoure Chronicle
The Minot Daily News
The New York Times
The Washington Post

Other Publications

A Festival at Ford's, March 21, 1981. The Ford's Theatre Society, Frankie Hewitt, Executive Producer.

Ford's Theatre's Reconstruction: Warehouse, Museum, Pilgrimage Site (1865-1968). Eva Reffell. Paper for The University of Michigan School of Information, Ann Arbor, 2004.

The Home Front in North Dakota During World War II. North Dakota Humanities Council, 2003.

Milton R. Young: Republican Senator from North Dakota. Ellen Szita. Ralph Nader Congress Project – Citizens Look at Congress. Grossman Publishing, Washington, D.C., 1972.

The National Cyclopedia of American Biography Being the History of the United States: As Illustrated in the Lives of the Founders, Builders and Defenders of the Republic, and of the Men and Women Who Are Doing the Work and Molding the Thought of the Present Time. Current Volume H, 1947-52. James T. White and Company, New York, 1952.

The North Star Dakotan. World War Two Through the 1960s. Issue Six. North Dakota Humanities Council, 2005.

E-Mail

Steven S. Allen, Staff Consultant, U.S. House Agriculture Committee 1973-75, to Andrea Winkjer Collin – November 4, 2003.

Harrison Mauzy Pittman, Director of the Agricultural Law Center at the University of Arkansas, to Andrea Winkjer Collin – December 10, 2008.

Michael J. Ganley, Fiscal Analyst, National Rural Electric Cooperative Association, to Andrea Winkjer Collin – November 12, 2009.

Donald A. Ritchie, Historian of the U.S. Senate, to Andrea Winkjer Collin – November 16, 2009.

Websites

lcweb.loc.gov:8081/ammem/amrlhtml/dtmcnary.html McNary-Haugen Farm Legislation, November 14, 2008.

www.nationalaglawcenter.org. National Agricultural Law Center at the University of Arkansas, December 10, 2008.

Unpublished Materials and Miscellaneous

"Commentary on ROC/NPL Factions of the North Dakota Republican Party," about the 1950 contest for the two North Dakota seats in the U.S. House of Representatives and the 1952 contest for a North Dakota seat in the U.S. Senate, written by Louise Aandahl Stockman, December 14, 2009.

Race of the Century:

Guy vs. Young

1974 North Dakota U.S. Senate Election

By Allan C. Young

Allan C. Young is a Devils Lake, North Dakota, native who managed his family's business, Manns Department Store, for many years. He also was active in state politics, having served as Chairman of the North Dakota Republican Party from 1972 to 1976. In the 1980s, Young moved to Grand Forks to attend graduate school at the University of North Dakota. He wrote the following thesis, *Race of the Century: Guy vs. Young 1974 North Dakota U.S. Senate Election*, in partial fulfillment of the requirements for his master of arts degree, which he received in 1989. He then earned his doctorate degree in 1992. Young taught American history at the University of North Dakota until his retirement in 2003. He and his wife, Harleen, continue to reside in Grand Forks.

◆ 1 ◆

The Republican Camp: Milton R. Young, November 1972 - December 1973

In mid-November 1972 Senator Young denied that he would not run for reelection and promised that he would make public his decision on the matter within the next three or four months, providing a clear signal that he did intend to seek another term. He made those comments at a one-hundred-dollar-a-plate dinner to a gathering of twenty-two supporters who formed an organization to push for the Senator's reelection. At that time Milton Young, also expressing an interest in the forthcoming election, raised the issue of his age, explaining that he would repeat his twenty-year pattern of annual health checkups at the Mayo Clinic and expected the report would agree with his personal feeling that he continued to enjoy excellent health. He declared that, should he be reelected in 1974, he would pledge to North Dakota's citizens that if because of impaired health he could not carry out his senatorial duties, he would offer his resignation immediately.[1] As an issue Milton Young's age maintained center stage throughout the campaign and no one worried about it more than the Senator. Even five years earlier in his 1968 reelection campaign his age had become an issue and he instructed one of his aides to do a study on the "average age of members of the United States Senate."[2] His manner of dealing, with the age question varied, but his positive view of his U.S. Senate seniority did not.

These two items surfaced the next month in a letter to Young from Gary Hendricks, a Republican Party activist and campaign director, who

353

suggested media strategies that the Senator could employ in a campaign against William Guy. He also pointed out that the Democrats would try to turn the Senator's seniority and age into liabilities.[3] Replying to Hendricks, Young agreed that age could be a factor, noting a Farmers Union resolution that opposed the election of any major candidate over the age of sixty-five. On the issue of seniority Young held that his many accomplishments for North Dakota came about because of hard work coupled with his seniority, and if he used seniority effectively, it could be an asset rather than a liability to him.[4] But age and seniority did not crowd out other matters on Young's political agenda.

Before his formal reelection announcement, Young in January 1973 took action to protect his perceived advantages over former Governor Guy. During that year's legislative session, the North Dakota Senate considered and passed a measure that would change the state's primary election date from September to June. The bill moved on to the House where the Chairman of the Judiciary Committee, Myron Atkinson, Jr., prepared to testify in favor of the legislation. But before he made his statement, he received a message that Young did not want the primary date changed. The Senator felt that holding the primary three months earlier would offer Guy more time to oppose him as the Democratic Party's official candidate. The House voted an indefinite postponement and sent the bill back to the Senate, where it died.[5]

On February 8, 1973, four days prior to his reelection announcement, Senator Young wrote to Ray Dobson, publisher of the *Minot Daily News*, enclosing a copy of the speech that Young intended to deliver at a Lincoln Day dinner in Bismarck. In the speech, Young announced for reelection but asked Dobson not to use any part of it prior to its delivery because he might change his mind about running. Young informed the Minot publisher that only he and the editor of the *Grand Forks Herald* had received an advance copy of the speech.[6] This indicated that in all likelihood Young would announce his reelection bid; however, some of his close political friends tried to persuade him not to run. He later recalled that John Rouzie, a former state Republican Party Chairman of Bismarck; Dr. Ben Clayburgh, Republican National Committeeman from Grand Forks; and Roland Meidinger, a former State Senator from Jamestown, met with him an hour before the dinner and "begged" him not to announce his candidacy. But they did not prevail because, as Young said, "I already planned to do it though and I did."[7]

"I will be a candidate for reelection," announced the seventy-five-year-old Senator Milton Young at a Republican Party Lincoln Day dinner honoring him in Bismarck's Grand Pacific Hotel on Monday, February 12, 1973. He pledged to resign if his health prevented him from fulfilling his senatorial duties and announced that the Mayo Clinic found him to be in excellent health. He said, "I had always expected to retire by the time I reached my present age. I find that isn't so easy, especially when my health is good." As Young continued his speech, he did not mention by name former Governor William Guy, whom the Senator considered his potential opponent; yet he clearly referred to him when he stated, "We sharply disagree on the fundamental philosophy of government and on almost every major issue or policy." Turning again to Guy, Young noted that he had entered the Senate at age forty-five and "that was a little too old." Guy would be fifty-five in 1974. Thus the incumbent again acknowledged that his age might be a factor in the campaign but counted his experience and seniority an asset for North Dakota, pointing out, "Few members of Congress have ever been very effective in their first years of service.[8] In 1970, Republican West District Congressman Thomas Kleppe had delayed his entry into that year's U.S. Senate race until just a few weeks before the Republican endorsing convention, creating hard feelings among those candidates who had announced much earlier for the office. To avoid a situation such as that in 1974, Young decided to make his announcement very early.[9] The Senator also claimed his turf to keep out other Republican candidates generally and North Dakota's lone Congressman, Mark Andrews, specifically.

It is not clear just what considerations prompted Young to decide in favor of running. again. In late January a group of eleven weekly newspapers conducted a poll, commonly referred to as the North Dakota

Poll, throughout their subscription areas on a choice between Guy and Young in the Senate contest. The results of the North Dakota Poll did not appear until the week of February and showed Guy leading Young 46.4 to 44.6 percent.[10] When Young made his Lincoln Day speech, he, did not know the results of the poll, and that is significant because it meant the veteran politician did not have any hard data that he would have serious problems in retaining his Senate seat. Commenting with hindsight about his decision to run, Young said, "That was one of the most difficult decisions I ever made" and his wife ". . . pretty much left it up to me."[11] Referring to the group of three who asked him not to run, the Senator commented that ". . . they probably had good reason for it because actually I hadn't realized that I was as darn old as I was."[12] In 1980 Young recalled in a television interview that he had decided to run in 1974 because the Democrats claimed that he could not win:

> My Democratic opponents used the wrong strategy,
> though. They said that I couldn't win again. That really
> was what prompted me to run again. At least, it started
> that way . . . It was their own strategy, but it backfired.
> They made it difficult for me to quit.[13]

For whatever reasons Young entered the race, he would continue to find them over and over again as the campaign proceeded.

Fargo's *Forum* did not find Young's announcement a surprise. Its editorial reviewed the strengths and drawbacks of Guy and Young and concluded, "The price of wheat, though, could well be a determining factor."[14] Taking another tack at the end of March, the paper admitted that while it appeared that the Republican Party would back Young at its 1974 convention, someone could appear from within Republican ranks to challenge Young in the primary. According to the *Forum*, this possibility depended to a large degree on an unnamed challenger's ability to raise enough money to conduct a credible campaign. [15] The Fargo paper was most likely referring to Bismarck auto dealer Robert McCarney, who had entered Republican primaries in 1968, 1970, and 1972 to challenge endorsed candidates for Governor and U.S. Representative. According to Jack Hagerty of the *Grand Forks Herald,* McCarney did receive an April telephone call from an unidentified person in Washington, D.C., asking about his availability as a primary opponent to Young. McCarney, however, rejected the idea, declaring his firm support for Young.[16]

The state's weekly newspapers generally wrote favorably about the Senator without being negative about Guy, reflecting the esteem in which they and the public held both men.[17] At the time, Young did not sense the wide support for Guy and underestimated what lay ahead of him. The *Kulm Messenger's* editor wrote that in referring to the upcoming contest between himself and William Guy, Young had said, "No doubt this will be a tough election, but in some respects it will be easier than some of the past ones. This is because of our sharply differing views on major issues and policies."[18] Young would not hold that attitude for long and soon began to confront the age issue.

Along with a dozen other federal legislators, Senator Young practiced Tae Kwon Do, a Korean self-defense art akin to karate. Young's involvement in Tae Kwon Do began several years before it became public and of it Young said, "It's one of the best physical arts I know of. It's good for self-defense, physical fitness, and good sportsmanship." He indicated that because he played twenty-seven holes of golf on weekends, his Tae Kwon Do activity did not take a high priority.[19] The Tae Kwon Do story presented an image of Young as a man capable of activities normally associated with men much younger than seventy-five. Photographs that accompanied an article of the Senator while engaging in Tae Kwon Do appeared in newspapers across North Dakota and received coverage nationwide.[20] Young also dealt with personal matters that he saw as possible campaign problems. In his March newsletter, Young turned to the matter of how he administered his Senate office. In response to questions that he had received asking if he employed his wife Pat on the Senate payroll, Young said he did and had done so for twenty-seven years. He pointed out that after they were married, he cut her salary in half although she continued on in the position of office manager. Young maintained that he could not run an efficient office of fifteen to twenty people without her.[21] During the balance of the campaign no more was heard about this topic.

As the year progressed the political climate of the United States revolved around the Watergate scandal. By April no public official could avoid commenting on it and least of all a Republican Senator running for reelection. Young saw Watergate as a threat to his reelection and whatever he said about it reflected this view. In mid-April he observed, "The Watergate affair seems to be one of the worst cases of political skulduggery in history."[22] At the end of the month, just minutes before news of the resignation of Presidential aides H. R. Haldeman and John Ehrlichman, White House counsel John Dean, and Attorney General Richard Kleindienst became public, Senator Young from his Capitol Hill office called for that same action in a telephone interview with the *Grand Forks Herald*. Sensing there would be decisive Presidential action in the Watergate affair, Young declared, "I've never known the President to wait so long to act on any major political problem." He also recognized that Watergate would affect his 1974 reelection bid but felt that it was much too early to ascertain in what way and to what degree.[23]

On April 21 a group of Republican state legislators met with Senator Young to discuss preliminary plans for Young's campaign. Discussing tactics, they mentioned his liabilities, including Watergate and age; however, they believed that these did not outweigh his record of attracting new industry into North Dakota, his seniority, and his appeal to farmers, which together would assure his reelection.[24] The group, meeting privately, consisted primarily of Republican state legislators. Others present included John Hjelle, editor of the *Bismarck Tribune*, who made an assessment of the Guy-Young contest. Hjelle indicated that the Senator's age would be both an advantage and disadvantage, that emphasis should be put on what Young could do for people "today, tomorrow, and next year," that a campaign plan should be prepared, and within six months a campaign chairman named.[25] No doubt Young took comfort from the advice and support of his one-time administrative assistant and editor of North Dakota's fourth largest daily newspaper. In the second week of May, temporary chairman Republican State Senator C. Warner Litten of Fargo announced the formation of a committee comprised of GOP legislators to assist Young's reelection effort. Litten looked forward to a close contest but stated, "We anticipate a victory for Senator Young."[26] After this announcement nothing more was heard from or about the committee. Young entered 1973 expecting few major problems, and his seniority enabled "him to use political pressure to obtain a tremendous amount of federal assistance for North Dakota. Holding elective office since 1924, never losing a reelection bid, known as Mr. Wheat, and carrying every county in North Dakota in several elections indicated to Young that in 1974 he would be reelected. However, the continuing Watergate revelations forced an adjustment in his campaign calculations. Returning to North Dakota over the Memorial Day recess, Young had anticipated that frequent questions concerning Watergate would greet him, but he was not prepared for what happened. "Everybody was talking about it. Everybody." His plan to spend in the $50,000 range during the campaign toppled under the Watergate problem and he believed that he would need to spend at least three times that amount. About the scandal he commented, "It'll hurt. It'll hurt the Republican Party and to some extent all its candidates and all incumbents, whatever their Party."[27] At the end of June, Young again repeated his view about Watergate: "There have been many messy cases of political skulduggery over the years, both alleged and proven, but this seems to be one of the worst. The public is entitled to a better answer than they have been given so far."[28] Indeed, political danger did exist as evidenced in a poll taken by Mark Andrews in the summer of 1973 which revealed the results of thirty-five thousand North Dakotan replies to the question, "What effect will Watergate have on 1974 N.D. elections?: 16.9 a great deal; 26.7 some; 19.8 none; 36.6 too early to tell." [29] Nearly 44 percent, seventeen months prior to the election, stated that Watergate would have an effect on their vote.

With experience and insight the *Minot Daily News*' political editor, columnist, and reporter Dick Dobson wrote consistently penetrating analyses concerning the Guy-Young race. As June came to an end, Dobson wrote that Young's age made him vulnerable because only three other members of the Senate were older than the North Dakota Republican. His article briefly covered Young's seniority but concentrated on statistically proving that at fifty-five Guy would be a bit younger than the average Senator. Dobson concluded, "It appears, therefore, that the age issue will help Guy and seniority will benefit Young in next year's election."[30] Young claimed that Guy, in his mid-fifties, was too old to begin a U.S. Senate career, but North Dakotans thought in terms of Guy as a young man, just forty-one when he was elected governor, and people continued to think of him as "young William Guy." He did not look fifty-fifty years old. The age issue just would not go away and neither would Senator Young stop providing reasons why he decided to seek another term.

Speaking to Republicans at their Summer Roundup in Medora and recognizing criticism that implied that at seventy-five he should not be running for reelection, he explained, "I have found that it isn't so easy to quit as to run again." He pointed out that if he were to leave the Senate, his power as the ranking member on the Appropriations Committee would be lost for North Dakota. Turning to personalities, Young speculated, "But, if I didn't run, it is almost certain that former Governor William Guy would be elected to the Senate, because Mark Andrews has always said he is not interested in running for the Senate. If Mark draws a tough opponent, Bill Guy, then you will want to devote more money to Congressman Andrews. If I draw the tough candidate, then I think you should give the bulk of your financial support to me."[31] In so saying, Young warned Andrews not to put designs on his Senate seat and made it clear that an important element in Guy's defeat depended on Republican faithfuls giving him the bulk of their campaign contributions. Over five months after his candidacy announcement, the incumbent still spoke as if a Republican challenger would appear.

During the summer the Young campaign canvassed fifty-seven hundred voters in every county, requesting that a stamped postcard be returned indicating preference between Guy and Young for the U.S. Senate. Senator Young believed that the 30 percent reply factor was unusually high for that type of survey and delighted in the results that put him ahead of Guy 53.5 to 46.5 percent – particularly because the Senate Watergate hearings paralleled the time span of the taking of the poll.[32] This piece of good news did not substantially raise Republican confidence nor their understanding of what Watergate meant to them on a statewide basis. Sixteen months before the next general election North Dakota Republicans expressed more concern about the outcome of the 1974 elections and continued success in fundraising than about the effect Watergate might play in determining these two activities. Acknowledging finances as a key ingredient in a winning campaign, Young observed that he never raised appreciable amounts of money in prior campaigns because he had no reason for such activity. But he said that anticipation of facing Guy caused many more offers of assistance to him than at any time in the past. As to the effect of Watergate, Young predicted, "I think it will hurt both Democrats and the Republicans in the election."[33] How or in what way Watergate could damage Democratic electoral prospects he did not explain.

During the final days of August, Young took yet another opportunity to expand on the reasons he rejected retiring from the Senate. Being the only Republican Senator from the six-state area of Iowa, Wisconsin, Minnesota, South Dakota, North Dakota, and Montana gave added importance to his reelection because ". . . it would be nice to have someone who can go in and talk to the President." Discussing the President's conduct of his office and not approving of Nixon's handling of Watergate during the first few months of the affair, he commented, "He is doing better now, but he should have spoken up before and told more about the operation of the White House. He delegated too much authority and trusted people too much."[34]

While Young put forth these views from his office in LaMoure, events taking place in his D.C. office would have long-range effects on the 1974 U.S. Senate election. On August 24 Bill Wright, Young's public relations assistant, wrote a thank-you letter to James (Jim) Jungroth for having sent him a *Jamestown Sun* column written by the paper's editor, Jack Evans, and a note from Jungroth himself. A Jamestown attorney, former chairman of the North Dakota Democratic-NPL Party, a Guy appointee to North Dakota's Water Commission, and yet an anti-Guy Democrat, Jungroth would enter the U.S. Senate contest in the 1974 general election as an Independent. Wright concluded the letter, "Jim, I discussed this with the Senator briefly on the telephone. He was real pleased at your thoughtfulness in providing us with the column, as well as your analysis. I will be leaving for Jamestown Saturday morning and hope we can discuss this further on the weekend." Evan's column quoted at length a speech that Guy had delivered at the grand opening of Summers Manufacturing in Maddock. Jungroth noted to Wright, "It is not the story itself but the fact that it was run. This is out of the circulation area. You will recognize this fellow is clever when he got this run in the *Sun*." Neither Jungroth nor Wright mentioned Guy by name in their correspondence.[35] Evans often used material of prominent people to fill his weekly "Buffalo Territory" column and because during 1973 Guy maintained a very low news profile Evans' use of his Maddock speech simply followed Guy's own format.

That Jungroth believed Guy somehow cleverly arranged to get Evans to print the speech represented his personal feelings about the former Governor rather than what actually occurred. But of more interest, Wright said he had told Senator Young about Jungroth's communication, confirming contact between the two (albeit through Wright) nearly a year before Jungroth's Senate candidacy; and Wright's intention to travel to Jamestown to discuss further matters pertaining to Guy indicated a close working relationship. Senator Young maintained throughout the campaign and after that he had nothing to do with Jungroth or Jungroth's campaign. But this Summer 1973 exchange puts that denial in question.

Just before Labor Day the *Washington Post* took a look at what the make-up of the U.S. Senate might be after the 1974 elections. The paper predicted that if former Governor Guy challenged Senator Young, the incumbent would have a tough race and could be beaten, but the paper rated the Republican a slight favorite.[36] In North Dakota, the first editorial endorsement in the 1974 U.S. Senate race appeared in the *Divide County Journal*, which aroused comment because the paper traditionally supported Democrats, but in the Guy-Young contest it backed Young.[37] Young used the August Congressional recess to make North Dakota appearances and dealt decisively with two political problems. His wife, Pat, canceled her appearances at the Republican Party's First Ladies Club events scheduled for September after the Senator learned the "Chat with Pat" social events actually would be fundraising affairs. He did not want to be associated with invitation-only meetings. The second item involved Senator Evan Lips and Robert McCarney, both of whom were from Bismarck and personally detested each other but shared a strong commitment to Young's reelection. In order to channel their talents and energies productively into his campaign, Young asked McCarney to form a committee of "Democrats, Independents, Nonpartisan Leaguers and miscellaneous renegades," while Lips took chairmanship of a Republican legislators' committee to promote Young.[38]

Seasoned political observer Dobson wrote in early October "that several former high-ranking officials in the state Democratic Nonpartisan League Party are going to support Senator Milton R. Young, R-N.D., for reelection next year." The reason for these defections stemmed, according to Dobson, from past fights between Guy and some members of his party and others who believed Young's seniority and record should be continued. Former state Democratic-NPL Party Chairman James Jungroth headed the list and could use both reasons to oppose Guy. Jungroth's intentions became clearer when he suggested he would even run as an Independent for U.S. Senator if that would cost Guy votes. Another unanswered question of who would support whom dealt with what Democratic Senator Quentin Burdick planned for the campaign in light of the uneasy relationship between Guy and Burdick through their years of public life. In fact, they did not have a close relationship, and

Burdick worried that if Guy won in 1974 his own chances of reelection in 1976 would be diminished because "North Dakota voters could decide then that two Democratic Senators is one too many." One option that some observers believed he would take would be for him to simply not become involved in 1974's campaign.[39] Young found more good news in a column written by nationally syndicated Jack Anderson, who praised the Senator as a bonus for North Dakota and told readers that if he lived in North Dakota, he would cast his vote for Young.[40]

Optimism (if not realism) infected the long-time incumbent Senator in late October. At a Fargo press conference Young discussed politics, saying he wanted former Governor William Guy as an opponent because "I think I know how to beat Bill Guy. A young man might be harder to beat. I'm sure they (Democrats) will make quite a campaign issue out of my age but I've had a physical recently and they could not find anything wrong with me." In the same tenor he assessed events on the national level, stating, "Apparently Watergate and Agnew hasn't hurt as much as I thought it would. It all looks very encouraging. I feel I have a better chance now than ever before to be elected. I don't think there's any possibility at all the House will start impeachment proceedings."[41] In press releases, speeches, and general correspondence Young gave the benefit of the doubt to President Nixon regarding the Watergate affair. What the Senator felt personally he expressed in a letter to former Republican Senator Frank Carlson and his wife of Kansas: "I am sure you have been following the Watergate mess and are concerned as we are. It is too bad that President Nixon can do so many things exceptionally well, especially foreign affairs, and mess up this whole Watergate affair. I think you would agree with many that he has handled that very badly."[42]

In November Kevin P. Phillips, the author of *The Emerging Republican Majority* (1969), in which he predicted long-term Republican control of the White House, reported in his periodic newsletter, *American Political Report*, that a public opinion poll conducted by Central Surveys (an Iowa-based firm) for Senator Young indicated Guy a victor over Young. This, according to Phillips, created concern among GOP planners who believed that Young did not understand his vulnerable position as he continued his candidacy. The newsletter implied that Young's wife kept him in the race because of her attachment to Washington, D.C. Phillips then pointed out that if Young quit the race, Congressman Mark Andrews, who had expressed an interest in the Senate seat if Young decided not to run, would enter the contest.[43]

According to the *Minot Daily News'* Dobson, "Young's response to Phillips was volcanic." The Senator sent a letter to his party's top officers, several Republican legislative leaders, two past state chairmen, and John Hjelle (but not Mark Andrews) expressing surprise at Phillips' newsletter and questioning the source of Phillips' information. Young dismissed the poll as non-representative and doubted its accuracy. Having brushed aside the poll, he strongly objected to Phillips' allegation that Pat Young was keeping the Senator in the race. Young was certain that Andrews "wanted to remain in the U. S. House of Representatives because of his ten years seniority and his seat on the House Appropriations Committee." Young concluded, "He didn't care what political strategists in Washington, D.C., thought but that he would step down if Republican Party leaders in North Dakota felt he should do so."[44]

More broadsides from the Eastern press hit the Young campaign during December. In an article that reported a meeting that President Nixon held with Republican campaign officials, the *New York Times* observed in mid-December "that the seat of Senator Milton R. Young, who is retiring, was in grave jeopardy."[45] Three days later the paper printed a correction stating, "Senator Young said yesterday that, contrary to earlier reports, he had decided to seek reelection."[46] He seemed unable to persuade national GOP leaders of the validity of his candidacy, and Washington reports reflected this. On the day after Christmas an article by Lee Egerstrom, the *Grand Forks Herald's* Washington correspondent, compared the style of seventy-seven-year-old North Carolina Democrat Senator Sam Erwin with that of Senator Young. Noting that their colleagues respected both, Egerstrom said Erwin's chairmanship of the Senate Watergate Committee created for him a large following nationally while Young's style kept him almost completely out of the national scene. But in their home states a different situation surrounded the two lawmakers. Erwin declined to run for reelection because, he said another six-year term for a man of his age would be too much to expect; this pleased North Carolina Democrats. In North Dakota Young announced early in the year that he would seek another term, and Republican rank and file solidly supported his decision. National Democratic leaders wanted Erwin to run but, when he decided not to, the support evaporated. Republicans on the national scene, however, were concerned that Young's age and a tough opponent could combine to lose a GOP Senate seat.[47]

Young's campaign people thought that the *New York Times* article originated from plants "by staffers for Senator William (Bill) Brock, R-Tenn., who heads the Senate Republican Campaign Committee, if not by Brock himself." Young's associates believed that Brock's motives for leaking negative information were Brock's desire for a younger Mark Andrews to be the Republican Senatorial candidate and his desire to establish a national power base for himself. Andrews, however, wanted to remain in the House and increase his seniority in that body. A close friend of Andrews said candidly:

> Young is the surest candidate against a tough opponent we have. All these national stories are doing, because the people of North Dakota do not read the *New York Times* daily, is drying up the national money. And that can hurt if this does become a nationally-watched fight. If everybody thinks we are in trouble, then we may be in trouble, because we won't be able to match the opponent's money. That's what the *New York Times* means to every state.[48]

Brock could very well have been influenced by news of the results of the North Dakota Poll in which Guy received 44.6 percent to Young's 47.6 percent. But in a trial heat plotting Andrews against Guy, the Congressman showed up as a strong Republican candidate with 55 percent to Guy's 35.8 percent and 9.2 percent undecided. [49] No comment on this poll came from Young, who concentrated on matters within his own party at the national level. By the end of the month, however, he learned that the national opposition party did not intend to ignore his race. National Democratic strategists listed Senator Milton Young of North Dakota as one of their prime targets, noting that he faced the "most vigorous challenge of his career from former Democratic Governor William Guy."[50]

Editorial comment on Egerstrom's article appeared in the *Bismarck Tribune* the day after it ran. Ripping into the chairman of the Republican Senatorial Campaign Committee, Hjelle opined, "William Emerson Brock the Third is an obscure United States Senator from Tennessee. The diminutive but handsome and nattily-dressed Brock is obscure because most freshman Senators are obscure and also because in the less than four years he has served in the Senate nothing of significance bears the Brock imprint." Accusing Brock of interfering in North Dakota internal politics, Hjelle condemned him for it. The editorial did include Brock's denial of mixing in North Dakota politics but dismissed Brock's position. The blistering column pointed out that Brock did not realize Mark Andrews did not intend to enter the Senate contest, and that by endangering Young's out-of-state financial support, Brock was playing into the hands of the Democrats. Hjelle ended the *Tribune's* editorial as he opened: "Thus, however, does a man whose name is not even known to most North Dakotans, a little known Senator from Tennessee, play a role in North Dakota politics."[51] Hjelle's opinion of Senator Brock had changed dramatically from the one he had formed earlier in the year when, at the request of Senator Young, he had met privately with Brock in Brock's office to seek funds for Young's campaign. Senator Young's response to the Egerstrom article changed Hjelle's attitude because Young became ". . . hopping mad at the GOP Senatorial Campaign Committee and its chairman Senator William E. Brock III, R-Tenn., who is suspected of being the chief promoter of the retire Young and run Andrews strategy."[52]

Notes

[1] Roan Conrad, "Young Hints at New Term, Promises Decision Shortly," *Mandan (N.D.) Morning Pioneer*, 12 November 1972, p. 1.

[2] Neal Bjornson, Memo to Senator Young, 27 June 1968, Folder 18, Box 600, MYP.

[3] Gary Hendricks to Milton R. Young, 5 December 1972, Folder 21, Box 615, MYP.

[4] Milton R. Young to Gary Hendricks, 5 January 1973, Folder 21, Box 615, MYP.

[5] Allan C. Young, "Changing North Dakota's Primary Election Date 1960-1984: A Partisan Struggle, Special Report #78", (University of North Dakota, Grand Forks, N.D.: Bureau of Governmental Affairs, March, 1987), 18.

[6] Milton R. Young to Ray Dobson, 8 February 1973, Unfiled, Box 61

[7] U.S. Senator Milton R. Young, interviewed by Dr. D. Jerome Tweton, 8 August 1979, transcribed tape recording, Folder 26, Box 794, MYP, p. 4.

[8] Gary Wolberg, "It's Official: Young Asks Re-Election," *Bismarck Tribune*, 13 February 1973, p. 1.

[9] Jack Hagerty, "Political Pulse: State Senate Race Discussed," *Grand Forks Herald*, 6 May 1973, p. 32.

[10] Phil Matthews, "Young-Guy Strength Assessed," *Fargo (N D.) Forum*, 19 February 1973, p. 9.

[11] U.S. Senator Young interviewed, p. 5.

[12] Ibid., p. 15.

[13] Boyd Christensen, *Boyd Christensen Interviews* (Bismarck, N.D.: Prairie House, Inc., 1983), 48, 49.

[14] "Forum's Editorial: No One Greatly Surprised At Sen. Young's Decision To Seek Re-election in '74," *Fargo (N.D.) Forum*, 15 February 1973, p. 4.

[15] "Forum's Editorial: There's Possibility Young May Be Challenged in 1974 Republican Primary Race," *Fargo (N.D.) Forum*, 26 March 1973, p. 4.

[16] Jack Hagerty, "Political Pulse: Teachers are Excited," *Grand Forks Herald*, 13 May 1973, p. 32.

[17] *Garrison (N.D.) McLean County Independent*, 15 February 1973, Clipping, Folder 2, Box 334, MYP; *Larimore Chronicle*, 15 February 1973, Folder 2, Box 334, MYP; *Langdon Republican*, 15 February 1973, Folder 2, Box 334, MYP.

[18] *Kulm Messenger*, 15 March 1973, Clipping, Folder 3, Box 334, MYP.

[19] "Muggers Better Steer Clear of These Congressmen," *Oakland Press*, 22 March 1973, p. B-13.

[20] *Bismarck Tribune*, 25 March 1973, p. 15; *Fargo (N.D.) Forum*, 22 March 1973, p. 1; *Minot Daily News*, March 23, 1973, p. 1; *Christian Science Monitor*, 27 March 1973, p. 10; Ibid.

[21] "Young Says He Cut His Wife's Pay," *Minot Daily News*, 26 March 1973, p. 2.

[22] "Young Sees Skulduggery in Bugging," *Fargo (N.D.) Forum*, 17 April 1973, p. 1.

[23] Jack Hagerty, "Election Effect Eyed: Young Called for House Cleaning," *Grand*

Forks Herald, 30 April 1973, p. 1, 2.

24 Jack Hagerty, "Political Pulse: Campaign Launched," *Grand Forks Herald*, 29 April 1973, p. 44.

25 James Backlin, to C. Warner Litten, 24 April 1973, Unfiled between Folders 24, 25, Box 615, MYP.

26 "N.D. Legislators For Re-Election Panel for Young," *Bismarck Tribune*, 10 May 1973, p. 7.

27 "GOP Plans for '74 Adjusted in Scandal's Wake," *Twin Falls (Idaho) Times-News*, 5 June 1973, p. 5.

28 *Garrison (N.D.) McLean County Independent*, 28 June 1973, Clipping, Folder 6, Box 334, MYP.

29 Jack Evans, "Buffalo Territory, Andrews Gets 35,000 Answers," *Jamestown Sun*, 17 July 1973, Clipping, Folder 7, Box 334, MYP.

30 Dick Dobson, "Inside North Dakota: Age, Seniority Factors," *Minot Daily News*, 23 June 1973, p. 7.

31 Phil Matthews, "Young Says It's Harder to Quit Than Run Again," *Fargo (N.D.) Forum*, 22 July 1973, p. 1.

32 "Senator Reveals Own Survey: Young Leads Guy By 53 to 46 Percent," *Bismarck Tribune*, 24 July 1973, p. 2.

33 Gary Clark, "Democrats Concern N.D. GOP More Than Watergate in 1974 Election," *Fargo (N.D.) Forum*, 5 August 1973, p. 1.

34 Gary Clark, "Young Considered Quitting the Senate," *Bismarck Tribune*, 27 August 1973, p. 3.

35 William I. Wright to James Jungroth, 24 August 1973, Folder 20, Box 411, MYP; James Jungroth, non-addressed memo, non-dated, Folder 20, Box 511, MYP.

36 Spencer Rich, "'74 Democratic Gains Seen," *Washington Post*, 27 August 1973, p. A2.

37 J .M.A., "John A. Dreams," *Crosby (N.D.) Divide County Journal*, 29 August 1973, Clipping, Folder 8, Box 334, MYP.

38 Dick Dobson, "Inside North Dakota Some Democrats May Back Young," *Minot Daily News*, 6 October 1973, p. 3.

40 Jack Hagerty, "Observations," *Grand Forks Herald*, 28 October 1973, p. 4.

41 "Bill Guy Beatable, Says Sen. Young," *Bismarck Tribune*, 20 October 1973, p. 7.

42 Milton R. Young, to Senator Frank and Mrs. Carlson, 7 November 1973, Folder 26, Box 528, MYP.

43 Dick Dobson, "Inside North Dakota: Young Would Retire If GOP Leaders Recommended It," *Minot Daily News*, 17 November 1973, p. 3.

44 Ibid.

45 R. W. Apple, Jr., "G.O.P. Aides Discuss '74 Outlook With Nixon; Watergate 'Never Mentioned'," *New York Times*, 12 December 1973, p. 27.

[46] *New York Times*, 15 December 1973, p. 33.

[47] Lee Egerstrom, "Young, Erwin Powerful Duo," *Grand Forks Herald*, 26 December 1973, pp. 1, 2.

[48] Ibid.

[49] "N. Dak. Poll Shows Andrews Favorite and Young Topping Guy," *Harvey Herald*, 6 December 1973, Clipping, Folder 39, Box 336, MYP.

[50] Carl P. Leubsdorf, "1974 Election Strategy 'Act Fast, GOP Chiefs Say'," *Washington Star-News*, 27 December 1973, p. 2.

[51] "Tennessee in North Dakota," *Bismarck Tribune*, 28 December 1973, p. 4.

[52] Dick Dobson, "Inside North Dakota: Erwin's Decision Affects Young," *Minot Daily News*, 29 December 1973, p. 9.

◆ 2 ◆

Towards a Long Sought Goal:
William L. Guy, 1962-1974

The possibility of William L. Guy running against Senator Young circulated across North Dakota long before any official announcements, and Young had seen Guy as a possible adversary quite early in Guy's political career.[1] As early as 1962, serious speculation had arisen over whether or not Governor Guy would challenge Senator Young instead of seeking reelection.[2] However, with only a little more than one year in the Governor's office, Guy chose to seek a second term (four-year terms did not go into effect in North Dakota until 1969). Still, even the remotest hint that Guy might have an interest in the Senate stirred political chords, as reflected in a March 1962 *Grand Forks Herald* editorial commenting on Guy's announcement for a second term. The paper was not surprised by the Governor's statement that he would run for reelection, but it praised him for displaying the political wisdom of not deciding to confront North Dakota's senior Senator because "there he would have finished an 'also-ran.' "[3] Senator Young also took more than casual notice of what might become a threat to retention of his Senate seat early in 1962 when the Senator challenged Governor Guy to debate him on the issue of how the mechanics of legislation which enabled farmers to hay soil bank land operated. Young did not deal gently with the young Governor: "If you persist in your continued partisan political approach and untruthful charges, you are not only confusing the issue but making it more difficult to work with you on all other important legislation affecting North Dakota."[4] These harsh words

371

came to characterize the Senator's attitude toward Guy.

Young handily won reelection in 1962, and as that term approached its end, rumors again tied Guy to a U.S. Senate contest. In early 1967 a report from North Dakota's political grapevine indicated Governor Guy might not run for a fourth term, and if that happened, he would run for Milton Young's Senate seat.[5] In February the *Dickinson Press* pointed out steps Governor Guy was taking to soften his liberal image in preparation for his race against incumbent Senator Milton Young.[6] These types of stories gained validity when in April of that year, Washington columnist Carl Rowan visited Guy in Bismarck, where he found the Governor "agonizing over whether to seek a new term as governor (he will have served eight years), whether to oppose Milton Young for the U.S. Senate, or to try to become one of the state's two Congressmen."[7] Reports circulated among the state's press during early 1967 that CBS newsman Eric Sevareid should return to his native North Dakota to seek a seat in the U.S. Senate. At a William Guy Day dinner attended by fourteen-hundred people in Fargo, Guy read a telegram addressed to the chairman of the event from Sevareid, who said he firmly and finally declined the suggestions that he consider a Senate race in North Dakota.[8] With speculation about Sevareid laid to rest, Senator Young predicted that Guy would be his opponent in the next year's Senate contest. Guy declined, however, to announce his plans for 1968.[9] Early in July Dobson forecast that Guy would not challenge Young, but Guy remained silent.[10]

The *Williston Herald* reported in mid-January that "a source close to the Governor commented . . . , 'I think Governor Guy has made up his mind. I believe the Governor will make a bid for Senator Milton Young's Senatorial seat rather than seek reelection to his present post.'"[11] Governor Guy himself contemplated the principal issue in a contest with Young when he noted the Senator's career in the U.S. Senate stretched back twenty-three years and predicted that if Young sought reelection, "I doubt if that would be held against him."[12] Whatever his personal preference might have been, it made no difference because in effect Governor William Guy found himself by May 11 being drafted by his own Democratic-Nonpartisan League. Of the twenty districts which held conventions, eighteen passed resolutions urging Guy to run for reelection. Not one party leader or officer made a public statement advocating that Guy run for any office but governor.[13] Guy eventually ran for governor, yet just days before he announced for reelection, a report by *Mandan (N.D.) Morning Pioneer* staff writer Joyce Conrad made it clear that Guy had told many of his party supporters that what he wanted to do in 1968 was to run against Senator Young.[14] At the press conference in which Guy announced his intention to seek another term for governor, he began by declaring, "Chances are much better than previously realized that North Dakota will send a new senator to Washington next year." He mentioned that while the current average age of a U.S. Senator was sixty-seven North Dakota would select a younger man to be its next U.S. Senator.[15] That did not happen and Young retained his Senate seat, but the stage had been set for Guy to seek the office which he so very much desired.

Governor William L. Guy dramatically changed North Dakota's political landscape on January 5, 1972, at a Bismarck news conference with his announcement that he would not be a candidate for reelection as governor and ruled out a Congressional candidacy. Citing family considerations as one reason for deciding not to seek a fifth term, Guy admitted his interest in a U.S. Senate contest, declaring, "I do not believe it would be proper to seek reelection as governor for another four-year term knowing that I might run for the United States Senate in 1974." However, the Governor explained, that statement should not be considered an announcement for the Senate contest.[16] Democratic State Chairman Richard Ista of Fargo expressed disappointment that Governor Guy would not seek reelection, but he also said, "We are extremely happy that he is planning to run for the Senate . . . At the age of 52, he is still a young man."[17] The North Dakota Poll taken prior to his announcement showed that after serving as the state's chief executive for eleven years, he remained very popular. In response to a question concerning Guy's job performance, 48.5 percent thought "he had done a good job and should be reelected"; 36 percent said "he has done a good job but should step down"; and 15.5 percent replied "he has done a poor job." To the question of whether or not the respondents would again support him, 49.6 percent said yes, 31.1 percent answered no, and 19.3 percent expressed no opinion.[18] North Dakota political writers recognized that Guy would be a "formidable candidate for U.S. Senate in 1974."[19] *Mandan's Pioneer*, North Dakota's only Democratic daily newspaper, thought that not being on the 1972 ballot would not harm him politically because "as a campaigner for his party's candidates and as Governor, he will command as much attention as if he were running himself.[20] Dobson commented, "Guy's chances against Young probably would be pretty good. A poll taken in 1968 for the state Republican Party showed the veteran senator leading Guy by only a 46-42 percent margin.[21]

Speculating on what direction Guy's career would take after he stepped down as Governor in January 1973, most observers believed he would not leave elective politics and would run for the U.S. Senate. The Governor himself commented, "I might do that, but I reserve the right to change my mind. Lately I've looked at Congress as a body trying to show the world that democracy does not work."[22] Interviewed in December, Guy said his plans for the future included going into business, accepting an invitation from a college to teach, and building a house in Casselton. On the political front, he indicated that even without an official position in his party he intended to stay in touch with people he had come to know during his twenty years in politics.[23] On the Republican side, no doubt existed as to what Guy intended; as 1972 came to a close, the first partisan attack on Guy appeared.

During 1973 Guy kept a very low news profile, yet his future remained part of North Dakota's political dialogue. Believing Guy's next political move would be as a candidate for the U.S. Senate, M. W. Thatcher, retired general manager of the Farmers Union Grain Terminal Association, sent a telegram to the soon-to-be ex-Governor enthusiastically endorsing such a development.[24] Just two weeks later, Dobson speculated on what Guy's defeating Senator Young would mean to North Dakota's Congressional delegation, especially Quentin Burdick, and reported that Young might possibly announce his reelection bid at a Republican Lincoln Day dinner on February 12.[25] Early in the 1973 legislative session, House Democratic Minority Leader Richard Backes spoke of building a positive record to assist electing Democrats in 1974 and predicted that William Guy running against Young in 1974 would be a bonus for his party.[26] At midpoint 1973, during their state convention, North Dakota's Democratic-NPL women dedicated the convention to Jean Guy and passed a resolution strongly urging former Governor William Guy to seek the party nomination for the U.S. Senate.[27]

Towards the end of the summer, Guy began to sound like a candidate. "As a livestock, grain and sugar beet farmer, I've never before sold hogs, wheat and soybeans at the exorbitantly high prices of today. I should be dancing in the streets, but I am not," declared former Governor Guy at the opening of Summers Manufacturing of Maddock. Speaking out for a more balanced, constant marketing and consumption system, he cautioned farmers to be wary because the economy showed signs of developing high interest rates.[28] During the week before Labor Day the state GOP Chairman stated that former Governor Guy would be Young's 1974 opponent and "Bill Guy will use the age issue against Senator Young because it's the only issue Guy has." The Republican spokesman went on to conjecture that Tax Commissioner Byron Dorgan would oppose Congressman Mark Andrews.[29] During this same period, in private conversations, Guy left almost no doubt that he would run against Senator Young. Democratic Party leaders in Bismarck made frequent calls to Casselton and stopovers at Guy's new home. Jean Guy observed she looked forward to the U.S. Senate campaign. Guy did not confirm rumors that he wanted Dorgan to challenge Andrews but did describe the state's Tax Commissioner as ". . . one of the brightest young lights on the horizon in either party."[30] Pinpointing the condition of the nation's economy as the major issue for 1974 campaign, Guy admitted that he did have an interest in Young's Senate seat but again did not make a formal announcement. Commenting on Young's statement that Guy's age made him too old to run for the Senate because he would not be able to attain meaningful seniority, the former Governor replied, "If I were to run for the Senate and if I were to win, I would be 55. If Senator Young were to run and win, he would be 78, so I don't quite understand the Senator's meaning." As to the matter of seniority, Guy asserted that he considered "the Congressional seniority system one of the gravest weaknesses in the federal government."[31]

Not yet an official candidate, Guy traveled the state during the fall of 1973, attending Democratic-NPL functions and explaining that he would focus on "visiting with old friends." As he made his appearances, national-level assessments gave encouragement to Guy's prospects. The *Washington Post* placed Young on its list of Republican incumbent Senators who faced strong Democratic challengers and possible defeat, and a liberal Republican publication, "The Ripon Forum," reported that a Republican-sponsored Spring 1973 poll "indicated an edge for Guy."[32] Throughout October Guy received strong encouragement from his party to enter the U.S. Senate contest. Early in the month Minot's Fifth District Democratic-NPL organization presented him with petitions signed by two-hundred and twenty-five people who urged him to take on Young.[33] At mid-month, the Twelfth District Democratic-NPL (Benson and Eddy counties) asked Guy to challenge Young,[34] and late in the month Lisbon Democratic-NPL party workers called for Guy to run for the Senate.[35] Also in October, a nationwide public opinion poll (Harris Survey) pointed to a Democratic landslide in the 1974 Congressional elections: 53 percent for the Democrats to 31 percent for the Republicans.[36] Guy's position seemed strong as he headed toward the election year.

Expressing a feeling held by quite a number of North Dakotans during late 1973, a weekly editor wrote, ". . . what the dickens are we going to do if Senator Young and former Governor Guy tangle for the Senate seat now held by Young? It's going to be a bad deal. I don't want to vote against either one of them. Wish I could vote for both."[37] Yet the approaching contest provided a choice of only one of the candidates, and Guy was gearing up for his efforts to achieve victory. Bob Valeu of Bismarck, former successful campaign manager for both Guy and Arthur Link, began making contacts in Washington on behalf of William Guy, arranging preliminary organizational campaign material for a Senatorial campaign, reciting that "if he (Guy) is a candidate, I look forward to being involved in his campaign." Valeu strongly hinted that Guy's formal announcement would take place in early 1974.[38] As 1973 came to a close, Guy's fortunes looked excellent with his campaign organization taking shape. In Wahpeton's paper, a columnist wrote that Senator Young received far more credit than he deserved in farm bill involvement and federal spending in North Dakota because both represented simple pork barrel legislation. The piece suggested the incumbent senior Senator "should gracefully withdraw and retire."[39] Guy hoped that this would become a widespread sentiment.

Notes

[1] Press Clippings, Folder 19, Box 287, MYP.

[2] *Grand Forks Herald*, 7 January 1962, p. 36; *Fargo (N.D.) Forum*, 19 January 1962, p. 14.

[3] "Editorial," *Grand Forks Herald*, 6 March 1974, p. 4.

[4] *Grand Forks Herald*, 6 March 1974, p. 3.

[5] *Mandan (N.D.) Morning Pioneer*, 14 January 1967, Clipping, Folder 3, Box 307, MYP.

[6] *Dickinson Press*, 8 February 1967, Clipping, Folder 3, Box 307, MYP.

[7] Carl Rowan, "Dakota Democrat Weighs Chances,11 *Washington (D.C.) Evening Star*, 26 April 1967, Clipping, Folder 5, Box 307, MYP.

[8] Memo Called to Young's Washington Office from his Fargo Office, 15 May 1967, Folder 6, Box 307, MYP.

[9] *Minot Daily News*, 27 June 1967, p. 1.

[10] Dick Dobson, "Inside North Dakota: Senate Bid By Guy Unlikely," *Minot Daily News*, 8 July 1967, p. 19.

[11] Jackie Anderson, *Williston Herald*, 11 January 1968, Folder 20, Box 314, MYP.

[12] "Guy Plans to Remain In Politics," *Minot Daily News*, 10 February 1968, p. 15.

[13] Dick Dobson, "Inside North Dakota: Demos Draft Guy For Fourth Term," *Minot Daily News*, 11 May 1974, p. 13.

[14] *Mandan (N.D.) Morning Pioneer*, 23 June 1968, Folder 24, Box 314, MYP.

[15] *Bismarck Tribune*, 25 June 1968, p. 1.

[16] "Guy Will Not Seek Fifth Term - Won't Run in 1972 But Eyeing 1974 Senate Race," *Minot Daily News*, 5 January 1972, p. 1.

[17] "Ista Has Mixed Emotions," *Fargo (N.D.) Forum*, 6 January 1972, pp. 1-2.

[18] "North Dakota Poll-Even After 11 Years Guy is Still Popular," *Harvey Herald*, 13 January 1972, Folder 25, Box 331, MYP.

[19] "Guy's Blockbuster," *Grand Forks Herald*, 6 January 1972, p.

[20] "Spinning Wheels," *Mandan (N.D.) Morning Pioneer*, 7 January 1972, Folder 13, Box 331, MYP.

[21] Dick Dobson, "Inside North Dakota: Big Year In State Politics," *Minot Daily News*, 10 January 1972, p. 7.

[22] Gen Joseph, "What Next for North Dakota's Guy?," *Minneapolis Tribune*, 12 November 1972, p. 14A.

[23] Frances Carrick and Milt Vedvick, "An Interview with Governor Guy," *North Dakota REC Magazine*, January 1973, pp. 10-13, 38-39.

[24] "Thatcher Sees Guy Capturing Seat In Senate," *Minot Daily News*, 2 January 1973, p. 11.

[25] Dick Dobson, "Inside North Dakota: Guy Topic of Speculation," *Minot Daily News*, 13 January 1973, p. 13.

[26] *Fargo (N.D.) Forum*, 22 January 1973, p. 9.

[27] "Guy Urged To Run By Democratic-NPL Women In Convention Here," *Carrington (N.D.) Foster County Independent*, 27 June 1973, Folder 6, Box 335, MYP.

[28] Jack Evans, "Buffalo Territory: Guy Comments on Agriculture, *Jamestown Sun*, 15 August 1973, Folder 8, Box 334, MYP.

[29] Jack Zaleski, Jr., "Allan Young Discusses Watergate, Dorgan, Guy," *Devils Lake Daily Journal*, 29 August 1973, p. 1.

[30] Jerry Hagstrom, "William Guy Plays the Waiting Game," *Mandan (N.D.) Morning Pioneer*, 9 September 1973, Folder 9, Box 335, MYP.

[31] "Guy Says Economy To Be Main Issue," *Mandan (N.D.) Morning Pioneer*, 10 October 1973, Folder 9, Box 335, MYP.

[32] Dick Dobson, "Inside North Dakota: Intrigue Surrounds Guy-Young Race," *Minot Daily News*, 5 October 1973, p. 5.

[33] *Minot Daily News*, 6 October 1973, p. 3.

[34] Doris Stadig, "Dems Urge Guy To Run For Senate Seat," *Minnewaukan (N.D.) Benson County Farmers Press*, 18 October 1973, Folder 12, Box 335, MYP.

[35] Jeff Carter, "Guy Keeps Candidacy Option Open," *Lisbon (N.D.) Ransom County Gazette*, 25 October 1973, Folder 10, Box 335, MYP.

[36] *Congressional Quarterly Weekly Report*, 3 November 1973, p. 2913.

[37] Richard M. Peterson, "Poor Richard's Almanac," *Minnewaukan (N.D.) Benson County Farmers Press*, 22 November 1973, Folder 11, Box 334, MYP.

[38] Phil Matthews, "Valeu Scouting for Bill Guy," *Fargo (N.D.) Forum*, 17 December 1973, p. 3.

[39] Chuck Coghlan, "As One Reader To Another," *Breckenridge-Wahpeton Daily News*, 19 December 1973, Folder 12, Box 334, MYP.

◆ 3 ◆

Controlling the Damage:
Young, 1974 to the Primary Election

As the election year began, Milton Young voiced concern over several political problems he felt might hurt his candidacy. He expected that the raising of campaign funds would be difficult and a goal of $100,000 nearly out of reach. Young hoped that his fundraising efforts to attract small donors would center around the themes of agriculture and his work on behalf of strengthening commodity prices. Accepting contributions from reputable sources, even if from outside North Dakota, posed no problems for him as long as he felt no special obligations to any organization.[1] Two days before his opponent entered the 1974 campaign, the Senator said that if President Nixon resigned it would benefit his Senate reelection bid, "but I'm not advocating that. Politically, I'd be better off right now with Gerald Ford as President." He maintained that as an issue his age, not Watergate, worried him most. Anticipating Guy's attack on the Congressional seniority system, Young planned to explain to the voters the advantages of power through seniority. Continuing to describe why he decided to run again, Young said, "You don't become a powerhouse in the U.S. Senate in your first term and that's really the compelling reason I'm running again. It's hard to give up the influence I've finally attained."[2] When Guy blasted Senatorial seniority in his candidacy announcement, the age and seniority issues received attention from several North Dakota leaders.

Welcoming Guy's announcement, Young repeated his defense of seniority, labeling it "a big issue in the campaign." The state's

Democratic Governor Arthur Link took the middle ground, suggesting seniority might become an important but not the principle issue. Tax Commissioner Byron Dorgan (correctly for everyone but Young) observed, "I think the principle issue, although it may not be spoken, will be Young's age." From North Dakota's Republican Attorney General Allen I. Olson came a different (but equally accurate) view: "It may or may not be a good system. But seniority is extremely important, especially to a small rural state like North Dakota."[3] Unwilling to allow the age issue to fade, Young hammered away at it in a Bismarck news conference: "Age will be a big issue. Some people are burned out. Others are still going strong at 80. It's hard for me to realize I am 76." Moving on to the seniority system, Young was emphatic: "The seniority system has its faults, but there's no other system you could devise that would give the small states better representation. I think it's the greatest system ever devised."[4] North Dakota's junior senator, Quentin Burdick, did not indicate whether or not he thought seniority the greatest system ever devised, but he believed that age should not be an issue in the Guy-Young contest.[5]

Little fanfare accompanied Bismarck businessman Robert McCarney's January 14 press release which said he might run for the U.S. Senate by entering the Democratic primary or running as an Independent. To political observers that brief statement made just one day prior to Guy's announcement signaled the beginning of yet another McCarney attempt to disrupt North Dakota's partisan electoral process.[6] Three days later Senator Young said he "understood all along he (Robert McCarney) was going to support me," adding that he told McCarney he should not go ahead with his plans of running for the Senate in the primary.[7]

William Guy's announcement of his candidacy came as no surprise to North Dakotans who recalled the former Governor's remarks at the time he announced in 1972 that he would not run for reelection but retained an interest in the U.S. Senate. He enjoyed recognition for his accomplishments and considerable support from all areas of the state.[8] It would, however, have surprised the public to learn the extent to which Senator Young saw the differences between himself and the former Governor. Not long after Guy's announcement, Young's attitude towards Guy surfaced in his reply to a constituent: "My opponent, former Governor Bill Guy, is 100 percent opposed to all of the views you express. He is a far-out liberal and opposed to everything you represent."[9]

During the first week of March, news reached North Dakota that Democratic Senator John C. Stennis of Mississippi, Chairman of the Senate Select Committee on Standards and Conduct, rejected Democratic State Chairman Richard Ista's accusations that Senator Young misused his franking privilege by distributing speeches made on the floor of the Senate to North Dakota news outlets. Regarding Stennis' statement, Young wrote Guy, urging "a clean and honorable campaign" and saying he intended to campaign on his record, taking full responsibility for what others in his campaign might say. He asked Guy to do the same "with those closely associated with your campaign." When Ista initially made his charges, Young called him a "stooge of Bill Guy" whose accusations were "not only inaccurate but malicious."[10] On a more positive note pertaining to use of the postal service, a fundraising committee calling itself "North Dakota Farmers for Senator Milton R. Young" sent a mass mailing to farmers asking them to contribute an amount equal to whatever number of bushels of grain they wanted to give to the Young campaign. The slogan used in the appeal was "Bushels for Mr. Wheat."[11] This was a timely appeal considering the information released by Young that the Department of Agriculture statisticians reported that from 1972 to 1973 North Dakota's net average farm income rose by over two and one-half times, marking the biggest increase of any state.[12]

Young's mail reflected citizen concern about Watergate, and many of them told their Senator that Nixon should leave the Presidency. Explaining that the House Judiciary Committee initiated impeachment hearings, Young told one North Dakota couple, "If the House voted to impeach the President and especially if they did so by a sizable majority, I am quite sure he would resign."[13] But he opposed Nixon's resignation to avoid impeachment proceedings, declaring that if the President resigned for that reason "it would set a bad precedent." As he so often did, Young talked about the effect of Watergate on his campaign: "It . . . can't help." Admitting that he faced a difficult race, Young reflected that "if the President wasn't in trouble, I don't think I would have any reelection problems." As evidence of that, the Senator mentioned support he received from Democrats and the National Association of Rural Electric Cooperatives.[14] He blamed Watergate and federal campaign regulations for inhibiting donors and making political fundraising more difficult; yet he insisted that in his personal campaign fundraising, he found little reluctance on the part of contributors.[15]

Two months after he implied he might run in the Democratic primary for the U.S. Senate nomination, perennial candidate Robert McCarney announced circulation of petitions to place his name in the Democratic-NPL column on the September 3 primary ballot. McCarney pronounced that his actions did not oppose Young but gave him a platform from which he could attack former Governor Guy; he pointed out that "the only way you can get the facts out is if you're a candidate." He charged Guy with Watergate tactics in his 1968 reelection campaign (Guy beat McCarney that year by a wider margin than any of his previous Republican opponents). Guy answered the accusation angrily: "None of these charges are true." When asked if he knew beforehand what McCarney planned to do, Young replied, "No, I did not ask Robert McCarney to seek nomination . . . I found out long ago that McCarney does as he pleases. If he had asked my advice, I would have advised against it." It fell to Democratic State Chairman Richard Ista to lower the partisan boom, declaring, "He is doing this as a ploy to assist Senator Young. I would say McCarney is about as phony as a three-dollar bill when it comes to being a Nonpartisan Leaguer. We have regular meetings. I have never seen him at one." Ista's Republican counterpart commented simply, "What can I say?"[16]

In a speech that Guy delivered at Washburn he mentioned something he and his wife Jean had experienced several months earlier during a vacation trip they made to California. The Guys spent some time with the Lawrence Welks, who invited them to a taping of the Lawrence Welk show on which a song would be sung in tribute to the former Governor while the Guys sat in the front row of the studio audience. Guy also told the Washburn rally that on April 20 (three weeks from the night of the rally) they could watch the show.[17] The story appeared on Thursday, April 3, and the following Monday an airmail letter left Senator Young's Washington office for Lawrence Welk in Santa Monica, California. Young erroneously told Welk that the Washburn paper's story could be considered "typical of the stories appearing in North Dakota papers since former Governor Guy's return to North Dakota. It seems apparent that former Governor Guy will use his friendship with you as a part of his forthcoming campaign."[18] The Senator went on to observe:

> Lawrence, I think it was real nice of you to have former Governor Guy appear on your program a couple of years ago when he was Governor, and again recently. Also, I thought it was real nice of you to play a number for Jean and him. If these films were to be used in the campaign this fall it would be quite a different matter, however. The great respect and admiration the people of North Dakota have for you could well be the deciding factor in this election if the films were to be used for political purposes.
>
> Last fall, I appeared on NBC's Today Show. I would like to have used this film for campaign publicity, but NBC has a rigid policy prohibiting such use of their film.[19]

Young explained further to Welk that Guy's position on abortion could not be determined but most probably was pro choice, while his record was one of actively supporting the right to life policies. Not until half way through the letter did the Senator get to the point:

> Lawrence, this is a very difficult letter for me to write to you, as I realize that though you are probably even more conservative than I am, you have always been very close friends with the Guys. My only purpose is to express the hope you will not permit the films concerning former Governor Guy to be used in his fall campaign.[20]

The promptness with which Young responded to the news of Guy's appearance on the Welk show reflected his realization of just how persuasive a Guy spot that incorporated a Welk appearance might be. Others shared the same concern and communicated it to the Senator. His campaign coordinator, Ray David, wrote the day after Young's letter went to Welk that he had seen the Washburn article, had talked to others about it, and that "Mac [McCarney] called and was concerned about the impact this might have on Welk fans across the State."[21] A communication pipeline existed between Young and McCarney.

Apparently the mood of anxious concern over the political ramifications of Guy's appearance on the Welk show did not reach the West Coast because Welk's reply to Young took nearly three weeks to appear. In a two-page letter, filled with chit chat, Welk wrote, "I can assure you the films you spoke of will never go out of our studios."[22] Several weeks later, Young responded, "I was real pleased to know that the films won't get out of your studio"; he also revealed his apprehension of events surrounding the Presidency:

> Everything looks good, but I am deeply concerned about this whole Watergate mess and impeachment. It's too bad this whole thing happened. In many ways Nixon has been a good President, but he certainly let certain things get out of hand. His handling of the tapes and their release, as well as other information, has been pretty bad. The news the last couple of days indicates the President is in deep trouble. It's just a question of how long he can last.[23]

Watergate took over the political agenda in the nation and in North Dakota during the spring of 1974, and as the climax drew closer Senator Young explained that how he might cast his vote in a Senate trial (after impeachment) troubled him because of the effect it could have on his reelection bid. Expressing his concern, he said, "If it comes to a vote in the Senate, no matter which way you vote, you'd be in trouble. I don't know how many solid Nixon supporters there are in North Dakota, maybe 25 percent. I figure maybe 35 percent." He thought that voting for conviction would turn many of the hard-core Nixon supporters against him.[24] Speaking to a convention of the North Dakota Federation of Republican Women in early May, Young noted that the mood of Congress changed after President Nixon released to the House Judiciary Committee edited transcripts of White House conversations. In a decidedly different tone than he expressed privately, Young told his partisan crowd, "There's been nothing yet to prove he President Nixon knew about the whole Watergate mess, that he encouraged it or had any responsibility for it."[25] On the second Friday in May the headline of the *Minot Daily News* read, "YOUNG URGES NIXON STEP OUT," and the lead story reported that Senator Young suggested President Nixon use the twenty-fifth amendment to step aside until the Watergate matter could be resolved.[26] In a related story Young (identified as a respected conservative) was reported as saying, "I think the President is getting in deeper trouble. I have been deeply concerned about how he has handled this whole thing."[27] In his May Senatorial newsletter to North Dakota, Young wrote that he did not himself know how he might vote should the Senate convene as a court after an impeachment of President Nixon. Then the Senator proclaimed, "I have been severely critical from the start of the whole Watergate mess."[28] As a Republican U.S. Senator running for reelection, Milton Young could not shake the Watergate scandal as summer approached in 1974.

Young again encountered opposition within the ranks of his own party at the national level. The *New York Times* reported on May 7: "Republicans at party headquarters in Washington wish 76-year-old Senator Young had stepped aside in favor of the state's popular at-large representative, Mark Andrews. They fear the worst against former Gov. William L. Guy, a Democrat."[29] Young did not reply to the *Times* story nor did he comment on opposition to him from a more traditional source, nationally organized labor, which targeted him for defeat.[30] But Young did handle the matter of candidates' making public their personal financial positions. After Guy released a statement of his financial assets, the Senator followed suit even though he strongly indicated he did not believe in such action. However, Young did not place a dollar value on his farm land, in contrast to the former Governor, who released the acreage he owned and its worth. Instead, the Senator made public the number of acres he owned, but not its value, explaining, "It would be very difficult to appraise the value of this farm. It has never been for sale and there have been no offers to purchase it."[31]

Young continued to cultivate and stay in contact with his friends in the North Dakota press as demonstrated by an incident which occurred in early July. The *Grand Forks Herald* noted Guy's statements that he saw inflation as the nation's number one problem and its solution as the combination of federal spending reductions and higher taxes to balance the budget, but the paper satirized Guy's position as inconsistent with his political history. The last line of the editorial made the observation: "Maybe since Guy started drawing $6,300 as a part-time director of a Fargo insurance agency he's joined the Chamber of Commerce.[32] A week later Senator Young wrote to the *Herald's* editor, Jack Hagerty, expressing admiration for the editorial. He also told Hagerty, "Jack, I would like to say something to you confidentially. My reason for asking you to keep this confidential is because I intend to use it at some time in the campaign." The something to which Young alluded consisted of a record of Governor Guy's having written him fifty-six letters asking him to vote for proposed federal expenditures but never a communication from Guy as Governor asking him to vote against a federal spending program.[33]

Even if Young did not believe that Guy's answers to reducing inflation were sincere, he did come to agree with his opponent that attention should be paid to the inflation issue. Both campaign camps took public opinion polls not only to discover who commanded the most support but also to find out what the voters considered to be the most important issues. A measure of Guy's superior polling data is that early in his campaign he singled out inflation as a key issue, but not until just before the Republican state convention in mid-July did Young join him in calling inflation the most important issue.[34] Parroting this view (and confirming the delay of polling results to the Republicans) the Republican state chairman said, "Inflation will be the number one issue at the convention and in the campaign."[35]

During the second day of the Republican state convention, George H.W. Bush, Chairman of the Republican National Committee, arrived in the convention city, Minot. Stressing recurring themes in Young's campaign, Bush stated that because of the Senator's seniority and his position as ranking Republican on the Senate Appropriations Committee, his reelection held special importance to the party nationally.[36] The next day, accepting his party's endorsement for the Senate, Senator Young defended the seniority system and repeated his disdain for North Dakota's losing the ranking position on the Senate Appropriations Committee, which he said counted as a major reason for his candidacy. He mentioned the damage caused by inflation but did not utter one word about Watergate or ethics in government. Stressing his strongest point, Young continued, "Ending the Cold War made possible the huge wheat sale to Russia which was strongly condemned by my opponent and his associates. . . As a direct result of the Russian wheat sale, we have the first five-dollar wheat in history. . . and the greatest prosperity in our state's history." Asking for "the biggest possible vote in the primary," the veteran Republican discouraged his fellow Party members from crossing over in the September primary elections to vote for Robert McCarney. Projecting optimism, Young claimed the pessimism expressed about his chances for reelection earlier were gone, and he concluded saying, "I see no problem in winning this election."[37]

Young received his endorsement by a unanimous vote, brought the convention to its feet cheering (he received the only floor demonstration during the convention), and touched the themes he felt worked best in his behalf.[38] As he left the Minot convention, Young believed his tactics would put him ahead of Guy and keep him there. This seemed reasonable, especially when in a quiet and almost unnoticed manner Robert McCarney, on July 22, filed petitions with North Dakota's Secretary of State to place his name on the Democratic-NPL ballot for U.S. Senator.[39] On July 25, U.S. Secretary of State Henry Kissinger and Senator Young made a brief visit to the Grand Forks Air Force Base. Kissinger, at a press conference, praised Young but denied his visit could be considered politically motivated. Despite the denial, Young received favorable political fallout from the visit of the famous Secretary of State, shoring up Young's claims that his seniority gave him powerful influence and through him all North Dakota.[40] Scott Anderson, a former North Dakota Democratic Party leader, received little attention as he supervised the filming of Kissinger's visit for TV ads in Young's campaign. In 1960 Anderson, as executive director of the state Democratic Party, had played a key role in Guy's election to the governorship. Anderson's appearance as an official of a Washington-based firm, Concept Films, Inc., working for Young, displayed that some important Democrats in the nation's capital did not want former Governor Guy replacing Young.[41]

Noting that his membership on the Senate Agriculture and Appropriations Committees consumed a large share of his time and his determination to maintain his high percentage of Senate attendance, Young announced in early August he would not have as much time to campaign as he had originally planned.[42] Perhaps the Senator anticipated the final moments of Nixon's Presidency and used the press of Senate business to allow him to remain in Washington and in his office when the President resigned. On the day of Nixon's resignation, in a brief press release, Young expressed an almost melancholy mood. He noted that because Nixon faced a House membership about to impeach him, a Senate in which his support continued to deteriorate, and an absence of public support, the President had no option but to resign. Young then repeated the thoughts he had included in his spring letter to Lawrence Welk: "Even though the President has brought most of this on himself, I cannot help but have a feeling of sadness. In many respects, especially on foreign matters, he has been one of our very best Presidents."[43] However, when asked how Nixon's resignation would affect his reelection campaign, Young's mood brightened immediately: "This should assure my reelection. I never at any time supported Watergate. I was always critical of Watergate. I never once defended it."[44]

Not until after the primary did Senator Young make an effort to reach out for extensive statewide press coverage. His statement that Nixon's resignation assured his reelection played a part, but more important to him was avoiding any publicity in the Democratic Guy-McCarney primary fight. But before that significant event, the Senator took note of an attitude that surfaced regularly as he campaigned across North Dakota in the fall. In the letter to the editor column published two weeks after Nixon resigned, a Ford dealer from western North Dakota, H. Spier, Jr. wrote:

> Who gave our farmers $5.00 a bushel for wheat? Isn't it much nicer to get $5.00 a bushel without a war than $2.00 like we had experienced years ago with a war? I've been in business for 25 years and I've never seen so much money in the country, and buying power, yet we don't appreciate it.[45]

Unlike the national economy in 1974, North Dakota's economy was booming because of the high prices of its agricultural products. While it is not possible to quantify the extent to which this influenced the outcome of the U.S. Senate race, there is no doubt that Milton Young, Mr. Wheat, could not have received the votes he did without it.

Notes

[1] Dave Bartel, "Senate Race Funding Poses Some Problems," *Grand Forks Herald*, 7 January 1974, p. 1.

[2] Chuck Haga, "Young Sees U.S. in 'Critical Situation'," *Grand Forks Herald*, 14 January 1974, p. 8.

[3] *Valley City Times*, 16 January 1974, Folder 6, Box 599, MYP.

[4] Dave Bartel, "Diversion Said in Danger," *Minot Daily News*, 17 January 1974, p. 1.

[5] Jack Hagerty, "Observations," *Grand Forks Herald*, 17 February 1974, p. 4.

[6] *Mandan (N.D.) Morning Pioneer*, 15 January 1974, Clipping, Folder 4, Box 599, MYP.

[7] *Mandan (N.D.) Morning Pioneer*, 18 January 1974, p. 1.

[8] *Grand Forks Herald*, 16 January 1974, p. 4.

[9] Milton R. Young to E. Standard, 22 January 1974, Folder 14, Box 50 , MYP.

[10] *Grand Forks Herald*, 9 March 1974, p. 1.

[11] Dick Dobson, "Inside North Dakota: 'Young, Andrews Gain in Seniority,'" *Minot Daily News*, 2 March 1974, p. 15.

[12] Bill Tillottson, "On the Hill," *Bismarck Tribune*, 29 March 1974, p. 15.

[13] Milton R. Young to Mr. and Mrs. Jack Redmond, 21 February 1974, Folder 12, Box 508, MYP.

[14] *Jamestown Sun*, 21 March 1974, p. l.

[15] *Jamestown Sun*, 22 March 1974, p. 2.

[16] Gary Clark, "McCarney Says Purpose Is Solely to Oppose Guy, " *Bismarck Tribune*, 12 April 1974, p. 5.

[17] Oliver Borlaug, "Guy Laments Lack of Leadership at Fund-Raising Dinner Attended by Nearly 200 in Washburn," *Washburn Leader*, 3 April 1974, Unfiled, Box 615, MYP.

[18] Milton R. Young to Lawrence Welk, 8 April 1974, p. 1, Unfiled, Box 615, MYP.

[19] Ibid.

[20] Ibid, p. 2.

[21] Ray David to Milton R. Young, 9 April 1974, Unfiled, Box 615, MYP.

[22] Lawrence Welk to Milton R. Young, 26 April 1974, p. 1, Unfiled, Box 615, MYP.

[23] Milton R. Young to Lawrence Welk, 8 May 1974, p. 1, Unfiled, Box 615, MYP.

[24] *Minot Daily News*, 3 May 1974, p. 7.

[25] *Minot Daily News*, 4 May 1974, p. 13.

[26] *Minot Daily News*, 10 May 1974, p. 1.

[27] Carl P. Leubsdorf, "GOP Joins Cry of 'Quit'," *Minot Daily News*, 10 May 1974, p. 1.

[28] *Minot Daily News*, 13 May 1974, p. 2.

[29] Dick Dobson, "Inside North Dakota: 'Naaden Campaign Horse Shot Down'," *Minot Daily News*, 18 May 1974, p. 14.

[30] *Grand Forks Herald*, 11 June 1974, p. 4.

[31] Gary W. Clark, "Young's Holdings Include But One Share of Stock," *Minot Daily*

News, 18 June 1974, p. 1.

[32] Jack Hagerty, "Conversion," *Grand Forks Herald*, 2 July 1974, p.4.

[33] Milton R. Young to Jack Hagerty, 9 July 1974, Unfiled, Box 615, MYP.

[34] J. D. Wilson, "GOP Expecting to Endorse Young, Andrews, and Wolf," *Grand Forks Herald*, 10 July 1974, p. 8.

[35] Jim Willis, "Inflation: Coal Development Key GOP Convention Issues," *Grand Forks Herald*, 10 July 1974, p. 8.

[36] Jim Willis, "Bush: Young Re-Election Top Priority," *Minot Daily News*, 13 July 1974, p. 7.

[37] "Speech For Republican Convention Senator Milton R. Young (R-N.D.) For Release," July 13, 1974, Folder 21, Box 615, MYP.

[38] Jack Hagerty, "Young, Andrews Endorsed," *Grand Forks Herald*, 14 July 1974, p. 1.

[39] *Grand Forks Herald*, 23 July 1974, p. 5.

[40] Jack Hagerty, "Kissinger Displays Both Diplomacy, Charm at Base," *Grand Forks Herald*, 26 July 1974, p. 8.

[41] Jack Hagerty, "In My Book," *Grand Forks Herald*, 31 July 1974, p. 6.

[42] "Young: Must Cut Back On Campaigning," *Minot Daily News*, 3 August 1974, p. 13.

[43] "Press Release," 8 August 1974, Folder 18, Box 503, MYP.

[44] "Young: My Re-election Assured," *Fargo (N.D.) Forum*, 9 August 1974, p. 1.

[45] *Washburn Leader*, 22 August 1974, p. 2.

◆ 4 ◆

Confidence to Altering Strategy:
Guy, 1974 to Primary Election

"William L. Guy will announce 'very soon, within a few weeks,'" forecast North Dakota's Tax Commissioner Byron Dorgan in the first week of January 1974, anticipating Guy's challenge for Young's U.S. Senate seat. Dorgan, certain that Guy would win, suggested that Young's age should convince the incumbent to retire and stated that Young's age would be a major campaign factor if he continued in the race. Expanding on the theme, Dorgan expressed his belief that it was "absurd" that "because a man has been around longer he's necessarily better."[1] Turning to his own political plans, Dorgan indicated that he considered a race against the Republican U.S. House member very appealing, but he did not say definitely that he planned to run for higher office.[2] Although Dorgan predicted that Guy was on the verge of announcing for the Senate, the former Governor himself maintained, ". . . I am not a candidate. I want to keep my options flexible." Acknowledging that two staff members of the Democratic Senatorial Campaign Committee had flown to North Dakota to consult with him, Guy denied that any arrangements, agreements, or funding had come out of the meeting. For the 1974 campaign he expected small contributions to finance the Democratic effort because ". . .we cannot go on allowing corporations to finance political campaigns."[3] According to the 1972 Federal Election Campaign Act, in North Dakota's general election (and in the primary election as well) U.S. Senate candidates could spend no more than $52,150 and of that amount only $31,290 for media. Both Guy and

Young agreed the limits did not pose any problems.[4]

Guy scheduled two press conferences for Wednesday, January 16, one at his home in the morning and another in Bismarck that afternoon, to unveil his political plans.[5] Thus, twenty-four months after he announced he would not run for Governor, William L. Guy used the living room of his Casselton split-level house to confirm that he intended to run for the U.S. Senate. Not mentioning Senator Young by name, Guy said he planned to campaign "on the issues and against no one" and that "I believe it would be helpful for North Dakota to have a Senator who is a farmer and who can speak out on our basic industry." Considering what the next eleven months held in store for him, the former Governor seemed unaware of the scope of the political battle into which he entered. Looking back over his twelve years as Governor, he told the twenty cameramen and reporters that the upcoming race did not seem as difficult as past contests. Stating flatly that he saw no reason to use Watergate as an issue, Guy did comment, "From my years of experience in North Dakota state government, I know it is possible to conduct the affairs of government and politics honestly."[6] Guy credited the urging of his family as an important factor in reaching his decision.[7]

Leaving Casselton by car and carefully observing the speed limit, Guy arrived at his Bismarck news conference at the Holiday Inn several minutes late. Primarily designed to give his candidacy announcement TV news coverage in western North Dakota, the Bismarck setting also provided a platform to raise the issue of the Congressional seniority system. As in Casselton, Guy did not mention Young by name nor did he mention age as an issue, but he found a way to put both squarely on the table, declaring, "I have long believed that the seniority system is one of the grave problems in Congress. It places too much responsibility on people who are neither willing nor able to carry it out." Attaining leadership in Congress under the seniority system, according to Guy, resulted from living longer than Congressional peers rather than displaying ability. Guy met head on Young's touting of his seniority, and used seniority to focus indirectly on the Senator's age. Having thrown down the gauntlet, Guy repeated his milder theme from earlier in the day: "I do not plan to campaign against anyone in the months ahead but simply for the privilege of representing North Dakota in the United States Senate."[8]

If nothing concrete had come out of Guy's meeting with representatives of the Democratic Senatorial Campaign Committee prior to his formal announcement, a month after he became an official candidate national level Democrats targeted North Dakota's Senate seat for a turnover.[9] Also on the national level Watergate held the attention of the two opposing Senatorial campaign camps, and signs of change could be detected. The North Dakota Poll showed that in late January a majority of respondents did not favor Nixon's resignation or removal from office. They also replied that if Nixon and McGovern should again face each other in a Presidential election, they would give North Dakota's electoral votes to Nixon. However, only 24 percent rated Nixon's performance as near average.[10] Eight months prior to election day Nixon's popularity did not show signs of collapse, but a downward trend appeared evident.

Lloyd B. Omdahl from Conway, former State Tax Commissioner, longtime Democratic-NPL activist, University of North Dakota assistant professor of political science, director of UND's Bureau of Governmental Affairs,[11] and a close friend of Guy acted, without salary, as the Guy campaign's media director. Eyeing the battle ahead, Omdahl told a meeting of the North Dakota Democratic-Nonpartisan League's policy committee in early March, "You're probably going to see one of the dirtiest campaigns for the United States Senate that you've ever seen in this state. Be prepared for a Watergate here only on a smaller scale." Later Omdahl explained that his remarks had referred to Republican Robert McCarney, who had announced earlier his interest in running in the Democratic primary for the party's U.S. Senate nomination.[12] During March Guy and his wife Jean crisscrossed North Dakota, attending party functions, mentioning few issues, and devoting time to fundraising efforts. The impression he gave to voters presented a serious, confident, and sensitive candidate who was concerned with the conditions in which he found the nation's politics.[13]

A campaign event in Washburn's Memorial Hall late in March reflected a typical North Dakota partisan meeting. Labeled a "Meet Bill and Jean Guy" meeting and priced at twenty-five dollars per couple, the evening included dinner, speeches, and a dance that drew a crowd of nearly two hundred people. Reverend Elmer Odlund, minister of Washburn's United Methodist Church, gave the invocation; county Democratic chairman Gerald Oberg emceed, and the ladies of the United Methodist Church served a ham dinner. It should be noted that no Jewish vote existed in McLean County and any effort to lure Catholic voters to the festivities went unreported. Providing the entertainment (not even the most partisan crowd thought political speeches entertaining) Turtle Lake (a McLean County community smaller than Washburn) residents Connie Hofer, Janeal Singer, Steve Hill, and Gail Orman sang popular songs and were followed by the political speakers. Candidate Guy's talk stressing the themes of Watergate, energy, leadership, and the power of the electorate broke no new ground. Washburn's weekly newspaper devoted more space in its coverage of the "Meet Bill and Jean Guy" night than Guy had received in any North Dakota daily or weekly between his formal announcement and the Democratic-NPL state convention.[14]

Prior to speaking before a thirtieth district Democratic-NPL dinner in Linton the next month, Guy told a reporter, "A junior member of a majority party could have more power than a senior member of a minority party." As he said, "Seniority works within a majority party." This seemed to be a change from Guy's earlier position but he added he would not limit "any Congressman's right to serve on committees [but] . . . if he is to serve on a committee, he should be elected by its members. At present, the party caucus names the chairman."[15] If the former Governor's position appeared fuzzy at times on the seniority issue, both he and Senator Young expressed strong support for the Garrison Diversion project, a proposal to divert annually 875,000 acre feet of Missouri River water to central and eastern North Dakota for municipal, recreation, and agricultural purposes. The Committee to Save North Dakota and its chairman, Richard Madson of Jamestown, attacked Senator Young for his pro-Garrison Diversion stand, but not Guy. Other than Madson's occasional protests, no partisan division took place on the issue of Garrison Diversion.[16]

In reply to questions concerning McCarney's intention to run against him in the September primary, Guy in early May answered, "So what's new? In every election I've been in since 1961, McCarney has played some role, always in violent opposition to me."[17] The lack of concern on Guy's part reinforced the picture of a confident candidate who could control the political agenda. Guy did just that when he continued to emphasize inflation as North Dakota's and America's most important problem. To combat inflation Guy proposed, "We must balance the federal budget by deciding what we can do without and then cutting back. Congress must adopt a budgeting system whereby it sets budget priorities, goals and ceilings on appropriations."[18]

The parallel between North Dakota's Senate contest and that of Arkansas's in 1974 caught the attention of North Dakota politicians and sent concern through the Young camp. James William Fubright of Arkansas's entered the U.S. Senate in 1945, the same year as Milton Young, but on May 28 Arkansas's forty-eight-year-old Governor Dale Bumpers defeated Senator Fulbright by a landslide in that state's Democratic primary.[19] From Guy's point of view his generational gap with Young matched the Fulbright-Bumpers example, yet Fulbright's national reputation worked against him with "back home folks" while Young did not suffer that type of liability. In order to grasp the opportunity to test his strength against Young, Guy realized that a decisive defeat of his primary opponent must take precedence over a final general election strategy; with just two months remaining before the primary, Guy pondered his campaign tactics because the McCarney factor could not be accurately calculated.[20] In the same vein political analyst Kevin Phillips commented on the North Dakota Senate race: ". . . 76-year-old GOP incumbent Milton Young is running like cold molasses. GOP insiders worry that he'll lose to Democratic ex-Governor William Guy unless Guy himself gets badly cut up in a primary challenge from Bismarck auto dealer Robert McCarney (who will be rehashing Guy Administration bank scandals)."[21]

On the eve of the Democratic-NPL state convention in late June at Minot, McCarney paid for a half-hour TV program titled "Special Political Broadcast" that accused Guy of corruption during his governorship. At a news conference the next day the former Governor responded:

> Last night with heavy hearts my wife Jean and I watched the vicious attack on me made by Robert McCarney in a paid political broadcast over several North Dakota TV stations. Nothing he said in that TV advertisement regarding me was true. Nothing! It was just one lie or crude innuendo after another.
>
> Mr. McCarney has apparently taken on the assignment to try to assassinate my character . . . I am very proud of my own personal integrity in politics and government service. I am even more proud of the extremely high standards of morality and honesty followed by the people of my administration for 12 years.
>
> McCarney's attacks on me raise some serious questions. Why is McCarney trying to blacken my name? Who is benefiting by his attacks? Certainly not him - certainly not me - certainly not the Democratic-NPL Party. Then who is benefiting? And why has the decision been made to conduct politics on this level?

Guy stated he would not debate McCarney because debates should be based on facts and McCarney had none.[22]

Turning his attention from Young to McCarney, for the first time in his campaign, the former Governor diverted his energies from the principle objective of defeating Milton Young, and he would be similarly side tracked again and again in the months leading up to November's election. Guy reached a turning point without realizing it, nor did he later recognize the pattern repeating itself. Unaware of any hidden pitfalls Guy went before the convention which gave him his party's endorsement for the U.S. Senate and pledged an "open-issue oriented campaign."[23]

Some days later Senator Young interpreted Guy's answer to McCarney's TV ad as an accusation of his having arranged McCarney's candidacy and shot back, "This kind of attack by innuendo is typical of Bill Guy's way of doing things." Carrying the matter further, Young charged, ". . . McCarney is now a Democrat candidate. Guy is barking up the wrong tree if he thinks I am responsible for all the goings-on within the Democratic Party," and he observed that the charges McCarney had leveled against Guy were serious.[24] Picking up on Young's statement about the serious charges, Guy in a telegram sent to the Senator declared, "Let me assure you that these charges are false, frivolous and shopworn." The telegram continued, "I propose that we meet at your convenience in Carrington or at any other place in North Dakota to have a friendly discussion of the seriousness of McCarney's charges. . . " He suggested Carrington because both his and Young's schedules placed them there at an annual legislative golf tournament. Such a meeting did not take place, however, because the Senator replied to his opponent, "This legislative golf tournament has always been a sociable, fun affair. I have no intention of using that gathering as a place for you to get me involved in a political debate over a problem that is entirely your own."[25]

In late July Guy returned to McCarney's candidacy being a front for somebody else when he remarked, "I'm convinced in my own mind Mr. McCarney is being used to carry out a special assignment against me by a group which I can't identify at this time." He did not speculate on which group, but he said his defeat could benefit the transportation industry, the military-industrial complex, and coal companies. He also announced the appointment of former Board of Higher Education member and State Senator George Sinner of Casselton as his campaign manager.[26]

In July an exchange took place within the Young camp which foreshadowed Guy's ultimate undoing. Jim Backlin, Senator Young's Bismarck field representative, sent Young information he had received verbally from Bob McPherson of the International Union of Operating

Engineers. Backlin informed the Senator that McPherson had revealed that ". . . he had learned that the environmentalists are pushing James Jungroth of Jamestown to run for the Senate in November. He said some Democrats don't think this was serious but he believes it is since he said the environmentalist groups are loaded with money and are looking hard for candidates supporting their viewpoint."[27] Several days later in a letter to McPherson, Young commented, "I had heard, too, from several different sources that Jim Jungroth of Jamestown was considering filing as an independent candidate for the Senate in the general election. Undoubtedly his major support will be from environmentalists.[28]

On August 5 James Jungroth announced his candidacy as an independent for the U.S. Senate in the November general election. Jungroth, explaining that he did not want to be involved in the issues between McCarney and Guy in the primary contest, said, "We don't want to get embroiled in the primary with the McCarney things." Explaining he planned to run on an environmentalist platform, Jungroth observed, "It seems necessary to me that there be a third candidate for the U.S. Senate in this fall's race. I find very little difference between the two party-endorsed candidates except for age, seniority and party affiliation." He continued, "Today North Dakota is at the crossroads. If industrialization comes, as has been proposed by the coal developers, major decisions affecting North Dakota will not be made in the city halls. . . county courthouses. . . nor the legislative chambers. . . , but instead will be made in out-of-state corporate board rooms." Jungroth advocated "Total nondevelopment beyond the water permits that have already been voted." That proposal took aim at Guy's support of a permit granted in July to United Power Association Cooperative.[29]

Minot columnist Dobson answered important questions concerning McCarney's motive for entering the Democratic primary and why Jungroth had chosen the general election and independent status. Dobson believed that McCarney's dislike of Guy – and not an assignment from Young - had played a paramount role in his decision to run in the primary, offering him an opportunity to attack the former

Governor. Dobson also noted that Jungroth had told Young in 1973 that his candidacy strategy would be to take votes away from Guy. Dobson went on to quote what he judged to be "an astute commentary" made by the executive editor of the *Grand Forks Herald*, Jack Hagerty: "It is true that Jungroth is likely to win most of his votes from Democrats. But given the antagonism which exists with a sizable part of the Democratic Party, those votes might otherwise go to Young - and the Republican incumbent might get them." Dobson concluded that "Independents usually take votes away from both major candidates, with the result that the outcome becomes more unpredictable. The simple truth is that many thousands of voters do not make logical, rational decisions."[30] Richard Ista expressed a different view; he believed Jungroth's presence on the ballot would hurt Guy more than Young; the *Forum* predicted the Jamestown man's candidacy would probably have no impact on the voter's decision.[31] Even though agreement did not exist in North Dakota political circles as to the outcome of the Senate contest in early August, national Democratic leaders at that time named North Dakota as one of the five states in which their candidates would have the best chance to take Republican Senate seats.[32]

The September 3, 1974 election marked the first time in North Dakota's history that the Democratic candidates polled more votes than Republican candidates in a primary. Guy identified independents, not Democrats, as responsible for his party's strong showing and saw it as "something quite profound. . . the emergence of an extremely large block of independent voters in North Dakota."[33] Young, running without primary opposition, received 51,705 votes as opposed to Guy's 55,269 and McCarney's 11,286, making a total Democratic vote in the Senate race of 67,555.[34] McCarney's ploy to deal the former Governor a mortal blow or at least to inflict major damage to him met with little success. On the day after his strong primary showing, Guy said that the election outcome was "extremely encouraging and reflects a showing of confidence of North Dakotans in their state government." He declared that he intended to emphasize issues that faced North Dakota and America in the general election campaign, putting inflation as the number one issue. He went on to point out, "I plan to spend an awful lot of time talking with people in the next few weeks to get their ideas of what they think should be done and what they want done."[35]

Labeling the primary election "An Historic Outcome," the *Mandan Morning Pioneer* editorialized that Guy's out-polling Young, even with McCarney as an opponent, pointed towards "an intensive political campaign."[36] Fargo's *Forum* took a different view, forecasting it would be logical that most of McCarney's primary votes would be cast for Young in the general election. However, the paper admitted that this did not negate the Democrats' primary vote ranking as their highest ever. The primary did settle who won the parties' nominations, but "didn't give a clear perspective on what will happen in November." Concluding, the *Forum* commented that, while Nixon's resignation should have cleared the air for Republican candidates, "President Gerald R. Ford's unconditional pardon of Mr. Nixon has shoved Watergate right back into the campaign."[37] Twelve years later political analyst Dobson would explain that a majority of voters in the 1974 primary had gone into the Democratic column because the Party had employed a get-out-the-vote drive to ensure William Guy's victory over political maverick Robert McCarney. The primary vote, therefore, had not adumbrated a Democratic sweep in the general election.[38]

Notes

[1] Chuck Haga, "Guy Predicted to Soon Enter U.S. Senate Race," *Grand Forks Herald*, 8 January 1974, p. 1.

[2] Jim Willis, "Dorgan Hints at Andrews Contest," *Grand Forks Herald*, 8 January 1974, p. 1.

[3] "Demos Eye Small Contributor in '74," *Bismarck Tribune*, 8 January 1974, p. 3.

[4] Dave Bartel, "High Cost Politics at An End," *Mandan (N.D.) Morning Pioneer*, Folder 6, Box 599, MYP.

[5] *Mandan (N.D.) Morning Pioneer*, 15 January 1974, Folder 1, Box 599, MYP.

[6] Phil Matthews, "Pledges Campaign Based on Issues," *Fargo (N.D.) Forum*, 17 January 1974, p. 1.

[7] "Senate N.D. Contest Set," *Washington Post*, 17 January 1974, p. 26.

[8] Dick Dobson, "Guy Blasts Seniority System," *Minot Daily News*, 17 January 1974, p. 9.

[9] *Congressional Quarterly Weekly Report*, 23 February 1974, p. 425.

[10] *New Rockford Transcript*, Clipping, 13 February 1974, Folder 9, Box 599, MYP.

[11] "Omdahl to Speak at Meeting of Democratic-NPL Women," *Grand Forks Herald*, 3 March 1974, p. 11.

[12] "Conclave Will Open June 21," *Minot Daily News*, 4 March, 1974, p. 2.

[13] Clippings, Folder 20, Box 599, MYP.

[14] *Washburn Leader*, 3 April 1974, Folder 32, Box 599, MYP.

[15] *Linton (N.D.) Emmons County Record*, 17 April 1974, Folder 32, Box 599, MYP.

[16] "Madson Lashes Out at Young For Statement on Diversion," *Fargo (N.D.) Forum*, 23 April 1974, p. 9.

[17] "So, What's New' Guy Says About McCarney," *Minot Daily News*, 2 May 1974, p.1.

[18] Dave Bartel, "Guy Terms Inflation As Nation's Largest Problem," *Minot Daily News*, 14 May 1974, p. 2.

[19] "Bumpers Fells Political Giant," *Bismarck Tribune*, 29 May 1974, p. 10.

[20] Dick Dobson, "Prairie Perspective: Guy to Face Multiple Challenges," *Minot Daily News*, 1 June 1974, p. 7.

[21] Kevin Phillips, "Doubtful Republican-Held Seats," *American Political Report*, 14 June 1974, p. 3.

[22] Dick Dobson, "Speech Blisters Guy; Republican Filing Million Dollar Action," *Minot Daily News*, 21 June 1974, p. 1.

[23] Dick Dobson, "Convention Backs Simonson; Knutson Refuses to Concede," *Minot Daily News*, 24 June 1974, p. 16.

[24] "Young Denies He Prompted Mac Charge," *Minot Daily News*, 27 June 1974, p. 2.

[25] "Young Declines Guy's Request," *Minot Daily News*, 29 June 1974, p. 9.

[26] "Guy Thinks McCarney Being Used By Group To Hurt Him," *Minot Daily News*, 25 July 1974, p. 2.

[27] Jim Backlin, to Senator Young, 16 July 1974, Folder 7, Box 508, MYP.

[28] Milton R. Young to Bob McPherson, 19 July 1974, Folder 7, Box 508, MYP.

[29] "Jamestown Attorney Runs With Independent Label," *Minot Daily News*, 5 August 1974, p. 1.

[30] Dick Dobson, "Prairie Perspective: Jungroth Race Could Backfire," *Minot Daily News*, 10 August 1974, p. 9.

[31] "The Forum's Editorial: North Dakota Confronted With 3-Candidate U.S. Senate Race in November," *Fargo (N.D.) Forum*, 10 August 1974, p. 4.

[32] "How '74 Senate Races Look Now," *U.S. News and World Report*, 5 August 1974, p. 39.

[33] Phil Matthews, "Guy, Andrews Score Impressive Wins: Knutson Captures Dem PSC Nomination," *Fargo (N.D.) Forum*, 5 September 1974, p.1.

[34] Jim Willis, "Official Primary Results Show Guy Top Vote-Getter," *Jamestown Sun*, 17 September 1974, Clipping, Folder 13, Box 597, MYP.

[35] *Williston Herald*, 4 September 1974, Clipping, Folder 10, Box 597, MYP.

[36] *Mandan (N.D.) Morning Pioneer*, 5 September 1974, p. 4.

[37] "Forum's Editorial: No Clear Perspective Gained from N.D. Primary Voting on November Election Outcome," *Fargo (N.D.) Forum*, 12 September 1974, p. 4.

[38] Dick Dobson, "Prairie Perspective: Advice to GOP: Don't Ignore June Vote," *Minot Daily News*, 15 June 1986, p. C-6.

◆ 5 ◆

Staying the Course:
Young, Primary to Election

Shortly after the primary, Senator Young, concerned that Guy had received more votes than he did, called a press conference in Bismarck to announce he would depend on local Republican organizations for turning out his vote in November. Earlier in the year Young had contacted the state GOP chairman about the party's get-out-the-vote program. Young said, "he wrote [GOP Chairman] they didn't have the money to get out the vote in the past campaigns, the Republican Party had the responsibility of getting out the vote, which they aren't doing now." Because his campaign did not have money or personnel to pursue a voter turnout program, Young explained that he would rely on his party's local units.[1] Young's representation of the Republican Party voter turnout program did not present clearly the situation which existed. The state GOP committee in early 1974 put into operation a program that delegated voter identification, absentee ballots, and voter turnout activities to its district organizations and offered assistance to districts in implementing those activities. At no time did Senator Young receive a letter from the state GOP chairman telling him North Dakota's Republican Party did not have a voter turnout program. In fact Young's interest in a voter turnout program did not surface until after the primary, and the rush of events soon removed the topic from the top of his campaign agenda.

On September 8 President Ford pardoned former President Nixon for all his possible crimes. The next day Young responded in a statement which provided him with considerable maneuverability. Recounting his earlier position that as a private citizen Nixon fell under the jurisdiction of the courts and "particularly Special Prosecutor Leon Jaworski," the Senator also reiterated his earlier stand of not wanting a former President put in jail. The reason he gave for opposition to imprisoning Nixon turned on this sentence: "A former President serving a sentence in jail would be difficult for the rest of the world to understand, and especially former President Nixon, who had probably done more for peace in the world than any President in history." That covered those North Dakotans who supported Ford's action, yet the old veteran politician knew enough to cover the other base. Backing away from the pardon, Young became less emphatic: "I can't help but think, though, that President Ford's pardon was premature and that former President Nixon's statement was not as forthright and complete as it could and should have been."[2] Giving himself a two-sided position on the pardon proved advantageous to the Senator, who just three days after the statement replied to a constituent who supported the pardon that to a large degree he agreed with her but "my mail right now is running heavily in opposition to the pardon."[3]

Several days after a luncheon with his top campaign personnel in early September, Young wrote to them, discussing decisions he made regarding the campaign. Rejecting a purchase of bumper stickers, he reflected, "I am afraid it is too late to do anything about it"; however, the Senator agreed to a political survey which he would use to target voters in areas not favorable to him. Analyzing the primary election results, he noted that while 12,000 more people voted in the Democratic column than in the Republican column. Guy out-distanced him by only 3,490 votes; and even though closely associated with Fargo, Guy did not carry the city. Young concluded that turning out his vote for the general election depended on raising the necessary money to get the job done. Quoting an April 6 memo from the Republican state chairman, the Senator recognized that party organization by itself could not deliver 100 percent of Republican voters to the polls, thus leaving his campaign organization with the problem of filling the gaps.[4] The incumbent expressed concern over money, but campaign finance reporting forms submitted to North Dakota's Secretary of State covering income and spending from January 1, 1974, to August 31, 1974, showed Senator Young's contributions topped former Governor Guy's $146,348 to $42,240. According to the reports, a St. Thomas farmer, William Grandy, made the biggest single contribution to Young's campaign - $100.[5]

Covering towns from Fargo to Dickinson along I-94 and Williston to Grand Forks along U.S. Highway 2, a Republican Ladies Caravan (September 16-20) that featured Pat Young drew a considerable amount of press attention during a week in which Senator Young tended to his Senatorial duties in Washington. From breakfast meetings to evening dinners, Republican women legislative candidates and incumbents joined Mrs. Young to promote both their own candidacies and Senator Young.[6] When the Senator returned to the state in October to campaign full-time, his schedule repeated the vigorous pace set by the women, crisscrossing the state to give him the greatest visibility possible. He stressed his themes of experience, seniority and constituent service, which qualified national political observers said ". . . is acknowledged to be among the best in Congress."[7]

Speaking to a meeting of Fargo's Chamber of Commerce on September 20, Senator Young told the group he did not want President Ford to campaign for his reelection in North Dakota. Young related, "I hated to do this, but some of President Ford's aides were planning to have him come out here. But I discouraged them. I don't want to get involved any more in the pardon and amnesty business than I am now." Because of Nixon's pardon, Young knew that many North Dakotans looked with disfavor on Ford, but he predicted Ford's popularity would return.[8] Just what signals Young's statement sent to the national press cannot be determined, but the status of North Dakota's U.S. Senate race became blurred as viewed by some national reporters. The *Christian Science Monitor* reported in late October that President Ford's decision to barnstorm for Republican incumbent U.S. Senators and Representatives recognized the problems hurting GOP candidates: inflation, an economic slow down, too much Watergate, and in some places apathy. In North Dakota's case the *Monitor* declared overconfidence produced Republican weakness and passed on the assessment of the Senate contest which the executive director of the Republican Senate Campaign Committee made. Buell Barrison noted that Young faced an uphill battle which "could go either way" and complained, "Our candidate doesn't even have a campaign."[9] Barrison must not have read *U.S. News and World Report* that reported while Democrats on the national level entertained hopes of picking up North Dakota's Republican Senate seat, Young would "win by a narrow margin."[10]

With a Fargo dateline a *Washington Post* staff writer filed a story on North Dakota's Senate race that went directly to the heart of the matter: "With few, if any, cutting issues emerging, the question of age is dominating the contest." The story outlined how a breach between Young and the Republican Senatorial Campaign Committee had occurred and ended when the committee, realizing Young would not step aside in favor of Representative Mark Andrews, put $50,000 into Young's campaign. Presented with a close race, Young for the first time in his political career returned home to campaign before Congress adjourned. With polls showing Guy running fourteen to sixteen percentage points ahead of Young, the Senator's main thrust stressed his seniority and reputation as "Mr. Wheat." But because the same polls indicated voters thought very highly of Young, former Governor Guy employed a strategy of not attacking the Senator directly and instead concentrated his assaults on the seniority system. Yet this caution did not mean that Guy thought highly of Young, who in his opinion had snubbed him during his twelve years as Governor and had engineered Jungroth's candidacy to draw votes away from him. To this accusation Young replied that Guy " . . . is the most sanctimonious, pompous liar I ever knew in politics." The *Post's* article ended with a telling prediction: "Guy's polls show Jungroth getting little more than two percent of the vote. Should the gap between Young and Guy close considerably between now and November 5, Jungroth's role could be pivotal."[11] Five years later, Young recalled calling Guy a sanctimonious liar and commented "that was a pretty strong statement which may have hurt me. Even though it was the truth, I think the statement was the kind that hurt me."[12]

An article in the *New York Times* called the Guy-Young race "basically a popularity issue" with the independent vote becoming more important with the major party candidates drawing closer as reflected in the North Dakota Poll. While North Dakota's tradition of voting Republican should assist Young, it might not, the *Times* reported, because of Watergate. The paper also emphasized a statement made by Edwin W. Smith, President of North Dakota Farmers' Union: "I can't see how the Republicans can win. I think you will see a great swing. But Jim Jungroth is in there now and that really fouls things up."[13] Senator Young also saw that the distance between him and Guy was closing; and, even though he had been a successful candidate each time he ran for the Senate, in late October he declared that the contest shaped up as the toughest race of his career. He announced, "Guy is not a big vote getter. The reason why he is tough for me is Watergate, Agnew, Nixon and the pardon . . . It's surprising it looks so good at this point. I denounced the pardon and perhaps that saved me" (Young apparently no longer had qualms about the effect on the American image if Nixon were in a jail cell). Young estimated that he gained ground during October, but the issues surrounding Watergate for him meant a loss of ". . . at least a 10,000 votes . . . Guy wouldn't be any problem if it were not for that." To counter the age issue he continued to emphasize his seniority: "My whole thrust is what seniority has done for North Dakota." Turning to Jim Jungroth, Young said two-thirds of the twenty-thousand votes he expected Jungroth to attract would come from people who otherwise would have voted for Guy. During the final weeks of the campaign, Young planned to increase his advertising so he could "peak at the end."[14] One of the ads he used to deflect the age issue showed Young breaking an inch-thick board with his hand, employing karate-type expertise learned through his association with the art of Tae Kwon Do.[15] In addition, 1974 was the first campaign in which Young used buttons and billboards.

Young was able to increase his ad frequency in the final weeks of the campaign when Bismarck businessman Harold Schafer contributed $3,000 to the Republican State Committee. The committee used the money to purchase seven hundred and thirty one spots on North Dakota's top eleven radio stations and to run seven different spots with Schafer as the announcer urging the reelection of Senator Young. However, on each spot, Schafer also mentioned the names of Mark Andrews and Ben Wolf, asking for their reelection, for the election of Republican legislative candidates, and ending with the phrase, "Vote Republican." Because the entire state Republican slate was included in the ads, the amount required for a federal candidate to list as a contribution became only 1/124 of the $3,000. Young needed only to report a campaign contribution from the state committee of $24.19, and because Schafer contributed to a political party, no reporting requirement applied to his donation.[16]

After an earlier concern about turning out the Young vote, the Young campaign made one gesture to assist that effort. A form letter from Senator Young went out to Republican block workers in Grand Forks praising their efforts and assuring that if he won, it would "be because of all the work that friends like you are doing in my behalf."[17]

Notes

[1] Bill Tillottson, "Young Cites Assistance Of Local Campaigners," *Bismarck Tribune*, 7 September 1974, p. 1.

[2] Milton R. Young, Press Release, 9 September 1974, Folder 15, Box 503, MYP.

[3] Milton R. Young to Mrs. Carlyle Johnson, 12 1974, Folder 15, Box 503, MYP.

[4] Milton R. Young, Form Letter, 9 October 1974, Folder 21, Box 49, MYP.

[5] *Bismarck Tribune*, 9 November 1974, p. 1.

[6] "Pat's Caravan," Folder 16, Box 597, MYP.

[7] *Congressional Quarterly Weekly Report*, 12 October 1974, pp. 2785-2786.

[8] *Dickinson Press*, 21 September 1974, p. 1.

[9] John Dillin, "Sliding Economic, Political Fortune Keep Ford on Go; He Rushes to Aid Faltering Republicans on Campaign," *Christian Science Monitor*, Eastern Edition, 21 October 1974, p. 1, p. 7.

[10] "Republicans Fear Disaster In Their Own Stronghold," *U.S. News and World Report*, 21 October 1974, p. 40.

[11] Leroy F. Aarons, "Age Issue Dominates Race for Senate in North Dakota," *Washington Post*, 20 October 1974, p. A2.

[12] U.S. Senator Milton R. Young, interviewed by Dr. D. Jerome Tweton, 8 August 1979, transcribed tape recording, Folder 26, Box 794, MYP.

[13] James P. Sterba, "Young Battles to Retain North Dakota Senate Seat; Guy, Democrat and Independent Make Race Close One," *New York Times*, 22 October 1974, p. 30.

[14] Gary W. Clark, "Senator Combats Watergate; Young in Toughest Battle," *Bismarck Tribune*, 23 October 1974, p. 1.

[15] Earl Flowers, "Two Giants of North Dakota Politics, Young and Guy, Matched in Senate Race," *Medford (Ore.) Mail Tribune*, 24 October 1974, p. 68.

[16] Allan C. Young to Milton R. Young, 25 October 1974, Folder 20, Box 511, MYP.

[17] Milton R. Young to Grand Forks block workers, 26 October 1974, Folder 21, Box 490, MYP.

◆ 6 ◆

The Lead Slips Away:
Guy, Primary to General Election

Guy's campaign did make an effort to interject substantive issues into the contest with distribution of nine position papers from mid-August to mid-September[1] but practically none of the material appeared in the media. Door-to-door campaigning became part of Guy's style during the fall campaign. Along with local Democratic-NPL legislative candidates, Guy moved into a community's residential neighborhoods for several hours of knocking on doors and then went to the town's business district to shake hands with voters.[2] Party workers often arranged a luncheon featuring the U.S. Senate candidate, or Guy would appear before a service club. At these noontime events Guy continued to stress his themes of open government and the unfairness of the seniority system.[3] Guy regularly appeared on radio talk shows or did interviews with the station news people. He repeated that routine on cable TV and commercial stations where available.[4] In the evening he attended party dinners and/or rallies sponsored by local party officials as pep rallies or fundraisers.[5] These dinners usually did not function as money raising vehicles but as methods to bring out as many of the party faithful as possible to reinforce their enthusiasm, to display the candidate's popularity to the community and its press, and to demonstrate to the candidate the strength and effectiveness of that area's party structure.

A North Dakota Poll taken in August but not released until the second week of September revealed an even contest in the Senate race with

Young 49.8 to Guy's 45.9 percent and 4.3 undecided.[6] The survey did not include Jungroth's name nor Kenneth C. Gardner, a Drayton public school social sciences teacher, who obtained the required signatures and filed for the U.S. Senate race as a member of the Freedom and Liberty Party.[7] Just what effect these Independent candidates would have on the election's outcome remained uncertain; however, Austin Engel, executive secretary of the Democratic-NPL Party, in late September predicted the result could hinge on Jungroth, who might receive as many as ten thousand votes. The Democratic official viewed the contest between Guy and Young as "a close race" and said, "Those (Independent) votes are going to be crucial. They could spell the difference."[8]

Seniority as an issue remained alive and well as the fall campaign proceeded. In Wyndmere, a reporter asked Guy what he could offer voters in lieu of Senator Young's seniority. He answered that in the U.S. Senate a junior member of the majority could carry the same influence as a very senior member of the minority: "After all, a Senator from the minority party never gets to be chairman of a committee, no matter how long he stays." Then, to the reporter's surprise, Jean Guy commented that a young man with good ideas could have influence simply by studying situations and knowing what the state and country needed.[9] On the Republican side Young continued his version of seniority, telling a "meet the candidates" forum at UND's Editor Day, "The main thrust of my campaign is what seniority means to North Dakota."[10]

During September the Guys campaigned across North Dakota in a whirlwind fashion, reaping extensive coverage in weekly newspapers and some dailies. Also that month the Guy campaign announced the creation of various letterhead committees supporting Guy's candidacy; Farmers and Ranchers for Guy, Senior Citizens for Guy, Students for Guy, and Women for Guy.[11] The purpose of these committees rested solely on having as many newspapers as possible print the names of those on the committees; they performed no other function. As the month drew to a close Guy's schedule continued at a rapid pace. On September 30, his fifty-fifth birthday, Guy visited Carrington, Fessenden, and

Harvey, and flew to Wahpeton for a birthday party banquet. On the next day he campaigned in Turtle Lake, Underwood, and Garrison, and the day after he made stops in Parshall, New Town, and Stanley.[12]

Jungroth spoke out in late September to convince his fellow party members to abandon their support of Guy. Using his campaign motto, "North Dakota's not for sale," he declared that his efforts to beat Guy and Young did not make him look foolish and declared, "I want to win." His attacks centered more on Guy than Young, who, he believed, had "lost touch with North Dakota," and on some Democratic Party leaders for "straying from the principles of the working man and the small farmer. They talk like a bunch of Main Street Republicans." Drawing a good deal of support from environmentalists, Jungroth stressed energy as his key issue. Commenting on the requirement that candidates for federal office report publicly contributions of one-hundred dollars or more, the Jamestown attorney explained, "The only reason people want to know is for political reprisals; to find out who in their office gave to me. Nobody has to be afraid to give to my campaign."[13]

With its October 3 endorsement of William Guy for the U.S. Senate seat the *Mandan Morning Pioneer* became the first daily in North Dakota to take an editorial stand in the Senate race. The paper wrote that the former Governor "would be an articulate spokesman for the state" and signal "the culmination of a period of change in this state which became apparent when he was elected Governor in 1960." Turning its guns on Young, the *Pioneer* stated that he "is not only old . . . but over the years he has consistently voted against every type of social program to benefit the people or the institutional structure of this country." Concerning Jungroth, the paper declared that if he drew enough votes to elect Young, it "would be a serious blow to the two-party system in this state."[14]

Bernie Shellum, a Minneapolis-based journalist, offered a view of the U.S. Senate race in early October that explained what caused the Senator's problems at the national level with his party and reiterated Young's age as the main issue of the campaign. Democratic-NPL polls, not disputed by Republicans, gave Guy a significant lead over the incumbent and Jungroth. In fact, the public opinion polls themselves "played an extraordinary role in the campaign, which has been characterized by political intrigue and personal animosities." Shellum wrote that a Republican-sponsored poll (he did not specify which Republicans) conducted in 1973 gave Guy a wide margin over Young but had him losing when matched against Representative Mark Andrews. The reporter revealed that "though suppressed in North Dakota, the poll inspired a Washington-based campaign to derail Young's plan to run for reelection. The results started to show up in newspaper columns, which suggested that Young defer to Andrews." In reaction, Young announced that he would not accept funds from the Republican Senatorial Campaign Committee and did not allow a head-to-head debate between Guy and himself to be included in a poll taken by the North Dakota Republican Party in early 1974.[15]

In April, the Democratic-NPL commissioned a Washington pollster, Peter Hart, to take a sounding of North Dakota voters in which he found Guy favored over Young 53 to 36 percent. The poll "also provided the D-NPL with choice and unexpected information that has guided the entire Guy campaign: among potential voters the overwhelming argument against Young is his age." To avoid providing ammunition that might take Young out of the race, Guy's forces "suppressed leaking the results until after the primary." In early September another Democratic-NPL poll showed the same results as the April poll, indicating that in the crucial months since the first poll a shift in voters' preference had not occurred. Also important to the Guy strategy, the September poll "confirmed the importance of the age question, camouflaging it by asking North Dakotans if they favored mandatory retirement of Senators and House members at age 75. Three-fourths of those polled, said they favored such a law." Concerning the effect Jungroth would have on the election's outcome, Shellum consulted what he termed experienced politicians in the Guy and Young camps. One of them said about Jungroth, "He can't possibly get enough votes to affect the race one way or another."[16]

In June, information appeared in the national press that the Council for a Livable World (CLW), recognized as a liberal fundraising organization, selected former North Dakota Governor William Guy as one of the U.S. Senate challengers whom it endorsed.[17] The national story broke in North Dakota on October 2 that the Council for a Livable World recommended to supporters that they contribute to the Senatorial campaign of William Guy. During his 1970 reelection campaign Democratic Senator Quentin Burdick had received more than $20,000 from the CLW but returned the money because he did not agree with what he considered its policy of unilateral disarmament. Burdick could identify the contributions he received from the CLW supporters because the contributors funneled their checks through the CLW headquarters; members mailed to the CLW offices their checks that were in turn transmitted to Burdick's campaign. Announcing its endorsement of Guy in a newsletter, the CLW asked its supporters whose last name began A through F to contribute to the North Dakota Democrat, instructed them to make their checks payable to "Friends of Bill Guy," and noted Guy "requested that none of the contributions be for more than $100."[18]

Meeting in Harvey three days later, the North Dakota State Republican Committee passed a resolution asking Guy to "have the political courage and integrity to return any money which might come from the Council for a Livable World to his campaign." The committee went on to accuse Guy of supporting the CLW agenda, protesting, "The Council informing its members of Bill Guy's strong opposition to the antiballistic missile and to the war in Southeast Asia leaves little doubt about his commitment to the Council's issues."[19] On the eleventh, Guy announced in Fargo, "I consider it a high honor to be endorsed by the Council" and that its out-of-state members' contributions averaged $15.78 per donor. He recalled that at the beginning of his campaign he had said he would not accept contributions from political action committees or special interest groups and stated, "we have adhered to that strictly, and the Democratic-Nonpartisan League Party has adopted that as its policy."[20]

Speaking to a Democratic-NPL district eighteen (City of Grand Forks) fundraiser the next evening, Guy made front page news as he characterized the CLW as an organization of "common interest," not a special interest group nor radicals. He then explained:

> They are only Joe and Jane Citizen from all 50 states. They do not back candidates as an organization, but as individual members. Their track record shows they endorse progressives in both parties. They've issued no demands as to what a candidate must believe in.
>
> Endorsements by common interests are important and legitimate. They then let their individual members make contributions as they like - that's perfectly alright.[21]

He said his endorsement by the Council and contributions from its individual members could be compared to ". . . a farm organization endorsing me and urging its members to support me with their checks. That would be proper. But if that farm organization were to levy against all its membership and then let a board decide to support one candidate with a block grant - that's not acceptable to me." Guy charged that Senator Young received such support from the defense industry and eastern banks. He admitted that an aide had contacted CLW officials concerning Republican allegations that the CLW supported unilateral disarmament and ". . . they said absolutely not. They said the Council is for a strong America." Guy charged that the *Grand Forks Herald* handled the disclosure of the CLW involvement in his campaign poorly.[22]

Several days later, in an editorial very critical of Guy, the *Bismarck Tribune* commented, "What is significant now, however, is that though federal law requires disclosure even of earmarked contributions, Guy has never yet reported a single contribution mailed him by the Council for a Livable World - though the Council raised more than $25,000 for him."[23] Joining the criticism of Guy's method of handling his contributions, the *Forum's* editorial on October 18 revealed that an associate of Jungroth's had visited the Council's headquarters in Washington, hoping to enlist its support for Jungroth's candidacy. He learned that CLW support could not be given to the Jamestown attorney because of the Council's prior endorsement of Guy. Jungroth then watched Guy's financial reports for indications of contributions from CLW members and noticed that the amounts received from donations under one hundred dollars jumped from just several-thousand dollars to nineteen thousand dollars in one reporting period. From this he concluded that the transfer of funds from the Council to the Friends of William Guy constituted ". . . a clumsy attempt at 'laundering' the source of the money." Jungroth took strong exception to the "hypocrisy" involved when Guy did not report the donations.[24]

The *Forum* editorial agreed with Jungroth's assessment and quoted a Guy campaign ad that sought financial contributions two days before the primary:

> Recent events in Washington have exposed the tremendous power special interest groups gained through political campaign contributions. This power can be curbed only through the cooperation of candidates and citizens.
>
> We are taking the first steps toward election reform in my campaign for the U.S. Senate. We have decided to conduct our campaign without contributions from interest groups even though their political action funds are perfectly legal under the present laws. Rather, we will rely on financial support of individual citizens to support us in this campaign.[25]

On the evening of October 22, after he had made his opening statement, the first question put to Guy on a Bismarck TV "Meet the Candidates" program dealt with the former Governor's acceptance of $25,000 from the Council for a Livable World, an explanation of what the Council stood for, and if it asked "for any commitment from you in exchange for their support." Guy began his answer inaccurately, identifying the Council's founder, Leo Szilard, as the man who asked President Roosevelt to appoint Albert Einstein to head the Manhattan Project that built the atomic bomb. Guy then correctly identified Szilard's concern with the prevention of nuclear war as the major factor in the formation of the CLW. He went on to defend both the Council's philosophy and his acceptance of the money sent to his campaign by

Council supporters, admitting, "I didn't realize that more than 1,600 Americans from all over the country would send me money as members of the Council for a Livable World that would total as much as they did."[26] As October drew to an end Jungroth held a press conference in Jamestown, announcing that he had notified Francis R. Valeu, Secretary of the U.S. Senate, of ". . . alleged violations involved in Council for a Livable World contributions" to Guy's campaign and that "I have been informed by the Secretary of the U.S. Senate's office that the auditors are now reviewing such earmarked contributions."[27] Robert L. Valeu, Guy's campaign manager, the next day quickly responded, announcing he ". . . had filed a formal complaint with the Fair Campaign Practices Committee at Washington, D.C., regarding accusations by James Jungroth." Valeu also charged, "James Jungroth, just seven days before the election, committed character assassination on Governor Guy when he falsely accused the Guy campaign of violating the federal campaign reporting law."[28]

Guy's interruption of his campaign schedule to call a press conference in Fargo just five days before the election reflected the importance he placed on the CLW issue. He felt it necessary to deal with the information in a letter from Valeu to the chairman of the North Dakota Republican Party. Valeu noted that while the funds Guy received did not pass through the Council's bank account, they were earmarked funds according to the federal regulations manual and were thereby subject to reporting requirements on the part of the Council. The letter continued, "In the interest of reasonable and timely disclosure, this office is requesting such committee to report promptly the total amount of funds forwarded to each candidate. In the future recipient candidates will be required to disclose the fact that reportable contributions in excess of $100 have been forwarded through an intermediary committee."[29]

Guy claimed that the charges against him made by Jungroth and the Republicans that he had violated federal campaign financing regulations contained no substance. He explained, "I must state that a letter from the Secretary of the U.S. Senate reaffirms our position that the Guy campaign financing and accounting set up by a certified public accounting firm, in accordance with federal law, continues to more than comply with federal law. We have not violated any law." He believed Jungroth had made the charges as a ". . . trumped up diversionary tactic . . . to divert voters from the real issues of the campaign."[30] The next afternoon, at a Grand Forks press conference, Minnesota Democratic Senator Walter Mondale, campaigning for Guy, said that if he were conducting a reelection campaign and the CLW supporters offered him donations, "I'd accept and be honored." Referring to the Council, Mondale stated it "is one of the most farsighted organizations in the country. It's made up of individuals from all over the country who are trying to prevent waste in the Defense Department. It wants a strong defense, but it doesn't want waste. It wants defense and detente."[31] Mondale made the final reference in the month-long controversy, but again Guy had diverted his time to answering charges rather than concentrating on Young's defeat.

During the second week of October the weeklies of the North Dakota Poll reported that their latest findings showed Guy 45.9, Young 45.9, and Jungroth 2.1 percent.[32] Several weeks later the editor of *Cass County Reporter* asked Guy why the North Dakota Poll indicated his popularity had risen four percent from September to October. He answered:

> You have to remember that the poll usually has a five percent Republican bias so we're even farther ahead. I really discount the changes in the poll, however, because it's not really scientific. This campaign is fairly well locked in and I think we'll see some desperation politics in the last ten days but think it will not change anything . . . desperation politics by my opponent I might add. I regard Jungroth and Young as a coordinated team out to beat me. Their joining together signifies the desperation of the Republican Party in this state.[33]

If doubtful about the accuracy of the North Dakota Poll, Guy displayed full confidence when he stated he would win a "substantial" victory because "we know from our polls already that the votes are here. It is a matter of turning them out."[34]

Congressional Quarterly equated Jungroth's shoestring campaign with a noose which if successful would ". . . throttle Senate hopes of Guy, a long-time political enemy of Jungroth." Having high hopes at the time Guy announced, Democrats felt 1974 would be the year they could pick off "Mr. Wheat." With Jungroth's entrance into the race in August their optimism cooled, but by mid-October it appeared that the former Democratic state chairman did not have the anticipated impact. Republicans viewed Jungroth's presence on the ballot as a device to siphon voters away from Guy, while Democrats saw him taking votes from Guy and Young because he attacked both men. Jungroth, found ". . . very little difference between the two-party endorsed candidates except for age, seniority and party affiliation."[35] Recapping and handicapping tight U.S. Senate races across the country, *Time* magazine observed that while Democratic challenger former Governor Guy did not say it directly, his principle issue was Senator Milton Young's age. Guy's campaign emphasized it repeatedly with the slogan of a need for a "future" leader. The national news weekly rated Guy as the leader because of Young's inability to fend off the age issue.[36]

Maintaining that age would not be an issue when he entered the Senate race, Guy's final campaign ads stressed the point. In a four-column-by-twelve-inch ad the headline stated, "For vigorous new leadership a proven leader . . . for the future." After briefly mentioning Guy's record as chairman of the Midwest Governors' Conference and his activities with the National Governors' Conference, the ad continued that "the time has come for North Dakota to look to the future by renewing its leadership in the U.S. Senate . . . Bill Guy can step into the U.S. Senate well-known and well-respected by its leaders . . . he will simply pick up where Milton Young leaves off."[37]

On October 31, Guy predicted that fellow Democrat U.S. Senator Quentin Burdick would endorse his candidacy which would ". . . be very beneficial to my race." Guy said that Congressional business had not permitted Burdick to campaign actively for him but that in any event he would be elected by a "significant margin."[38] As forecast, Senator Burdick five days before the election appeared before a fifth district

Democratic-NPL luncheon in Minot and announced that North Dakotans should elect the former Governor to the U.S. Senate, where he would be ". . . not only a North Dakota Senator but a United States Senator."[39] Not placing all their hopes in Burdick's less than ringing endorsement, the Guy campaign made a defensive move the next day. Guy's campaign chairman, George Sinner, charged Jungroth and Young with conspiring to defeat the former Governor and explained, "If this weren't so serious, I assure you I wouldn't make the accusation." Sinner admitted he did not have tangible evidence of collusion but knew of brothers-in-law, one of whom had worked in the Jungroth campaign and one in the Young campaign. In response, Young thundered, "It is difficult to understand how any reasonable person could blame me for all the troubles within the Democratic Party. When serious charges are levied against Guy involving his honesty and integrity, his only answer is a diversionary counter-attack and more spots on television sanctimoniously telling the people how pure he is."[40]

On the Saturday prior to election day the *Minot Daily News* announced in large bold headlines that a poll it had commissioned from the University of North Dakota's Bureau of Governmental Affairs showed the Senate race too close to call because of the size of the undecided vote.[41] In his political column that day Dobson commented on the tenor of the Senate campaign:

> This has been a strange campaign. It has been a campaign largely devoid of substantive issues. Inflation is probably the foremost problem, but it's difficult to start an argument about it. Nobody is for it.
>
> Most of the political debate in this post-Watergate autumn has been over campaign financing. Each candidate strives to appear purer than his foe. Actually, it's pretty much a pot vs. kettle contest.

He went on to note that the sizable margin Guy had held over Young during the summer and early fall seemed to be declining with Young's effort picking up "momentum" in the closing weeks of the campaign. Dobson continued, "The Senator's campaign was nicely orchestrated to 'peak' in the final fortnight. The race has now become what many spectators felt all along; it would be a toss up." He did not predict the outcome but forecast a total vote of 250,000 and urged his readers to watch the results from Barnes County, which he termed a bellweather along with Cass and Ward counties for indications of which candidate would win.[42]

An Associated Press article from Washington predicted Guy would win North Dakota's Senate race but expected Jungroth to pull votes away from him.[43] Secretary of State Ben Meier forecasted that voter turnout would be "about 225,000" compared to 289,205 in the Presidential election year 1972 and 225,859 in the off-year 1970.[44] Senator Young in New Rockford at his last rally as a candidate told his audience, "I am encouraged by polls taken in the last two weeks and other developments which indicate I will win, although there are no cinches in politics."[45] Guy said the 1974 campaign for the U.S. Senate had created more interest than any previous campaign in which he had been involved.[46]

As election day - Tuesday, November 5, 1974 - dawned, low clouds and fog greeted North Dakota's early voters.[47] According to morning reports from Wahpeton, Fargo, Minot, Williston, and Devils Lake, voter turnout was running ahead of the 1970 pace.[48]

Notes

[1] Campaign Position Papers, Folder 9, Box 1, Democratic Nonpartisan League Party Papers, Orin G. Libby Manuscript Collection, Elwyn B. Robinson Department of Special Collections, Chester Fritz Library, University of North Dakota, Grand Forks, North Dakota.

[2] *West Fargo Pioneer*, 11 September 1974, Clipping, Folder 10, Box 597, MYP.

[3] *Jamestown Sun*, 13 September 1974, Clipping, Folder 10, Box 597, MYP.

[4] Ibid., 17 September 1974.

[5] *Cooperstown (N.D.) Griggs County Sentinel Courier*, 11 September 1974, p. 6.

[6] *Stanley (N.D.) Mountrail County Promoter*, 11 September 1974, Clipping, Folder 13, Box 597, MYP.

[7] "Gardner Against Tax Proposed," *Grand Forks Herald*, 1 November 1974, p. 7.

[8] *Williston Daily Herald*, 26 September 1974, p. 4.

[9] Louise Frost, "Over the Back Fence," *Lidgerwood Monitor*, 12 September 1974, Clipping, Folder 8, Box 597, MYP.

[10] "Young Cites Seniority in Editor's Talk," *Bismarck Tribune*, 14 September 1974, p. 5.

[11] Clippings, Folder 10, Box 597, and Folder 6, Box 598, MYP.

[12] *Minot Daily News*, 28 September 1974, p. 3.

[13] Stuart Smith, "Staunchly Opposes Strip Mining: Jungroth Runs Against Guy, Young Because of Coal Issue," *Grand Forks Herald*, 29 September 1974, p. 11.

[14] "An Editorial," *Mandan (N.D.) Morning Pioneer*, Clipping, Folder 1, Box 598, MYP.

[15] Bernie Shellum, "Can Karate Cut Age Issue for a Not-So-Young Young?", *Minneapolis Tribune*, 6 October 1974, p. 1, 4A.

[16] Ibid.

[17] *Congressional Quarterly Weekly Report*, 15 June 1974, p. 1552.

[18] Jack Hagerty, "In My Book," *Grand Forks Herald*, 2 October 1974, p. 6.

[19] *Dickinson Press*, 9 October 1974, p. 9.

[20] "Clayburgh 'Socked' by Remark," *Grand Forks Herald*, 12 October 1974, p. 4.

[21] Chuck Haga, "Guy Defends Receipt of Contribution," *Grand Forks Herald*, 13 October 1974, p. 1.

[22] Ibid.

[23] Editorial "Secret Funds Become Public," *Bismarck Tribune*, 15 October 1974, p. 4.

[24] "Forum Editorial: There's a Difference Between Pledges, Performance in Case of U.S. Senate Candidate Guy," *Fargo (N.D.) Forum*, 18 October 1974, p. 4.

[25] Ibid.

[26] KFYR-TV Bismarck, "Meet the Candidate, William Guy The Guest," 7:00-7:30 p.m., 22 October 1974, p. 2, 3, Transcript, Folder 19, Box 511, MYP.

[27] Bill Tillottson, "Guy Distorts Truth to Win, Says Jungroth," *Bismarck Tribune*, 29 October 1974, p. 1.

[28] *Jamestown Sun*, 30 October 1974, Clipping, Folder 6, Box 598,

[29] "Guy Refutes Charges On Campaign Money," *Fargo (N.D.) Forum*, 1 November 1974, p. 13.

[30] Ibid.

[31] Chuck Haga, "Guy Will be Recognized as Leader in U.S. Senate, Sen. Mondale Says," *Grand Forks Herald*, 2 November 1974, p. 1.

[32] *Casselton (N.D.) Cass County Reporter*, 11 October 1974, Clipping, Folder 6, Box 598, MYP.

[33] Gary Wright, "William Guy Critical of Senate Seniority System," *Grafton Record*, 31 October 1974, Clipping, Folder 6, Box 598, MYP.

[34] Ibid.

[35] *Congressional Quarterly Weekly Report*, 12 October 1974, pp. 2784-2786.

[36] *Time*, 21 October 1974, pp. 35, 36.

[37] *Hillsboro Banner*, 31 October 1974, p. 9.

[38] "State Campaigns Nearing Wrapup," *Bismarck Tribune*, 31 October 1974, p. 2.

[39] "Burdick Endorses Guy," *Minot Daily News*, 1 November 1974, p.12.

[40] "Sinner, Guy Aide, Sees Conspiracy," *Minot Daily News*, 2 November 1974, p. 3.

[41] Dick Dobson, "Young And Guy Race Tossups-Polls Shows Undecided Hold Key; Andrews and Knutson Ahead," *Minot Daily News*, 2 November 1974, p. 1.

[42] Dick Dobson, "Prairie Perspective: Guy-Young Contest Undecided," *Minot Daily News*, 2 November 1974, p. 3.

[43] Carl P. Leubsdorf, "State-By-State Summary on Key Election Contests," *Fargo (N.D.) Forum*, 3 November 1974, pp. A-16, 17.

[44] Jim Willis, "Election Spending Nearly $1 Million Average Turnout Foreseen," *Bismarck Tribune*, 2 November 1974, p. 3.

[45] "Political Roundup," *Minot Daily News*, 4 November 1974, p. 15.

[46] Jim Willis, "Decision Day On Tuesday: Mild Weather Seen; 225,000 Turnout Predicted," *Bismarck Tribune*, 4 November 1974, p. 1.

[47] Jim Willis, "Andrews vs. Dorgan Also Highlight on State Ballot; N.D. Vote Spotlights Young-Guy Race - Two Will Win, Two Will Lose," *Williston Daily Herald*, 5 November 1974, p. 1.

[48] "Vote Heavy Locally and Around N.D.," *Grand Forks Herald*, 5 November 1974, p. 1.

◆ 7 ◆

Confusion:
The Recount

As the first scattered returns from 687 precincts came in on election night, Young took a 500-vote lead, but as the number of reporting precincts increased, Guy moved ahead and steadily pulled away. At 2:50 a.m. the next day Guy's margin over Young lengthened to 2,700, at which point the Associated Press declared him the victor. But, as the count continued, that lead diminished. When the AP closed its election night reporting bureau, Guy's margin stood at 1,200. When counting resumed later in the morning, it slipped to 801 by 11 a.m.; at that point confusion took command as to who had won the Senate seat.[1] By early afternoon the AP counted Young ahead by four votes, with the totals Young 114,670, Guy 114,666, Jungroth 6,576, and Gardner 858.[2] Nationally, the AP stated, "In North Dakota, Senator Milton Young, one of the Senate's most senior Republicans, was unseated . . . beaten in his bid for a fifth full term by former Governor William Guy, 55, after a campaign in which age was the dominant issue."[3] A more accurate assessment appeared in a Williston weekly:

> Right now, at this moment at 4:30 p.m. Wednesday, as the newspaper goes to press, William Guy has 14 more votes than Senator Young.
>
> That's an unofficial tally.
>
> Naturally there will be mistakes on both sides when the canvassing boards meet within the next few days. And there still are some absentee voters ballots to be counted.[4]

In the early morning hours of that day Jack Hagerty wrote:

... it is apparent that - unless there has been a massive error in the unofficial tabulation - Sen. Milton R. Young has been defeated for reelection. It is the first time he ever has been beaten for reelection to an office he has held in a political career extending back more than half a century. And we are sad, for Mr. Young, for North Dakota and for the nation.

But we offer our congratulations to former Gov. William L. Guy, the victor by a narrow margin. Like Senator Young, he has had an all-winning political career for the past 20 years, having served four terms as governor and now, after a two-year layoff from public office, winning his way to the Senate.[5]

The next day Young pulled ahead and Hagerty opened his column "WOOPS! Hold on to your hat"; he noted that the winner in the Senate contest would have such a small margin that the state could expect a recount after the State Canvass Board issued its report. He ended the column, ". . . we accepted the AP's decision Wednesday morning to the extent of saying Guy apparently had been elected and offering our congratulations. Whatever happens in the next five weeks or so, those congratulations stand for making such an exciting race of it."[6]

According to North Dakota statute, each county's canvassing board, consisting of Democratic and Republican district chairmen, clerks of the county courts, and chairmen of the county commissions, would convene within seven days after the election. The boards did not handle the actual ballots, which remained in the custody of the county judges, but verified that the figures in the poll books agreed with the slash marks, and corrected any errors. In addition, if the county auditor received absentee ballots postmarked prior to election day, the board would open the ballots and add them to the official tallies.[7] All of the canvass boards' reports had to be received in the Secretary of State's office by November 13, and the State Canvass Board's report was due by November 19; candidate recount requests could not be submitted until after the State Canvass Board had completed its work.[8]

When the first county canvassing board meeting in Bowman increased Young's lead over Guy by six votes (Guy lost five and Young picked up one), providing the Senator a 96-vote edge, state officials and both candidates fixed their attention on the canvass boards. Governor Arthur Link, Secretary of State Ben Meier, and Attorney General Allen Olson issued a joint statement that urged election officials to take ". . . 'extreme care' and to be 'vigilant' " in the handling and counting of ballots. Meier warned, "It is vital that every precaution be taken in processing election returns correctly." Guy reflected his concern: "I just hope all the judges in the election precincts recognize the seriousness of the situation and keep tight security on the ballots." This, of course, was an unnecessary admonition since election-day judges did not at any time have possession of the ballots. Young showed no less concern (or more understanding of the process) over the operations of the canvass boards and expressed suspicion of vote totals that seesawed. He declared, "I want to check all of these counties personally. It surprises me that a county can change its votes like this. They are supposed to have those ballot boxes sealed and with the county auditors after the votes have been counted."[9]

Five days after the election, with 48 of 53 county canvass boards reporting, the incumbent held a 240-vote margin over the challenger.[10] That very narrow margin turned attention to North Dakota's recount statute passed in 1971 and amended in 1973. It provided that if in a Congressional election the spread between the winner and the next candidate was less than .005 percent, the runnerup could request a recount within ten days after the State Canvass Board's report. The legislation required the applicant to make a demand in writing to each appropriate district judge in North Dakota's six judicial districts. When the recounting of the ballots took place, the county canvass boards, or other persons named by the judge, would open and count the ballots in the judge's presence. Candidates or their representatives could challenge ballots which would then be presented to the judge for his decision whether or not they would be included in the final tally. When completed, within fifteen days of receiving the recount application, the judge would certify the results to the Secretary of State.[11] However, the statute did not require a record to be made of the judge's rulings on challenged ballots, nor contain provisions for an appeal of the rulings, thus making it difficult for the state's Supreme Court to make discretionary rulings in an appeals case.[12]

After the election, in a letter to the editor distributed across the state, Guy wrote:

> The final outcome of the United States Senate race will not be known for several weeks. My wife Jean and I extend our sympathy to Senator Young and his wife Pat for the anguish that this waiting period is causing them. It is hard to get on with life as usual while this matter hangs in the balance.
>
> . . . Looking back, I don't think we would carry out our campaign any differently. We stuck to the issues and the voting records. That's what our American system of free democratic elections should be all about. We had a great go at it - and no matter what the final outcome might be - my wife and I have no regrets.[13]

To a vastly more restricted audience Young expressed himself in the *Kulm Messenger*:

> This was my last campaign for public office. You have always given me a good majority ever since I first ran for the Legislature in 1932.
>
> Win or lose in the recount, I want to express my deepest appreciation to my friends and neighbors all over LaMoure County who have supported me all these years - through all these campaigns your friendship and support has meant more to me during my public life than anything else.[14]

The mood of gratefulness and reflection did not prevail as the ever-lengthening 1974 Senate contest continued.

Ten days after the election the Secretary of State released the 53 county canvass board results, which put Senator Young ahead of former Governor Guy by 176 votes. Young knew Guy would request a recount, but Guy announced that his decision concerning a recount would not be made until after he had consulted with the state Democratic Policy Committee. The Senator commented that he believed a recount would not change the outcome of the election, while Guy observed that he did not expect any major change and added, "I've been in politics many years, and I'm conditioned to accept things as they come." Young declared, ". . . the swarm of COPE workers and Farmers Union leadership" caused the close election, but he reflected, "I was pleased that I got that big a vote with that kind of opposition."[15] When the Democratic-NPL State Committee met in Bismarck, it urged Guy to ask for a recount of the U.S. Senate election.[16]

Looking ahead, political reporter Dobson predicted what he believed would occur during the recount, focusing his attention on totals from machine and paper ballots separately. In the 114 precincts that used voting machines, Guy led Young 41,203 to 37,982, but in 1,529 polling places that used paper ballots, accounting for 65 percent of the total votes cast, Young led Guy 76,868 to 73,472. Because recounting voting machines just involved rechecking printout totals, Dobson doubted those counts would vary from the reports of the canvass board. However, in the case of paper ballots several possibilities presented themselves for challenges that could result in ballots being disallowed. Ballots could be thrown out if not initialed or stamped by election officials, if the voter placed the "X" outside the box provided, or if the voter's candidate selection could not be determined; the recount would also correct any tallies previously miscounted. Because of those elements, Dobson concluded that Guy would be in the best position to increase his total.[17]

The State Canvass Board, chaired by the Secretary of State and composed of the two political party chairmen, the State Treasurer, and the clerk of the State Supreme Court, met during the morning of November 19. It reported Milton Young the winner in the U.S. Senate election by a margin of 177 votes - 114,852 votes for Young to Guy's 114,675. Because the winning margin was less than one-half of one percent, Guy could avail himself of North Dakota's recount statute, which gave him ten days to petition the district courts for a recount.[18] That same day Young told a Washington-based reporter that he planned to ask the Senate's Rules Committee, Privileges and Elections Subcommittee to send observers to be present at the recount. He expressed concern over recount procedures, noting that Democratic Governor Arthur Link would select the six judges who would have "final authority" over the recount outcome. Contacted at his home in Casselton, Guy joined Young in requesting that observers be sent by the Rules Committee to oversee the recount but corrected him on his statement concerning Link. Guy explained that Young was ". . . misinformed when he says that Governor Link has anything to do with the recount . . . only the Supreme Court can name lead judges in each Judicial district." He went on to say lead (presiding judge of a North Dakota Judicial District) judges came from the state's nineteen judges but ". . . are not named because of the recount, but to have supervisory responsibility for all judicial affairs in their districts." The lead judges, Guy said, would establish procedures governing the recount, but "the actual responsibility for overseeing rests individually with the 19 district judges."[19] When the recount took place, the lead judges both set the recount procedures and conducted it.

The following day Young again voiced his concern that Guy, as Governor, had appointed many of the district judges and so had Governor Link. He related, "I am somewhat concerned about the recount law itself. For example, Bill Guy can pick the six judges for the recount but I have no recourse." Yet he did add, "I have every confidence in all the judges."[20] That prompted both Guy and Link to issue statements that they resented Young's implications.[21] Infuriated, the Senator issued a blistering statement from his Washington office, proclaiming that Guy and Link deliberately tried ". . . to discredit me with the recount judges and the public." Quoting from letters he had sent to both Democrats, Young's release lashed out:

> According to press statements, you charged that I question the integrity of the district judges who will handle the forthcoming recount of votes for my U.S. Senate seat.
> This is a complete misrepresentation of my position. On at least two occasions I have publicly expressed confidence in the judges' integrity.[22]

He repeated his concern that Guy had selected the six judges who would handle the recount and that in the recount procedure he did not have an equal voice in their selection. Additionally, Young observed, "The most serious objection to the procedure . . . is each judicial district has sole and final jurisdiction over the validity of the contested ballots." He noted that the statute did not contain a "specific provision" for an appeal which upset him because "a cardinal principle of our judicial system is the right of appeal, which is denied under this statute."[23] Senator Young did not understand the recount legislation.

In preparation for the recount, Guy employed Fargo attorney P. W. (Bill) Lanier, Jr., as his chief counsel, and Young hired a Jamestown attorney, Kenneth M. Moran, as his principal counsel. The Guy camp established a William Guy Recount Center in the former Democratic-NPL headquarters in Fargo to organize volunteers who would represent Guy at all 53 county recounts. Moran followed a different strategy and selected an attorney in each of the six judicial districts who would be personally involved in the recount proceedings.[24] Meeting in Bismarck, the six presiding (leading) district judges drew up the rules by which recount procedures would be conducted. Once an official demand reached a presiding judge, he would issue a directive to each county auditor in his district to deliver the general election ballots and the poll books to the district court. Proceedings would be open to the public and subject to rules maintaining order. Candidates would be allowed representatives who could challenge ballots upon which the judge would then rule; an exhibit number would be assigned to each challenged ballot; and an official record would be made of each decision.[25] North Dakota's district courts were prepared to accept a petition for a recount.

On Wednesday, November 27, twenty-two days after the general election, Guy set the wheels in motion to decide who had won the election. He sent a formal demand for a recount to Secretary of State Ben Meier and an application for a recount to the six presiding judges on this day before Thanksgiving.[26] On the day after Thanksgiving, District Judge Ralph B. Maxwell began recounting ballots in Fargo, where Guy and his recount manager David Strauss looked on as one of Young's attorneys, Frank Magill, made a motion challenging the constitutionality of North Dakota's recount statute. Judge Maxwell denied that motion.[27] After two days work, Steele County became the first to have its ballots recounted; Guy added one vote to his tally.[28] Four days into the recount two themes emerged. One dealt with judges rejecting paper ballots on which the voter had marked more than one U.S. Senate candidate. The make-up of the ballot gave Young and Guy a separate column each but both independent candidate names appeared in the third column. Even though "vote for one" appeared at the top of the ballot, some voters apparently selected either Young or Guy and then marked their preference for one of the independents in the third column. Three recount centers reported this phenomenon and it damaged Guy's count. He observed that the ballot make-up ". . . did lend to the confusion of some voters," and his recount manager went to the heart of the matter pointing out, "It's killing us."

The other theme involved daily reporting of who gained or lost votes; the press, however, did not have an ability to identify what daily results meant vis-a-vis the final result.[29] Headlines gave a sense of election night returns: "Young Recount Lead Gains 5," "Ramsey County Recount Shows Gain for Young," and "Young Lead Drops to 160." Such reporting reflected a sense of excitement without offering a trend that could indicate who would finally win.[30] When recounts of 37 counties had been completed their results could only be compared to the totals previously reported by the State Canvass Board, putting Young's lead at 177 votes.[31] On December 10, with 44 counties recounted, Young's lead increased to 201, but the next day, as the completion of ordeal neared, Young's margin fell to 185.[32]

The suspense ended at 6 p.m. on December 11, thirteen days after the recount began and two days before the statutory deadline. "It's Young by 186, Recount Shows," announced the *Bismarck Tribune*, reporting Young's final total of 114,117 votes to Guy's 113,931; in November the State Canvass Board, however, placed the total at Young, 114,852; Guy, 114,675.[33] Secretary of State Ben Meier announced that he intended to reconvene the State Canvass Board as quickly as possible.[34]

During the recount process Senator Young made no public comments, but after its completion he released this statement:

> I am most grateful to the people of North Dakota for reelecting me to the United States Senate. My razor-edge majority is not like the more than 60-percent margins I have received in every election in the last 30 years. This was the worst possible year for an incumbent Republican to be seeking reelection and especially when I had a formidable opponent.
>
> This was the longest and most difficult campaign I have ever been involved in and I am happy it is over.
>
> I plan to continue working hard in the Senate the same as I always have, using my position of seniority to help people with their problems as well as the State of North Dakota and its communities.[35]

In a telephone interview the day before the meeting of the State Canvass Board, Richard Ista suggested he did not consider the door closed to further challenges of the recount results. However, Ista made it clear that "the ultimate decision will be made by Bill Guy and he won't make a decision until after the weekend."[36] But Guy did not delay his decision and held a press conference in Fargo on Friday afternoon, December 13, saying he did not plan to challenge the recount results. He then presented his prepared statement:

> I wanted to win that election and it would be dishonest of me if I said I was not deeply disappointed to lose.
>
> It is difficult to understand the figures that swirl around a statewide recount unless you follow the process very closely. For instance there was a shrinkage of 1,479 votes from the State Canvassing Board totals. But this figure does not reveal that 1,884 votes were rejected . . . because the voters had voted accidentally for two candidates for the U.S. Senate instead of only one. The double vote tabulation shows that 710 voters cast their ballots for Milton Young and either Gardner or Jungroth. But a whopping 1,174 voters cast a double vote for William Guy and either Gardner or Jungroth. Many of those double votes were rejected at the precinct level and do not show up in the shrinkage of the State Canvassing Board.
>
> Even though Senator Young will be declared the winner, it is consoling to me to know that more voters turned out on Election Day and put their X behind the

name of William Guy than turned out and put their X behind the name of Milton Young. By voter preference, I won the election but by the technicality of the law, I lost it.[37]

Next Guy took aim at what he viewed as one of the primary reasons for his defeat:

James Jungroth, a former Democratic Party official and recipient of much Democratic Party patronage over the years, also added to the confusion. Many Democratic voters did not realize that he had turned against his party. They thought he was running against Gardner and not against Guy. It will be interesting to see how the Republicans show their appreciation to Jim Jungroth in the years ahead.

He expressed his appreciation for the efforts of the party and volunteers who worked for him. Taking a philosophical look at the campaign, Guy reflected that for himself and his wife, "We have no regrets at all - only great memories and satisfaction in the achievements we've made. Our plans for the future are indefinite. As soon as we get on top of the mountain of work that has accumulated this past year we've been campaigning, we will take a couple weeks of vacation."[38] In a question and answer session that followed, Guy reiterated his belief of what had actually happened on Election Day: "If all the voting had been by machine, I would have won."[39]

Because the recount statute did not state how the results of a recount should be certified, Attorney General Allen I. Olson advised Meier to recall the State Canvass Board to make the recount tallies official. Consequently, as the former Governor held the last press conference of the campaign, the board reconvened in Meier's office. Immediately after Meier called the board to order, state Democratic Party Chairman Richard Ista declared, "My participation on the canvass shall be under protest. It is my opinion the recount figures as provided by the judges . . . in the recount are not accurate." He cited reasons to support his contention: judges had permitted uninitiated ballots in voting machine precincts to be counted contrary to state law; judges had exhibited extreme inconsistencies in allowing ballots to be counted because of errors on the part of local election officials; in the case of double voting, voter intent had not been protected, and the recount statute did not provide for judicial appeal. Stressing his dissatisfaction, Ista continued, "It is also my opinion that the judges were acting in an administrative position and not in a judicial capacity and directly ruled part of North Dakota election laws unconstitutional by allowing uninitiated ballots to be counted." After completion of the canvass that certified Young the winner, Ista refused to sign the canvass, declaring, "I don't think a winner has been selected . . . therefore I feel the rights of William L. Guy have been taken away from him as well as (the rights) of the Democratic Party." The last of the board members to sign the canvass, the Republican Party representative, commented, "I feel the judicial system in North Dakota is adequate, the judges were honest and they conducted the recount." Ista shot back, "In no way am I challenging the ethics of the judges."[40] Three days later, on December 15, Governor Link certified to the U.S. Senate that North Dakotans had elected Milton R. Young on November 5.[41]

An early explanation of why Senator Young had done better than polls predicted came from Lloyd Omdahl. He saw the late concentration of Young's direct mailings, newspaper ads, and TV spots as responsible for the surge. Omdahl noted that Young deflected Guy's essentially low key attack on the age issue by promoting his Washington experience and seniority. Young's press secretary, Bill Wright, credited his boss' diminution of Guy's lead to the conduct of a ". . . well-planned campaign that was intended to peak late, and he broke his neck getting around the state, showing that he's healthy."[42] Jungroth commented on his impact on the outcome: "I don't know if I'm the difference in this race . . . the difference I made in this election is that I said essentially 'pox on both houses.' Maybe I added a little leavening to the race."[43] Both independent candidates disputed Guy's contention regarding the double voting issue. Jungroth spoke right to the point: "It's terribly presumptive on his part for him to believe he was going to get all those votes. How can he say that those votes would not have gone to either myself or

Mr. Gardner if there had been only one vote? There was a legitimate following for both of us." In a prepared statement, Jungroth struck back at Guy's suggestion that he expected future favors from the Republican Party: "As to the innuendo that I have or had some arrangement with Young or the Republican Party for a job, I state categorically that I do not have nor have I ever had any such desire for a political job, other than U.S. Senator. Nor did I have any relationship with Young or with the Republican Party other than as political opponents."[44]

Only two incumbent U.S. Senators, both Republicans, lost their reelection bids in the 1974 general election: Marlow W. Cook of Kentucky and Peter H. Dominick of Colorado.[45] Across the country voting by those eligible to vote was the smallest percent since 1942.[46] North Dakota did not follow the national trend.

1974 North Dakota U.S. Senate Election[47]

Milton R. Young (R)	114,117	48.4 percent
William L. Guy (D)	113,931	48.3 percent
James R. Jungroth (Ind.)	6,739	2.9 percent
K. C. Gardner (Freedom and Liberty)	874	.4 percent

The voter turnout of 1974 topped that of 1970 by nearly ten thousand votes and was higher than Meier's prediction by the same amount. Considering the funds expended by the candidates, each vote Young received cost him 44 percent more than Guy.

Campaign Expenditures[48]

Milton R. Young	$300,121
William L. Guy	$115,561
James R. Jungroth	$13,187

Several days before Christmas, Young replied to a letter from a woman in Golden Valley: "Just a note to thank you for . . . your congratulations on my winning the recount. This was quite a campaign and with the recount it certainly was a long one . . . those 186 votes look more like 186,000 now."[49] The Senator believed that his victory came in the recount rather than at the polls on November 5.

Two-thirds of North Dakota's broadcast news directors and newspaper editors voted the Young-Guy race as the state's number one news event of 1974, calling it the "race of the century."[50]

Notes

[1] "Guy, Young Down to Wire," *Minot Daily News*, 6 November 1974, pp. 1-2.

[2] *Jamestown Sun*, 6 November 1974, p. 1.

[3] "U.S. Senate Gains Fall Short of Hopes," *Grand Forks Herald*, 6 November 1974, p. 20.

[4] Corinne Shemorry, "There's Never Been a 'Cliff-Hanger' Like This," *Williston Plains Reporter*, 6 November 1974, Folder 19, Box 600, MYP.

[5] Jack Hagerty, "In My Book," *Grand Forks Herald*, 6 November 1974, p. 4.

[6] Ibid., 7 November 1974.

[7] "Burleigh To Canvass On Friday," *Bismarck Tribune*, 7 November 1974, p. 1.

[8] "Who Won Senate Seat," *Bismarck Tribune*, 7 November 1974, pp. 1-2.

[9] Ibid.

[10] "Young Still Holds Lead Over Guy," *Fargo (N.D.) Forum*, 10 November 1974, p. 1.

[11] Phil Matthews, "Outcome of Senate Race to Take Time," *Fargo (N.D.) Forum*, 10 November 1974, p. 1.

[12] Bill Tillottson, "Senate Could Settle Recount Question," *Bismarck Tribune*, 15 November 1974, pp. 1-2.

[13] *Mandan (N.D.) Morning Pioneer*, 10 November 1974, Clipping, Folder 5, Box 600, MYP.

[14] *Kulm Messenger*, 14 November 1974, Folder 17, Box 600, MYP.

[15] "Young Wins by 176 in Complete Tally," *Bismarck Tribune*, 15 November 1974, p. 1.

[16] *Mandan (N.D.) Morning Pioneer*, 16 November 1974, Clipping, Folder 20, Box 600, MYP.

[17] Dick Dobson, "Prairie Perspective: Young's Lead in Paper Ballots," *Minot Daily News*, 16 November 1974, p. 3.

[18] Bill Tillottson, "Canvass: Young by 177 Votes," *Bismarck Tribune*, 19 November 1974, p. 1.

[19] Al Eisele, "Young Asks Senate to Observe Recount." *Grand Forks Herald*, 19 November 1974, p. 1.

[20] "Young Voices Concern Over Recount Law," *Bismarck Tribune*, 20 November 1974, p. 2.

[21] "Young Claims Discredited by Link, Guy," *Grand Forks Herald*, 22 November 1974, p. 2.

[22] Ibid.

[23] Ibid.

[24] *Jamestown Sun*, 25 November 1974, Clipping, Folder 17, Box 600, MYP.

[25] Phil Matthews, "Guy Files Petitions Asking Recount," *Fargo (N.D.) Forum*, 27 November 1974, p. 12.

[26] Bill Tillottson, "Guy Files Request for Recount," *Bismarck Tribune*, 27 November 1974, p. 1.

[27] "Recount Challenges Voiced: Whole Process Is Alleged Illegal As Steele County Work Starts," *Minot Daily News*, 30 November 1974, p. 1.

[28] Phil Matthews, "Recount Changes So Far Minor," *Fargo (N.D.) Forum*, 1 December 1974, p. 1.

[29] "Recount Trims Young's Margin By Five Votes," *Bismarck Tribune*, 3 December 1974, p. 2.

[30] "Young Recount Lead Gains 5," *Bismarck Tribune*, 4 December 1974, p. 2; "Ramsey County Recount Shows Gain For Young," *Devils Lake Daily Journal*, 5 December 1974, p. 1.

[31] *Jamestown Sun*, 9 November 1974, Clipping, Folder 14, Box 600, MYP.

[32] "Young's Margin Jumps to 201," *Bismarck Tribune*, 10 December 1974, p. 1; "Young's Lead Moves to 185," *Bismarck Tribune*, 11 December 1974, p. 1.

[33] "It's Young by 186, Recount Shows," *Bismarck Tribune*, 12 December 1974, p. 1.

[34] "Meier Plans Quick Action to Certify," *Fargo (N.D.) Forum*, 12 December 1974, p. 2.

[35] "Thanks Are Given People," *Minot Daily News*, 12 December 1974, p. 1.

[36] Bill Tillottson, "Will Guy Challenge Young's Victory?", *Bismarck Tribune*, 13 December 1974, p. 1.

[37] William L. Guy, Press Statement, 13 December 1974, Folder 18, Box 600, MYP.

[38] Ibid.

[39] Phil Matthews, "Guy Contends Double Voting Cost Him N.D. Senate Race," *Fargo (N.D.) Forum*, 14 December 1974, p. 1.

[40] Bill Tillottson, "Canvassing Board Says Young Winner," *Bismarck Tribune*, 14 December 1974, p. 1.

[41] "Vote Count Certified By Governor," *Bismarck Tribune*, 17 December 1974, p. 9.

[42] "Who Won Senate Seat," *Bismarck Tribune*, 7 November 1974, pp. 1-2.

[43] Hal Simons, "Jungroth Says His Role Was 'Leavening' in N.D. Senate Race," *Fargo (N.D.) Forum*, 10 November 1974, pp. 1-2.

[44] Hal Simons, "Independents Doubt Effect of Double Voting on Election," *Fargo (N.D.) Forum*, 15 December 1974, p. 1.

[45] *Congressional Quarterly Weekly Report*, 18 January 1975, p. 151.

[46] Ibid., 1 February 1975, p. 246.

[47] Ibid., 5 April 1975, p. 721.

[48] Ibid., 19 April 1975, p. 721.

[49] Milton R. Young to Agatha Welgum, 21 December 1974, Folder 1, Box 508, MYP.

[50] "Young-Guy Race Top Story in 1974," *Fargo (N.D.) Forum*, 31 December 1974, p.1.

◆ 8 ◆

Reflections:
Heen, Guy and Wright Look Back

Fourteen years after the Guy-Young race three significant participants who had been involved in the process, Judge Douglas B. Heen, former Governor William L. Guy, and Senatorial aide William Wright reflected on what had happened in that "race of the century." These three provide personal perspective to the three key elements of the 1974 North Dakota U.S. Senate election: Guy's campaign, Young's campaign, and the recount. Heen directed and presided over the recount of more paper ballots than in any other judicial district; Guy best represented the story of his campaign; and without Young (the Senator died in 1983) to speak for his campaign, Wright adds to that story.

As presiding judge of North Dakota's Northeast Judicial District (Bottineau, Cavalier, McHenry, Pembina, Pierce, Ramsey, Renville, Rolette, Towner, and Walsh counties), Douglas B. Heen conducted the 1974 U.S. Senate election recount for his district in his chamber city, Devils Lake. Heen detailed the meeting of the six presiding district judges (prior to Guy's request for a recount). They promulgated rules which governed the recount procedure. To the best of his knowledge, each judicial district followed those rules. While aware of Senator Young's comments that Guy and Link appointees would be in charge of the recount, he said the meeting disregarded them because the judges felt, "that they were bound by our oath as judges to fairly and impartially and honestly administer the judicial affairs of the State of North Dakota and that included the recount procedures."[1]

In Heen's district all of the ballots were paper and required hand counting that took seven days. Zeroes or check marks between the boxes on the ballot and ballots that contained no mark in a box were the errors that most often caused him to disqualify ballots. Considering Guy's claim that double voting hurt him more than Young, Heen said "they weren't sufficient to really cause me to remember that as a significant discrepancy in voting to void the ballot." Recalling the effectiveness of the candidates' representatives during the recount, he observed that both sides fielded quality men but a law student from Valley City representing Guy, Earl Pomeroy, impressed him the most. Safeguarding the ballots presented Heen with the most difficulty because he "wanted no hint that any tampering had been done with the ballots after they had been delivered here to court members in the city of Devils Lake."[2]

Asked to respond to the charges Richard Ista made at the State Canvass Board meeting in December 1974, Heen stated that he did not permit uninitiated ballots to be included in tallies, and that he followed North Dakota law and case law established by the Supreme Court "assiduously" in dealing with errors on the part of local election officials. On the issue of the recount statute not providing for judicial appeal, Heen declared:

> . . . I was not concerned with judicial appeal. That did not influence my ruling one whit . . . that was not my problem. My problem was . . . supervising recount of the votes -- to see that it was accurate and that each ballot measured up legally to the requirements of law.

When he heard the Ista charge repeated that the judges did not act in a judicial capacity but in an administrative position, thereby ruling part of North Dakota law unconstitutional, the judge said, "That point was made, but so what else is new?" To him his decisions met the standard of legal requirements; he rejected any implication of having declared statutes unconstitutional. As to the denial of rights of the Democratic Party and William Guy by the recount, Heen observed, ". . . that's perhaps not an unexpected statement by a representative of the defeated candidate."[3]

Judge Heen believed that the courts' time would have been better used if all the state's district judges would have been employed in the recount procedure, instead of only the presiding judges.[4] Heen displayed considerable pride in the manner in which he conducted the recount in his district and expressed confidence that the other five presiding judges also did a very credible job. Praise and respect of the presiding judges did occur at the time in the press, and criticism of the judiciary did not appear after the final meeting of the State Canvass Board.[5]

Comfortably seated in the den/office of his north Bismarck townhouse, former Governor Guy reminisced about events and people that shaped his bid for the U.S. Senate a decade and a half earlier. He related that in 1962 he did not have an interest in running against Young and that while some Democratic-NPL leaders thought he should challenge Young in 1968, he wanted to run for reelection. Guy considered that 1974 would be the year to run for the Senate because he did not believe he could run, as a sitting Governor, for Congress nor resign his office and make a Congressional bid. The former Governor thought his tenure as the state's chief executive would make a move to Congress a natural progression because of his having acquired ". . . some very valuable experience and information and knowledge of the people of the state that could be put to good use as a Representative or a Senator in the United States Congress."[6]

As noted previously, Guy kept a very low news profile in 1973. He explained that during his twelve years as Governor he had made a great deal of news and for several years the press recognized him as the state's number one newsmaker. But in 1973 Arthur Link became Governor, and Guy wanted to create no doubt that Link should be acknowledged as the leader of the Democratic-NPL Party and head of the state's executive branch. Guy said that he " . . . very studiously tried to stay away from commenting on any activities of state government and any activities of Governor Link so there would be no conflict that might arise between the two of us or any misunderstanding that could arise and I wanted all the loyalty of the people that I left behind to be solidly to Governor

Link, the new Governor, and not to me. And so, yes, I did in a calculated way just tried [sic] to stay out of the news."[7]

The only polling Guy recalled in 1973 gave him a 73 percent approval rating and Young 72; that indicated a close race, but in early 1974 polling showed that he commanded a substantial margin over Young. With that in mind the former Governor discussed some of the background that dictated his campaign strategy. Not having a close association with Young, Guy assessed him as " . . . very partisan, very political, in his views." Guy revealed that Young never phoned him or consulted with him concerning Congressional matters that affected North Dakota, even though Guy paid the Senator a courtesy call every time he went to Washington. Guy nevertheless believed that at seventy-six Young deserved to retire with the public respecting him and appreciating the years of service that he gave to North Dakota. That conviction led Guy to tell his campaign lieutenants "that we would not attack Senator Young in any way on the basis of his record or on the basis of his age because I felt we could win the election without doing that. And, in retrospect, of course, that was not good planning."[8]

Because of prior experiences, Guy knew Young to be skillful "in generating public sympathy" for himself. As a case in point, Guy noted that Young used his speech impediment as a positive factor in eliciting sympathy from the public who did not expect Young to "project well" in interviews or on the stump. Guy realized that if he attacked Young personally, the Senator would turn it around on him, and that included age, which Guy viewed as "such a personal vulnerability" for Young. Guy remembered:

> So, to my knowledge, nobody said anything about Senator Young's age in that election; that is, in our campaign organization. I am sure that a lot of people talked about his age, but that was not an organized sort of thing. Toward the final days before the election, I think Senator Young actually felt frustrated that nobody was attacking . . . his age, and so he started to talk about it himself, saying that I and the Democratic-NPL Party campaign was [sic] attacking him on the basis of his 76

years, but that is not true[9]. . .

Well, in retrospect, it might have been effective to use his age. That is something that we will never know. I've never blamed anybody for losing the election other than myself. But I do realize that if other people had done certain things, it might have turned out differently. I don't know that the age issue was one that could have made it turn out differently.[10]

Moving on to personalities, Guy recalled his appearance on the Lawrence Welk Show in 1974 but stated he did not ask Welk for a copy of the film and did not know of anyone on his staff who did. Even though Welk and he were close friends, Guy said Welk's political views were "so extremely conservative that he would have done nothing to assist my campaign but he also felt the band leader would not have acted to harm his chances of being elected."[11] Young's deep concern that Guy would obtain the film from Welk appears to have been without foundation.

No person occupied Guy's attention more than Robert McCarney. He declared that because of his standing in the 1973 poll, his opposition [Milton Young] gave McCarney the mission of doing "whatever was necessary" to lower Guy's approval rating. Recalling the contest with McCarney, Guy insisted that McCarney:

. . . was a totally media-created political person. He came into his candidacy with absolutely no experience in government . . . He wasn't a precinct committeeman or legislator or anything like that. He knew very little about state government. I recall one statement that he made in which he said the state does not need new taxes . . . because it has a $60 million surplus. . . The fact of the matter is that he was referring to the resources of the State Land Department . . . all of which was dedicated to . . . public education. That is just an example of how he could go out and with no knowledge of state government make statements like that. He was almost like Yogi Berra when it came to making statements . . . the press liked that sort of thing and so they just kind of made a political person out of him.[12]

Guy believed that after he had defeated McCarney in 1968, the

Bismarck auto dealer became willing to take on the assignment of reducing Guy's popularity. But in order to do that with a sense of credibility, McCarney decided to enter the Democratic primary, and as Guy put it, ". . . in order to attack me legitimately and be heard, he couldn't be Joe Citizen." Having filed his candidacy in 1968, McCarney paid for a full page ad that made an indelible impression on Guy. He recalled that the ad implied " . . . that my wife was doing something illegal" concerning the financing of a headquarters for the Democratic-NPL Party; it also implied that McCarney had obtained a letter from Hubert Humphrey's 1968 Presidential campaign manager that thanked the Guys for lining up prostitutes, and he accused Guy of accepting illegal airplane trips. Guy deeply resented the ad and mentioned that Fargo's *Forum* had refused to publish it. What astounded Guy the most appeared at the top of the ad in fine print: "I, Robert McCarney, do not vouch for the truthfulness of anything on this page." Guy felt at the time that people would not believe that type of negative campaigning but over time his view changed: " . . . on looking back, I should have . . . nailed that right now, but I didn't." Guy made that statement shortly after the 1988 Presidential election, and, making a very revealing reply as to whether or not Governor Dukakis might in the years ahead have similar feelings, said, "Well, no question about it. I think he conducted his campaign with the same naivete and parochial viewpoint that I used back in 1974."[13]

Not expressing surprise that his position papers received very little press coverage, Guy charged that the media showed slight interest in positive campaigning or issues on which candidates ran. Instead, Guy saw negative advertising or accidents, such as "falling down and tearing your trousers just before . . . a speech" as the topics that would appear in the papers. Continuing, Guy broadly indicted North Dakota journalists who covered his campaign but did not report the positions he considered were important:

> They never had and, frankly, I don't think they ever
> will in this state. We used to put out what you might
> call sound bites, although at that time they were not put

out for television consumption, but we knew that if we would put out just a sentence or two that described the position that the news media might use a sentence or two or might send that sentence or two on to the radio newsrooms or the TV newsrooms, but the news media was totally incapable of digesting anything more than one or two sentences a day in a political campaign.[14]

Guy related another event that reflected his displeasure with the press in early September of 1974. An AP reporter interviewed him by phone at some length as to his stand on lignite coal development. He felt comfortable with the interview because only a few days before he had met with Governor Link and Democratic Public Service Commissioner Bruce Hagen to ensure that they presented a unified front on the development issue. However, several days later in Harvey, Guy read the story, based on the interview, in Fargo's *Forum*, and it shocked him because of the inaccuracies. He called the AP, asking for the reporter who had conducted the interview, and learned he was no longer in North Dakota but had been assigned to another state. Then Guy complained about the story and asked what he should do. The AP answered that he should write a letter to the editor correcting the story. He did not find time to do this because of his campaign schedule and hoped that few people would read the article, diminishing its impact. He regretted the decision because, according to Guy, Jungroth used the article as the centerpiece of his campaign at North Dakota State University and the University of North Dakota, portraying Guy as an anti-environmentalist. Still bothered by the incident, Guy said:

> I have always wondered why the Associated Press sent this reporter in here to take that story and to write the story wrong and then to leave the state after writing the story and then refuse to interview me again to set the story right. I might have called a press conference. But we didn't call a press conference very often in those days because the press were reluctant to show up during campaigns.[15]

Speculating on whether his stand against seniority worked for or against him, Guy first thought it worked against him but did not know just how it affected voters.[16] However, he displayed no confusion over the effect of James Jungroth who, he declared, " . . . was the diversion candidate. His mission was to divert votes from me." Pointing out that Jungroth did not campaign for himself or against Senator Young, but directed his fire on him, Guy declared that Jungroth's strategy involved stirring up college students against him to ". . . divert sufficient Democratic votes from the young people at the colleges, that would be the richest ore in which to mine. . ."[17] Thinking about who did the most damage to his campaign, Guy stated, "Well, there is no doubt about the fact that Jim Jungroth is the one that won the campaign for Senator Young."[18]

No issue occupied more of Guy's conversation than the Council for a Livable World. He retold the story of how he came to be aware of the CLW, decided to accept its endorsement, and was surprised at the number of contributions he received. He went on to explain that, as he remembered, the CLW became an issue because the *Grand Forks Herald's* Jack Hagerty thought " . . . he had really found the Achilles heal in the Guy campaign when he found out the Council for a Livable World had endorsed me and the membership were sending me individual checks." Guy recalled that Hagerty's first story concerning the CLW received little attention so the editor later ran a front page story that implied the Council was a subversive organization that advocated unilateral disarmament. The former Governor then went to Hagerty's office and asked him about the source of his information. Hagerty, after he "hemmed and hawed," admitted he ". . . just accepted the far right's description of this Council . . . instead of doing any investigative reporting on his own."[19] Guy's account is not accurate. Hagerty did run the first CLW story in North Dakota. No doubt Guy visited him, but the front page story to which Guy referred reported a speech he had made pertaining to the CLW.[20] Furthermore, it is not possible that Hagerty told Guy that his story on the CLW was based on descriptions given him by the far right.

Guy's recollection of events surrounding the CLW issue became even murkier when he was asked if the uproar over the CLW had surprised him. He replied, "I don't even recall that there was an uproar, but maybe there was." He stated that the issue really represented ". . . negative advertising that existed at that time" which he felt ". . . causes the negative advertising of the 1988 campaign to pale a little in comparison . . ." Guy remembered that he did feel the issue had hurt him and ". . . did peel off a few votes" because four years earlier Senator Burdick had returned the money he had received from the CLW. That, said Guy, gave his opponents ". . . an extra leg up . . ." because they could say that when Burdick learned the nature of the CLW, he returned their money. But Guy didn't think Burdick understood what they stood for. Rather:

> . . . he just didn't want to fight the battle of trying to defend the Council. And I decided if they were good, if they were right, then that's one of the battles that I was willing to fight. And to this day, I think that the Council for a Livable World is one of the finer public service organizations that we have.[21]

Turning next to why Senator Burdick took no part in his campaign, Guy explained that only Burdick could provide the correct answers, but he ". . . felt that Senator Burdick worried that the state of North Dakota would not send two Democratic Senators to the U.S. Senate and I have always felt that Senator Burdick felt that I represented a threat to his keeping that seat and, therefore, he would prefer that I didn't win the election."[22] The record indicates that on this point Guy is correct. In October of 1973 Dobson wrote that reports in political circles said some Democratic-NPL leaders would not back Guy and that another factor that could hurt Guy revolved around whether or not North Dakota's junior Senator Quentin Burdick would support Guy's Senate bid. He and Guy did not have a close relationship, and Burdick worried that if Guy won in 1974 his chances of reelection in 1976 would be diminished because "North Dakota voters could decide then that two Democratic Senators is one too many."[23]

Guy's disappointment with and resentment toward Burdick became evident as he continued to relate the Senator's role in 1974:

> So, it is true that Senator Burdick did not really pull

an oar in that election on my behalf, that he would arrange
for a television studio appointment to cut some tape in
my behalf and then he would fail to show up. That was
twice and it is true that Party leaders did, several of them,
corner Senator Burdick in the closing weeks and ask him
to come out with a strong statement on my behalf . . . on
television and radio, and again he refused to do that . . .
I have always felt that Senator Burdick, as far as I was
concerned, was always paranoid in all of the years that
he was in the Senate and I was in the Governor's Office.
I said earlier that Senator Young never contacted my
office at any time during those years. Neither did Senator
Burdick. Now, I called his office many times and talked
to him about things that I thought the state was interested
in regarding federal legislation . . . But, at no time did the
Senator ever call my office or me to ask what I thought
. . . Every time I went to Washington, I always made a
point to stop in and talk to Senator Burdick just as I did
Senator Young.[24]

In spite of Burdick's non-supportive role, Guy commented he
always supported Burdick and that Burdick may not have been elected
to the Senate in 1960 if he and his wife had not campaigned so tirelessly
for him. His support of Burdick reflected a belief that it would make
the Democratic-NPL Party a stronger contender in legislative, state,
and Congressional contests. Guy related that Burdick's reaction to him
did not develop from his lack of support for the Senator. What effects
Burdick's actions or lack of action made on the outcome of the election,
Guy did not know. He noted that a shift of ninety-five votes would have
altered the results, but, he added, "I don't blame Burdick."[25] Yet when
he turned his attention to Kissinger's Grand Forks Air Force Base press
conference filmed by Scott Anderson for the Young campaign, Guy's
charity towards Burdick vanished. Repeating his feeling that Young
and/or his supporters drew Jungroth into the race, Guy lashed out:

Scott Anderson and Tom Bergum, and I can't think
of some others, used Senator Burdick's office as their
Washington headquarters almost. For the Jungroth
operation. But I'm not accusing Senator Burdick of being
the instigator of the Jungroth mission. I'm just saying that
whether Burdick realized it or not, his offices were the

gathering place for the group supporting Jim Jungroth's candidacy. Yes, that is well known.[26]

Discussing the recount, Guy stated that he did not have any hesitation requesting the recount, that volunteers represented him during the recount, but that he nevertheless acquired a $10,000 debt which took four years to bring down to $600, which Guy then paid himself.[27] He did question the recount process, relating that Judge Burdick at Williston allowed "a couple hundred" ballots to be counted even though they did not have the required election judge stamp on them and that those votes ". . . went heavily to Young." Guy did not suggest that anything illegal occurred, but he did believe Judge Burdick ". . . went around the law a little bit in order to have those votes counted." He said other judges he had talked to agreed with his assessment.[28] The former Governor also reiterated his position taken at his last press conference in 1974 concerning the effect on the election produced when a voter marked both Guy and Jungroth on the ballot.[29]

Trying to sort through the reasons why he lost the election, Guy thought he could have campaigned more strenuously and energetically because ". . . the campaign plan and tactics that we used were not the effective tactics that were available to us." First saying lack of funds did not hamper his campaign, Guy reversed himself and suggested more advertising would have garnered him enough votes for a victory.[30] Zeroing in on one polling place in Enderlin, in which the students of Trinity Bible College voted, Guy said Young carried it solidly because when he campaigned there he claimed to be a born-again Christian. He said that if the college at Enderlin had remained a state school ". . . the vote out of Enderlin . . . would have been different."[31] Guy knew he could have done more but was not able to define how he would have accomplished that.[32] Unsure of what reasons he should single out that lost him the election, Guy declared, "I really thought I would win that election, so it's hard for me to say what were the reasons I lost. I really don't know why I lost."[33]

When asked if he could redo the campaign of 1974 what he would do differently, Guy replied:

> I would react to Bob McCarney's negative advertising in the primary very strongly and with a high degree of outrage. I would go on to the college campuses following Jim Jungroth and try to unravel the tale that he was spinning to the college students, although I did go on to the college campuses, but I could have done that more vigorously than I did. I would have corrected statements like the AP story on my position on lignite development (by calling) a press conference and ... correct that. Other than that, I don't know how much more I could do.[34]

Guy cited possible actions that would have been reactive and defensive, but none that involved Senator Young or the CLW.

William (Bill) Wright began his journalistic career as sports editor with the *Jamestown Sun* in the 1950s and advanced to editor. Wright's friendship with Senator Young began when his editorials defended the Senator against attacks from the John Birch Society. He joined Young's 1962 reelection campaign as a press secretary, and a short time later accepted a full-time position in Young's D.C. office.[35] Looking back to Young's effort to gain a fifth term, Wright recalled that in 1972 he told the Senator that important friends of his in North Dakota did not believe he would be able to win reelection.[36] Wright reflected that within days of that conversation Young made up his mind to go ahead with a reelection bid. Young's wife Pat disapproved of Wright's having told the Senator what his North Dakota supporters said because she did not want him to run and believed she had come close to convincing the Senator to retire.[37] However, Wright stated "a case of Senatorial ego" caused Young to run. "I don't want to call it an illness, but something that affects United States Senators. It isn't just peculiar to our North Dakota Senators. They really hate to leave. It is quite a life and I must say with all due respect to the gentleman from Berlin that ego had a great deal to do with it."[38]

Taking up the age issue, Wright said that Young did not "disparage his age but used it as a plus and to counter any negative effects saying 'Bill Guy . . . was too old' - of all the incredible things . . . a masterpiece of political judgment." As to what notice Young took of polling data, Wright remembered that Senator Young ". . . was dangerously behind in the beginning of polling season for the 1974 election"; yet, faced with a twenty-point spread, he ". . . didn't pay a whole lot of attention to it." Wright ascribed Young's poor showing to Guy's popularity and Watergate. As a former member of North Dakota's press, Wright enjoyed a close friendship with Dick Dobson and kept the Minot newsman " . . . advised of certain activities and events and strategies" used in the campaign that at times ran in Dobson's column, which Wright described as "wonderful." He realized:

> It was extremely influential in terms of the politically astute community of North Dakota and so it was to our advantage whenever Dick would write something that was either optimistic or showed the potential for the Senator to defeat the very popular Governor, and my recollection is that he did that fairly often, . . . Dick started out being a Guy supporter. In fact, in that very election, he was one of the last people to be convinced that Senator Young would win that election.[39]

Wright did not recall to what degree Young encouraged McCarney in his campaign against Guy, nor did he remember "it being a major contribution to the overall picture of trying to diminish your opponent's standing."[40] But he remembered with greater clarity Jungroth's role and shed some light on why Jungroth went to the lengths he did to prevent Guy from being elected to the U.S. Senate. Having met Jungroth at UND in the late 1940s, Wright renewed their friendship when he moved to Jamestown and they became "very close hunting friends" as well as social companions who did not agree on political matters. Wright declared that Jungroth's opposition to Guy stemmed from a philosophical base that resulted in their becoming "severe antagonists." He described Jungroth as a "true liberal" not only in a political context but also in the way he "defied many of the tenets of societal acceptance whereas the Governor, in those days, was a model of good behavior." At one point, Guy proposed to the Legislature doubling the size of the Highway Patrol, whereas Jungroth advocated cutting it in half, denying patrolmen firearms, and making them purchase their own uniforms and the gas their patrol cars used. The former Senate aide observed, "This is a sort of a violent demonstration of how much they did not get along. Jim considered the Governor terribly stuffy and cold and Jim, of course, is just exactly the opposite."[41]

Thinking back to the summer of 1973 and the letter he wrote to Jungroth about visiting him in Jamestown, Wright said he recalled talking to Jungroth on his patio. Asked who first brought up the idea of Jungroth being involved in the 1974 campaign, Wright stated, "Well, legend is that I had initiated that thought. I just refute that. It was Jim's idea all the time. Obviously, it was a fascinating possibility . . . I wish I could claim credit for that but I deny credit." Wright reported that when he told Senator Young of the possibility of Jungroth's candidacy, the Senator said nothing but his facial expression conveyed the sense of "my, that would be interesting." He recalled only one phone call between Jungroth and Young[42]; however, Wright stayed in touch with Jungroth and kept Young informed of those communications. As an example, Wright learned of the CLW connection with the Guy campaign from his friend, Jungroth.[43]

At the time Tom Bergum, Scott Anderson, James Jungroth, and William Wright lived in Jamestown, they became part of what Wright called a "small cabal"; when all but Jungroth moved to Washington, the association continued. Bergum and Anderson shared Jungroth's disdain for fellow Democrat Guy, and they also favored incumbents achieving reelection. Those two reasons, Wright maintained, formed the bases of their working for Young's reelection; but he stated that they were "devotees of Senator Burdick," and had Burdick opposed their favoring Young, they would not have proceeded. As for Guy's contention that Bergum and Anderson used Senator Burdick's office as Jungroth's campaign headquarters, Wright indignantly asserted ". . . there is just nothing to that. That's beneath the dignity of Senator Burdick and those two people. There is nothing to that."[44]

Anderson's firm, Concepts, Inc., filmed Kissinger's visit, and Wright claimed he made the suggestion to hire the firm. As to how the visit of Secretary Kissinger came about, Wright explained:

> Not easily. It was through the higher -- much higher -- levels of Republican politics than I was swimming, between the Senator and the Administration and then Secretary Kissinger himself. It was worked out. It was considered to be a strong plus in the political atmosphere . . . there is a whole lot of detail involved in that of which I was a part, but not a principle part. That's high level stuff. Staff people don't really get that intimate with Cabinet members.[45]

Wright could not remember the reason or circumstances surrounding Senator Burdick's dislike of Guy, but he knew it existed and had spanned quite a few years. The Burdick and Young association Wright described as close yet not intimate. He related that the two Senators conversed often and that Burdick "was not particularly interested in having then-Governor Guy defeat his colleague."[46] The impression he projected put Burdick for Young and against Guy.

Notes

[1] Douglas B. Heen interviewed by Allan C. Young, 27 October 1988, Folder 1, Box 1, 1974 North Dakota Senatorial Election Interviews, Orin G. Libby Manuscript Collection, Elwyn B. Robinson Department of Special Collections, Chester Fritz Library, University of North Dakota, Grand Forks, North Dakota, pp. 1-2. Hereafter referred to as SEI.

[2] Ibid., pp. 2-4.

[3] Ibid., pp. 4-6.

[4] Ibid. , p. 6.

[5] "Scrutinize Election Laws," *Minot Daily News*, 21 December 1974, p. 4.

[6] William L. Guy interviewed by Allan C. Young, 21 November 1988, Folder 2, Box 1, SEI, pp. 10-12.

[7] Ibid., p. 11.

[8] Ibid., pp. 12-13.

[9] Ibid., pp. 13-14.

[10] Ibid., p. 17.

[11] Ibid., pp. 14-15.

[12] Ibid., pp. 36-37.

[13] Ibid., pp. 37-40.

[14] Ibid., pp. 15-16.

[15] Ibid., pp. 26-28.

[16] Ibid., p. 16.

[17] Ibid., pp. 31-32.

[18] Ibid., p. 33.

[19] Ibid., pp. 19-21.

[20] Chuck Haga, "Guy Defends Receipt of Contribution," *Grand Forks Herald*, 13 October 1974, p. 1.

[21] William L. Guy interviewed by Allan C. Young, 21 November 1988, Folder 2, Box 1, SEI, pp. 21-23.

[22] Ibid., p. 23.

[23] Dick Dobson, "Inside North Dakota: Some Democrats May Back Young," *Minot Daily News*, 6 October 1973, p. 3.

[24] William L. Guy interviewed by Allan C. Young, 21 November 1988, Folder 2, Box 1, SEI, pp. 23- 24.

[25] Ibid., pp. 24-25.

[26] Ibid., pp. 41-42.

[27] Ibid., p. 35.

[28] Ibid., pp. 40-41.

[29] Ibid., pp. 29-30.

[30] Ibid., p. 31.

[31] Ibid., p. 34.

[32] Ibid., p. 35.

[33] Ibid., p. 3l.

[34] Ibid., pp. 34-35.

[35] Randy Bradbury, "Longtime Political Aide Comes Home," *Fargo (N.D.) Forum*, 9 October 1988, p. 1.

[36] William Wright interviewed by Allan C. Young, 22 November 1988, Folder 3, Box 1, SEI, p. 2.

[37] Ibid., pp. 3-4.

[38] Ibid., p. 3.

[39] Ibid., pp. 7-8.

[40] Ibid., pp. 15-16.

[41] Ibid., pp. 9-10.

[42] Ibid., Pp. 8-12 .

[43] Ibid., p. 14.

[44] Ibid., pp. 12-13.

[45] Ibid., pp. 13-14.

[46] Ibid., pp. 4-5.

◆ 9 ◆

Conclusions

The 1974 U.S. Senate race was an election for former Governor Guy to lose and Senator Young to win. Until September 1974 Guy retained a substantial margin over Young in the polls, even though Young's campaign had begun in February 1973. Guy's domination through that period remained solid because no effective damaging information appeared to hurt him. But in the summer of 1974 the former Governor altered his successful strategy in response to Robert McCarney's attacks. His decision to crush McCarney in the primary led to an Election Day get-out-the-vote drive that produced, for the first time in a North Dakota primary, a larger Democratic vote than Republican. Although Guy hailed this as signaling the emergence of the Democratic-NPL as the state's majority party, he missed the fact that an undetermined number of Republicans had chosen to vote in the Democratic-NPL column for McCarney. Guy also did not appreciate that, after his party's primary election efforts, its organization would enter the all-important fall campaign, not fresh, but in need of a rest; volunteers who work from August to a September primary require time away from campaigning for their interests and energies to recharge. Guy reacted to McCarney's attacks as if they posed a political threat to his candidacy when, in fact, they did not dent his popularity. Certainly McCarney's ads and statements qualified as personal assaults on Guy and his wife, but the polls showed that in August his lead over Young remained solid. His personal outrage overshadowed his political judgment.

Guy might have been able to overcome the votes he lost to Jungroth with strong and active support from Senator Burdick. That did not occur, and the history of their relationship should have alerted Guy that only extraordinary measures on his part would have provided even a temporary rapprochement. Success in politics is based on addition, not subtraction, multiplication, or division, and Guy faced open warfare from one Democratic leader, Jungroth, and disdain from another, Senator Burdick. His attack on Jungroth for lack of Party loyalty had no effect on the constituency to which Jungroth's campaign appealed. Guy's personal attacks on Jungroth diminished his statesman image without tarnishing the Jamestown attorney.

Confronted in October with his acceptance of $25,000 that was from outside North Dakota and not included in his campaign finance report, Guy stepped into quicksand. After he had made statements that his campaign would not accept funds from special interest groups, he then righteously defended the propriety of receiving the money from the Council for a Livable World. Because Burdick had returned his CLW contribution just four years earlier, Guy's constant explanations of the issue reinforced his opposition's contention that Guy was putting up a smoke screen. As with McCarney and Jungroth, the CLW controversy prevented Guy from concentrating his time on Young's defeat. That, more than anything else, accomplished what Guy called the missions of McCarney and Jungroth, and if Jungroth's votes denied Guy a victory, Young's campaign had to have boosted Young to a vote total where he could take advantage of it.

The answer to how Senator Young won the 1974 U.S. Senate election is that he persevered. Accustomed to landslide victories, Young went into the 1974 election cycle aware that the match up with Guy would be difficult and that he could face opposition from within Republican ranks. Unlike Guy, Young did manage to achieve unity within his party both nationally and in North Dakota. It took Young over a year and involved him in some stormy sessions to convince national Republican leaders he would not step aside, but when Republican National Committee Chairman George H.W. Bush appeared in July 1974 at Minot to speak for him, Young had no further distraction from Republicans. The problems that he did experience involved the issue of his age, which remained the central issue of the campaign. Young met it head on with a variety of tactics that kept it before the public. From publicizing his practice of Tae Kwon to engaging in a final vigorous campaign schedule, Senator Young reduced the negative image his age posed.

Another negative factor, Watergate, Young could not remove. He talked about it often as reducing his chances of being reelected, and as a Republican he had no options to counter its effects. He did have his seniority, and that he used skillfully with Guy assisting him by taking a stand against Congressional seniority; the tenure in office that provided the seniority worked well for Young, as did a booming agricultural economy. Capping off the campaign with a rush of appearances and heavy advertising, Young peaked at the last moment, winning reelection.

Contrary to comments and statements made by the candidates during the recount, the voters on November 5, 1974 had selected the winner of the "race of the century." A breakdown in the elective process did not happen in the recount procedure; the recount served only as the last and final inspection of the ballots and computation of the candidates' total votes.

Bibliography

Manuscript Collections

Democratic-Nonpartisan League Party Papers, Orin G. Libby Manuscript Collection, Elwyn B. Robinson Department of Special Collections, Chester Fritz Library, University of North Dakota, Grand Forks, North Dakota.

Milton R. Young Papers, Orin G. Libby Manuscript Collection, Elwyn B. Robinson Department of Special Collections, Chester Fritz Library, University of North Dakota, Grand Forks, North Dakota.

1974 North Dakota Senatorial Election Interviews, Orin G. Libby Manuscript Collection, Elwyn B. Robinson Department of Special Collections, Chester Fritz Library, University of North Dakota, Grand Forks, North Dakota.

Newspapers

Bismarck Tribune, 25 June 1968 - 17 December 1974.

Breckenridge-Wahpeton Daily News, 19 December 1973.

Carrington (N.D.) Foster County Independent, 27 June 1973.

Casselton (N.D.) Cass County Reporter, 11 October 1974.

Christian Science Monitor, 23 March 1973; 21 October 1974.

Cooperstown (N.D.) Griggs County Sentinel Courier, 11 September 1974.

Crosby (N.D.) Divide County Journal, 29 August 1973.

Devils Lake Daily Journal, 29 August 1973; 5 December 1974.

Dickinson Press, 8 February 1967 - 8 December 1974.

Fargo (N.D.) Forum, 19 January 1962 - 31 December 1974; 1 June 1983; 9 October 1988.

Garrison (N.D.) McLean County Independent, 15 February 1973; 28 June 1973.

Grafton Record, 31 October 1974.

Grand Forks Herald, 7 January 1962 - 22 November 1974; 1 June 1983.

Harvey Herald, 13 January 1972; 6 December 1973.

Hillsboro Banner, 31 October 1974.

Jamestown Sun, 17 July 1973 - 9 November 1974.

Kulm Messenger, 15 March 1973; 14 November 1974.

Langdon Republican, 15 February 1973.

Larimore Chronicle, 15 February 1973.

Lidgerwood Monitor, 12 September 1974.

Linton (N. D.) Emmons County Record, 17 April 1974.

Lisbon (N. D.) Ransom County Gazette, 25 October 1973.

Mandan (N.D.) Morning Pioneer, 14 January 1967 - 16 November 1974.

Medford (Ore.) Mail Tribune, 24 October 1974.

Minneapolis Tribune, 12 November 1972 - 6 October 1974.

Minnewaukan (N.D.) Benson County Farmers Press, 12 November 1972; 18 October 1973; 22 November 1973.

Minot Daily News, 10 January 1967 - 21 December 1974; 15 June 1986.

New Rockford Transcript, 13 February 1974.

New York Times, 12, 15 December 1973; 22 October 1974.

Oakland Press, 22 March 1973.

Stanley (N.D.) Mountrail County Promoter, 11 September 1974.

Twin Falls (Idaho) Times-News, 5 June 1973.

Valley City Times, 16 January 1974.

Washburn Leader, 3 April 1974; 22 August 1974.

Washington Evening Star, 26 April 1967.

Washington Post, 27 August 1973; 20 October 1974.

Washington Star-News, 27 December 1973.

West Fargo Pioneer, 11 September 1974.

Williston Daily Herald, 11 January 1968; 5 November 1974.

Williston Plains Reporter, 6 November 1974.

Magazines and Journals

Phillips, Kevin. "Doubtful Republican-Held Seats." *American Political Report*, 14 June 1974, 3.

Carrick, Frances, and Vedvick, Milt "An Interview with Governor Guy." *North Dakota REC Magazine*, January 1973, 10-13, 38-39.

Congressional Quarterly Weekly Report, 3 November 1973, 2913; 23 February 1974, 425; 15 June 1974, 1552; 12 October 1974, 2784-2786; 18 January 1975, 151; 1 February 1975, 246; 5 April 1975, 721; 10 April 1975, 790-793.

Laugtug, Denise, and Wright, Boyd L. *North Dakota Election Statistics Report #1*, University of North Dakota, Grand Forks, North Dakota: Bureau of Governmental Affairs, Election Research Division, September 1977, 6-49.

Time, 21 October 1974, 35-36.

U.S. News and World Report, 5 August 1974, 39; 21 October 1974, 40.

Young, Allan C. "Changing North Dakota's Primary Election Date 1960-1984: A Partisan Struggle, Special Report #78." University of North Dakota, Grand Forks, North Dakota: Bureau of Governmental Affairs, March 1987, 18.

Books

Christensen, Boyd. "Boyd Christensen Interviews." Bismarck: Prairie House, Inc., 1983.

Dubofsky, Melvyn, and Theoharis, Athan. "Imperial Democracy: The United States Since 1945." Englewood Cliffs, N.J.: Prentice Hall,1988.

Guy, William L. "Governor William L. Guy." Vol. 1, in *Ramsey County, North*

Dakota: 1883-1983, 38-39. Devils Lake, North Dakota: Centennial Heritage Book Committee, 1983.

Robinson, Elwyn B. *History of North Dakota*. Lincoln: University of Nebraska, 1966.

Rylance, Dan. "Fred G. Aandahl and the ROC Movement" in *The North Dakota Political Tradition*. Thomas W. Howard, ed. Ames: Iowa State University Press, 1981.

Appendix

Milton R. Young Chronology

December 6, 1897   Milton R. Young is born in Berlin, North Dakota, to early LaMoure County settlers John and Rachel Young.

Spring 1915   Graduates from LaMoure High School, finishing in three instead of four years with the intention of becoming a lifelong farmer.

Fall 1915   Enrolls at North Dakota Agricultural College in Fargo (now North Dakota State University) and plays college football. Drops out when football season concludes at the end of October.

October 1915   Leaves Fargo Halloween night to enroll in Graceland College in Lamoni, Iowa, in order to play another month of football.

July 9, 1919   Marries Malinda V. Benson in Moorhead, Minnesota.

December 18, 1919   First of three sons, Wendell "Mix" Young, is born in Berlin, North Dakota.

November 28, 1921   Second son, Duane "Toad" Young, is born in Berlin, North Dakota.

November 26, 1923   Third son, John "Scoop" Young, is born in Berlin, North Dakota.

1924   Elected to first public office at age 26, the Henrietta Township Board of LaMoure County, serving 15 years.

1926   Elected to Henrietta Township School Board, serving nine years.

November 8, 1932   Elected to North Dakota House of Representatives.

November 6, 1934   Elected to North Dakota Senate, eventually serving on seven committees and becoming ranking member of the Appropriations Committee.

January 1941	Elected President Pro Tempore of North Dakota Senate.
1942	Instrumental in forming new faction of North Dakota Republican Party, named Republican Organizing Committee (ROC) in 1943, to wrest control of the Party from William Langer and the Nonpartisan League.
January 1943	Elected Majority Leader of North Dakota Senate.
1944	Manages Fred Aandahl's successful campaign for Governor.
March 12, 1945	Appointed by Governor Aandahl to the United States Senate to fill the vacancy left by the death of John Moses.
March 19, 1945	Sworn in by Vice President Harry S. Truman as the 40th Republican Senator in the 79th Congress.
June 25, 1946	Wins special statewide election to complete the unexpired U.S. Senate term of John Moses. Defeats Democrat William Lanier, Jr., and Independent candidate, former Senator Gerald P. Nye, with 67 percent of the vote.
1946	Elected Secretary to the U.S. Senate Republican Conference, serving until 1971, the longest period any Senator of either party served in a Senate leadership position in the 20th Century.
1947	Named to U.S. Senate Appropriations Committee. Served longer on this and the Agriculture, Nutrition, and Forestry Committee than any other member at the time of his retirement in 1981.
November 7, 1950	Defeats U.S. Senate Democratic candidate Harry O'Brien of Park River, with 68 percent of the vote.

November 6, 1956	Defeats U.S. Senate Democratic candidate Quentin Burdick of Fargo, with 64 percent of the vote.
November 6, 1962	Defeats U.S. Senate Democratic candidate William Lanier, Jr., of Fargo in a rematch of their 1946 contest, this time winning 61 percent of the vote.
November 5, 1968	Defeats U.S. Senate Democratic candidate Hershel Lashkowitz of Fargo, with 65 percent of the vote. Receives the highest vote percentage of any Republican Senator in the nation facing an election opponent.
June 4, 1969	Malinda Young dies in a Fargo nursing home at the age of 73.
December 27, 1969	Young marries Pat Byrne, a Bowman, North Dakota, native and personal secretary in his Senate office since 1945.
November 5, 1974	General election against former Governor William Guy for Young's sixth term in the U.S. Senate. Election results too close to call and goes into recount.
December 11, 1974	Recount completed, with Young winning re-election by a margin of 186 votes out of 237,059 votes cast, or 48.4 percent to Guy's 48.3 percent. It is the closest race to date for a Congressional seat in the history of North Dakota.
December 30, 1979	Announces he will not resign early, and will complete his full term in the U.S. Senate.
December 5, 1980	Named President Pro Tempore in honor of his retirement – the only time in U.S. Senate history that a member of the minority party presided over the majority party.
January 3, 1981	Last day in the U.S. Senate, serving two months short of 36 years.

Including his 12 years in the North Dakota Senate, Young served 48 years as a lawmaker. He continuously held elective office for 56 years, and was never defeated for re-election. At the time of his retirement, he was the Republican Dean of the Senate. Only 14 Senators in the history of the U.S. Senate had served longer, and he served longer *consecutively* than any other Republican in Senate history. He remains the longest serving U.S. Senator in North Dakota history.

January 1981   Moves back to LaMoure, North Dakota, and establishes a winter home in Sun City, Arizona.

Fall 1981   Visiting professor of history and political science at the University of North Dakota, Grand Forks.

May 31, 1983   Dies of prostate cancer at age 85 in Sun City, Arizona.

June 4, 1983   Funeral in LaMoure at the high school attended by 1,400 people. Laid to rest in Berlin Cemetery in Berlin, North Dakota. Simple obelisk marker reads: "Served With Honor and Distinction."

January 19, 2005   Son Duane "Toad" Young dies at age 83 in Berlin, North Dakota.

November 22, 2005   Son Wendell "Mix" Young dies at age 85 in Berlin, North Dakota.

Interview Transcripts

Dr. D. Jerome "Jerry" Tweton, Professor Emeritus of History, University of North Dakota. Interviewed May 13, 2004, by Andrea Winkjer Collin and Richard E. Collin.

Below are excerpts from the interview where Dr. Tweton discussed the oral interviews he conducted with Senator Milton Young on August 8-10, 1979, and November 7, 1980.

JT: Why don't I start by saying how this came about. I got a call from the Senator's office wondering if I would go on staff for an oral history-type project. They would put me on staff enough time so I could run through *The Congressional Record* for key things, look at votes and how he stood on issues. I spent a couple of months doing that prior to talking to him. Then I would have my list of questions and others that would come up. So we did it that way over two sessions, 15 months apart. The tapes that we made were the property of his office and his staff would type up the tapes. I would then get a copy of it and some things were changed for clarification. He would add some things, usually that were not very nice to Mark Andrews. He would just add those in. So that's the only thing he really added were those kinds of comments about Senator Andrews.

Q: Before we get started, give us some personal and professional background about yourself.
JT: I went to the University of North Dakota in 1965 after six years in Nebraska. I taught there for 30 years, actually 29-and-a-half, took early retirement. I was chair of the department most of that time, and ended up being the Chester Fritz Distinguished Professor of History. Since retirement, we have a bed and breakfast in Fessenden, the Beiseker Mansion, which I run with my wife. I have worked as senior consultant with the North Dakota Humanities Council for several years.

Q: What are your first recollections of Senator Young?

JT: My first run-in with Senator Young was in 1946, as a kid. I got a job working for the Republican Organizing Committee, putting up posters and distributing handbills in Grand Forks. The first time I really talked to him, or met him on a one-to-one basis, was in 1974 in his office. At that time, I was the chair of the North Dakota Humanities Council and we were there for some national meeting, and we were encouraged to visit the delegation when we were there. So I was in his office, and right away, being friendly and interested in history, he didn't want to talk about anything else but his own history. And so I came into the office and we chatted, and he started pulling out old photographs, I think one was of a 1920s-something Studebaker, he was very proud of. We talked about early politics and so forth. Right in the middle of that, a call came in from General Westmoreland. The conversation went something like this – Senator Young answered the phone, "Hi, Westy. Yes, I am in a very important conference right now, I will call you back." So that was sort of fun. The thing that came out, and this was right after Watergate and the Nixon fiasco. He was really worried if any Republicans would win in 1974 and how this would damage his chances of getting reelected to the Senate. He was very concerned about that. This was in the springtime, before Nixon actually resigned.

Q: What was your general impression of him, as a teacher of history?

JT: I thought he was terribly charming. A down-home, earthy-type person. He sort of bemoaned the fact that the Senate now took so much time. When he was first in, he could go home and harvest. He talked about how complicated things had become. I thought he was very open and frank. I had on my list of questions some things about his relationships with women, his first wife and that type of thing. I very gingerly got into that at the end, after I had intended to, but he was the one that said I really want to talk about some of those things. So then we did. I thought it was interesting that after two or three Scotches in the evening, his stutter disappeared.

Q: How many hours total did you spend with him in the interviews?
JT: I think about a week each time. We did them at the Omega Hotel, in his hotel room, in LaMoure. A significant amount of time was spent playing golf, eating, talking to people around town, that kind of thing. It was mostly in the evenings that we sat down and talked about things. It was a very relaxed atmosphere, very relaxed.

Q: And he was very interested in sharing all of this with you?
JT: Oh, yes. No pulling teeth at all.

Q: Anything he retracted?
JT: No, not a thing. There were a lot of things over dinner and so forth that you would talk about that never got in. One of his political enemies was William Langer, who died in 1959. Although enemies, he got along very well with him. And in many ways, patterned his office after Langer's. Sending congratulations to high school graduates and all that very personal type of thing. There was none of that from someone like Gerald Nye at all and Lynn Frazier. They didn't do that kind of thing.

Q: Did you have any certain objectives when conducting these interviews with Young?
JT: No, I didn't have a plan to write a book. I just thought that we need to get as much of this now as we can. So it was to get his viewpoints and his reactions to questions and so forth without any real thought of using it myself.

Q: It seems like you spent a lot of time researching the issues and preparing for the interviews.
JT: Yes, I spent about two months every day in *The Congressional Record*, going back to what I thought were the key pieces of legislation that he would have voted on. He didn't say much in *The Congressional Record*, and so I thought why did you vote this way on that and would try to get into what made him tick. One of the most interesting things – I

suppose it maybe says something about the value, or the limitations of oral history – I asked him the question of why he voted against NATO. He was sure he hadn't. He was absolutely certain he had not voted against NATO, he said, "No, you've got that wrong." I said, "Senator, I think I have it right." He had a terrible temper, so you had to be a little careful. I said, "I don't think I made a mistake, but of course I could have." He said, "Why don't I have my office check on that?" And so the next day he came in, "Doggone, I voted against NATO. I shouldn't have done that. I should have voted against SEATO, because that was ridiculous." He had voted for SEATO. And so I tried to find out why, and he said, "You know, I can't tell you why I voted against NATO." I have a feeling, sort of interpreting why he voted against it without him saying anything is that in North Dakota, it was pretty isolationist. Nye, Langer. And I think when he got there he was perhaps in those sentiments of being very leery of foreign entanglements. And then by the time SEATO comes several years later, he is sort of into the internationalist mode where he stayed.

Q: Didn't he say that World War II changed it? As much as you wanted to be an isolationist, it was no longer practical.
JT: Oh, yes. I think he came to accept the fact that isolationism just wasn't going to work after the war was over.

Q: One of the things we've come across is the strong alliance he had with Southern Senators, supporting them on agricultural issues, but also supporting them consistently in voting against civil rights legislation. Why was that?
JT: He felt he needed their votes on wheat. He would support them on agriculture, but he felt he had to go beyond that and – I don't know if it's on the tapes or not – but he said it didn't make much difference how he voted on that because there weren't many blacks in North Dakota. A very practical thing for him. And then with the Civil Rights Act of 1964, he voted for the final bill, but he voted with the Southern Senators on

every amendment to water it down. You have all the Southern Senators and Milton Young. And two, I think, he became a very good friend of Richard Russell, who he had great respect for. I remember when Gilbert Fite wrote his biography of Russell, he mentioned in the Russell Papers what looked like a very strong relationship between Young and Richard Russell of Georgia. So I think it was very practical.

Q: He came under criticism from Republicans about working with these Southern Democrats. We saw a tape of him at a rally in Washburn in 1962 where he says, "I plead guilty to working with these Southern Democrats" because it benefited North Dakota.

JT: It was true. The same was true of William Langer. He had very strong relationships with some of the really reactionary Southern Senators, and he of course was quite liberal. Let me interject something here before I forget it. When I was in Washington, and this must have been after the interviews, about 1980 when he decided not to run again. I stopped by to drop off a book or something for him. He said, "Let's go out to lunch," so we went to the Senate Cafeteria, I think it was, and he sat down with (Senator Edward) Kennedy. Kennedy put his arm around him, talked back and forth, called him "Milty" and so on. So I asked Young after that, how do you get along with the liberals? He said, "Oh, they're wonderful people. Oh, Kennedy, he's wonderful." He'd never say that in public, I'm sure in North Dakota, but there Kennedy was wonderful.

Q: During your interviews with him, were there any surprises that came out?

JT: I should have read them through again. Surprises, I suppose, came from looking at the record, because I was very surprised he voted against NATO. Not shocked, but I found it interesting his civil rights approach with the Southern Senators. I was a little surprised at the animosity that had built up between Mark Andrews and himself. I think largely over the closing of the Nekoma site and the SST (Supersonic Transport), I think were the two things where they split. As a matter of fact, I think he said over lunch or something, that he got along better with Burdick than he did Andrews.

Q: He really could get along with almost all the other North Dakota politicians. Was it just a basic chemistry that didn't hit off with those two?

JT: I think so, it must have been. I think Young, as the senior North Dakota Senator being from the same party, thought that Andrews ought to go along with him. And I think until he didn't, things were pretty good.

Q: How was his memory by the time you sat down with him for those interviews in 1979-80? You mentioned NATO ...

JT: Other than that, really sharp.

Q: We get the sense that he really loved being a Senator, the issues, working with the Washington people and the North Dakota people, it was something that really fitted him well.

JT: I think it did. Especially what he enjoyed most was he and his staff helping North Dakota people, and of course, bringing home the bacon. That reminds me, one of the things that did surprise me was the fact that he claimed to have nothing to do with the placement of air bases in North Dakota. That was mid-1950s, and he'd only been there 10 years. He said, "No, people think that, but it's not true."

Q: How good a Senator do you think Young was in the history of the state and in the Senate and in what way?

JT: That's a tough question. He was effective for North Dakota. He was really the first to bring home in substantial sums the bacon, obviously a very high priority with his office was to get money for North Dakota projects. Why else would there be a Coast Guard station at LaMoure and so on? He sort of set the pace for that. Langer couldn't have cared less. He would help people out, and get them a tractor during the war and get a lot of immigrants in from Europe, working with the State Department, but he never placed a very high priority on getting the federal-type monies for North Dakota projects. I think in that respect Young was successful. I think the second thing of importance was, or maybe co-equal, was handling problems for North Dakota people. Then I think farm legislation. I don't think he was terribly interested in the larger picture. He became a relatively important player as far as intelligence and the CIA and that kind of thing. But except for agriculture, he didn't see himself as one who would generate legislation. He would react to what others did. There's no Young Bill, or Young Act of such and such.

Q: A former staff person said he thought Young would have been a lot more prominent nationally if it hadn't been for his stuttering. That he sort of held back on the national scene.
JT: Well, I think there's something to that. He would never go on *Meet the Press* or anything like that.

Q: Was he ever on any of those type of shows?
JT: I don't think so. I think it did hold him back from being in the public eye. But I think even if he didn't have a stutter, I don't see him as being really a self-promoter in that way.

Q: We've heard people also say that, oh, he had far more power than Burdick when they were together. Do you see that?
JT: I think he was a lot harder worker than Burdick. I think Burdick only in his later years as Senator really used his position to get things done. I think Young saw that right away. Very clearly, Young's office was more efficient, more active, more competent, I thought anyway. You'd go over to the Burdick office and it was gloomy and slow moving.

Q: They obviously got along . . . we talked back in January about your (Christopher) Sylvester interview that is not around, where Sylvester talked about how Burdick had worked behind the scenes,

to actually help Young in that '74 campaign against his fellow Democrat William Guy *(Author note: We were unable to locate the tape that Tweton referred to having recorded with Sylvester the same time he was interviewing Young in 1979-80).*

JT: As I recall, Burdick did not want to see Guy in the Senate. His support of Guy came very, very late too, when he did come out and support Guy, I think in the last week or so. As I recall, Sylvester talked about being sort of liaison with Burdick's people, and that they would actually hold sort of strategy meetings, off the Hill, about how Young could best defeat Guy, what role Burdick might play in supporting Young, but not really appearing to.

Q: One of the things that Allan Young mentions in his master's thesis, which you directed, is that Burdick set up some taping sessions where he would actually say I will go to some TV station and tape some ads for Guy, and then he'd cancel and not show up. He did this more than once. It was almost like this feeling that Burdick was trying to indicate, "Well, I'm supporting Guy," but when push came to shove, he wouldn't do the ads. Any thoughts on why he wouldn't be supportive of him? Was it an inter-party thing?

JT: I suppose. It's just like I don't think Young wanted Andrews in the Senate. I think he tried to talk him into staying in the House.

Q: You mentioned earlier that Young would take back the transcripts and put in even harsher criticisms of Andrews. Were there any specific incidents where you can remember Young talking about where he felt that Andrews had crossed him or upset him?

JT: Yes, there were those two issues that I mentioned, the SST and the closing of the Nekoma site. He was really angry about those. Those are the only two I remember.

Q: How about observations about his relationships with other state politicians? Relationships with the Governors?

JT: I get the impression that he would always say, "These are good fellows, he's a good fellow." I think, other than on Garrison Diversion, there was very little between the Senate office and the state. He talked about that too, generally. I was talking about how, when you go to the Senate and stay there, what is your relationship to people in the state who are politicos, and the issues? As I recall, he made the point that anybody that goes to Washington really tries to stay above that for obvious reasons. You don't want to get into the lottery question if you're in Washington. I do remember talking about that with him.

Q: How about his relationship with the media?
JT: I don't recall anything about that, other than that he talked once about doing his first TV thing where he talks about Ezra Taft Benson (1954), that he really didn't like to do that because of his stuttering. *(Author note: This TV film footage is included in the DVD enclosed with this book).*

Q: It seems, though, that his staff was pretty media savvy.
JT: Oh, I'm sure. They were very protective. I tell you, that was a protective staff. Much more media successful than Burdick was or Langer was.

Q: Going back to the '74 race. What are your views on that? Did you think that going into that that Young was going to win, any observations on Guy and the way he conducted the race?
JT: I think that Guy came off, if age were to be an issue, as sort of being an old young man. Which has always sort of been his problem, I think. Slow of speech, and that kind of thing. I thought Young would win. I thought in North Dakota the incumbent never loses, rarely does. I was really surprised it was that close, I really was. I didn't think that Guy had much charisma. Of course, Young didn't have much. I thought Guy didn't come across very fiery or take advantage of Young being older, less articulate and so on. And he was sort of dull.

Q: How do you think the history of the state might have been different if Guy had won, if Young hadn't been a Senator those last six years?

JT: I suppose if there were swing votes on any legislation, like Art Link, when he went to Congress, just sort of vote the Party line. I would guess that would have happened with Guy as well, especially when you're there for a short time, or you just get there. You sort of fall in line on voting. It probably wouldn't have made much difference.

Q: I've heard people say that Young had many successes in bringing things to the state, but perhaps one of his greatest disappointments was Garrison Diversion.

JT: I think that's been the bugaboo for all the people in Washington. [Senator Byron] Dorgan was on C-SPAN or one of those stations within this past week, talking about Garrison Diversion and North Dakota not getting its fair share. I don't think he's alone in that. That's one thing that certainly the Congressional delegations have pulled together on, whether they're Republican or Democrat or what have you, on Garrison Diversion.

Q: It seems like he had a pretty good relationship with Johnson, that Southern Democrat connection.

JT: That I do recall. You've jogged my memory a bit. This was tempered somewhat by Watergate and so forth, but I remember in casual conversation, maybe it's on the tape, that he never trusted Richard Nixon. He couldn't be trusted. Johnson you could trust. His word was golden.

Q: There's a wonderful photograph of him with Eisenhower, with his arm wrapped around him. *(Author note: This photograph is on the back cover of this book).*

JT: Yes, that's a great one! ... He didn't vote for Goldwater. I remember that. That did surprise me, that he didn't vote for Goldwater. I said, "Well, did you vote for Johnson?" And he said, "I'm not telling you."

479

Q: Did his being Mormon ever come up in his political campaigns?
JT: I don't think so. I found it very interesting that here's North Dakota, that there's two Senators. One's a Roman Catholic, Langer, and the other is a Reorganized Mormon. I don't think the religious question ever came up with either of them.

Q: As we finish up today, Young came in as a member of the Old Senate, and we've heard about the New Senate that came in during his time, his 36 years in the Senate. How do you think it changed, from the Old Senate to the New Senate?
JT: The main thing is the complicated government. When Young first went, all he had to know about, really, was agriculture. The longer he was there, the more he was pulled into intelligence and defense and those kinds of things. He said many times it was overwhelming, you can't know all this stuff. And he sort of looked back on the days when he could go back and dig into his wheat crop, and just say, " 'bye, guys." And I think Burdick, although he went there later, was still sort of like the Old Senate as well. And Andrews, of course, wasn't. Maybe that was part of the friction there.
JT: One more thing. He really wanted me to go away with the impression that he was a very early opponent of the Vietnam War. I think he stretched that, but he wanted to be known as one who really early recognized that this was bad. That's the only thing I think he tried to sway me on, and would bring newsletters and so forth and wanted me to really know that.

Q: Do you remember any of his specific comments about our involvement there and how Johnson had conducted the war?
JT: No, no. Just that he was early on the opposition.

Donald A. Ritchie, then Associate U.S. Senate Historian. Interviewed January 22, 2004, by Andrea Winkjer Collin and Richard E. Collin.

Q: Tell us about where you think Milton Young fits into the context of the history of the U.S. Senate and some of his most important contributions and achievements.

DR: The authors of the Constitution I think saw the Senate and the Senators as essentially ambassadors from their state. We were originally a very loose union of states, and the Senate was going to be equal and there would be two Senators who would represent the interests of those states. It's different from the House of Representatives from the very beginning and when you look at the history of the institution, there are some members who are associated with a particular issue or who had Presidential ambitions or who had some sort of national program. But I'd say the largest share of Senators have really seen that their main function in Washington was to represent the interests of their state and their constituents and to make sure that when national issues were decided, that their state was included and not trod upon by the larger states or other interests along the way. And in that sense, I think Milton Young really did have a very good track record as an ambassador, in a sense, from North Dakota. He understood North Dakota issues, he understood farming, he was a farmer, he made sure they were included in what went on, he made sure the federal money went back into the state, and that the interests of his constituents were always represented. That's probably his largest contribution, and it's a very solid one. It's a very traditional and a very important one. It's really what the Senate was created for.

Q: Any particular achievements that you think stand out during his 36 years in the Senate?

DR: Well, of course he was known as Mr. Wheat, and I doubt that there was an agricultural bill that ever went through that didn't deal with wheat that he didn't have his hands on it somehow. There's a lot of Senators who like to have their name on the title. But someone up here once said you can get an awful lot done if you're willing to let others have the credit for it. And I think Senator Young was a person who worked most comfortably in committees, the Appropriations Committee, and on anything dealing with agricultural issues and wheat issues. Every other Senator knew that if you were talking about wheat and agriculture, you had to talk to Milton Young. So in that sense, I think that was probably his biggest contribution, protecting the interests of his state and particularly the farming community in his state. I remember him. He was still a Senator when I first got here. He was a very large man, but he was not an intimidating man in any way. He was a very gentle man. He spoke in a very low voice. He had something of a lisp. He wasn't the kind of person who stood up on the floor of the Senate and gave long speeches or anything like that. Very pleasant. His wife was well liked by everybody on Capitol Hill because she had been his secretary before she had married him. Everybody up here knew Pat, and they were a very pleasant couple in so many ways. And he had an ability, I think, to sit down with people and make them agree with him. His greatest strength was in the committee room, sitting around the table. The funny part about his career – he was here for a very long time – but only I think about four years of his entire service in the Senate was his party in the majority. He was always perpetually in the minority, which is a real disadvantage. Today, the two parties are at loggerheads. They won't give each other an inch. But I think there was a very good sense of accommodation that developed over time in the years that Milton Young was here, and that it didn't make any difference in many ways whether he was in the majority party or the minority party. I think people respected him for what he stood for, and they respected the issues that he was promoting, particularly agricultural issues. And they deferred to him on issues that related to North Dakota because I think he had a great deal of stature. Friendships cut across party lines, they cut across regional lines. He was close to people like Richard Russell from Georgia. He was not known as an intense partisan, even though he held the party leadership position. He was one of those people, I think, who worked as part of the institution rather than necessarily as part of the party.

Q: Young did of course enjoy longevity in the Senate and seemed to have the respect of his Senate colleagues. What was it about his personal style and work ethic that might have contributed to that?

DR: People knew that he was serious about what he was doing. He knew the issues. A very important thing is that some Senators don't feel a necessity to be a generalist, they don't feel they have to say something about everything. They really learn the subject matters that their committees are dealing with, and when they speak about those issues, they speak with authority. I think that was one of his strengths. He was not the kind of person to jump up and give a speech on every issue that was going on. He served all during the Vietnam War, but you really don't associate Senator Young with any of the big fights over the Vietnam War. He talked about military issues, particularly because he was interested in military bases in North Dakota. But for the most part he stuck to the issues that he was most concerned about and specialized in them, and in that sense, his speeches carried weight. There are Senators that people listen to when they talk about the subjects that they are most closely associated with. He didn't have an intimidating, blunderbust style. He was just the opposite, very polite, deferential, courteous, a very nice man. It would be hard for anyone to mad at Milton Young. So I can understand why, in a body where sometimes people get on each other's nerves, that people enjoyed his company and found him a very collegial Senator. And that's very important, it is a very collegial institution.

Q: You mention, of course, that he was called Mr. Wheat. Why was that the case? Do you know where that originated?

DR: Newspapers and cartoonists love to be able to reduce everybody to a symbol, and of course politicians also like to be able to do that because they want their constituents to think of them in a certain way. I don't know who thought up the term originally, but everybody embraced it.

The Senators used to call him Mr. Wheat, and Senator Young liked to call himself Mr. Wheat. I'm sure he probably put it in his newsletters, and the newspapers, the editorialists and everybody else used it as a nice device. It's sort of like the Republican elephant and Democratic donkey and Uncle Sam and other symbols like that. The one place I can remember where he got in a little trouble for that was there was sort of a wicked article that appeared in, I think, *The Washington Monthly*, called "Separating Mr. Wheat from the Chaff." The author had sent out contradictory letters to all of the Senators on a hot issue, I think it was gun control or something like that, and basically got back letters from the Senators saying "I agree with you" or "I disagree with you," except for Senator Young, who agreed with both of the positions that he sent out. This was not a big issue for him, but his staff tried as hard as possible not to disagree with anybody who wrote in on that issue. It made it seem almost like he had taken contradictory positions. It wasn't an issue that he felt very strongly about. If it had been an agricultural issue, then it would have been a different matter, I think. So they used the name Mr. Wheat in a little twist in separating the wheat from the chaff. But actually, in a state like North Dakota, being known as Mr. Wheat was a terrific asset in his campaigns. Really, the only time he ever had any major trouble running for re-election was his last run, and that was really not his record, it was his age. I think once a person has been in Washington for a long time and reaches a certain age, you do become vulnerable to it in a campaign. I remember that campaign very vividly because he used karate to establish the fact that, despite his age, he was quite vigorous and he won. It was a narrow election that time around, but all the other races that he ran in were quite solid. One of the reasons for that is because the voters knew they were voting for Mr. Wheat.

Q: You mentioned that *Washington Monthly* article. Any idea when that appeared?
DR: Yes, that was just before he left office, it was 1979 or 1980, and it was a little piece about the whole question of constituent mail. One

aspect of Senator Young's career was that he represented a very small state, not geographically, but in terms of population. It was one that was fairly stable in terms of its politics, although it was a two-party state. For the most part, once you got elected in either party, you had a very good chance of getting re-elected. There are different pressures on Senators from small states as opposed to big states. When I first started to work here was in 1976, and I remember very shortly after that we produced a brochure about the office. We divided all the Senators up into two or three categories, and each of the staff members went around to leave several stacks of these brochures in each of the Senators' office. And it was a very interesting experience for me, because I wound up going into about 30 Senators' offices in the Russell Building and the Dirksen Building. I don't believe it was Senator Young's office, because I know it was in the Russell Building, and I think it was probably Quentin Burdick's office. But I remember going into Ted Kennedy's office, which looked like an insurance company. There were so many people on so many desks in so many rows. The lights were up, the phones were ringing, it was a really intense space. I went upstairs to Senator Burdick's office. It was the exact same room. There was one desk in the middle of the room, and it was a woman secretary, and she was knitting when I came into the door. Clearly, there weren't as many calls coming into a North Dakota Senator as there were to a Massachusetts Senator or a California Senator or a New York Senator. That gives you a certain degree of, I think, a little more independence, a little less pressure, than some of the other Senators. You don't have as many conflicting constituent interests that you have to deal with. I think Senator Young had a really good sense of who lived in North Dakota, what the issues were, what mattered to people. He knew about economics, he knew about agriculture, and he knew about jobs. I don't think he had to question his positions in any of those areas at any particular time. It might have been different if he had been a Senator from California, where there are a lot of different positions that you have to deal with, and if you make a decision one way, you are going to make people unhappy the other way.

Q: The Senate was a very different place when Young left the institution in 1981 as opposed to when he arrived in 1945. How did it change?

DR: It grew considerably. One of my interviewees said it grew from a small barnyard to a metropolis. It really was a very small institution when he first arrived in 1945. At that time, the Senate worked out of one building, the Russell Building. There was one cafeteria, all of the staff went over there. There was a Senators dining room in the Capitol Building, there was one subway. You constantly saw people in the halls. Each Senator had two rooms, and so there really was not a lot of room for large staff. As the government grew, they were sticking staff everywhere. They began to partition off the ends of the corridors to create rooms to put the overflow of the staff. They worked people out of the attic and the basement. Some staff worked in bathrooms in the Senators' offices, because there just was not a lot of space.

Q: Do you attribute that to the growth in the federal government, basically?

DR: Oh, yes. The federal government and particularly the legislative branch have grown enormously since the end of World War II, because the issues grew enormously. When Senator Young came, it was in the days when the Senate was in session for about half of the year, and then they would go home for half of the year. Nowadays, you have to be here all year round essentially. In those days, transportation was a lot more difficult. A Senator from North Dakota couldn't go home every weekend, so you came at the beginning of the Congress and you stayed pretty much until the end of the Congress and then you went home to your home state. At least since the late 1950s, with jet planes, a Senator from North Dakota could fly home pretty much every week. It was a different calendar for the Congress then. They tended to do work on Saturday mornings as well. You were around your colleagues a lot more, you got to know everybody. It was a much more intimate place, I think, when he first got here.

Q: What about the political atmosphere, the partisanship level?

DR: It was certainly a partisan era. You were coming out of the New Deal era when the Democrats had dominated the Congress. Starting in 1937, there had been a split in the Democratic Party between the conservative and liberal wings, and Republicans were pretty much able to forge some strong alliances with conservative Democrats. So even though the Republican Party was in the minority in 1945, it actually had a lot of clout because there were probably a majority of Senators, when they got together, who were on the conservative side and it would prevail. In 1946, the Republicans won, and for the next decade it was very close. There was never a period when either party had more than, say, a two-vote margin in the body. But both parties were internally divided. The Democrats had a conservative, Southern wing and a Northern, liberal wing. The Republicans had a moderate, what they later called an Eisenhower wing, and a conservative Taft wing. Senator Young is a hard person to place in this. I think he was what we would call a conservative today, but I don't think he was very uncomfortable with the Eisenhower moderate wing of the party. He fit into the party as a whole, and I think he was probably somewhere right smack in the middle of the Republican Party, which made him also very close to a lot of Democrats at that time. So you didn't have the extreme partisanship I think that you have today where the two parties are very internally cohesive. The Republican Party is solidly conservative, and the Democratic Party is pretty solidly liberal, and so there's not much of a middle ground for compromise and bipartisanship as there was when he first came here in 1945. That doesn't mean that there wasn't a lot of partisanship and that it wasn't rancorous. But he was never part of the rancor.

Q: Toward the end, do you feel that the institution had almost moved beyond him, because times had changed so much?

DR: I think it was an extremely different institution by the time he left. Actually, 1980 was a big divide, and I think he would have found it more uncomfortable if he had stayed longer. The last six years that he was here were a tough time, first with the end of the Vietnam War, and then Watergate, and then a lot of rancor in the post-Watergate era, a lot of filibusters, a lot of posturing, and all the rest. There were things that were a little uncommon for some of his experiences previously. I don't know that he would have enjoyed the Senate much after 1980. A lot of the people that he served with were also retiring at that point and a whole younger generation of politicians were coming in.

Q: He had an interesting alliance with key Southern Senators regarding a variety of issues, defense and agriculture especially. He was an independent, in some ways populist politician from the Northern Plains joining with Southern Senators again and again to support key legislation in areas involving these issues and others. Why was that the case, and why did it work so well so often?

DR: Those Senators looked on their role very much the way he looked on his role in that a Senator from Georgia was interested in cotton and also military issues, because there are a lot of bases in Georgia, in particular. A Senator from North Dakota was interested in wheat and military issues, and so you can understand why one would defer to the other one on cotton, and the other would defer to the other one on wheat and they would agree in general in terms of a strong defense. They would also agree that would support projects in each other's state. There was a great deal of reciprocity that existed at that point as part of the collegiality and as part of what we call Senatorial courtesy. Senators always defer to their colleagues in terms of things that happen that relate to their state. But in many cases what is relating to their state is similar to what is relating to other states. Essentially, North Dakota was a rural, agrarian state and that made it very similar to a lot of the rural, agrarian states in the South. The South, because it has changed dramatically in the last few decades in terms of in-migration and the whole social scene, has changed in many ways. If you look at it when he first got here in the 1940s, the South was essentially a rural, agrarian society.

Q: Weren't a lot of the deals and agreements really cut in the committee room and the hallways back in the old Senate?

DR: There's still a lot deals cut in the hallways and the corridors and the backrooms. A lot of what goes on in the backrooms really determines what happens. Ninety percent of a piece of legislation is written in the committee, maybe 10 percent might be argued on the floor, if that. In many cases, the arguments are over a very narrow part of what the bill is all about. Especially if you're dealing with appropriation committees, most all that work goes on in private conversations between members. Even with the sunshine legislation, there's an awful lot of dealmaking that goes on. Part of that has to do with how much you trust your colleagues. Can you trust them on their word? If they say they are going to support you, will they follow through? They say a U.S. Senator's word is his bond. I think no one ever accused Senator Young of ever going back on a deal once he had agreed to it. He felt very comfortable in the backroom. He was a committee-oriented Senator. There still are a lot of them. In the Senate, they divide people up between work horses and show horses. The show horses are the ones who are out in front of the microphones, who are speaking out on the big issues of the day and who are so busy promoting the big issues of the day that they are not around in the committees to actually work on the legislation. The work horses in the backrooms are the ones who really make the legislation. In many cases, they achieve a lot because they are not out there trying to take credit for everything.

Q: And where did Young fit in?

DR: He was definitely a work horse in the Senate. No one would have questioned that.

Q: Would you characterize the Congress, pre-Watergate and post-Watergate, a bit further, particularly in the committees? I had heard reference to people saying to Senator Young, "whatever you think is best for wheat, you just go ahead and put it in." Have those

kind of things changed in this new era?

DR: I think so. Things are much more partisan today than they were. People are more suspicious of each other and they're less willing to put complete faith in a colleague than they were in those days. It takes awhile to get to that level where people have that much confidence in you. He had to earn that kind of respect. I think there still are some Senators who would probably meet that description. Maybe there were a few even then, I'm not sure, but it's not necessarily the norm. I think it was in many ways a more collegial place at that stage. There always were hot button issues. When he first got here, McCarthyism was a huge issue, it was very divisive. On the other hand, there were also huge areas of consensus. The Cold War came about just about the time he came to Congress, and that sort of got the largest share of people in the center. They pretty much decided that the United States had to play an active role in the world, that it had to have a strong defense, that it had to be involved in international agreements and defense alliances, that it had to join the United Nations. There was this bipartisan foreign policy that developed. Senator Vandenberg of Michigan was really a proponent of that, but I think Senators like Young and others who might, if he had come into the Senate in the 1920s coming from North Dakota, might have been an isolationist. But I think he realized coming in after World War II that he had to be an internationalist, and that I think created a large consensus that the vast majority of Senators joined in on. That lasted into the middle of the Vietnam War, when that began to unravel in a very negative way. And then of course we went into the Nixon years, and there was a lot of tensions between the executive and legislative branches. People stopped believing what the executive branch was telling them, which is one reason why the staff here started to grow. If you can't trust the information you're getting from the executive branch, then you have to have some independent form of information, so you create a larger staff, committee staff and individual staff, and you build new buildings to house all that staff. There were certainly some very dramatic breakdowns. But for a large share of when he was here, at least for the first 20 years, there was a fairly broad consensus that I think helped keep people together and helped avoid some of the really partisan rancor that we have up here now.

Q: Talk some about his relationships with the Presidents who were in office during his time in the Senate. He went from Franklin Roosevelt right up the very last days of Jimmy Carter. Did they rely on him much for support or counsel or insight?

DR: He would see Presidents because he was in a leadership position in the Republican Party. That meant he would see Republican Presidents a lot more. He would see someone like Eisenhower or Nixon or Ford as President than perhaps he would the Democrats just because leaders were invited to the White House on a regular basis. I think Presidents and their Congressional liaison who had anything that was going to deal with agriculture or anything that was going to deal with North Dakota most likely would stop at Senator Young's office at some point. He probably had very good relations with the Presidents. I can't imagine one of them that he didn't have good relations with. Of all of them, I suspect he was probably happiest during the Eisenhower years. Eisenhower was someone who he respected and agreed with, and he had complete faith in. But I think he probably worked well with all Presidents, Democrats as well as Republicans, some of whom of course had been his colleagues. John Kennedy had been in the Senate with him, Lyndon Johnson had been in the Senate with him, Richard Nixon had been in the Senate briefly with him. Gerald Ford was in the House leadership at the time Young was in the Senate leadership. So he had personal dealings with most all of them before they became President.

Q: What were some of the key agricultural and defense legislation that Young was involved in during his time in the Senate?

DR: I really can't name anything particular. But I doubt that there was an agriculture bill during that period that he didn't have something to do with in terms of protecting farmers rights and parity and making sure that the federal government remembered its responsibilities to the farm communities. I can't really think of a specific bill that I would say he was the spearhead on, but I'm sure that there's not one of them that doesn't have one of his amendments in there somewhere. I think also in terms of appropriations bills and especially military appropriations that involved military bases he had real impact. North Dakota of course became a front line of the Cold War with the missile sites and all the rest of it. I'm sure that he was very much involved in all of that.

Q: Is there any legislation that he might be remembered for today that you might recall?

DR: There really isn't a Young bill. But there are a lot of Senators here like that. Even Senator Byrd, you don't really think of him in terms of specific bills. He is much more interested in the internal operations of the Senate and the power of the purse. Senator Byrd in many ways is a Senator who is similar to Senator Young, although Senator Byrd tends to speak out a little bit more on some of the issues. But he believes very strongly in the power of the purse, that the single most important power that the Congress had was the ability to appropriate federal funds and not a penny would be spent by the federal government that was not appropriated by the Congress, and that Congress had to keep an eye on all of that and that they had a responsibility in parceling that money out so that it was spread around the country and not concentrated in just a few places. I think in terms of that, just like Senator Byrd is identified with bringing federal projects back to West Virginia, and Senator Ted Stevens is identified with bringing federal projects back to Alaska, I think Senator Young did that for North Dakota. Even though he was never Chairman of the Appropriations Committee, he was almost a co-chairman of that committee because I think people deferred to him on so many issues. As a result, because appropriations are often done on a quid pro quo arrangement, he got a much larger share of federal funds back into his state than would have gone there otherwise. I think that is a very good and healthy part of the system. The press attacks things they call pork, they love to reduce it to that issue. But when you look at the small states, for the most part, they have kept their Congressional delegations in office a lot longer than the large states have. And as a result, Senators who come from small states tend to become senior. They're either chairmen of committees or ranking members of committees, and that gives them much more influence than the junior Senators. That means that when the federal dollar is cut up, their states get a very healthy share of it. Carl Hayden, who was in the Senate for most of the time that Senator Young was here, represented Arizona in the same way that Senator Young represented North Dakota. His big issues were building roads in Arizona and getting water pumped into Arizona. If you look at what the population of Arizona was when Carl Hayden first came to Congress, it was a tiny little group of people living in the desert. And now there are millions of people living in the state. The state couldn't have sustained that population if it hadn't been for the federal funds that Carl Hayden put into that state. Otherwise, the population of California would have a few more million people in it right now than it does. I think that has really helped to spread essentially population and projects and jobs around the country by having Senators from these small states who are bringing back perhaps a larger share than they would have gotten otherwise from the federal dollar.

Q: You raise an interesting point about Young's similarities with other Senators. Any other Senators you can think of over the years that Young was similar to?

DR: There was a moderate group of Republicans in the 1970s, Mark Hatfield was one of them, John Chaffee was another, John Warner today in the Senate. They're not known as hard edged idealogues. They work deals on both sides of the aisle, they're respected by both sides. They're known as men of principle. And they get a lot done because they're in the middle, and it's easier to work bipartisanship arrangements when you can bring in some people from the other side of the aisle. I think Senator Young stood out in that respect. It's harder to judge him in part because if you look through *The Congressional Record*, you're not going to find as much of Milton Young as you will of, say, Hubert Humphrey or Wayne Morse or any of the Senators who loved to get up and speak on every issue. That just wasn't his style. He really was much more comfortable in a committee room. For much of the time he was in the Senate, the doors were closed. We didn't have sunshine rules on committees until the 1970s. So much of what he did was done away from the public glare. But he didn't need the public glare to get himself re-elected. People knew where he stood and they knew that he was doing his job. So he didn't have to go out and beat the drum and get press releases out there and have everybody think he was doing everything by himself, in a sense. That kind of self-effacing style makes it very hard to go back and judge and say, "A ha, the Taft-Hartley Act is a bill that has his name on it." That wasn't the way he worked. But that certainly doesn't mean that he wasn't effective. He understood the system and he made it work for him very well. There are Senators like that today who are in that mold as well, who are not the ones who are in the headlines every day, but they really are shaping the legislation. You were asking about Senators Young was like. One other person that I would say he was very much like was George Aiken of Vermont. He was another Senator who was very much interested in agricultural issues and had the same kind of philosophy and personality, although Aiken was a little more garrulous and tended to talk a little more to the press and is remembered for some of his statements a little more in that respect. But I think fundamentally very much the same type of person.

Q: Any other anecdotes or stories about Milton Young as Senator that come to mind?
DR: I met him on a number of occasions, usually at receptions. He always enjoyed chatting. But you would have to strain a little bit to listen to him, because he didn't have a loud voice. I think he was much better when he was sitting down in a quiet room with a few people. I still remember him in his karate suit. I think that's kind of an interesting part of him. A lot of Senators are involved in athletics. They play tennis,

or they play squash to get away from the stress and strain around here. But there aren't many who take karate lessons and he did that well into his 70s. And he had a group of Senators and Representatives who used to get together, and they had a trainer come in and all the rest of it. I've seen pictures of him in his costume. He was very proud of that, the fact that he could break a board. It wasn't a trick, he could do that. So you had the suggestion that this is a lot tougher, stronger guy than his mild appearance made him seem. There is one other thing. When people get hired around here – staff members move around as Senators and Representatives retire and leave office – you get known for whom you work. And there are certain people, you look at their resume, and if they worked for Milton Young or they worked for Mark Hatfield or they worked for Howard Baker or people like that, you know that, okay, these people are going to be reasonable, they are going to institutionally oriented, they're not going to be hard edged partisans, they're not going to be idealogues. They're going to be pleasant and thoughtful and intelligent people. I think that the staff winds up being a reflection of the Senators that they work for. And it serves you well to be identified with a Senator like Milton Young. I've known quite a few people around here whose heritage went back to Milton Young. A lot of the doorkeepers, some of the secretaries, all sorts of folks who stayed on here as career staff on Capitol Hill, and they were very proud that they once worked for Milton Young.

(On Young and Burdick working so well together) Quite often, it's a lot easier for Senators if they are from different parties in the same state. The fact that Burdick was a Democrat and Young a Republican probably suited them very well. Because that meant they never had to go to the same sources to raise campaign funds, they probably were never going to be invited to the same speeches and events, unless they were clearly non-partisan events, and they were never going to run against each other. So that really makes for a sort of comfortable area, and they usually tend to agree that they will vote any way they want on any issue except an issue that relates to the state, in which case they will support each other because they are supporting the state. While a Democrat will go out and campaign for the Democratic candidate, and the Republican will campaign for the Republican candidate, they're often quite relieved when the other party wins. Many of them would find that it would be difficult to have that candidate as their colleague. Certainly Senator Burdick was very happy to have his colleague on the Appropriations Committee, that was big asset. Senator Young must have helped Senator Burdick on any number of occasions on projects that were important to him because they were important also to the state of North Dakota. I can understand why Burdick was very happy to have Senator Young there.

Q: They were known to have gotten along quite well?
DR: Yes, and I think part of that was the nature of the two men and part of it was the fact that they were both from different parties. I think it would have been different if Senator Young had served in the Senate with, say, Mark Andrews. Then he would have had another Republican, and the question would be who was going to announce nominations that relate to the state, who was going to announce appropriations, who was going to be invited to speak at the Republican Convention, who was going to do this and that. A lot of jealousies can develop when two Senators are from the same party representing the same state. So I think it was probably very satisfactory to him that he had a Democratic colleague for much of his career. It was probably more difficult during the years that he was dealing with William Langer than it was when he was dealing with Quentin Burdick.

Q: Even when Senator Andrews was over on the House side, there were reports of quite a bit of acrimony, and it's probably because, like you say, they were both from the same party?
DR: Of course, in a smaller state, where you only have one or two Representatives, then of course that Representative is almost like a Senator because they have to run on sort of statewide basis. And there's

a lot of places where you can step on people's toes. That's not unusual, people who actually think alike politically, but who otherwise really can't get along with each other. Senator Wayne Morse of Oregon, who was a very liberal Democrat, one of his former students, Richard Neuberger, who was also a very liberal Democrat from Oregon, had the worst fights, they just trashed each other terribly while they were here, even though they voted exactly the same on every issue. So just thinking alike doesn't necessarily give you an automatically good relationship. Senators are always looking over their shoulder, because you've got to worry about the Governor, and you've got to worry about the Representatives in your state. Senators only run every six years, and a lot happens in that six-year period. A lot of your voters aren't there after six years, or new voters have moved into the state. Whereas, Representatives run every two years. Their name is up before the public more frequently, and the Governor of course gets a lot of press, so Senators are always sort of looking over their shoulder. On the other hand, you get someone like Andrews, who probably felt that Young was sitting on that seat, and that was his seat and he ought to have a chance to run for it. Why wasn't he going to retire, etc., etc. That kind of builds bad blood as well, and that certainly has happened in other situations in other states.

Index

Bennett, Tony 207

Benson, Ezra Taft 120-126, 138, 300-301

Benson, George 207

Benson, Paul 197, 231-232, 336-337

Bergland, Bob 146

Bergum, Tom 450, 454

Bier, Howard 263

Bjella, Arley 198, 336

Bjornson, Neil 105-106, 129, 131, 138-139, 141, 143, 146-147, 219, 284, 336, 341-342

Block, William 336

Boardman, William 33-34

Booth, John Wilkes 201

Borah, Senator William 149-150

Bowman Haley Dam Project 132, 188

Boyd, B.W. 30

Braaten, Oswald 49

Bradley, Omar 78-79

Brannan, Charles 110, 115-116, 142

Brannan Plan 110, 138, 229-230

Braun, Jonathan William "Billy" 53, 61, 79

Bridges, Senator Henry 102

Bridston, Joseph 56, 60-62, 64-65, 93, 95-96

Brock, Senator William 366-367

Brunsdale, Governor, Congressman Norman 61, 65, 231, 299-300, 313

Brunsman, A.A. 25

Brunswick Corporation 325

Buechler, M.A. 30

Bulganin, Nikolai 173

Bullis, Harold 242, 336

Bumpers, Senator Dale 397

Bunker, A.G. 263

Burdick, Congressman Usher 39, 104, 231, 233-234, 238, 305, 308-309

Burdick, Eugene 309, 451

Burdick, Senator Quentin 123-124, 166, 214, 232-239, 280, 282, 300, 309, 311, 336, 363-364, 375, 381, 416, 421-422, 449-450, 454-455, 459, 468, 475, 477, 480, 485, 495-496

Burgum, Leslie 20

Burke, Governor John 337, 339

Burke, Thomas 241

Burlington, Dan 188

Burnham, John 112

Burning Tree Golf Course 213

Burtness, Congressman Olger 23-24

Bush, George H.W. 265, 388, 459

Butterlegging 112–115

Butz, Earl 139, 145

Byrd, Jr., Senator Robert 295, 330, 492

Byrne, M.S. 75-76, 336

Byrne, Patricia (Pat) *see* Young, Pat Byrne

C

Cain, James 48, 55

Calver, Dr. George 303

Capehart, Senator Homer 79, 97

Capper, Senator Arthur 97, 106, 124

"Carloads of Coffins" Speech, Senator William Langer 307

Carlson, Senator Frank 364

Caro, Robert 285

Carswell, Harold 221

Carter, Lynda 207

Carter, President Jimmy 145-146, 189, 214, 225-226, 491

Casey, Senator Lyman 104

Cash, Johnny 207

Castro, Fidel 215

Cattlemen's Association, National 129-130

Cavalier Air Force Station 167

Central Intelligence Agency 157, 159-160, 170, 174, 214-215, 246, 292, 476

Chaffee, Senator John 493

L

M

247, 250, 310

O

Oasis Restaurant 54
Oberg, Gerald 396
O'Brien, Harry 228-229
Odland, Elmer 396
Office of Price Administration 99
Old Soldiers Golf Course 76
Olson, Governor Allen 234, 336, 381,
    428, 435
Olson, Governor Floyd 51
Olson, Governor Ole 37-44, 47-48
Omdahl, Lloyd 252, 395, 436
Omega Coast Guard Navigation Sta-
    tion, LaMoure 163-164, 475
Omega Motel 163, 472
Onassis, Aristotle 253
O'Neil, Thomas 232-233
Opdahl, Carl 31-35
Orlady, Benjamin 59-60
Orman, Gail 396

P

Panama Canal 196-197, 225
Pansandak, Ferd 71
Park River Dam 184
Paulsen, P.M. 76
Paulson, Lester 336
Pavarotti, Luciano 207
Park, Tongsun 194
Pearl Harbor 82, 148, 151
Pearson, Drew 73
Pearson, Richard 338
Pembina Dam 184
People's Republic of China 175-176,
    221
Pepper, Senator Claude 97
Percy, Senator Charles 204
Perimeter Acquisition Radar Station,
    Concrete 165
Perlman, Itzhak 207
Phillips, Kevin 364-365, 397-398

Pick, Lewis 184
Pick-Sloan Missouri Basin Program 184-
    191, 324
Pipestem Dam 188
Plum Grove School 11
Pomeroy, Earl 442
Pressler, Senator Larry 329
Project Azorian (Jennifer) 159-160
Prowse, Juliet 207

R

Raschko, Mike 290
Reagan, President Ronald 320
Redlin, Congressman Rolland 310
Redlin, Earl 250
Reed, Ed 31, 229
Reeder, Don 243
Reffell, Eva 208-209, 342
Reichert, William 243
Reimers, Robert 249
Reiten, Chester 198-199, 266, 341
Reorganized Church of the Latter Day
    Saints 7-8, 10, 14, 110, 327, 336,
    480
Republican Organizing Committee 60-65,
    70, 76, 80, 86, 91-93, 96, 229, 297-
    299, 301, 307, 467, 471
Republican Senatorial Campaign
    Committee 281, 408, 415
Reserve Officers Association of the United
    States 167
Rhodes, Congressman John 224
Ribicoff, Senator Abraham 102
Richey, Charles 190
Ringling Brothers Barnum and Bailey
    Circus 201
Ritchie, Donald 343, 481-497
Roach, Senator William 104
Robards, Jason 204
Robinson, Elwyn 55, 340
Robertson, Congressman Charles 62, 298
Robideau, C.J. 229
Rockefeller, Nelson 249

507

Roosevelt, President Franklin 24, 26, 34, 53-54, 60, 78, 89, 98, 101, 106, 201, 210, 418
Roosevelt, President Theodore 100
Rouzie, John 260, 267-268, 317, 336, 354
Rowan, Carl 372
Rue, Milt 62, 64, 212
Rumper Leaguers 63, 298
Rural Electrification Administration 72, 132, 189, 231, 236
Rural Telephone Act 120
Rusk, Dean 255
Russell, Senator Richard 77, 103, 117-118, 152, 159, 202, 285-287, 294, 328, 335, 474, 482

S

Sadat, Anwar 222
Saltonstall, Senator Leverett 196, 302
Sandness, A.J. 25, 229
Sandness, Claire 25, 274, 336, 340, 342
Sands, Ernie 336
Sanstead, Wayne 258
Saud, King Ibn 172
Schafer, Harold 242, 336, 410
Schatz, George 86, 88
Schiebold, Karl 336-337
Schlesinger, James 161
Schnell, Ray 230
Schockman, August 28-29, 50
Schommer, Nick W. 37
Schultz, Art 129
Schweiker, Senator Richard 326, 328
Scott, John 123, 250
Select Committee on Investigations, Senate 193
Sevareid, Eric 247-248, 372
Shellum, Bernie 414-416
Short, Congressman Don 242, 247, 310
Simon, K.W. 193-194

Simons, Hal 320
Simons, Ken 76
Singer, Janeal 396
Sinner, George 252, 399, 422
Sioux Manufacturing Corporation 200
Sloan, William 184
Smart, W.M. 229
Smith, Edwin 409
Smith, Senator Margaret Chase 158-159
Smith, Senator Willis 202
Snyder, Bill 228
Soil Bank Act 122-123
Solem, Custer 308
Sorensen, Theodore 214
Sorlie, Oscar 337
South East Asia Treaty Organization 150, 473
Southern Democrats 131, 199, 285, 473-474, 488
Soviet Union 140, 220-221, 245, 316
Spier, H., Jr. 390
Stalin, Joseph 98, 173, 212, 290
Stallman, Tom 282
Stambaugh, Lynn 63-64
Stanley R. Mickelsen Safeguard Complex, Nekoma 165, 474, 477
Stanton, Edwin 205
Stassen, Harold 64
State Canvass Board 427-428, 430, 433-435, 443
State Mill and Elevator 28
Steagall Amendment 107, 111, 118
Steagall, Congressman Henry 107
Stennis, Senator John 199, 325, 382
Stern, Ben 94
Stevens, Senator Ted 176, 492
Stevenson, Adlai 214, 237, 305, 307
Stockwell, Walter 11-12
Stoudt, Dick Jr., 337
Strategic Arms Limitation Treaty 169-170
Strauss, David 432
Strinden, Earl 336
Struble, H.B. 25